ART IN TRANSFER IN THE ERA OF POP

ART IN TRANSFER IN THE ERA OF POP

Curatorial Practices and Transnational Strategies

Edited by
Annika Öhrner

Södertörn Studies in Art History and Aesthetics 3
Södertörn Academic Studies 67
ISSN 1650-433X
ISBN 978-91-87843-64-8

This publication has been made possible through support from
the Terra Foundation for American Art International Publication Program
of the College Art Association.

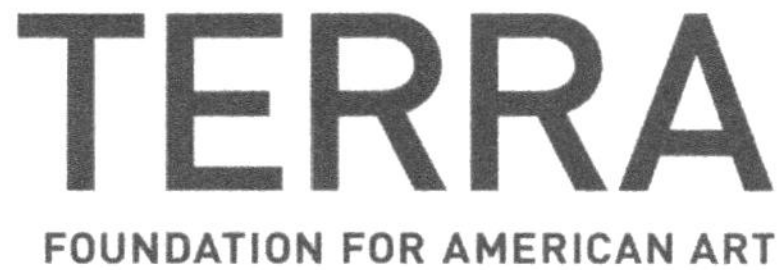

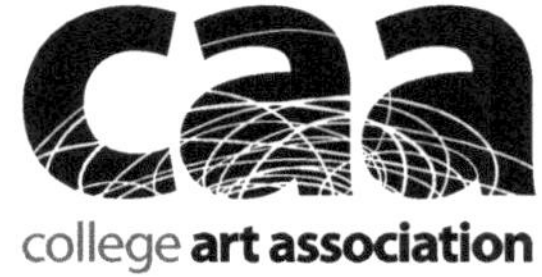

Södertörn University
The Library
SE-141 89 Huddinge

www.sh.se/publications

© The authors and artists

Copy Editor: Peter Samuelsson
Language Editor: Charles Phillips, Semantix AB

No portion of this book may be reproduced, by any process or technique,
without the express written consent of the publisher.

Cover Image: Visitors in *American Pop Art: 106 Forms of Love and Despair*,
Moderna Museet, 1964. George Segal, Gottlieb's *Wishing Well*, 1963.
© Stig T. Karlsson/Malmö Museer.

Cover Design: Jonathan Robson
Graphic Form: Per Lindblom & Jonathan Robson
Stockholm 2017

Contents

Part 1
Exhibitions, Encounters, Rejections
37

Introduction

Annika Öhrner

The writing in *Art in Transfer in the Era of Pop* focuses on cultural transfers in the extended 1960s. This decade, stretching back to the 1950s and forward into the 1970s, covers the "Era of Pop," a period of new, intense, artistic engagement that is often characterised by the breakthrough of American art and popular culture in Europe. The title of this volume was likewise inspired by the film *Stockholm à l'heure du Pop* (Swedish title: *Popen kommer till stan*), produced and filmed in 1964 by a Belgian artist by the name of Olivier Herdies (1906–1993), who had lived in Sweden since 1937. The film, running for 33 minutes, starts out with long shots from the city life of Stockholm, picturing Stockholm's *tunnelbana* (the Metro, also known as T-Bana) and the crowds of the 800,000 inhabitants of this city as modern and urban. Shots from exhibitions in numerous independent art galleries follow, combined with interiors from the very first presentation in a European museum of American Pop Art: the show *Amerikansk pop-konst: 106 former av kärlek och förtvivlan* (American Pop Art: 106 Forms of Love and Despair), at the Moderna Museet.

The film's construction of affinities between art and urban life and culture, as well as between the local and the international, is what makes *Stockholm à l'heure du Pop* a suitable emblem for the thinking and writing that has been gathered together in this book. New art did not *just arrive* in Europe in the guise of American Pop in the early 1960s; it was already happening in numerous ways. In addition, the film represents these processes in the capital of Sweden, a "neutral" country between the West and the East. While some of the essays in this volume are consequently about events, art, and cultural transfers that took place in Scandinavia, others examine curatorial and artistic practices from a wide range of other geopolitical situations in Brazil, France, Germany, Hungary, Japan, and Poland. Thus, in a certain respect, the authors have a privileged position compared to that of historians placed in the centre, in the sense that they are sensible to the fact that their statements are written from specific locations. Their case studies thus unpack a web of conflicts, critiques, resistances, mutable agencies and contradictory patterns that were present in the practices concerned.

Critical attention has been increasingly directed to questions of how power structures were reshuffled in the long 1960s, as new production forms, positions and liaisons emerged in the markets and fields of art. Over the last years, a critical field has developed within art history which concerns methods for challenging the established narrative of modern art, a narrative that has been structured on ideas of centre and periphery, the nation, and aesthetic development. Since Serge Guilbaut's pivotal *How New York Stole the Idea of Modern Art: Abstract Expressionism, Freedom, and the Cold War* (1983), some of these assumptions have been questioned and new spatio-temporal models have been proposed.[1] While Guilbault's book put forward an intricate sociopolitical argument for why American art gained power in the Western art world—an argument which changed how these events are perceived today—it did not provide models for understanding the nature of local situations, the cultural transfer of art and the complex relations between agents involved.[2] This anthology has

[1] Serge Guilbaut, *How New York Stole the Idea of Modern Art: Abstract Expressionism, Freedom, and the Cold War*, Chicago: University of Chicago, 1983. Recent art exhibitions have served to widen the scope of the art ordinarily connected to Pop, see *International Pop*, produced by the Walker Art Center, Minneapolis and *The Ey Exhibition, The World Goes Pop*, Tate Gallery, London, both in 2015.

[2] The concept of cultural transfer, central to art history, was developed within a group of international researchers that published their work in Michel Espagne and Michael Werner (eds.), *Transferts: Les relations interculturelles dans l'espace franco-allemand (XVIII et XIXème siècle)*, Paris: Editions recherche sur les civilisations, in 1988. Within the field of literary history, the term is used to study circulatory implications, turning away from comparative studies and instead highlighting cross-mixing between cultures. Béatrice Joyeux-Prunel developed theories of cultural transfer for the circulation of the works of the great modern artists in her *Nul n'est*

the ambition to work in that gap, offering case studies using different methods but with the common notion that they combine local knowledge, archival research, and micro stories to open up new transcultural perspectives on the Pop art of the 1960s. The project is firmly located in the field of *horizontal art history*.[3] Piotr Piotrowski, in his book *In the Shadow of Yalta: Art and the Avant-garde in Eastern Europe, 1945–1989* (2009), takes a stand against the tendency of many projects to reinforce a universal perspective by reproducing the opposition between the centre and the periphery. He even asserts that the interest in "peripheral" portions of the continent is inversely proportional to, as is his example, the absence of East-Central European art from the textbooks on European art history.[4]

There are still scholarly and methodological problems with how global art is framed by stylistic premises originating in North Atlantic Art History, in the general art historical discourse. Thus, the challenge for the art historian is twofold. First, important theoretical and empirical work is still urgently to be performed, in order to describe and analyse the process and its effect on the art life and art discourse of the 1960s and today. Secondly, research has to be done on various conceptual, artistic and curatorial processes in the Era of Pop, to tell new, other, and multiple stories. These are the challenges that the scholars contributing to this anthology, working on this field from different cultural positions, are responding to in various and deeply intriguing ways.

Among the methods employed in these studies, one finds the use of a multiplicity of sources in order to enhance the possibility of understanding several social, cultural, financial, and political contexts, and articulates the kind of work that needs to be done in order to reassess the period. Many of the essays take a dual perspective, pairing a thorough knowledge of the

prophète en son pays? L'internationalisations de la peinture des avant-gardes parisiennes 1855–1914, Paris: N. Chaudun, 2009. For a further discussion of theories of art in transfer and circulation, see Thomas DaCosta Kaufmann, Catherine Dossin and Béatrice Joyeux-Prunel (eds.), *Circulation in the Global History of Art*, Farnham: Ashgate, 2015.

[3] Piotr Piotrowski, "On the Spatial Turn, or Horizontal Art History," Umeni/Art (Prague), No. 5, 2008, pp. 378–83, and his "Towards a Horizontal History of the European Avant-Garde," in Sascha Bru and Peter Nicholls, *Europa! Europa? The Avant-Garde, Modernism and the Fate of a Continent*, Berlin: De Gruyter, 2009, pp. 49–58.

[4] Piotr Piotrowski, *In the Shadow of Yalta: Art and the Avant-garde in Eastern Europe, 1945–1989*, London: Reaktion Books, 2009, p. 15.

particular and the local with a horizontal perspective on how art historical writing and concepts of cultural transfer can be further developed. This horizontal perspective varies between authors, but the dual approach in and of itself serves to open up mechanisms and strategies in the material. The contributions present a web that, to refer to Piotrowski once again, serve to resist the concept of universalism and change the established narratives of the period. As Piotrowski puts it in his introductory essay in the book, something that Agata Jakubowska also emphasises in hers: "peripheral art works are caught in a kind of trap between a general vocabulary of style, which originated elsewhere [...], and local specificity that is not readable from the outside."[5]

Considerations such as these serve as a point of departure for reassessing the East–West cultural transfer with regards to the Neo-Avant-Garde, its exhibition forms and artworks. In the Era of Pop, artistic regeneration spread in networks both outside and inside institutions, between metropolises and peripheries. Most of the studies in this anthology have *the exhibition* and *curatorial strategies* in focus, not just as a practice of aesthetic decision-making, but as performative, active position-taking in the art world as such. While Part One of this volume focuses on how exhibitions articulate positions in an emerging field, sometimes gaining force and in other cases not, Part Two presents readings of artists' practices as reactions, reflections, criticisms, or creations of imagery concepts connected to Pop. Here, alternative readings and understandings of these practices are put forward.

In her chapter, Mathilde Arnoux scrutinises an excellent example of Piotrs Piotrowski's "trap" from the period just before Pop art exploded, that is, from the congress of the *International Art Critics' Association* in Poland in 1960. The congress was held at a particularly interesting moment in history, when major shifts in East–West relations were beginning to take effect. It exemplifies the end of the Abstraction/Figuration dichotomy that had dictated the artistic identities of the opposing blocs. Arnoux assesses the two models of representation, figuration and abstraction that

[5] Piotr Piotrowski, "Why Were There No Great Pop Art Curatorial Projects in Eastern Europe in the 1960s", pp. 21–36 and Agata Jakubowska, "Personalising the Global History of Pop Art. Alina Szapocznikow And Maria Pinińska-Bereś", pp. 237–262, in this volume.

were still so critically important in the 1950s. The theme of the conference was "Modern Art as an International Phenomenon," and the hosting Polish branch of *Association Internationale des Critiques d'Art* (AICA) had intended to let it represent the Thaw after the death of Stalin. In the Polish context, representation, even if "abstract," preserved its mimetic connection to a referential physical reality as in the case of artwork by Marian Bogusz and Tadeusz Dominik. The Western critics at the conference, however, did not allow their own perspectives of internationalism to be challenged by an alternative model of an art form that embodied different values than their own. Even the French critic Restany, despite being well versed in the Polish context, described it as an inferior situation and a belated copy to what had already happened in the West.

The arrival of new art from the U.S. has occasionally been described as a cultural invasion in the framework of popular culture, and, as stated above, a matter of rivalry between art in Paris and New York. The artist Robert Rauschenberg and his early appearances in Europe, for example, in 1961 on the occasion of the *Rörelse i konsten* (Movement in Art) exhibition at the Moderna Museet in Stockholm, have been seen as embodying these processes. In her chapter, Catherine Dossin takes the occasion when Rauschenberg received the Grand Prize of Painting at the Venice Biennale in 1964 as her point of departure, and when the French critic Pierre Cabanne questioned whether the jury had given the award to the indisputable painter or to the pop artist. Through close readings of texts and archival documents and quantitative and distant readings, methods developed in Artl@s, a research project on spatial-digital art history at École Normale Supérieure in Paris, directed by Béatrice Joyeux-Prunel and Dossin herself, she points to the 1964 Biennale as a decisive moment in the history of Western Art, where young artists for the first time could be artistically consecrated.

Hiroko Ikegami takes on the position of an outsider in relation to the dominant culture while visiting a claimed periphery, arriving in Stockholm to follow Robert Rauschenberg's artwork *Monogram* through the history of the Moderna Museet. The study takes the famed *combine* as well as other works of Rauschenberg through its more or less scandalous performances in the museum in the 1960s, to a harsher, more political criticism of the American part of the museum's programme during the period of the anti-American climate around the beginning of 1970. It ends with the appropriation by the Moderna Museet of Robert Rauschenberg's signature for a new logotype in connection with the reopening of the museum in a new building on the old site in 2004. Ikegami also follows Rauschenberg's visit to her native Japan, offering an over view of a number of Japanese artists whom she designates as *Tokyo Pop* and whom Rauschenberg, visiting Tokyo in 1964, failed to give any real recognition. Within the local art scene as well, through the connotations that the Japanese perceived in Pop art to earlier military aggressions, these artists failed to receive any appreciation.

Amerikansk pop-konst: 106 former av kärlek och förtvivlan (American Pop Art: 106 Forms of Love and Despair) was the very first showing in a European museum of pop art, opening on 29 February 1964 at the Moderna Museet in Stockholm. In Sweden's national narrative, this exhibition has been inscribed as a pioneering moment, opening a new space for an "Open Art" in Sweden, as well as constituting a triumphant moment for American art in Europe. My own contribution, a close study of archival documents and texts connected to the exhibition, scrutinises the conception, production and reception of the show. It intends to reveal how the period of conception of the "Pop show" in Stockholm not only coincides with, but also plays a direct role in the negotiation and development of Pop art as a phenomenon and label—in the U.S. After about two years of preparations, the show's opening symbolised a *consolidation* of a previously open art concept and art market rather than the *beginning* of a period of openness and inclusion of art forms and artistic actors which has been the standard story. Due to the exhibition, pop art became identified in Sweden with the American artists it presented, while several early local shows and initiatives by young artists, such as the ones presented in the film *Stockholm à l'heure du pop* referred to above, presenting a diverse variety. The new space that had been consolidated was gendered male.

Reactions to the American Pop invasion were occurring all over the world. Hannah Abdullah's contribution to this volume begins in November 1964 during *New Realists & Pop Art*, the first Pop Art exhibition in West Germany, at the Akademie der Künste in West Berlin. At the opening, the gallerist and curator René Block protested against the lack of German artists in the show while wearing a gas mask with a poster strapped to his back that advertised New German Realists at Gallery Block. On his front, he wore a poster for "Images of Capitalist Realism," Gerhard

Richter's first solo-exhibition at Galerie Block. The action was received as "in keeping with the Pop Art style." Block's opening of a new gallery was calling for a broader perspective on Pop as well as a clear political content. Abdullah asks whether Block, through his activities and those within graphic arts, was seriously proposing a Western parallel or an alternative to Eastern Bloc Socialist realism. She concludes that by mobilising the new realist idiom to thematise pressing social and political issues in Cold War Germany, Block tried to push pop to its limits. Politics and pop coexisted in his programme of Capitalist Realism.

Öyvind Fahlström was something as unique as a Swedish artist who was strongly connected to the American Pop field through his close friendships with artists like Rauschenberg, Oldenburg, Rosenqvist, and Lichtenstein. He lived and worked in Manhattan from 1961 almost until his premature death in 1976. Sophie Cras's contribution to this anthology sheds new light on the "cartographic" dimension of Fahlström's work, in particular his *World Map* (1972). Cras argues that although Fahlström was often considered part of the of international pop art scene, his use of comics and his appropriation of American counterculture were part of a strategy to propose a new visualisation of the Cold War. Fahlström mimicked and subverted the techniques of visualisation of economic data initiated by the German economist Otto Neurath in the 1920s. He thus built a very personal, politically engaged and fantasised cartography of the violent imperialist politics of the early 1970s, suggesting that given categories and divisions could be traversed, condemned, or ridiculed. In his case, the situation between local and global was not a trap, but a way to open new semiotic dimensions in painting.

Another "local" perception and deep transformation of American Pop and Robert Rauschenberg, was the one performed by Brazilian artists. Oscar Svanelid's chapter manages to reformulate the Brazilian reception of U.S. pop art in the early period of the military dictatorship (1964–1968) in "AnthroPOPhagous" terms. He argues that Brazilian artists not only rejected pop art, but then simultaneously incorporated it into their work, thus revealing complex aesthetic and strategic processes. This idea is scrutinised in two case studies of the art of Waldemar Cordeiro and Hélio Oiticica. Far from regarding pop art as nothing more than commercial images, as is often assumed, Oscar Svanelid suggests that these Brazilian artists used pop as a political instrument—as did Fahlström—but in a completely different and unique manner.

The trap between the specificity of the local and the general style vocabulary developed elsewhere, was a position in which many artists in Europe found themselves. Another "trap" was constituted by the strongly male inflected space of pop art and the art scene as a whole in the 1960s, which failed to foster female agency. However, pop art practices were also adopted outside this space, to the oblivion of dominating art history. In her chapter, Agata Jakubowska departs from a recent international feminist exhibition which claimed to break the dominancy of Anglo–American pop while presenting female pop artists, but failed to take into account Eastern Europe, as it was not fully addressed in their local or national context. Jakubowska's study is rigorous, comprising an analysis of two highly interesting exponents of art production in the actual Era of Pop, outside the established explanatory conventions.

Katarina Wadstein MacLeod, in her turn, uses the non-spatial and trans-national figure of "the home" to approach art that was made locally, in Stockholm, during the peak era of American art import. The domestic, truly highlighted in American pop art, was not only scrutinised and questioned by the Swedish Women's Movement, but also reoccurred as a problem and tradition within the work of artists such as Marie-Louise Ekman and Anna Sjödahl, who adopted pop-related elements in their art. In the course of the remapping of Western art history, studies like Jakubowska's and MacLeod's are essential.

A tendency towards abstraction could be found in other European contexts, as in the post-war modernism that saw the advent of artist groups that opted for spatiality through the synthesis of the arts that would engage with citizens and form a ground for democracy. Many of the most celebrated artists from the period were engaged in these questions, and yet little of their collaboration is visible in art history due to the tendency to emphasise "American" art history. Håkan Nilsson's chapter looks into two of these groups, *Groupe Espace* in France and *aspect* in Sweden. He argues that the groups were important for transferring art ideals and disseminating ideas that would reach outside the art community and into the urbanist strategies for the reconstruction of Europe, a trait that was non-existent in their American counterparts. Nilsson discusses how the idea of a joint visual language functioned with the ideal of pluralism and he reflects on the groups' relationship to the "open" art scene of the 1960s, as well as to the much-debated suburbs from the same time.

Tania Ørum's chapter establishes how the 1964 American Pop Art show and other exhibitions at the Moderna Museet in Stockholm, were disseminated to Denmark and the Netherlands, where they had a considerable impact. "Most pop art came to Denmark through Sweden," Ørum explains and points out that artist networks developed over the border between the two nations. Despite this, she suggests, different conceptions of pop art and minimalism developed in the two countries. In the introduction of a Swedish edition of texts by John Cage, written by Torsten Ekbom and Leif Nylén, she finds a very open and inclusive use of the term *pop art*, which she contrasts with how in Denmark, *minimalism* was used as a term for what was new and American, at least to the extent that it was understood in the writings of Hans-Jorgen Nielsen, who was influenced by artists like Smithson, Judd and Morris.

In his chapter, Dávid Fehér's deals with both exhibitions and image structures. He investigates transformations of pop art in Hungary through key exhibitions of the late 1960s. In the focus of the study is the so-called "Iparterv circle" that was named after two legendary semi-official group exhibitions held in Budapest, as well as solo exhibitions with the "Ipartev-artists" György Kemény, Endre Tót and László Lakner. He explores the extent to which the exhibitions can be interpreted as peculiar local responses to international artistic trends, viewing them as instances of *cultural transfer*. He also analyses, at the level of aesthetic strategies seen within the artworks, how these artists transformed the "Western" notion of Pop art and how they were related to local artistic traditions. Hungarian pop-related exhibition projects of the 1960s and similar exhibitions in the Eastern bloc are essential for understanding pop art's reception in the region. The analysis of such events might shed light on hidden perspectives of "international pop" and his chapter, as many chapters in this volume, will contribute to comparative studies on the internationalisation of pop art.

As has already been obvious for the reader, the work of Professor Piotr Piotrowski has played an invaluable role in this anthology, not only because of the impact and importance of his own authorship to our field of art historical research, but also for the central part he played as keynote speaker and discussant, as colleague and friend, during a conference at

Södertörn University and Moderna Museet in Stockholm in 2014.[6] We were all looking forward to future readings, meetings, and interchanges with him, and were immensely saddened and shocked by the news of his passing in May 2015.

The anthology *Art in Transfer in the Era of Pop* is dedicated to his memory.

Stockholm, November 2016
Annika Öhrner

[6] The scholars contributing to this volume gathered during 6–8 November 2014 at the *Art in Transfer: Curatorial Practices and Transnational Strategies in the Era of Pop* conference held at Södertörn University and Moderna Museet, Stockholm, arranged by the Department of Art History, School of Education and Culture at Södertörn University, in cooperation with the Terra Foundation for American Art and the Centre for Baltic and East European Studies (CBEES). My deepest gratitude to Charlotte Bydler, Senior Lecturer and former research leader in Cultural theory, CBEES, and Oscar Svanelid, PhD Candidate, for their invaluable contributions to, and joyful exchanges during, the conceptualisation and realisation of the conference. I would also like to thank Anna Tellgren and Annika Gunnarsson, Moderna Museet, Helena Mattson, KTH School of Architecture and Francesca Rose, Terra Foundation for American Art.

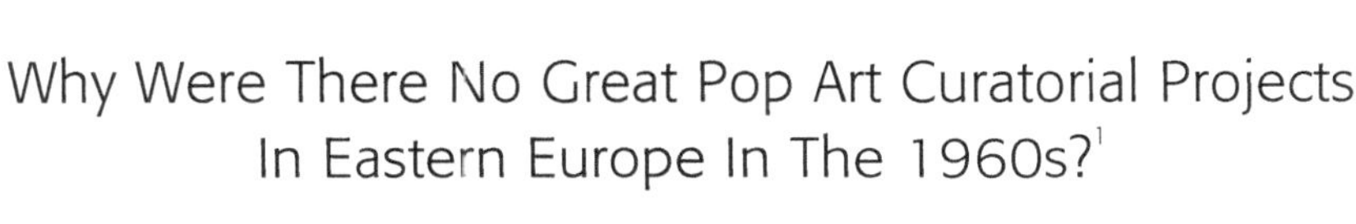

Why Were There No Great Pop Art Curatorial Projects In Eastern Europe In The 1960s?[1]

Piotr Piotrowski

[1] The late Piotr Piotrowski (14 June 1952-3 May 2015) gave this lecture as a keynote speech at the conference *Art in Transfer: Curatorial Practices and Transnational Strategies in the Era of Pop*, at Moderna Museet, 6–8 November 2014. The conference was arranged by the Department of Art History, Södertörn University, Stockholm. During this period, while he was a guest researcher at CBEES. Professor Piotrowski has modified and reworked his lecture for dual publication in Baltic Worlds (Issue 4–5, 2015, p. 10–16) as well as in this anthology. The text has been very lightly edited for the present publication. Published with the kind permission of © Maria Żuk-Piotrowska.

The 1960s had more than one face. Although pop culture rapidly spread throughout the world during the decade, this did not mean that pop art, which, by the way, is of course not the same thing as pop culture, followed. On the contrary, we still are faced with a big issue here: American and Western European methodological imperialism frames global art via stylistic premises that originated in North Atlantic art history. One of the groundbreaking texts dealing with the question of methodological imperialism and pop art was recently written by the Hungarian author Katalin Timár: *Is Your Pop Our Pop?*[2] This was followed by the work of the Polish scholar Anna Kołos, in her (regrettably unpublished) M.A. thesis, *Quoting Pictorial Tradition in the Poetics of Pop Art in Polish, Hungarian, and Slovak Art in the Age of Socialism.*[3] The idea these two authors share is that acceptance of the term "pop art" by local art history is problematic. Peripheral art works are caught in a kind of trap between a general vocabulary of style, which originated

[2] Katalin Timár, "Is Your Pop Our Pop? The History of Art as Self-Colonizing Tool," www.artmargins.com/index.php/archive/323-is-your-pop-our-pop-the-history-of-art-as-a-selfcolizing-tool [November, 2014]

[3] Anna Kołos, *Cytowanie tradycji obrazowej w poetyce pop artu w sztuce polskiej, węgierskiej i słowackiej doby socjalizmu* (Quoting Pictorial Tradition in the Poetics of Pop-art in Polish, Hungarian, and Slovak Art in the Period of Socialism), unpublished MA thesis, Poznań: Instytut Historii Sztuki, Adam Mickiewicz University, 2011.

elsewhere (in the case of pop art, the origins are of course North America and Britain), and local specificity that is not readable from the outside. This constitutes a challenge for local art critics, who must find a way out of this trap. While Timár's article is largely critical of Hungarian art-historical discourse, in her thesis Kołos tries to analyse particular techniques shared by both North American and Central-East European artists, such as "quoting pictorial tradition," rather than depicting a general view of this sort of art in the region. Finally, in the precise and detailed analysis Kołos provides, we are able to find some general, international similarities between artists working in those two art-historical contexts, as well as differences. Nevertheless, there are some art historians who have no objection to the use of the term "pop art" in local contexts, such as Katalin Keserü in Hungary, or Sirje Helme in Estonia.[4] In other countries, although this vocabulary is used (for example in Slovakia), there are no monographs on local pop art like those by the foregoing authors.

Whatever might be said of pop art techniques and the art-historical discourses used in Hungary, and later in Estonia (and less frequently in other countries), one would be hard-pressed to say that the 1960s was an era of pop in the region, especially one with North American influences. In Eastern Europe, pop art did not reach the level of being a significant style, and there were no large-scale international curatorial projects dealing with it.

The first question might then be: Why were artists in Eastern Europe in the 1960s not so interested in North American pop art, as opposed to artists in, say, Sweden? Concerning Sweden, let me simply point out that, although formally speaking it was a neutral country, especially from the military point of view, (and still is), from the Eastern European perspective, it was (and still is) seen as a Western country. Although the West was idealised in the East, and the US has enjoyed a great prestige in Eastern Europe (and still does), the cultural map at that time, at the beginning of the 1960s, was more complicated. A simplistic answer might at first present itself as to why there was no North American art (e.g. pop art) here:

[4] Respectively: Katalin Keserü, *Variations on Pop Art: Chapters in the History of Hungarian Art Between 1950 and 1990*, Budapest: Ernst Museum, 1993; Sirje Helme, *Popkunst Forever: Estonian Pop Art at the Turn of the 1960s and 1970s*, Tallinn: EESTI Kunstmuuseum KUMU, 2010.

there was not enough pop culture background in the region, at least not to the same extent as in the U.S. and Western Europe. Yet the situation is more complicated. Pop art was definitely “charming” for local artists (as was pop culture for general audiences), and some of them, such as László Lakner, who had the opportunity to see Robert Rauschenberg’s famous exhibition in Venice in 1964, were influenced by it. It was a sort of *new* Western art. If we take into account, on the one hand, that pop art referred directly to popular reality, that is, to non-artistic reality, which was fascinating for the artists, and—on the other hand—that Eastern European artists strongly supported modernist values, such as art autonomy, which in turn was a reaction for socialist realism understood as political propaganda (i.e. engaged in reality), we could understand that the epistemological status of pop art might be complicated for Eastern European artists. Allow me to further develop these ideas in a couple of arguments.

1. The background of pop art was a sort of cultural trash—popular iconography, everyday, ordinary objects, and so on. It was a way to understand the contemporary, present-day reality; that is, it was quite a different approach to the world from that expressed by high modernism—in case of the U.S.: abstract expressionism. In Eastern Europe the point of departure for postwar modern art—which actually began in the post-Stalinist period, simultaneously, curiously enough, with the emergence of pop art in the U.S. (that is, during the late 1950s/beginning of the 1960s)—was high modernism, as an alternative to socialist realism. The trauma of the mandatory, the only art that could be shown publicly, which went together with political terror, was so strong that it resulted in a conviction that only autonomous high art is able to defend the high culture values that at the same time guarantee artistic freedom. The popular culture at the beginning of the 1960s was extremely pure, and it would be very difficult to become fascinated by it. If there is something precisely similar to the methodology of pop art—that is a sort of critical analysis of everyday realities—it would be soc-art, which emerged much later in the USSR. Artists such as Eric Bulatov, in the mid-1970s and later, referred to the ambiguities of the everyday communist iconosphere of the Soviet Union.

2. That was of course the desire for American trash, such as Coca-Cola cans, popular comic books, illustrated magazines with movie stars, etc. It

was not, however, the everyday realities here, rather a charming cult of the reach of free culture. If we thus look at—let's say—Gyula Konkoly's pictures (a Hungarian artist), and some of the references to Western popular culture found in them, we see Western influences and popular culture, almost as iconography, quoted as stylistic references (i.e. pop art), *très-à-la-mode* Western art, art novelty coming from the West.

3. It has also happened that these references have been combined with *informel* painting (Figure 12.5), as in the case of Endre Tót, to mention another Hungarian of that period. This is important since the *informel* style was able to elevate any art production to the level of high culture, i.e. free art, so important in the post-socialist-realism period. If we now take into account Robert Rauschenberg's *combine paintings*, which in some sense were behind Hungarian art experiments, we can see that the relation between the everyday object and abstract expressionist references was in fact the reverse. The idea wasn't to elevate the banal reality to the level of high art, but on the contrary, to discredit high art itself.

4. The foregoing is in no way meant to suggest that there was no "figurative" painting in Eastern Europe in the 1960s. The figurative painting that existed, however, was of course based on a different tradition—I would call it non-socialist realism—and referred to different problems, mostly existential, usually suppressed by genuine American pop artists.

The second question I would like to raise here might be: "Shall we draw the conclusion that there was no interest at all within Eastern Europe in North American culture, again, as opposed to the interest in Sweden at the beginning of the 1960s?" At that time, to be sure, Eastern Europeans did not buy into the idea of New York's having "stolen the idea of modern art." They still believed that the capital city of international contemporary art was Paris. If we look at Entre Tót's painting, it is not even clear whether we are seeing a North American echo of pop art, or French *Les Nouveaux Réalistes*—something entirely different, of course, having become very popular in the 1960s in Slovakia because of the close relation of local artists to Pierre Restany. Katarzyna Murawska-Muthesius, one of the authors of the book *Paris: Capital of the Arts, 1900–1968*, wrote polemically to Serge Guilbaut:

> Despite the supposed impenetrability of the Iron Curtain, a steady exchange between Paris and Eastern Europe took place from 1946 onwards. A plethora of exhibitions travelled in both directions; periodicals and catalogues were privately circulated; artists and critics, sponsored by cultural and political bodies, travelled both West and East. Relations were never broken off completely, even during the "darkest nights of Stalinism," although they were closely monitored by the authorities. The Iron Curtain might be compared to a two-way mirror, able to hide and reveal several Parises: the dreamt-of "fount of modernity," the "communist" Paris of Daumier and socialist realism; and finally the "forbidden" Paris of existentialist anxiety and of the liberating gestures of *Tachism*. These diverse ways of looking at Paris from the position of an Eastern European observer might be aligned chronologically to form a tentative sequence which would unfold from the brief episode of the return to modern Paris in the period directly after the war (1945–8), through the rise of the "Iron Curtain Paris" constructed by Stalinism (1949/50–5), to the Paris "regained" with the post-Stalinist "Thaw" (from 1956).

In terms of the 1960s, our primary interest, she added:

> During the 1960s, however, the absolute hegemony of the Parisian dream was beginning to turn into a nostalgic memory, even in Poland. The freedom to look at Parisian art mattered increasingly, but so did the chance to be seen there. Throughout the 1950s and the 1960s, Paris was undeniably the city in which artists from Eastern Europe were exhibited by both state museums and private galleries. At the helm was Denise Rene, with her successive displays of the pioneering Polish Unism (1928) and geometrical abstraction in 1957, of abstract Yugoslavian art in 1959, and of work by the Hungarian constructivist László Kassák in 1960 and 1967. A young Polish artist, Jan Lebenstein, received the Grand Prix at the Première Biennale de Paris in 1959.[5]

Naturally, this does not mean that there was no relationship at all between Eastern Europe and New York—the famous exhibition of Polish contemporary painting at the MoMA in 1961 attests to this—but it was definitely less visible and less recognised by both art criticism and the authorities than—let's say—the exhibition of Polish painters at the Musée National d'Art Moderne in Paris the same year. However, in the course of the

[5] Katarzyna Murawska-Muthesius, "Paris from behind the Iron Curtain." in: Sarah Wilson et al. (eds.) *Paris: Capital of the Arts 1900-1968*, London: Royal Academy of Arts, 2002, pp. 250, 259.

1960s, the situation gradually started to change. By the end of the decade, London and New York had replaced Paris as places of privilege for Eastern Europeans. It was not, however, pop art (with the exception of Hungary, as noted) but rather happenings and conceptual art that captured the attention of Eastern Europeans. Therefore, the real change of "art-geographical desire" or the change in both virtual and real cultural trajectory, took place here by the end of the 1960s, and was connected with an entirely different aesthetics and art theory.

Now, let's come back to the beginning of the 1960s, and ask the third question: if transnational pop art curatorial projects were not to be found in Eastern Europe as the crucial art-historical experience, were there others in the "Era of Pop," instead? I assume that the only large-scale transnational, indeed global, curatorial project at that time in Eastern Europe was the *New Tendencies* Biennial in Zagreb, established in 1961 and running through 1973. It was organised—and this is extremely interesting from an art-geographical point of view—on the basis of the South American artist, Almir Mavignier. (However, it was based in West Germany, actually in Ulm, which is extremely important because of the Hochschule für Gestaltung, founded by Max Bill in the 1950s, an artist extremely important for Latin American concretism).[6] Let's look into this a bit more closely.

Almir Mavignier, a Brazilian artist who moved to Germany, is one of many who created a sort of bridge between Europe and Latin America, especially in the field of—generally speaking and broadly understood – neoconstructivism. To live in Ulm was, as noted, significant because of Max Bill, whose influences over Latin American concretism cannot be overestimated. Another theme might be the argument about how relationships between Latin America and Eastern Europe looked in the 1950s/ 1960s in terms of the above-mentioned broadly understood neoconstructivism. And then we have the striking comparison of the background of two curatorial projects, namely the Biennial in São Paulo, established in 1951, and, ten years later, the *New Tendencies*, also organised in the bien-

[6] Margit Rosen (ed.), *A Little-Known Story about a Movement, a Magazine, and the Computer's Arrival in Art: New Tendencies and Bit International, 1961–1973*, Karlsruhe/ Cambridge MA: ZKM| Center for Art and Media/ The MIT Press, 2011.

nial format, albeit with a much shorter lifespan. In both cases, there was an ambition to be modern, universal, and global; in both cases neoconstructivism (in Brazil's case concretism) was the vehicle of inter-national culture, i.e. "international" and "national" at the same time, or an attempt to internationalise the local; in both cases emerging and modernised countries wanted to be recognised as the protagonist of the utopia of technology, science, industrialisation, and so on. Of course, there were significant differences, too. The São Paulo Biennial was initiated by a private, very successful, businessman, and its structure followed the Venice Biennial format with national delegations from around the world. Its crisis came in 1969 because of the international boycott caused by the increase of terror and censorship, introduced by the local junta in December, 1968. However, the biennial still exists, as a large global event. The *New Tendencies* was much more specific, focusing on particular art only, organised by the artists and critics, with the support, of course, from the local administration. It was definitely a smaller-scale event, showing invited artists and their art, not national teams. Its failure resulted from internal artistic causes, but the failure was also connected to the end of the relatively liberal policy in Croatia, called "Croatian Spring," followed by stronger centralisation of Yugoslavia. Let's save these observations, however, for a different occasion.

Nevertheless, Almir Mavignier, because of his role in founding *New Tendencies* in Zagreb, would play a very important role in art developments in Eastern Europe. He had become familiar with the local art scene –probably the most vivid, international, and dynamic in Eastern Europe at the end of the 1950s and the beginning of the 1960s –ever since he stopped there on his way from the Venice Biennale to Egypt in the summer of 1960. While returning to Ulm, he wrote, on 24 February 1961, a famous letter to Matko Meštrović, a young art historian and art critic, the key person in creating this series of exhibitions, actually in French, a language widely used in Eastern Europe at that time.[7] He suggested the idea of organising a global show in Zagreb with artists from Germany, Italy, France, Switzerland, Austria, and Brazil. In *New Tendencies 1* (this one written in the plural), there were only two South American artists, and

[7] Ibid., pp. 59–61.

they were the ones who used to live in the West, actually in Western Europe: Almir Mavignier himself and Julio Le Parc, an Argentinean living in France. In the next exhibition, *New Tendencies 2* (still in the plural), in 1963, there were, in addition to Mavignier and Le Parc, Martha Boto (Argentina/France), Carlos Cruz-Diez (Venezuela/France), Luis Tomasello (Argentina/France), and Gregorio Vardanega (Argentina/France/Italy). In the third exhibition, *New Tendency*, in 1965, Martha Boto and Waldemar Cordeiro were present from South America, though the exhibition was open to Eastern European countries other than Yugoslavia: the Group Dviženije from the Soviet Union, as well as Edward Krasiński from Poland and Zdeněk Sýkora from Czechoslovakia were shown.[8] The third exhibition, organised as *Tendencies 4* (in the plural again, but without the adjective "new") was not put together until 1969, already in a different historical context and along with different theoretical questions. Let me just mention that it was anticipated by a couple of different events and side projects (workshops, symposia, shows), also under the title "Bit International," and the slogans "Computers and Visual Research" and "The Theory of Information and the New Aesthetics."

To return to the beginning of the New Tendencies, it is worthwhile to focus on a couple of general questions. As Margit Rosen has written in the enormous retrospective catalogue of this series of events, which she also edited, new technology and new hopes and expectations in terms of aesthetic, social, and political potential were the main backdrop to the *New Tendencies*. From an art-historical point of view, this project was clearly distinct from abstract expressionism, or—in French terms—*Tashism*, because it rejected the idea of "genius," replacing it with a concept of "research," as well as industrial production and science, and connecting them with "democracy," because of widely accessible mass-reproduction and multiplicities of serially produced art works. The artists believed their efforts were part of a struggle against the elite-oriented art market.[9] In my opinion, however, neither neoconstructivism nor pop art had anything to do with democracy. Technology, which lay behind neoconstructivism, led to technocracy, rather than to democracy, and the consumerism that informed

[8] Ibid., respectively pp. 65, 111, 179.
[9] Margit Rosen, "Editorial," ibid., 10–11.

pop art was populist, not democratic. They both were somehow anti-elite (in different ways), but far from democratic, if by the latter we mean an agonistic agora, rather than shopping mall or perfectly organised factory.

Let me add that it was not only *Tashism* that was a negative point of reference of the *New Tendencies*; it was also—what is important for us and what is much more generally characteristic of neoconstructivism—pop art. This sort of art (i.e. neoconstructivism) was somehow close to *The Responsive Eye* organised by William Seitz at the MoMA in New York City in 1965, promoting what he has called "optical art," or "op art." Also in Europe, as Jerko Denegri argues in the above-mentioned retrospective, the *New Tendencies* movement was connected with such projects as the Moving Movement exhibition at the Stedelijk Museum Amsterdam (1961), later shown at the Moderna Museet in Stockholm and elsewhere. There were more post-Art *Informel* abstract artists consistent with the focus of both Almir Mavignier and Matko Meštrović, such as the ZERO Group from Germany, the Paris-based Groupe de recherche d'art visuel founded in 1961, Padua Gruppo N, people around *Azimuth & Azimut* in Milan, and others.[10] The local situation should be also on the agenda, if not the primary point of reference. If Zagreb had not been so interesting for Almir Mavignier, he would not have proposed Matko Meštrović as organiser of the exhibition. In the text mentioned above, Denegri cites the Exat 51 group, which emerged shortly after Josip Broz-Tito broke his relation with Stalin and left the Eastern Bloc. Exat 51 was a very influential group of artists in Zagreb who formed the immediate art-historical context for the *New Tendencies.*[11] Allow me to also add another Zagreb group of artists that emerged in the city in 1959, namely the Gorgona group. Although these artists had declared a different type of art, different theory and attitudes, and different politics and aesthetics—including rejecting the visual from the artwork (actually conceptual approach)—some of them, such as Julije Knifer, took part in the exhibitions. Also, Matko Meštrović himself was connected with the Gorgona group.

[10] Jerko Denegri, "The Conditions and Circumstances That Preceded the Mounting of the First Two New Tendencies Exhibitions in Zagreb 1961–1963," ibid., pp. 20–21.
[11] Ibid., p. 19.

Now allow me to draw your attention to the position of neoconstructivism itself in the region as a whole, i.e. Eastern Europe, in the 1960s, in order to provide the broader geographical framework of this curatorial project. Constructivism as such has a very strong tradition in Eastern Europe. Because of its Soviet origins, very quickly it became widespread in the region in the 1920s, especially in Poland, where Henryk Stażewski, Katarzyna Kobro, and Władysław Strzemiński had close relationships to Russian artists, especially Kazimir Malevich, but it also quickly became important in Hungary because of Lajos Kassák. Kobro and Strzemiński died at the very beginning of the 1950s, but Stażewski in Poland and Kassák in Hungary were still very much alive in the 1960s, and they created strong circles of younger artists who became responsible for the revival of constructivism. Their personal role in the revitalisation of constructivism was very important. To a lesser extent, we can say the same about Czechoslovakia, which does not mean, however, that in the 1960s neoconstructivism was not visible there. In 1963, several outstanding Czech artists founded the group Křižovatka, then the Synteza group in 1965, and finally the Club of Concretists in 1967. The first attempt towards a constructivist revival (aside from the Exat 51 group in Zagreb) appeared in Poland in 1957. Julian Przyboś, a close associate before the war of Katarzyna Kobro and Władysław Strzemiński, wrote an essay called "Abstract Art – How to Get Out." Przyboś argued against the French-oriented Informel style and one of its main Polish protagonists, Tadeusz Kantor, advocating instead attention to local artistic heritage, the Polish avant-garde tradition, namely constructivism. However, the first exhibition that manifests this was organised not in Poland, but in Paris—at Denis René Gallery in the same year: *Précurseurs de l'art abstrait en Pologne*, 1957.

Paris, as noted, did indeed host a couple of exhibitions like that. The Zagreb artists from the Exat 51 group showed their work in *Salon des Réalités Nouvelles*—in fact, the same year the group was formed (1951). And allow me to mention the abstract Yugoslav art in 1959, and the work of the Hungarian constructivist László Kassak in 1960 and 1967, all shown at Denis René Gallery. It is hard to pinpoint the end of neoconstructivism in Eastern Europe, since even in the 1970s it was very popular throughout the region; however, its role changed around the end of the 1960s in the face of neo-avant-garde art: conceptual art, body art, performance, and other poetics.

Now, let me raise the final question: what is the art-historical significance for the Old Continent of the popularity of neoconstructivism, as well as a Parisian as opposed to the North American geo-cultural trajectory, in Eastern Europe in the "Era of Pop," i.e. in the 1960s?

The first and most general answer is quite banal: there was no one, monolithic, Europe. Art history in Sweden in the 1960s, for example, was different from the art history in Yugoslavia. This also means that both virtual and real art geography looked different in different parts of Europe. If Sweden tended to focus on the North American art scene, Eastern Europe was—let's say—more "traditional" and viewed Paris as the eternal capital of culture with a capital "C". Because it was cut off from its Western part, it petrified the old, continental, imagined cultural relations, which at the same time were symbolic, and compensated for the loss of the paradise that Europe without the Iron Curtin was thought to perhaps be. The next answer is not terribly sophisticated either. While pop culture was behind pop art, there was no pop culture in Eastern Europe in the 1960s, or at least not to the same extent as in the West, although pop music gradually began to become more and more widespread, but this started later in the 1960s. Nevertheless, it was more desirable than easily accessible, in some places maybe even elitist, rather than popular. Only later in the course of the 1960s did the situation change, but not to the same extent as in the U.S. To put it more metaphorically, Coca-Cola was still more expensive in the region –if it was even accessible at all—than vodka.... In a word: it was not a "natural" background for pop art, even if we can find something, especially in Hungary and later in Estonia, resembling it in terms of style.

There is a deeper problem. Pop art acknowledged art with a lowercase "a". It wanted to be anti-elitist, immersed in everyday imaginary and street poetical art manifestation. However, art written with a lowercase "a" was suspect for Eastern Europeans. In addition, they needed art with a capital "A" as a manifestation of a defence of culture with a capital "C". Even if they used ordinary everyday objects in their art production, they elevated them to "Great Art," and placed them in the symbolic, aesthetic, and poetic order. They felt that they had a mission to defend art, not to discredit it, since they knew that the latter was a goal of the powers that be, the regime originating with the Soviets.

All of this was more or less obvious. I would like, however, to conclude with a different observation. Of course, as already noted, neither pop art nor neoconstructivism was democratic. While the former was populist, identifying equality with consumption—changing art galleries into commercial galleries, museums into shopping malls—the latter stood for a technological utopia, and believed that technology would solve the problems of humanity, changing it into fabricated machinery, transforming existential issues into technocratic discourse. Both of them were criticised as such around 1968.

Neoconstructivism was of course not exclusively Eastern European. On the contrary, it was global, originating in Western so-to-speak rationalist, scientific, technocratic, and industrial utopian thought. Its functions were, however, different. While in the West it was connected with capitalism, in the East the same utopia supported communism. Here, thus, we touch upon the core problem. Was the popularity of neoconstructivism connected with the reigning system of power? I would argue that in Yugoslavia and in Poland in particular, it was. The artists, and the powers that be, shared the same conviction that technology, science, and industrialisation would be the way forward. Additionally, neoconstructivist art did not appear dangerous—squares, circles, rectangular, straight lines, and so on were neutral and devoid of direct political meaning. Of course, the situation was dramatically different in such countries as the GDR, where socialist realism was mandatory in art in the 1960s, at least in the public sphere. In countries like the GDR, neoconstructivism manifested the desire for freedom, which also shows that in Eastern Europe there were internal borders, too. In both cases, i.e., a little bit more free, as well as a little bit less free communist countries, neoconstructivism manifested the desire to participate in the global art scene, to share the same universal culture, since these possibilities were limited–though of course to a lesser extent in Yugoslavia. I would like to stress that neoconstructivism gave the Eastern European artists a strong conviction that they are modern. To be modern, made possible both a utopian prospect for the future, as well as references to the tradition of modernism from the past; and modernism, as I noted above, was the main framework of post-socialist-realist art in Eastern Europe. To put it simply: the problem with pop art would not be that it was modernist; indeed, it was anti-modernist, and as such would not address the typical Eastern European trauma experienced at that time of the discrediting of universal art by communist cultural politics.

Bibliography

Denegri, Jerko, "The Conditions and Circumstances That Preceded the Mounting of the First Two New Tendencies Exhibitions in Zagreb 1961–1963," in *A Little-Known Story about a Movement, a Magazine, and the Computer's Arrival in Art: New Tendencies and Bit Internationa*l, 1961–1973, Margit Rosen et.al, Cambridge, MA: MIT Press, 2001, pp. 20–21.

Helme, Sirje, *Popkunst Forever: Estonian Pop Art at the Turn of the 1960s and 1970s*, Tallinn: EESTI Kunstmuuseum KUMU, 2010.

Kołos, Anna, *Cytowanie tradycji obrazowej w poetyce pop artu w sztuce polskiej, węgierskiej i słowackiej doby socjalizmu* (Quoting Pictorial Tradition in the Poetics of Pop-art in Polish, Hungarian, and Slovak Art in the Period of Socialism), unpublished MA thesis, Poznań: Instytut Historii Sztuki, Adam Mickiewicz University, 2011.

Keserü, Katalin, *Variations on Pop Art: Chapters in the History of Hungarian Art Between 1950 and 1990*, Budapest: Ernst Museum, 1993.

Rosen Margit, (ed.), *A Little-Known Story about a Movement, a Magazine, and the Computer's Arrival in Art: New Tendencies and Bit International, 1961–1973*, Karlsruhe and Cambridge, Mass.: ZKM Center for Art and Media/ and The MIT Press, 2011.

Timár, Katalin, "Is Your Pop Our Pop? The History of Art as Self-Colonizing Tool," www.artmargins.com/index.php/archive/323-is-your-pop-our-pop-the-history-of-art-as-a-selfcolizing-tool, November, 2014.

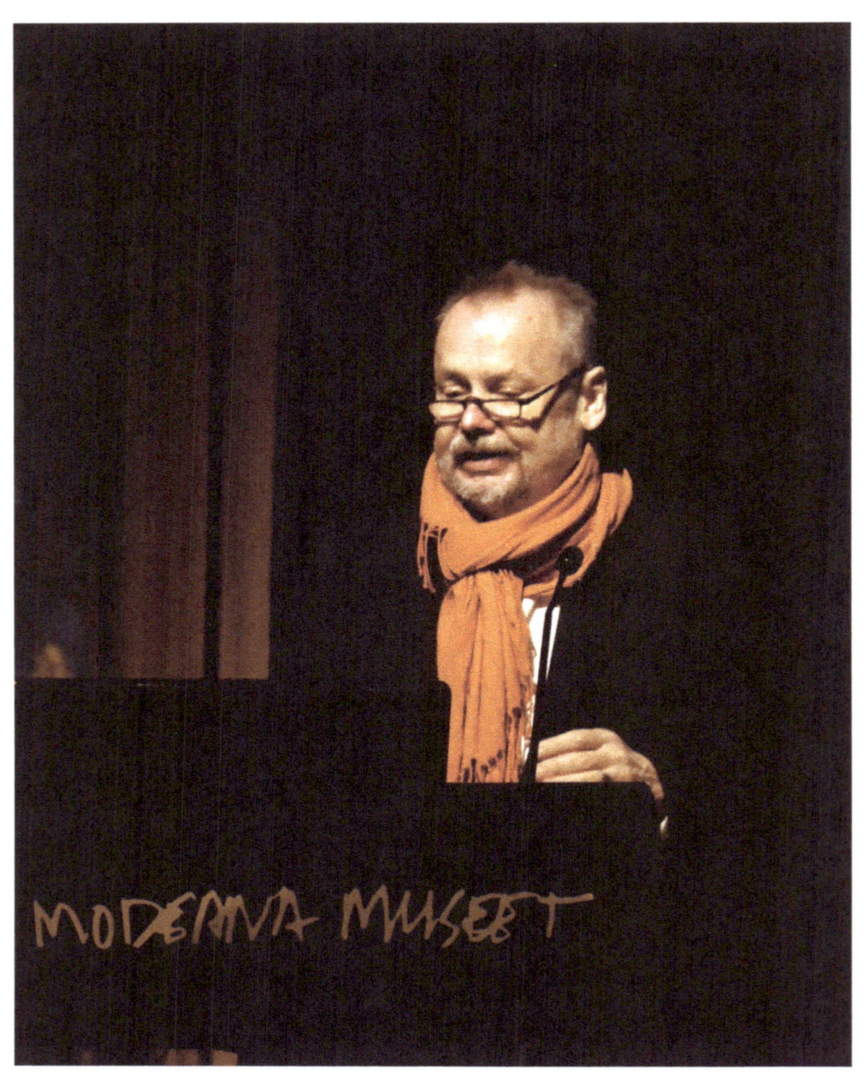

Piotr Piotrowski (14 June 1952–2 May 2015)

Part 1

Exhibitions, Encounters, Rejections

1
Contemporary Polish Art Seen Through the Lens of French Art Critics Invited to the AICA Congress in Warsaw and Cracow in 1960[1]

Mathilde Arnoux

[1] The research leading to these findings has received funding from the European Research Council under the European Union's Seventh Framework Programme (FP7/2007-2013/ERC Grant Agreement No. 263560. We would like to thank the Archives de la Critique d'Art in Rennes for granting us access to their archival collections and libraries for the purpose of this research: www.archivesdelacritiquedart.org/ The chapter is translated by Sarah Tooth Michelet.

While the Cold War did not lead to armed conflict in Europe, it was essentially driven by an ideological opposition, a conflict between models of representation. Both superpowers utilised art as an instrument of soft power to propagate their own particular values. Art institutions and the cultural policy-makers of the 1950s tended to oversimplify the artistic context of the period by pitching abstraction in the Capitalist West against figurative representation in the Communist East. However, these forms of expression were not so clearly divided between the two dominant systems. On both sides of the Cold War divide, there was competition between different models of representation, combined with a borrowing and re-appropriation of terminology. At the International Meetings organised by the *Ownreality Research Project* in 2013, Sophie Cras showed how, in 1960, the art critic Pierre Restany gave the name "Nouveau Réalisme" to the movement he championed—a name that had already been adopted by a group of artists supported by the French Communist Party in the late 1940s-early 1950s, whose painting style was deliberately traditional.[2] She

[2] Sophie Cras, "Le Nouveau Réalisme: du réalisme socialiste au réalisme capitaliste," *Own-Reality (6),* 2014, accessible online: www.perspectivia.net/content/publikationen/ownreality/6/cras-fr (English translation: "Nouveau Réalisme: From Socialist Realism to Capitalist Realism": www.perspectivia.net/publikationen/ownreality/6/cras-en/view).

explained that by doing this, Restany reinterpreted the original meaning of the movement's name to support his promotion of "true" realism, which directly opposed the realism of the communists. Such re-appropriations are difficult for us to contemplate if we view the Cold War period as limited to direct confrontations. The directions followed were often not as clearly-defined as we imagine them to be. An event such as the International Art Critics' Association (AICA) Congress held in Poland in 1960 is particularly interesting from this perspective, as it allows us to examine what happened to these models of representation that were so critically important to the identities of the opposing systems at an event that brought representatives of the two blocs together.

This is what we aim to explore here, by paying particular attention to how the art critic Pierre Restany, founder of Nouveau Réalisme, responded to the event. It is only possible to analyse this if we understand the motivations of the Polish branch of the AICA at the Congress, and the extent to which the different viewpoints of participants were constructed in relation to each other.

What the Polish critics desired to show: The AICA Congress as a reflection of the period of thaw

The 7th AICA Congress marked the first time since the Association's establishment in 1948/1949 that the event was held in a country east of the Iron Curtain. Affiliated with UNESCO as a non-governmental organisation in 1951, the AICA organises regular international gatherings of art critics from member countries based on a particular theme.[3] So, from 6 to 15 September, art critics from around the world attended the congress in Warsaw and Cracow at the invitation of the Polish branch of the AICA led by Juliusz Starzyński.[4]

[3] See *Histoires de 50 ans de l'Association internationale des critiques d'art: dédié à Abraham Marie Hammacher (1897–2002)*, Paris: AICA, 2002.

[4] Stanisław Mossakowski, "Juliusz Starzyński," in *Rocznik Historii Sztuki*, 1976/11, pp. 5–8; Joanna Sosonowska, "Juliusz Starzyński (1906–1974)," in *Rocznik Historii Sztuki*, t.XXXVI, PAN WDN, 2011; Marta Leśniakowska, Władza Spojrzenia – władza języka. Juliusza Starzyńskiego obraz sztuki i jej historii, "Modus.Prace z Historii Sztuki," T. XII–XIII (2013), pp. 27–52.

The programme presented by the Polish critics aimed to showcase the liberalisation of cultural life that Poland had enjoyed since the death of Stalin, during the period known as the Thaw (Figure 1.1–2).[5] This is seen

[5] See Rennes, Archives de la Critique d'Art, AICA Collection, Warsaw 1960, 7th Congress (Folder 1), programme of the *7th International Congress of Art Critics, VIIe congrès international des critiques d'art, VII międzynarodowy Kongres krytyków sztuki*; and Restany PREST. XS EST 49, a folder containing the typescript "Informations concernant les collections des musées et les expositions ouvertes à Varsovie et à Cracovie du 1 au 15 septembre 1960" (Information concerning museum collections and exhibitions open in Warsaw and Cracow from 1–15 September 1960), Rennes: Archives de la Critique d'Art, Archives of Pierre Restany. This folder contains details about exhibitions of historical and contemporary art provided to critics at the congress. Historical art exhibitions in Warsaw: *Polish Painting from the Mid-18th Century to the Present Day*; *Polish Prints of the 20th Century*; A Retrospective on the Work of Tadeusz Makowski (1882–1932) at the Warsaw National Museum, encouraging visitors to also explore the museum's collections of Medieval art, decorative arts from the 17th to 19th centuries and ancient Egyptian and Greco-Roman art; *The Early Days of the Polish State*, held at the State Archaeological Museum in celebration of the 1000th anniversary of the Polish State; an exhibition of documents presenting the history of the city of Warsaw from the 17th century to the present day at the City of Warsaw's Historical Museum; an exhibition of work by Juliusz Słowacki "honouring the life and work of one of the greatest Romantic poets," held at the Adam Mickiewicz Museum; *The Artist in Industry*, an "exhibition of works by students and graduates from the National Visual Arts Academies in Łódź (fabric and fashion design) and Wrocław (ceramics and glass work) held at the Zachęta Gallery run by the Central Bureau of Art Exhibitions; *Folk Inspirations in Polish Industrial Design and Crafts* held in the foyer of the Warsaw National Theatre. Contemporary art exhibitions in Warsaw: the Fine Arts Gallery held an "an exhibition of paintings and prints by artists who took part in individual and group shows held at the gallery," curated by the Warsaw branch of the Union of Polish Visual Artists; *Confrontations 1960* at the Krzywe Koło Gallery; *Poland in Artistic Photography*, held at the Warsaw Institute of Technology, portraying "the life of the nation and its people and revealing the transformations that have taken place. This exhibition has a retrospective character, presenting an artistic review of work by members of the Union of Polish Art Photographers from the fifteen years following the war"; an exhibition hosted by the journal *Współczesność* presenting a selection of paintings by Marek Oberländer; an exhibition-sale of work by Henryk Musiałowicz at the Bristol Hotel; and an exhibition of paintings by Mieczysław Antuszewicz at the Klub Literatów (Writers' Society) – "As part of a series of popularisation activities initiated by the Union of Polish Visual Artists, these small-scale exhibitions are organised in various parts of the city, particularly in company clubs." Exhibitions held in Cracow: *Gallery of Polish Painting 1750–1895* at the National Museum, focusing on developments in Polish painting in the 18th century and its place within European art history, as well as on the work of Jan Matejko, leading Symbolist artists and Realists of the 19th century; the exhibition hall devoted to modern Polish painting at the new National Museum presented Polish paintings from the period of "Impressionism to the present day," with a room dedicated to painters working in the Impressionist style and the reaction to Impressionism, Symbolist painters and key examples from the "Young Poland" movement; the first twenty years of the 20th century, featuring the Realist move-

in their decision to include exhibitions held in galleries that had opened as a result of the Thaw, such as the Krzywe Koło and Krzysztofory Galleries.[6] It is also reflected in the catalogues signed by Aleksander Wojciechowski, editor of the Warsaw-based art journal *Przegląd Artystyczny*, which documented artistic debates of the period. Certain aspects of their discourse on abstraction and the theme of the congress itself are indicative of the period of liberalisation that was underway in the political arena.[7]

The theme of the AICA Congress

We must therefore consider the theme of the 1960 AICA Congress—whose title was "Modern Art as an International Phenomenon"—within the context of the Thaw and the promotion at that time of a non-uniform image of socialist culture. When Juliusz Starzyński suggested holding the congress in Communist Poland to the Association's president James Johnson Sweeney during the 1957 AICA Congress in Palermo, with the idea of debating "the international character of modern art and the role of the different domestic environments in the creation of this art,"[8] it an-

ment dominated by the Colourists, a large collection of works by Olga Boznańska and landscapes from the "Young Poland" movement; sculptures by Xawery Dunikowski; Polish painting from 1912 to the present day, tracing issues "From Formalism to the work of T. Makowski and F. Kowarski, among others," the Colourists and the most recent painters from Cracow (names are not mentioned); sculptures and paintings from the Szołayski House collection; the Czartoryski collection; national art collections from the Wawel Royal Castle; an exhibition of traditional and contemporary folk art at the Ethnographic Museum; an exhibition of contemporary Polish prints at the Fine Arts Palace organised by the Union of Polish Visual Artists, presenting an overview of work in this field from the two previous years; the Krzystofory Gallery presented *The Cracow Group*; and the Exhibition Centre presented work by the *MARG* group.

[6] Witold Jedlicki, *Klub Krzywego Koła*, Paris: Instytut Literacki, 1963; Galeria "Krzywe Koło," ed. J. Zagrodzki, Warsaw: Muzeum Narodowe, 1990; B. Wojciechowska, "Marian Bogusz i Galeria 'Krzywe Koło,'" in *Marian Bogusz 1920–1980*, Poznań: Muzeum Narodowe w Poznaniu, Centralne Biuro Wystaw Artystycznych, 1982.

[7] On the effects of the period of Thaw on the Polish art scene and the gradual process of liberalisation, see *Odwilż. Sztuka ok. 1956 r.*, exh. cat., Poznań: Muzeum Narodowe, Sztuki Współczesnej Gallery, 1996, in particular, the essay by Piotr Piotrowski, "The 'Thaw'," pp. 243–259.

[8] See Juliusz Starzyński, Introduction to the typescript "VII Congrès International des critiques d'art Varsovie-Septembre 1960. L'Art - Les Nations - L'Univers. Enquête international, Section Polonaise de l'AICA" (7th International Congress of Art Critics, Warsaw, September

nounced the position he would defend during the exhibition *Art in Socialist Countries* held in Moscow in 1958. This exhibition caused a major stir and was condemned by the Soviet authorities as a "betrayal of socialist ideology and aesthetic values."[9] At this exhibition, Starzyński desired to show works that drew inspiration from the sources of modern art, notably from the Colourist School, which used forms that contrasted sharply with Socialist Realist works. Drawing upon Marxist-Leninist terminology, he thus asserted his position in favour of a "national path towards socialism," of a renationalised socialist Polish art.[10] At the Warsaw Congress in 1960, he brought an international dimension to this debate, as well as increased visibility and credibility by bringing it to the attention of Western critics. Starzyński felt it was important—without calling into question the socialist system—to assert Poland's freedom to choose not to conform to Moscow's perception of international art as restricted to a single style.[11]

The thaw at the core of the exhibitions: the reality of abstraction

Indications of the Thaw are also apparent in the texts that accompanied the exhibitions, such as the *Confrontations* show held at the Krzewy Koło

1960. Art - Nations - Universe. International Survey, Polish Branch of the AICA), p. 1, Rennes: Archives de la Critique d'Art, AICA Collection.

[9] Katarzyna Murawska Muthesius "Paris from Behind the Iron Curtain," in Sarah Wilson et al. (eds.), *Paris: Capital of the Arts 1900–1968*, exh. cat., London: Royal Academy of Arts, 2002, p. 258.

[10] Starzyński declared: "The art from twelve socialist countries presented at the Moscow exhibition does not, and cannot, convey a uniform image. We must look to history to understand the reasons for this, namely, the varying conditions of social and economic development, which are the result of differences in consciousness and which influence the current artistic situation in each country in specific ways." ["Dyskusja nad wystawą sztuki krajów socjalistycznych," *Życie Literackie*, 1959, No. 14], cited in *Odwilż. Sztuka ok. 1956 r.*, exh. cat., Poznań: Muzeum Narodowe, Galeria Sztuki Współczesnej, 1996, in the essay by Piotr Piotrowski, "The 'Thaw'," pp. 243–259.

[11] Starzyński's position was made clear at the congress's second work session led by Giulio Carlo Argan on the theme of "Modern art as the result and expression of the multiple traditions and approaches of different peoples," at which he stated that "Only those artists who associate themselves with the historical reality of their own people, while at the same time participating in the mainstream movement of their era, will have a lasting presence in the history of art," illustrating his arguments with examples from Polish art. See Rennes: Archives de la Critique d'Art, AICA Collection, Warsaw 1960, 7th Congress (Folder 1), programme of the *7th International Congress of Art Critics, VIIe congrès international des critiques d'art, VII międzynarodowy Kongres krytyków sztuki, Bulletin No. 3*, n. page.

Gallery in Warsaw. The publication released with this exhibition includes a collection of excerpts from the gallery's catalogues from previous exhibitions held in 1960.[12] Polish abstract art is presented as participating in the international art scene: a connection is drawn between Tadeusz Dominik's work and the international travel of the Action Painting artists in New York is documented, and high-quality texts describing works in great detail were made accessible by being translated into French. One striking feature of these descriptions is the frequent use of the word "reality" in reference to abstract practices. This is, however, not the same view of the reality of abstract art as was formulated by Western critics, such as Werner Haftmann, to describe its autonomous, spiritual dimension and give tangible content to non-figurative art; a reality that was seen as distinct from the mimetic, material reality attributed to realism.[13] Instead, it was an endeavour to identify a subject whose representation was the focus of abstract work by artists such as Marian Bogusz and Tadeusz Dominik and whose treatment justified their abstract approach. To quote from one of these texts: "Five years ago, during the exhibition entitled *Group 55* in which Marian Bogusz took part, we were struck by the notion of space that was explored with such intensity in this artist's paintings. This space was described as an imaginative, "philosophical" space filled

[12] This publication gathers together catalogues of exhibitions by the painters Marian Bogusz, Tadeusz Brzozowski, Tadeusz Dominik, Stefan Gierowski, Tadeusz Kantor, Bronisław Kierzkowski, Adam Marczyński, Jerzy Nowosielski, Jan Tarasin, Jerzy Tchórzewski and Rajmund Ziemski, and the sculptors Tadeusz Łodziana, Alina Szapocznikow, Alina Ślesińska, and Magdalena Więcek, *Konfrontacje 1960*, exh. cat., Warsaw: Krzywe Koło Gallery, 1960.

[13] Under the direction of *documenta* founder Arnold Bode, Werner Haftmann was responsible for formulating the art-historical discourse and the ideological position of the first three documenta exhibitions in Kassel – *documenta I* (1955), *II* (1959) and *III* (1964) – which helped to communicate his point of view to the general public. Haftmann is also author of a highly successful book, *Painting of the Twentieth Century*, which focuses on Western art practices. This book was republished many times, originally published in German: Werner Haftmann, *Malerei im 20. Jahrhundert*, Munich: Prestel Verlag, 1954. See, in particular, Haftmann's Introduction to the 1955 edition. On the subject of Werner Haftmann, see Harald Kimpel, "Werner Haftmann und der Geist der französischen Kunst," in Martin Schieder and Isabelle Ewig (eds.), *In Die Freiheit geworfen. Positionen zur Deutsch-französischen Kunstgeschichte nach 1945*, Berlin: Akademie Verlag, 2006, pp. 129–150. See also Gregor Wedekind, "Abstraktion und Abendland," in Nikola Doll et al. (eds.), *Kunstgeschichte nach 1945. Kontinuität und Neubeginn in Deutschland*, Cologne and Weimar: Böhlau Verlag, 2006, pp. 165–181.

with thoughts rather than objects. Yet it was also a real space, which was just as real as the artist's intellect."[14] Space in Bogusz's work was seen as an object of representation (Figure 1.3–1.4), as were the forms and colours of nature in Dominik's paintings (Figure 1.5–1.6). Representation was thus seen to preserve its mimetic connection with a referential physical reality, from which it could never fully break free. The progression of Socialist Realist figurative artists towards abstraction was thus presented in a form that was acceptable to Marxist-Leninist doctrine. Through these texts, Wojciechowski ensured a sense of continuity, and, like Starzyński in Moscow, allowed for the possibility of integrating abstract practices into Marxist-Leninist phraseology. The term "afiguratism"—or "afigurative" art—was employed to clarify the situation. The use of this term, which was borrowed from the French communist art critic Raoul-Jean Moulin's review of the Polish section at the Paris Biennale in 1959, made it possible to avoid using the word "abstraction"—and even implied its opposition to abstraction—and ensured that Polish art practices did not conflict with the mimetic representational requirements of the realist doxa.[15] It was a rhe-

[14] Cat. Marian Bogusz, in *Konfrontacje 1960*, exh. cat., Warsaw: Krzywe Koło Gallery, 1960.

[15] Wojciechowsk made reference to "afigurative painting" in an article published in the journal *Przeglad Artystyczny*, in which he reported on the 1st Paris Biennale: "At the Biennale, victory has been claimed by the opposite movement to that of abstraction, a movement defined by some critics as "afiguratism." The Polish section's exhibition, among others, was seen to be associated with this movement. I take this opportunity to quote from a viewpoint that is representative of reactions to our exhibition: "References to the real are constant, revealing an imaginary space in the work of Teresa Pągowska and inventing curious blossoming forms in the work of Tarasin. Yet the artists refuse to express these references in the usual ways; a movement, a climate or a colour interest them more than representing or interpreting reality. In this way, Ziemski brings forth in front of our eyes streaks of red, yellow and green set against earthy backgrounds that are delicately worked and infinitely evocative. Furthermore, the extreme refinement of materials in the work of Gierowski and Kierzowski, and, particularly, the highly structured symbols in the work of Lebensztejn, which are created through an endlessly diversified treatment of thick textures, are far from gratuitous. These paintings express the new reality of these artists' lives with a proud commitment to aesthetic values," writes R. J. Moulin in "Les Lettres Françaises" (No. 793). The term "afiguratism" attracted the attention of art critics for some time during this period. It was mentioned in the same issue of *Przeglad Artystyczny* in a text by Mieczysław Porębski, which describes the Polish paintings presented at the São Paulo Biennial in similar terms (pp. 70–71 of the same issue of the journal, "Biennale in Sao Paulo"), as well as in an essay by Tadeusz Dominik published in the catalogue produced for the Krzywe Koło Gallery.

torical strategy directed against the standardisation of an exclusively Western concept of abstraction.

In this way, the question of the international dimension of art and the Polish critics' views on abstraction were profoundly influenced by the specific socio-political context of the Thaw era. The archives of the AICA contain transcripts of debates held at the congress. They conclusively prove that critics from Western Europe and the United States showed no particular concern for these issues. They did not consider that their own perception of internationalism could be challenged by an alternative model that embodied different values. No mention was made of art scenes east of the Iron Curtain, apart from Poland, and the brief references to realist practices portrayed them as anachronistic.[16] The desire of certain artists to return to traditional sources or national references as a means of breaking free from a totalitarian perception of internationalism was not addressed.

Pierre Restany's point of view

Nonetheless, a close examination of the personal archives of Pierre Restany reveals a more complex situation.[17] Restany was well aware of the implications of the period of Thaw, as well as the intentions of its representatives to support developments in artistic practice while remaining loyal to communism. He fully understood what the terms "international-

[16] Jean Clarence Lambert, "The greatest hope for modern art is that is has rediscovered a sense of the universal," in typescript "VII Congrès International des critiques d'art. Varsovie-Septembre 1960. L'Art – Les Nations – L'Univers. Enquête international, Section Polonaise de l'AICA," pp. 46–47, Rennes: Archives de la Critique d'Art, AICA Collection.

[17] See the handwritten document "Notes de voyage. La Pologne et la tentation de l'Occident," signed and dated "October 1960, Cannes"; typescript "La Pologne et la tentation de l'Occident," Nov. 1960; handwritten document "La Pologne en plein tachisme," Paris, 11 November 1960; typescript "La Pologne et la tentation de l'Occident," n.d. [1964], grouped together in the report on the trip to Poland for the AICA Congress in 1960, in the Folder entitled "La Pologne et la tentation de l'Occident," Nov. 1960, see Restany PREST. XS EST 55; texts published in *Cimaise*, January–February 1961, under the headings "Notes de voyage: Pologne-Tchécoslovaquie," pp. 78–90, and "Le VII Congrès de l'AICA," pp. 96–99; and in *Das Kunstwerk*, under the heading "Die Situation der Kunst in Polen," February 1961, Notebook 8/XIV, pp. 16–22. Restany's trip to Poland is described by Henry Meyric Hughes in "Pierre Restany, l'AICA et l'aventure est-européenne," in *Le demi-siècle de Pierre Restany*, Richard Leeman, ed., Paris: INHA, Les Editions des Cendres, 2009, pp. 387–401.

ism" and "afiguration" meant to the Polish critics. But rather than giving particular consideration to the topics presented by the Polish critics, he interpreted them according to his own modernist, progressive viewpoint. Polish artists' return to embracing national traditions was seen as archaic.[18] In Restany's opinion, art should not be considered as a manifestation of the national psyche. He believed that art practices driven by a search for a Polish identity had no place in any modern tradition. His writings combine historical accounts and discussions of contemporary art, through which he portrays an image of Poland as peripheral and backward, a nation whose identity was defined by sources from a past era.

Poland is presented as an epigone, or inferior imitator, of France and the United States—which Restany saw as the two hegemonic powers in the art world—a view he reiterated in the discussions held during the congress. He considered Poland to be provincial, marginal, and the particularities of the socialist system and the national characteristics he mentions—Catholicism, a young nation, romanticism—in no way alter his interpretation of Polish abstract art in terms of Western models. Poland is viewed exclusively through the prism of what he perceives as the cutting edge of international art, which he limits to the work of French, American, German, Italian and Japanese avant-garde artists in the Dada tradition.[19]

[18] Archives de la Critique d'Art, "Le VIIe congrès de l'association internationale des critiques d'art," PREST-XSEST57/23. In a report on discussions held during the congress, Restany clearly expresses his views on the subject of returning to tradition. He explains that during the three work sessions, which were "led, respectively, by Jacques Lassaigne (France), H. L. C. Jaffé (the Netherlands) and G. C. Argan (Italy), debate arose around the general issue of expressiveness: is modern art an international language in itself (in its spirit and purpose) or does it identify itself as the transcendental sum total of diverse traditions? A trend appears to have emerged from these discussions favouring the search for a renewal of art through a return to the primary elements of national tradition. This is the justification today for so many cases of artistic nationalism and explains why we see such a proliferation of cultural inferiority complexes. Yet tradition has always stifled new art, and it is only by breaking free of the straitjacket of localism that geographically localised art movements have been able to play their historical role to the full. However, it would be futile to expect any avant-garde proclamations from a congress (held by the AICA or any other organisation)." Restany, see Archives de la Critique d'Art, "Le VIIe congrès de l'association internationale des critiques d'art," PREST-XSEST57/23.

[19] Restany's responses to questions in a survey sent out by Starzyński prior to the congress, in which he states his opinion regarding the theme of the Congress, provide some clarity on these questions. Only Lyrical Abstraction and the Dada movements are described by Restany as international movements, with geometric abstraction eliminated from consideration as it had

Poland's presumed allegiance to the West therefore did not prevent it from remaining backward, since Polish artists had not realised that Lyrical Abstraction and Tachisme had already been replaced by new practices.

In 1960, Restany believed that he had progressed beyond abstract painting. After seeking to assert his critical view of Art Informel over that of other critics, such as Michel Tapié, Julien Alvard, Charles Estienne and Michel Ragon, he turned his back on abstraction and focused on building the reputation of the group of artists he named Nouveaux Réalistes, for whom he wrote a manifesto in April 1960.[20] Restany's disparaging comments about Polish Art Informel cannot only be attributed to the country's "backward" state; they primarily reflect his dissociation from abstraction. Restany was no stranger to the rhetoric of Polish art critics, who drew their references from the Parisian communist press. At the time of the AICA Congress, he was fully aware that the abstraction/figuration polarity no longer carried the same messages. Communist doctrine had evolved with the Thaw, and Restany had no alternative but to dismiss that which communism now tolerated. His position was fuelled by antagonisms resulting from the Cold War, and his views on art and the practices he defended were radically opposed to communism.

When Restany founded Nouveau Réalisme in 1960, the effects of the Thaw were discernible in Eastern Europe, and some Eastern states began to accept abstract art. Yet abstraction had already ceased to embody the values of independence, freedom and subjectivity that the West sought to represent. In founding this movement, Restany was motivated by a strong desire to distance himself not only from abstraction, but also from all that communism had appropriated.

Furthermore, it is important to consider why Restany gave only cursory mention to geometric abstraction and paid little attention to the ironic and

rapidly reached "the peak of its international expansion, [...] having at the same time become ossified and conformist," with its "precarious dominance" overthrown by pictorial lyricism, which came to the fore after 1945. See Rennes: Archives de la Critique d'Art, AICA Collection, Warsaw 1960, 7th Congress (Folder 2), Pierre Restany, "L'art moderne, langage international du lyrisme et de l'irrationnel," in "L'Art – Les Nations – L'Univers. Enquête internationale, Section polonaise de l'AICA, Varsovie, 1960," pp. 14–20, p. 15.

[20] See, Richard Leeman (ed.), *Le demi-siècle de Pierre Restany*, Paris: INHA, Les Editions des Cendres, 2009; Richard Leeman, *Le Critique, l'art et l'histoire: De Michel Ragon à Jean Clair*, Rennes: Les Presses Universitaires de Rennes, 2010.

dark side of Polish art practices, which he would have observed in a performance staged by Miron Białoszewski at his apartment, and at Tadeusz Kantor's Cricot 2 Theatre.

Restany's understanding of "international" art—which, as we have seen, was far from complete—did not include geometric abstraction or the sense of post-utopian melancholy, or eccentricity, that were expressed by some Polish artists. These forms of expression embodied values that Restany refused to acknowledge as part of contemporary art. His criticism of the "the pessimism of the immediate past"[21] and his campaign for an optimistic, constructive and progressive outlook led him to take a dim view of the way in which Warsaw chose to come to terms with its destruction.[22] Moreover, the theme of destruction, which was so prevalent in Polish art practices, was not referred to anywhere else in his writings. Restany vir-

[21] "Working in various ministerial offices placed me in a good position to assess the pulse of the nation and the national structures of production. The end of the 1950s marked the end of the period of reconstruction and the onset of economic growth, the beginning of the great technological adventure into space. [...] In other words, I opted in favour of optimism, [...] in reaction to the pessimism of the immediate past." Restany, *1960: Les Nouveaux Réalistes*, Paris: MAMVP, 1986, p. 267. Jill Carrick eloquently explains how the *Manifesto of Nouveau Réalisme* and other essays offered a "new" vision of a "new" France, a France of the post-war period that was revitalised and full of optimism and energy, turning away from the defeat, humiliations and tragedies of the war. With Charles de Gaulle proclaimed first president of the 5th Republic in January 1959, and again on his re-election in 1965, the new regime endeavoured to detract from the internal conflicts that had disrupted France during and following the war. This was articulated through the propagation of myths of the promotion of social cohesion and national unity. See Jill Carrick, "Vers un art de l'intégration?," in *Le demi-siècle de Pierre Restany*, Richard Leeman, ed., Paris: INHA, Les Editions des Cendres, 2009, pp. 77–88, p. 82 (English title: "Towards an Art of Integration?," published in the proceedings of the 2006 international symposium "Pierre Restany's Half-Century," INHA).

[22] "Since 90 % of the city centre and the main districts had been destroyed, it was the last chance to follow the course of history and officially list the site as a commemorative monument, and to reconstruct a new capital at another location as a symbol of renewal. But nationalist sentimentalism won the day—Warsaw was reconstructed on its original site and the Old City was rebuilt stone by stone based on sketches by Canaletto (produced around 1770). These reconstructed facades bring to mind a theatre set that is artificial and soulless, dehumanised, just like the metaphysical cities of de Chirico. Elsewhere in the New City, the Baroque churches of Visitandines and Sursum Corda offer a strange contrast with the MDM block (a Socialist Realist architectural ensemble), the Muscovite-style Palace of Culture (a gift from the Russians) and the housing developments in the suburbs, which are still new but on the verge of collapse. All of these inconsistencies in town planning, which make Warsaw one of the most depressing cities in the world, reflect the intellectual uncertainties of the nation." Typescript "La Pologne et la tentation de l'Occident," Nov. 1960.

tually ignored Polish geometric abstraction, which, according to him, never took hold in an enduring way. Constructivism was described as a temporary phenomenon that, in Restany's view, could not compete with the deeply-entrenched influence of France on Polish art. While reasserting his state-hegemonic view of the situation, he discredited the legacy of Russian Constructivism, which is perceived as digressions from the main currents. In this way, Restany relegated all revolutionary art practices to the fringes of the international movement. The primary aim of his contribution to art theory was to disengage "avant-garde art" from the role of social confrontation, as shown by Jill Carrick in her essay, "Vers un art de l'intégration?" [Towards an Art of Integration?].[23] The Polish artists who captured Restany's interest were defined as "non-activists" (non-engagés in French)—as opposed to the "intellectual communists"[24]—who followed in the tradition of the interwar French Colourists. While Restany's evaluation of the Polish art scene was highly influenced by his personal convictions, it can only be fully understood by taking into account the stance of the Polish branch of the AICA.

The 1960 AICA Congress was held at a particularly interesting moment in history, when major shifts in East—West relations were beginning to take effect. It exemplifies the end of the abstraction/figuration dichotomy that had dictated the artistic identities of the opposing blocs. It offers a picture of the Thaw era, while bearing witness to the deterioration of gains made during this period of liberalisation. Although Polish artists' increasingly apparent interest in modern modes of expression had been more willingly accepted since 1956–1957, these practices met once again with disapproval after the *Art of Socialist Countries* exhibition in Moscow in 1958. Even if it was out of the question for the Polish authorities to change their policy on the small degree of independence from the USSR that had been obtained by Poland's leader Gomułka after intense negotiations with Khrushchev in the wake of the insurrection of October 1956, they had no intention of extending this freedom. After Gomułka had reaffirmed his faith in Marxist-Leninist principles at the Polish Party Congress in March

[23] Jill Carrick, *Le demi-siècle de Pierre Restany* (*Pierre Restany's Half-Century]*), Richard Leeman (ed.), Paris: INHA, Les Editions des Cendres, 2009 (note 21), pp. 77–88.
[24] Typescript entitled "La Pologne et la tentation de l'Occident," Nov. 1960.

1959, the guidelines issued by the Soviet Central Committee one year later explicitly expressed the Polish United Workers' Party's loyal support for realist art. The art journal *Przegląd Artystyczny* changed its editorial board, with its new editor, Helena Krajewska, an ardent supporter of Socialist Realism from its very inception. The same year, Starzyński was removed from his position as director of the Instytut Sztuki Pan, which he resumed in 1968 after the dismissal of Jerzy Toeplitz. In 1960, the Polish government enacted a restriction that no more than 15 percent of artworks in public exhibitions could be abstract. Although this Directive saw limited compliance, it remained in effect until the collapse of the socialist system in Poland. The AICA Congress was thus held at a pivotal moment. It reveals a prism of complex relations between art critics from the East and West as they focused on a common subject (Art Informel) and expressed their own perspectives, demonstrating at times their interdependencies (such as the fact that both Restany and the Polish critics were familiar with Raoul-Jean Moulin), which threatened to aggravate existing antagonisms. Furthermore, by turning our attention to the artistic debates that took place within a divided Europe, we are able to take into consideration the fragile interrelationships, the subtleties of viewpoints and the interactions that were played out on the frontline of the Cold War, which were of a different nature to the relations that existed between the two rival superpowers, the United States and the Soviet Union. This interpretation of these connections and interdependencies cannot suffice, but it represents a process of vital and fundamental importance for the construction of Europe today.

References

Primary sources

Rennes, Archives de la Critique d'Art, AICA Collection, Warsaw 1960, 7th Congress.

Rennes, Archives de la Critique d'Art, Pierre Restany : PREST. XS EST 49 ; PREST. XS EST 55; PREST-XSEST57/23.

Secondary sources

Jill Carrick, "Vers un art de l'intégration?," in *Le demi-siècle de Pierre Restany*, Richard Leeman, ed., Paris: INHA, Les Editions des Cendres, 2009, pp. 77–88.

Sophie Cras, "Le Nouveau Réalisme: du réalisme socialiste au réalisme capitaliste", *OwnReality* (6), 2014, accessible online: www.perspectivia.net/content/publikationen/ownreality/6/cras-fr (English translation: "Nouveau Réalisme: From Socialist Realism to Capitalist Realism": www.perspectivia.net/publikationen/ownreality/6/cras-en/view).

Galeria Krzywe Koło, ed. J. Zagrodzki, Warsaw: Muzeum Narodowe, 1990.

Werner Haftmann, *Malerei im 20. Jahrhundert*, Munich: Prestel Verlag, 1954.

Histoires de 50 ans de l'Association internationale des critiques d'art: dédié à Abraham Marie Hammacher (1897–2002), Paris: AICA, 2002.

Henry Meyric Hughes in "Pierre Restany, l'AICA et l'aventure est-européenne," in *Le demi-siècle de Pierre Restany*, Richard Leeman, ed., Paris: INHA, Les Editions des Cendres, 2009, pp. 387–401.

Witold Jedlicki, *Klub Krzywego Koła*, Paris: Instytut Literacki, 1963.

Harald Kimpel, "Werner Haftmann und der Geist der französischen Kunst," in Martin Schieder and Isabelle Ewig (eds.), *In Die Freiheit geworfen. Positionen zur Deutsch-französischen Kunstgeschichte nach 1945*, Berlin: Akademie Verlag, 2006, pp. 129–150.

Konfrontacje 1960, exh. cat., Warsaw: Krzywe Koło Gallery, 1960.

Richard Leeman (ed.), *Le demi-siècle de Pierre Restany,* Paris: INHA, Les Editions des Cendres, 2009.

Richard Leeman, *Le Critique, l'art et l'histoire: De Michel Ragon à Jean Clair*, Rennes: Les Presses Universitaires de Rennes, 2010.

Marta Leśniakowska, *Władza Spojrzenia – władza języka. Juliusza Starzyńskiego obraz sztuki i jej historii*, "Modus.Prace z Historii Sztuki", T. XII–XIII (2013), pp. 27–52.

Stanisław Mossakowski, "Juliusz Starzyński," in *Rocznik Historii Sztuki*, 1976/11, pp. 5–8.

Katarzyna Murawska Muthesius "Paris from Behind the Iron Curtain," in Sarah Wilson et al. (eds.), *Paris: Capital of the Arts 1900–1968*, exh. cat., London: Royal Academy of Arts, 2002.

Mieczysław Porębski, "Biennale à São Paulo" , in *Przegląd Artystyczny*, n°1, 1960, p. 70–71.

Odwilż. Sztuka ok. 1956 r., exh. cat., Poznań: Muzeum Narodowe, Sztuki Współczesnej Gallery, 1996.

Pierre Restany, "Notes de voyage: Pologne-Tchécoslovaquie" and "Le VII Congrès de l'AICA," in *Cimaise*, January–February 1961, pp. 78–90, pp. 96–99.

—. "Die Situation der Kunst in Polen," in *Das Kunstwerk*, February 1961, Notebook 8/XIV, pp. 16–22.

—. *1960: Les Nouveaux Réalistes*, Paris: MAMVP, 1986.

Joanna Sosonowska, "Juliusz Starzyński (1906–1974)," in *Rocznik Historii Sztuki*, t.XXXVI, PAN WDN, 2011.

Gregor Wedekind, "Abstraktion und Abendland," in Nikola Doll et al. (eds.), *Kunstgeschichte nach 1945. Kontinuität und Neubeginn in Deutschland*, Cologne and Weimar: Böhlau Verlag, 2006, pp. 165–181.

B. Wojciechowska, "Marian Bogusz i Galeria 'Krzywe Koło,'" in *Marian Bogusz 1920–1980*, Poznań: Muzeum Narodowe w Poznaniu, Centralne Biuro Wystaw Artystycznych, 1982.

Aleksander Wojciechowski, "La Biennale de Paris," in *Przegląd Artystyczny*, n° 1, 1960, p. 71–72

VIIe CONGRES INTERNATIONAL DES CRITIQUES D'ART
Varsovie-Cracovie, septembre 1960

Programme provisoire

LUNDI 5			Arrivée à Varsovie, inscription, installa
MARDI 6	matin	9 h.-	Réunion de la Commission des Admissions
		10 h.-	Réunion du Comité de l'AICA
		11 h.-	Séance inaugurale du Congrès
		12 h.-	Conférence sur l'architecture de Varsov
	ap.midi	15 h.-	Visite de la ville précédée d'une séanc des courts métrages sur la reconstructi de Varsovie
MERCREDI 7	matin	9 h.-	Ière Séance de travail; thème: l'art mo en tant que phénomène international
	ap.midi	15 h.-	Visite au Musée National de Varsovie
		18 h.-	Cocktail
JEUDI 8	matin	9 h.-	Réunion des Commissions de Travail
	ap.midi	15 h.-	Assemblée Générale de l'AICA
VENDREDI 9	matin	9 h.-	IIème Séance de travail; thème: l'art m ne en tant que résultat et expression d traditions et tendances des différents peuples
	ap.midi	15 h.-	Visite des expositions
SAMEDI 10	matin	9 h.-	IIIème Séance de travail; thème: l'art derne et les perspectives du developpem de l'art des différents peuples
	ap.midi		libre
DIMANCHE 11	matin	8 h.-	Départ pour Cracovie /déjeuner en route visite de la ville
	ap.midi		
LUNDI 12	matin	10 h.-	Visite des expositions
	ap.midi	15 h.-	visite de la ville
		18 h.-	Cocktail
MARDI 13	matin	9 h.-	Visite du chateau Wawel
		10 h.-	Conférence au sujet de l'art polonais
		11 h.-	Séance de clôture
	ap.midi		libre
MERCREDI 14			Commencement du circuit touristique

Figure 1.1: Programme of the AICA Congress, PREST.XS EST 49.

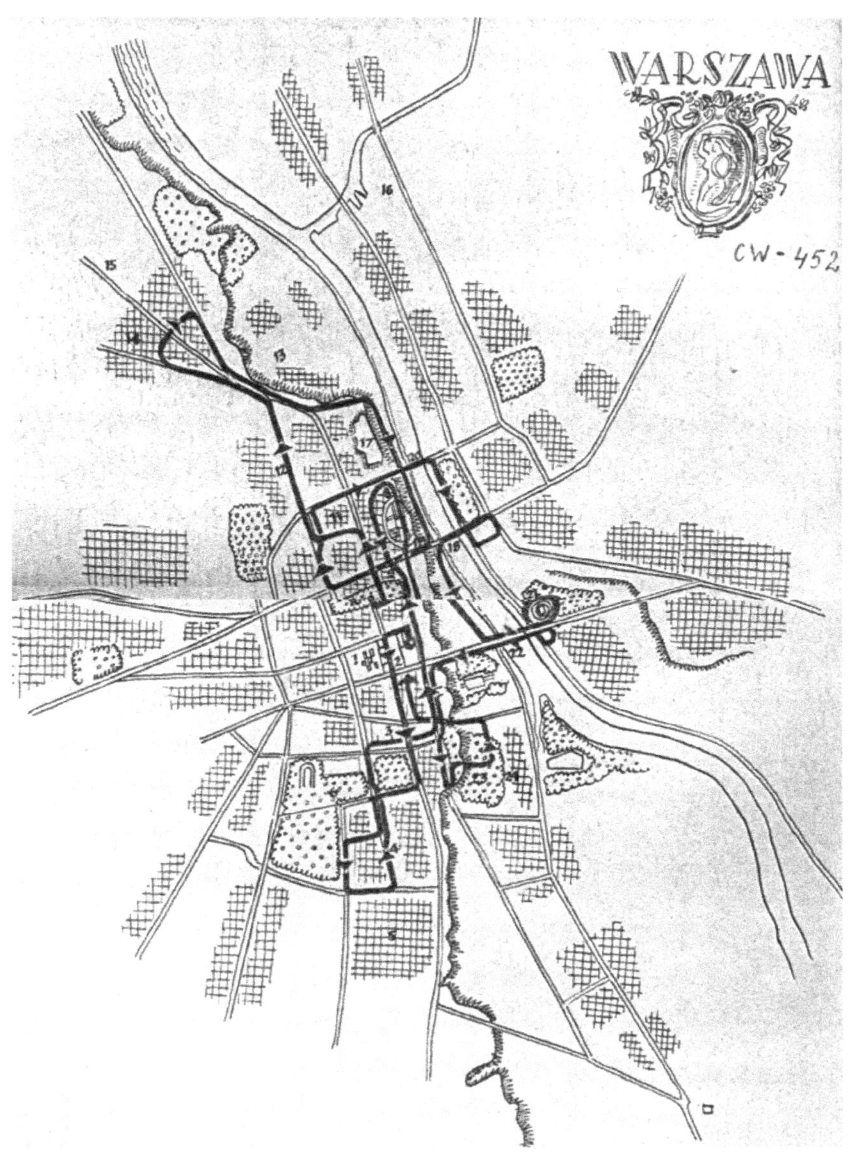

Figure 1.2: Warsaw Map, PREST.XS EST 49.

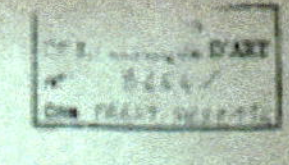

marian bogusz

galeria „krzywe koło"
warszawa — czerwiec 1960

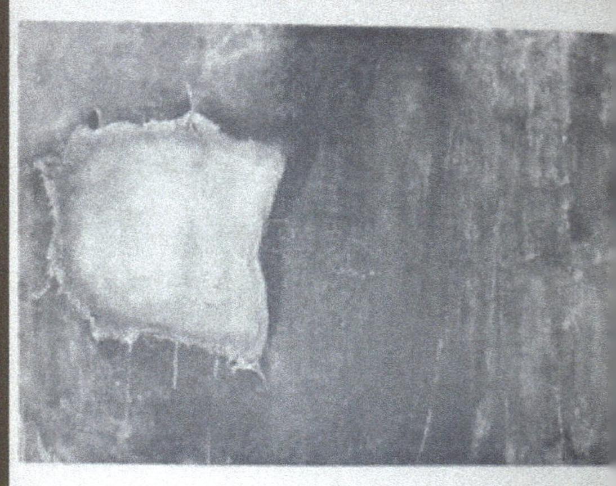

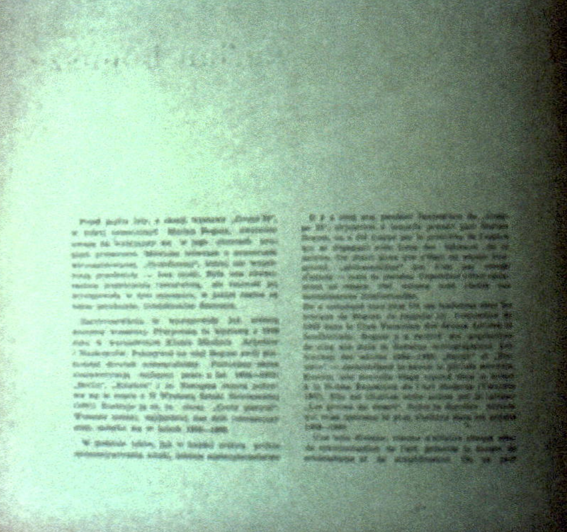

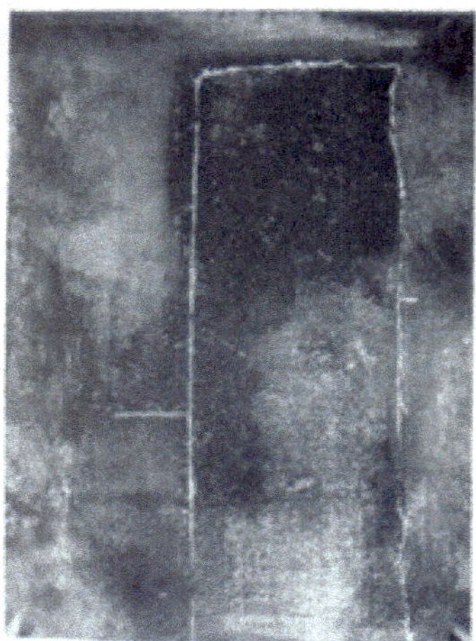

Figure 1.3: Konfrontacje 1960, Restany Library, Rennes, PREST.S EST 211.

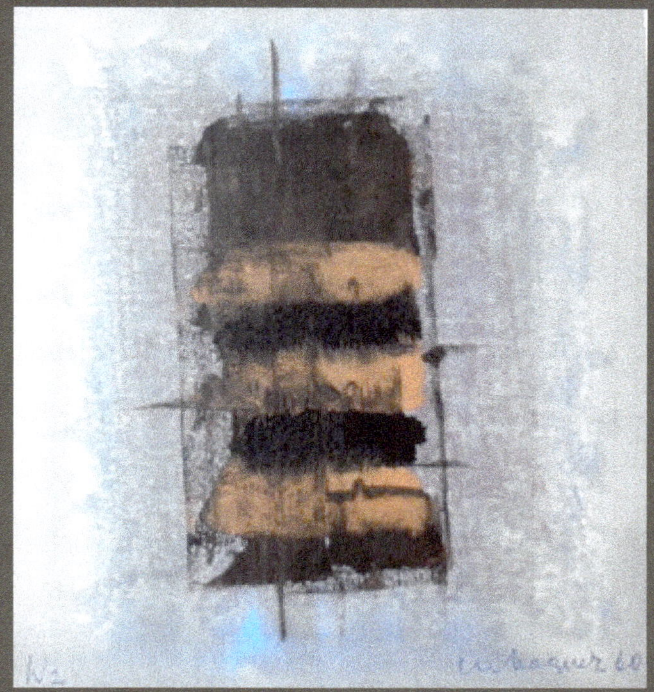

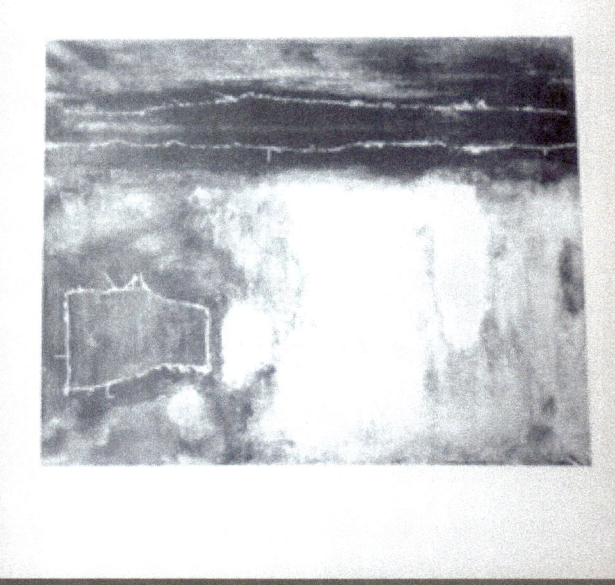

Figure 1.4: Konfrontacje 1960, Restany Library, Rennes, PREST.S EST 211.

tadeusz dominik

galeria „krzywe koło"

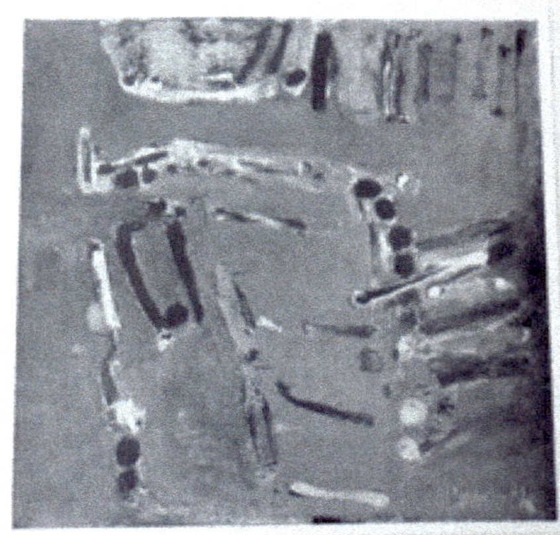

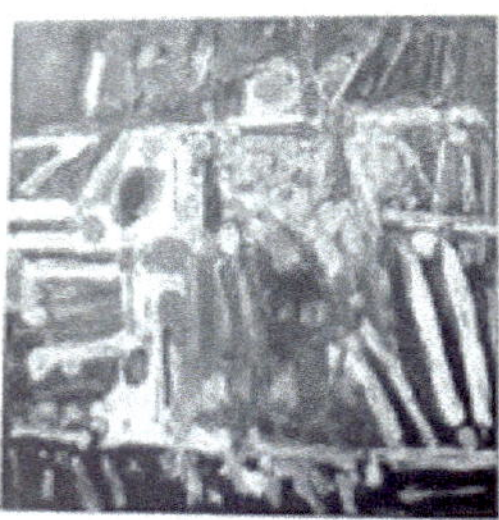

Figure 1.5: Konfrontacje 1960, Restany Library, Rennes, PREST.S EST 211.

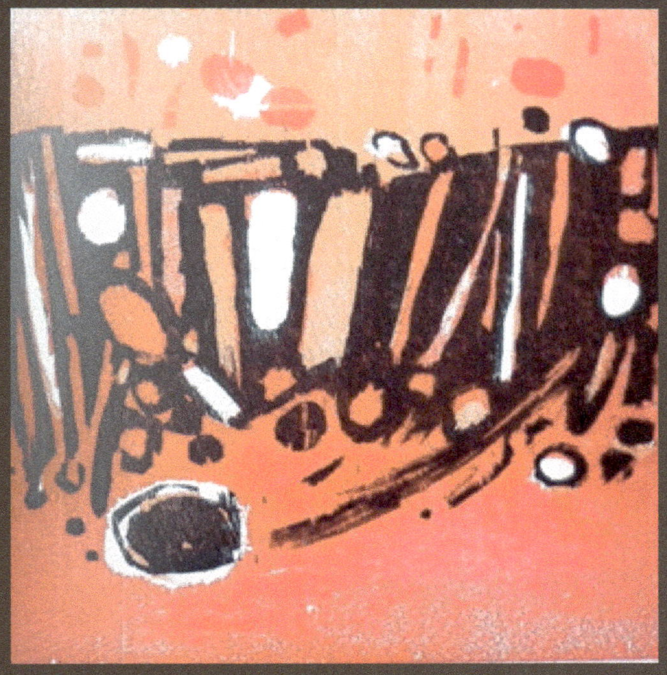

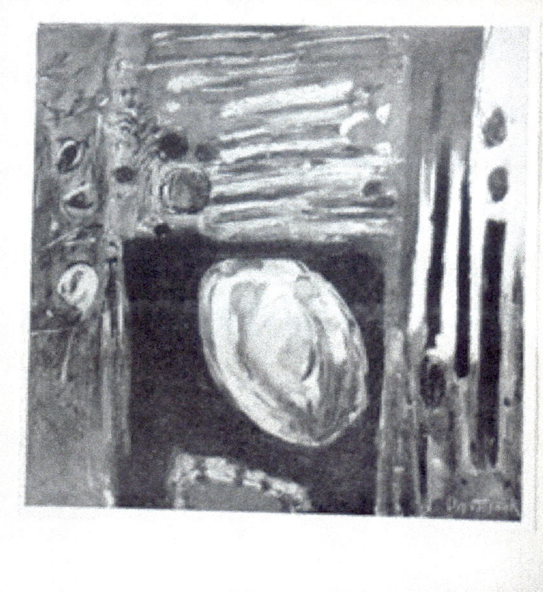

Figure 1.6: Konfrontacje 1960, Restany Library, Rennes, PREST.S EST 211.

2
"Be Young And Shut Up"
Understanding France's Response to the 1964 Venice Biennale in its Cultural and Curatorial Context

Catherine Dossin

In his review of the 1964 Venice Biennale, in which Robert Rauschenberg received the Grand Prize of Painting, French critic Pierre Cabanne asked: "But which man did the jury […] want to crown? The painter who is indisputable, or the pop artist?"[1] This question summarised the complicated nature of this award and the ambivalent responses it generated. On the one hand, it did not come as a total surprise: Rauschenberg was greatly appreciated in Western Europe where he was regarded as a leading figure of the new international avant-garde. His receiving this major honour nonetheless caused a stir, or rather, to echo Cabanne, the fact that a Pop artist would be awarded this prestigious prize was disturbing and even shocking to many, even among those who appreciated the young American. Although they enjoyed his work, they did not see him as a proper candidate for this particular recognition.

Traditionally, negative responses to Rauschenberg's prize have been read in the context of the rivalry between Paris and New York as fits of chagrin and resentment from the defeated Parisian clan, while the award was regarded as a symbol of the triumph of American art. Without con-

[1] Pierre Cabanne, "A Venise. L'Amérique proclame la fin de l'Ecole de Paris et lance le Pop'Art pour coloniser l'Europe," *Arts*, no. 968 (24–30 June 1964): 16. Unless otherwise noted, translations are the author's.

testing the validity of such an interpretation, we must recognise that it does not explain everything. First, it was not the first time that an American was rewarded in Venice;[2] consequently the symbolic value of the award did not rest merely on Rauschenberg's citizenship. Second, the French pavilion could not have won that year, because Roger Bissière, who represented France, had asked to remain out of the competition due to his advanced age. Furthermore, as Hiroko Ikegami showed very well, Rauschenberg's prize aroused negative reactions in the United States.[3] But in Paris, conversely, some people were actually quite happy with the result. Rather than a victory or a triumph, Rauschenberg's award is better described as a contentious event that revealed major ideological divides within the Western art worlds. Of course, each biennale had its share of recriminations, but not to that extent and, while most of these scandals were quickly forgotten, the disputes surrounding the 1964 Biennale remain a decisive moment in the history of Western Art.

The controversy caused by Rauschenberg's receiving the Grand Painting Prize should not be dismissed as mere anti-Americanism and jealous bitterness. It needs to be taken seriously and to be studied carefully, using not only close reading of published texts and archive material, but also distant reading of data pertaining to the curatorial practices and transnational strategies of the time, as found in exhibition catalogues, following the methodology promoted by ARTL@S.[4] Distant reading in the

[2] Alexander Calder had won the Grand Prize for Sculpture in 1952, and Mark Tobey was awarded the Painting Award of the city of Venice in 1958. This recognition was particularly important, since that year all the international prizes had gone to Italian artists and thus regarded as invalid by the international community. Tobey is thus sometimes wrongly listed as the winner of the Grand Prize for Painting.

[3] See in particular the chapter entitled "Disbelief and Dismay: American Responses" in Hiroko Ikegami, *The Great Migrator: Robert Rauschenberg and the Global Rise of American Art* (Cambridge: The MIT Press 2010), 94–97.

[4] Launched in 2009 at the Ecole normale supérieure in Paris by Béatrice Joyeux-Prunel, ARTL@S promotes a Spatial (Digital) approach of global art history. In a nutshell, ARTL@S offers art historians a collaborative, integrated digital environment in which they can trace, compute, and map the transnational circulations of artists, artworks, and styles. At the core of the project is BasArt, a relational, geo-referenced historical database of exhibition catalogs. BasArt centralizes, processes, and further disseminates information that art historians have theoretically at their disposal but do not have the means to practically access or process on their own. For more information on ARTL@S, see Catherine Dossin, Béatrice Joyeux-Prunel, and Sorin A. Matei, "Spatial (Digital) History: A Total History? The ARTL@S

forms of maps, charts, and graphs allows us to study the information contained in these catalogues in a systematic and dispassionate way, and to thereby escape official narratives and purely theoretical speculation and to replace, as Franco Moretti put it, the "old unnecessary distinctions (high and low, canon and archive, such-and-such national literature...) by new temporal, spatial and morphological distinctions."[5] ARTL@S provides a great tool to rethink the 1964 Venice Biennale in this way.

Unlike previous and successive prizes awarded in Venice that recognised the achievements of an artist, Rauschenberg's success never totally belong to him. As Cabanne hinted, it was the symbol of something that went far beyond him and, I contend, beyond Paris and New York.[6] It marked a shift in curatorial practices that resulted from the socio-cultural transformations, which the Western world was then undergoing. The late 1950s and early 1960s was indeed a period of social and cultural changes that was marked by the arrival of a new generation and the emergence of a distinct youth culture which sparked a crisis of values, strongly resisted by the older generations, and announced the social unrest and radical upheavals of the late 1960s.[7]

To fully understand the decision of the jury of the 1964 Venice Biennale and the reactions it generated, we thus need to see them as part of a larger social and cultural context, rather than as a symbolic moment, and consider how this specific context affected the curatorial strategies and museum practices of the time.

Project," *Visual Resources: Digital Art History Special Issue* (Spring 2013): 47–58. And consult the website at www.artlas.ens.fr

[5] Franco Moretti, *Graphs, Maps, Trees: Abstract Models for a Literary History* (London; New York: Verso, 2005), 126.

[6] I have elsewhere already advanced this idea, which is further developed in this paper. See the chapter entitled "This Is Tomorrow: The Triumph of the American Way in the 1960s" in Catherine Dossin, *The Rise and Fall of American Art, 1940s–1980s: A Geopolitics of Western Art Worlds* (Burlington, VT: Ashgate, 2015), 151–88.

[7] In his study of the 1960s, Arthur Marwick draws a clear distinction between "the first stirrings of a cultural revolution, 1958-1963" and the "High Sixties, 1964–1969." See Arthur Marwick, *The Sixties: Cultural Revolution in Britain, France, Italy and the United States, c.1958–c.1974* (Oxford, New York: Oxford University Press, 1998).

The rise of a younger generation

One major change that occurred at this time was a shift in the timing and sources of artistic consecration. Whereas official recognition used to come at the end of one's career and museum retrospectives to acknowledge movements and trends long after their time, around 1964 we see young artists being recognised and new artistic movements, such as Pop art, being glorified immediately. We can take stock of this transformation by comparing two retrospective exhibitions that took place in 1964, namely *'54–'64: Painting and Sculpture of a Decade* which took place in London in April and *Bilanz Internationale Malerei seit 1950* that opened in Basel in June. While *Bilanz* and *'54–'64* shared the ambition to provide an overview of the art produced in the last decade or so, the two exhibitions were radically different.

The Basel show presented a small selection of established artists who had dominated the international art scene of the past fourteen years, including the *Vieux Maitres* (Picasso, Braque, Matisse, Léger, Chagall, Miró, and Rouault), the postwar generation of Parisian artists (Bazaine, Estève, Dubuffet, Giacometti, Poliakoff, de Staël, van Valde, and Vieira da Silva), the American Abstract Expressionists (Pollock, Rothko, Kline, de Kooning, Newman, Tobey and Still), as well as major Europeans figures such as Nay, Hundertwasser, Jorn, and Tàpies. Sam Francis and Jean-Paul Riopelle represented the North-Americans from Paris. *Bilanz* did not include any young or upcoming artists; no Pop artists, not even Rauschenberg who had been awarded the Grand Prize in Venice just a few days before the opening. Yet, the show did not generate any controversy or receive any special attention. It was regarded as a successful, standard retrospective.

In contrast, *'54–'64* caused a stir. As the Paris based critic Herta Wescher explained in her review of the show, abstraction that had dominated the international art scene since the late 1940s was relegated to a position of secondary importance. Parisian abstraction was particularly mishandled. Bissière, who represented France at the Biennale, was absent and, with him, the whole French lyrical abstraction. Fautrier, who had won the Biennale in 1960, was not included either. For Wescher, the show was biased: "Seen in this way, the arbitrary suppression of so many artists of the Paris School seriously indicts the historical duty incumbent upon such an exhibition."[8] Worse, even British abstraction and American Abstract Expressionism were misrepresented. Wescher commented: "It is inadmissible that Pollock, who had the deepest influence on the new generation, be presented by no more than a narrow panel which is lost in the ensemble."[9] The major fault of the show was the overwhelming representation of young American Pop artists, who outnumbered the more established Abstract painters, be they French or American. In a show that was supposed to present the artistic production of the past ten years, to give such precedence to artists who had emerged only two years prior was regarded as deplorable, and this was because it did not reflect the history of the past ten years, but rather recent taste.

As Tables 1 and 2 show, the difference between *'54–'64* and *Bilanz* was less about the origins of the artists (Paris or New York) than about their ages. And if artists from Paris dominated in Basel, it was in no small part because artists from the older generations were often based in Paris. The strong representation in Basel of American Abstract Expressionism, which was slighted in London, brings further evidence that the shift was less geographic than generational. Switzerland was one of the very few European countries where American art had been very visible since the War. Arnold Rüdlinger, the organiser of *Bilanz*, had been one of the earliest European supporters of American art. In 1947, as director of the Kunsthalle in Bern, he had organised a show of Alexander Calder. In 1954, he had organised a show titled *Tendances 3*, which featured three American artists: Jackson Pollock, Mark Tobey, and Sam Francis. In 1955, Rüdlinger became the director of the Kunsthalle in Basel, where he continued to regularly exhibit American artists.[10] As a result of Rüdlinger's efforts, and the work of several commercial galleries including the Galerie Beyeler, American art was very well represented in Switzerland in the 1950s, even more so after Tobey settled in Basel.

In contrast, little had been seen of American Abstract Expressionism in London before the late 1950s, when several important shows organised by

[8] Herta Wescher, "Pauvre Ecole de Paris," *Cimaise*, Spring 1964, 64.

[9] Ibid., 63.

[10] For more information on Rüdlinger's relations with American art, see Eberhard Kornfeld, "Rüdlingers Reise nach New York 1957" in Lukas Gloor, *Die Geschichte der Basler Kunstvereins und der Kunsthalle Basel, 1839–1988* (Basel: Kunsthalle Basel, 1989), 228–29.

the International Program of the Museum of Modern Art (MoMA) came to Great Britain. As a result of this late "discovery," the British art worlds had the feeling of having missed something and a strong desire not to repeat the same mistake.[11] After seeing Rauschenberg's first exhibitions at the Sonnabend Gallery in Paris in 1963, Bryan Robertson, the director of Whitechapel in London, decided to give him a show in his institution.[12] He actually postponed a retrospective of Kline in favour of the young artist. Robertson considered that Kline's show sent by MoMA, like Rothko's 1961 retrospective, should have taken place years earlier and thus could wait a few more months. It was far more urgent to show Rauschenberg while he was still current and relevant.[13]

The selection for *'54–'64* reflects a similar thinking: an urgency to present what was most current and relevant, rather than distributing official accolades to established artists. The victims of this new approach to curatorial practice were the older generation, Parisian and American, who were likewise overshadowed by the novelty of the rising stars. The London exhibition then exemplified the shift in the values of the Western art worlds, where museums were starting to pay more attention to novel than historical trends, so much so that success and recognition were more closely linked to the future rather than the past.

Postwar figuration under the Pop Art banner

The growing importance given to the most recent artistic developments becomes particularly obvious when considering a series of exhibitions devoted to figuration that also took place in 1964. After years when abstraction had dominated the international art scene, figuration was making a strong comeback that several European institutions attempted to

[11] On the European reception of American art in the postwar period, see Catherine Dossin, "To Drip or to Pop? The European Triumph of American Art," *The Artl@s Bulletin* 3, no. 1 (Spring 2014): 79–103.

[12] He had actually already mentioned the idea to Castelli and Rauschenberg in autumn 1962 while he was in New York. Brandon Taylor, "The Rauschenberg Retrospective in 1964," in *The Whitechapel Art Gallery Centenary Review* (London Whitechapel Art Gallery, 2001), 71.

[13] Ibid., 71–75. On the European reception of Rothko, see Catherine Dossin, "Mark Rothko, the Long Unsung Hero of American Art," in *Mark Rothko. Obrazy z National Gallery of Art w Waszyngtonie*, ed. Marek Bartelik (Warsaw: National Museum of Warsaw, 2013), 101–12.

document, including the Gemeentemuseum Den Haag, which showcased *Nieuwe Realisten,* curated by Wim Beeren, and the Museum Voor Schone Kunsten in Ghent, which presented *Figuratie Defiguratie. De Menselijke Figuur Sedert Picasso,* organised under the headship of Karel J. Geirlandt. If both exhibitions manifested a similar desire to examine the renewed interest in figuration, their ways of approaching current interest illustrated two very different curatorial outlooks.

Figuratie Defiguratie represented the more traditional genre of exhibition, in which the historical perspective dominated. As Geirlandt explained in his introduction, the show came from the fact "that quite a number of artists feel a renewed urge to practice figuration currently." It was the organisers' desire to remind people that "even when abstract art was at its zenith a form of modern figuration was very active," and to "look back at figurative art during the period from the beginning of the century up till now."[14] Consequently, the show featured "Three categories of artists. The older artists whose work is now part of the history and source of the art of today; the younger artists whose art is in full evolution and promises new possibilities. In between is the generation of mature and established artists."[15] The show did indeed cover the entire century up to 1964. In fact, the earliest works exhibited was James Ensor's *De intrige* dated 1890, and almost half of the works on display had been made before 1945. Picasso was the best represented artists, with nine works from 1908 to 1963, including his *Femme accoudée* of 1921 which provided the cover of the catalogue. In the youngest generation, Yves Klein and Niki de Saint-Phalle represented the Nouveau Réalisme, while Rauschenberg, Roy Lichtenstein, Andy Warhol and George Segal exemplified American Pop art, with each one or two works on display. The most important part of the show was what Geirlandt called the "mature and established" artists, that is to say Giacometti, Dubuffet, Bacon, Jorn, Guttuso, Staël, Fautrier, Tobey, and the like. As such, the show provided the perfect example of a historical outlook in which recognition came from the past. Works by Klein and Rauschenberg were validated by being exhibited next to more established

[14] Karel J. Geirlandt, "Figuration and Disfiguration," in *Figuratie Defiguratie. De Menselijke Figuur Sedert Picasso* (Ghent: Museum Voor Schone Kunsten, 1964), XLVI.
[15] Ibid., XLVII.

painters like Dubuffet and Fautrier, who in turn were presented as the heirs of Picasso and Matisse.

In contrast, *Nieuwe Realisten* represented a newer type of show strongly grounded in the present, even though legitimacy was historically based. The idea for the exhibition came about in the autumn of 1959, when Wim Beeren visited *New Images of Man.* Organised by Peter Selz at the Museum of Modern Art in New York, it featured de Kooning, Dubuffet, Appel, Bacon, and Richier, among others. Intrigued, Beeren undertook to further explore and then exhibit the diversity of postwar figurative trends. In planning his show, he decided to supplement Selz's selection with works by Dutch, Belgian, Soviet and Yugoslavian realist artists. In addition to these mature and established artists, the young Dutch curator also wanted to showcase the young Nouveaux Réalistes and the British Pop artists. As he was finalising his selection, Beeren experienced the opportunity to view works by Lichtenstein, Warhol, Segal, Oldenburg and Rosenquist at the Gallery Sonnabend in Paris, and was completely taken aback. The new American Pop art therefore became the centre of the exhibition, along with the Nouveau Réalisme.

The exhibition, which opened in The Hague in June 1964, just a few days after Rauschenberg won the Grand Prize in Venice, was divided into four sections: "Traditioneel Realisme," represented by Léger, Rivera, Guttuso, Shahn, etc.; "Nouvelle Figuration" dominated by Bacon and de Kooning; "*De werkelijkheid als gevonden voorwerp*" (Reality as found objects), placed under Duchamp's leadership and featuring Joseph Cornell, Man Ray, and the "Groep Restany Parijs," which featured the Parisian Nouveaux Réalistes; and finally "Pop" divided between the founders of the movement (Dine, Johns, Rauschenberg, and Rivers), and its U.S., British, and French representatives.[16] Compared with *Figuratie Defiguratie,* whose ambition was to present a panorama of 20th century figurative art, *Nieuwe Realisten* focused on current figurative trends, which were discussed and placed in their historical context. The core difference between these outlooks is best exemplified in the exhibition catalogues: while in Ghent, the cover featured a Picasso from his 1920s *retour à l'ordre*, or Return to Order, period; in The Hague, the catalogue took the

[16] Wim Beeren, ed. *Nieuwe Realisten* (The Hague: Haags Gemeentemuseum, 1964).

form of a newspaper, thereby making the now and the new the most important.

The topicality of Beeren's exhibition pushed other institutions to take it on. In September, a slightly modified version opened at the Museum des 20. Jahrhunderts/Museum of the 20th Century in Vienna under the title *Pop, etc.* As this new title suggested, the Viennese show placed further emphasis on the newest trends gathered under the generic Pop banner. In fact, Beeren's historical, geographic, and stylistic distinctions had been preserved on only one page of the catalogue, which now simply featured the artists in alphabetic order. Moreover, several historical figures such as Rivera and Shahn had been omitted.[17] After Vienna, the show went to the Akademie der Künste/Academy of Arts in West Berlin in November 1964. In Berlin, the organisation and composition of the Vienna venue were preserved, but the title was changed to *Neue Realisten & Pop Art*, although the exhibition featured many artists who did not belong to either the Parisian or the American group.[18] Despite their different titles, the German and the Viennese exhibitions placed, in what could appear as a rather irreverent gesture, all postwar figuration under the patronage of the most recent realist developments.

The place of the mature and established artists was further reduced when the show was presented at the Palais des Beaux-Arts in Brussels/Centre for Fine Arts, Brussels in February 1965 as *Pop Art, Nouveau Réalisme, etc.* The selection for this last iteration, reworked by Belgian curator Jean Dypréau, was very different from the original Dutch exhibition. With the exceptions of Duchamp and Bacon, the older generation was not presented at all. De Kooning, a key figure of Beeren's show, was absent, and, with him, Appel, whose work had been on the cover of the Berlin catalogue. The works of the older generation were replaced by works of the younger Parisian and American artists. Thanks to additional loans from the Sonnabend Gallery in Paris and Belgian private collectors, including Dypréau himself, the American contingent had increased dramatically: Rauschenberg, Lichtenstein, and Dine had now five works on display

[17] Werner Hofmann, ed. *Pop, etc.* (Vienna: Museum des 20. Jahrhunderts, 1964).
[18] Werner Hofmann, ed. *Neue Realisten & Pop Art* (West Berlin: Akademie der Künst, 1964).

instead of two, while Warhol and Rosenquist had three instead of two.[19] Nonetheless, the shift was less a geographical matter (from Paris to New York) than a generational one—Paris was indeed very well-represented in Brussels through the new generation, as seen in Table 3. More than New York, it was youth that triumphed in Brussels. Beeren's historical survey of New Realist trends had been transformed into a presentation of the most current artistic trends. The shift was clearly manifested in the physical appearance of the catalogue, a stylish pink booklet, next to which, the original Dutch catalogue looked like an old newspaper.[20]

Considering the overall age ranges of artists featured in these exhibitions, we can grasp the extent to which curatorial practices were switching from an historical to a contemporaneous outlook (Table 4), but we can also see what Christophe Charle has dubbed "the temporal discordance" at work.[21] Changes never happen at the same rhythm everywhere. Comparing the curatorial approaches of *Figuratie Defiguratie* and *Pop Art, Nouveau Réalisme, etc.*, the two Belgian shows devoted to figuration, we can indeed see how, even within the same country, two institutions could exist with very different cultural and social frameworks.

The place of youth at the Venice Biennale

The temporal discordance apparent in the curatorial practices and approaches to contemporary art of the time was particularly obvious in the French and the American selections at the Venice Biennale.

Jacques Lassaigne, the curator of the French pavilion, had selected Julio González, who had passed away in 1942 and was consequently not eligible for a prize, and Roger Bissière, who had asked to remain out of the com-

[19] Jean Dypréau, ed. *Pop Art, Nouveau Réalisme, etc.* (Brussels Palais des Beaux-Arts, 1965).

[20] For a more detailed discussion of the changes that occurred during the touring of this exhibition, see Catherine Dossin, "*Pop Art, Nouveau Réalisme, etc.* Comment Paris perdit le pouvoir de nommer les nouvelles tendances," in *Le nom de l'art*, ed. Vanessa Theodoropoulou and Katia Schneller (Paris: Publications de la Sorbonne, 2013), 49–62.

[21] See for instance Christophe Charle, *Discordance des temps. Une brève histoire de la modernité* (Paris: Armand Colin, 2011); Christophe Charle, "Spatial Translation and Temporal Discordance: Modes of Cultural Circulation and Internationalization in Europe (second half of the nineteenth and first half of the twentieth century)," in *Circulations in the Global History of Art*, ed. Thomas DaCosta Kaufmann, Catherine Dossin, and Béatrice Joyeux-Prunel (Burlington, VT: Ashgate, 2015), 113–32.

petition because of his advanced age.[22] The French also exhibited the work of a young sculptor, Jean Ipousteguy, and two young painters, René Brô and Bernard Dufour, who were little known outside France and so clearly not in a position to compete for the Grand Prize. Whereas the French presented artists at the ends of their careers, the Americans presented artists at the breakthrough moments of theirs. In 1964, the American pavilion accordingly featured two exhibitions programmatically titled "Germinal Painters" and "Young Painters." For them, the Biennale was a showcase for new ideas and discoveries. In contrast, for the French, it was a place of consecration and honours.

Until 1964, the historical approach had dominated the Biennale. In the years following the War many countries, including Italy, saw this event as the opportunity to look back at their previous national artistic production and to educate the public about modern art which had so often been mishandled at the time of its creation before being suppressed by Fascist governments. In 1948, for the first postwar Biennale, the organisers accordingly planned a didactic panorama of the visual arts in Europe since the late nineteenth century. As Giovanni Ponti, the Extraordinary Commissary of the Biennale from 1946 to 1954, explained in his preface to that year's catalogue: "We have accumulated works of every current and of every trend. [...] I don't believe that I exaggerate if I state that, for the first time after the war, one has both a wide and complete vision of what has been created by the greatest artists of the Modern era. [...] the panorama of artistic trends is complete."[23] The focal point of the Biennale was an exhibition of Impressionism in the German pavilion, featuring ninety-eight paintings from the public collection of Cologne, where the museums remained closed. The exhibition, the first important presentation of Impressionism in Italy, was a popular success.

[22] The jury nonetheless gave Bissière, who would die in December 1964, an honorary award in recognition of his long career. For more information on all the awards presented that year, see "Prize winners at the XXXII Venice Biennale," *Art International*, 25 September 1964. And Didier Schulman, "La France à Venise," in Association Française d'Action Artistique, *La France à Venise: le pavillon français de 1948 à 1988* (Rome: Edizioni Carte Segrete, 1990). 213

[23] Quoted and translated in Adrian R. Duran, *Painting, Politics, and the New Front of Cold War Italy* (Burlington, VT: Ashgate, 2013), 76.

A similar need to understand and showcase the history of modern art motivated the exhibitory programme of the German pavilion at the Venice Biennale throughout the 1950s. After the vicious Nazi attack on the visual arts, there was a strong desire to look back at the history of modern art, especially at the German contributions. In 1950, for their first official participation at the Biennale since the war, the Germans asked Eberhard Hanfstaengl, who had been the curator of the German pavilion in 1934 and 1936, to serve again. He organised a retrospective of Der Blaue Reiter, which was followed by a presentation of Die Brücke in 1952. Through these two exhibitions, Hanfstaengl distinguished between the Apollonian (Der Blaue Reiter) and the Dionysian (Die Brücke) poles of German Expressionism. In 1954, he opposed the abstract and figurative trends of modern art through a retrospective exhibition of Paul Klee and Oskar Schlemmer. In 1956, he examined the Surrealist vein with Max Ernst.[24]

The French pavilion followed a similar pattern, using the Venice Biennale to pay homage to the masters of the first School of Paris. These historical presentations, responding to the need of the public and the general curatorial practices of the Biennale, received public and critical acclaim. As a matter of fact, throughout the postwar period, French artists scooped up most of the major awards: Georges Braque (painting, 1948), Marc Chagall (printmaking, 1948), Henri Matisse (painting, 1950), Ossip Zadkine (sculpture, 1950), Raoul Dufy (painting, 1952), Jean Arp (sculpture, 1954), Jacques Villon (painting, 1956), Hans Hartung and Jean Fautrier (both painting, 1960), and Alfred Manessier (painting, 1962).[25] In 1962, the organisers of the Biennale held a retrospective of the winners of the Grand Prizes since 1948 in the central pavilion, thereby historicizing their own history.

In 1964, things changed with most of the pavilions adopting the contemporaneous outlook that had been that of the U.S. pavilion for some time, and were showing *promising* rather than *established* artists. That year, Edouard Tier became the curator of the German pavilion. Breaking

[24] On the German contribution to the Venice Biennale, see Christoph Becker and Annette Lagler, eds., *Biennale Venedig: Der Deutsche Beitrag (1895–1995)* (Stuttgart: Institut für Auslandsbeziehungen/Cantz Verlag, 1995).

[25] For a detailed list of Grand Prizes, see "Gran Premi dal 1938 al 2003," in *Storia della Biennale die Venezia, 1895–2003*, ed. Enzo di Martino (Venice: Papiro Arte, 2003), 129–30.

with the tradition of historical shows, he started to present young West German artists.[26] Following suit, the Belgian pavilion presented Pol Bury, who represented the new kinetic and optical trends. As for the Italian pavilion, it featured "Nuova Figurazione," a group show of young Italian artists, as well as "Arte d'oggi nei musei," for which Giulio Carlo Argan had asked several museums to send works from their collections that had been created in the past fourteen years. While the French Musée National d'art Moderne sent recent works by established Informel artists, most European museums chose younger artists, such as Tinguely (Moderna Museet, in Stockholm), Johns, César (the Tate, in London), Twombly and Arman (Galleria Nazionale d'Arte Moderna, in Rome).[27] Rauschenberg's award that year was thus part of a larger curatorial trend, in which it was more important to present what was most current and relevant, rather than distributing official accolades to established artists.

In an unpublished essay, Pierre Restany analysed the events of Venice with great insight: "By the anachronism of his choice, Jacques Lassaigne is the indirect craftsman of the American victory. The indignation of the Parisian journalists won't change anything. The school of Paris was not betrayed by the decisions of the international jury, it was harmed (on good faith, this is the worst!) by the one who had the responsibility to represent it by establishing an official selection. The presence as guest of honour of the old master Bissière is to say the least aberrant in Venice in 1964."[28] If Restany had been in charge of the official selection, he would have taken a competitive position and presented the Nouveaux Réalistes, thereby giving the French pavilion an opportunity to participate actively in the laboratory of contemporary art that Venice was becoming. But to have entrusted the young Restany with that selection would have required the French officials to change their perspectives not only on the function of the Venice Biennale, but also on the place of youth in the art worlds, and in the society at large.

This was all the more difficult for the French since in 1959 they had created the Biennale de Paris, which was restricted to artists under thirty-five years of age, in order to counterbalance the Venice Biennale and to

[26] Becker and Lagler, *Biennale Venedig: Der Deutsche Beitrag (1895–1995).*

[27] Ikegami, *The Great Migrator*, 94.

[28] Quoted in Henry Perier, *Pierre Restany, l'Alchimiste de l'art* (Paris: Cercle d'Art, 1998), 242.

provide opportunities to younger artists. In their mind, young artists such as Rauschenberg should be presented in Paris in a space devoted to the discovery of new experiments, while Venice should be reserved for the consecration of established artists. In Venice, young artists could be recognised through the David Bright Prize, which recognised artists under age forty-five in the three categories of painting, sculpture, and print. In 1964, Ipousteguy was awarded the David Bright Prize for sculpture—an honour which was seen as an appropriate recognition for a young artist at that moment of his career. Had he received the Grand Prize of Sculpture, it would have been deemed inappropriate, French or not French.

In the catalogue of the XXe Salon de Mai, which took place in Paris in May 1964, Gaston Diehl, the president of the Salon, conveyed the anxiety that many felt at seeing novelty being embraced everywhere as the highest artistic value: "In a period dominated by the acceleration of time, must any link with the past be cut? Is all that lasts suspicious and is it important to deny as soon as possible ideas introduced the previous day in order to respond the demands of the current area and eternal youth?"[29] Diehl's questions summarise to my mind the reason why so many French (and not French) were dismayed by Rauschenberg's receiving the Grand Prize of Painting: beyond the so-called triumph of American art, it was the triumph of values associated with the new and the young. Under the growing demographical pressure of the baby-boomer generation, the Western world was undergoing social and cultural transformations that overwhelmed and frightened the older generation. Rauschenberg, as an American Pop artist, embodied both youth (his own and that of his country), and modernity. As long as the Pop artists remained confined to space and position deemed appropriate for young artists, such as commercial galleries like the Sonnabend Gallery in Paris or the Paris Biennale, their works could be appreciated for what they were: a fresh and stimulating take on modern life.[30] But that they could garner official recognition at major international events such as the Venice Biennale was unaccept-

[29] Gaston Diehl, "Vingt années d'efforts en commun," in *XXe Salon de Mai* (Paris: Musée d'art moderne de la ville de Paris, 1964), unpaged.
[30] On the critical reception of Pop art in France, see Clémence Bigel, "Le Pop'Art à Paris: une histoire de la réception critique des avant-gardes américaines entre 1959 et 1978" (Master, Université Paris 1 – Panthéon-Sorbonne, 2013).

able. Not only did it contradict all established values, it also tapped into a rampant anxiety surrounding youth.

The Young Face of France

Following the débâcle of 1940, the humiliation of four years of German Occupation and the shame of Collaboration, there was an urgent need to reinvent France. The younger generation was seen as the one capable of renewing France culturally, spiritually, and politically.[31] For decades, France had been an elderly country with a low birth rate, but the Baby Boom of the post-war years was rejuvenating the old nation and bringing hope for the future. In 1959, the French government published a book in English entitled *The Young Face of France*, which bragged about the economic and political potential of the country's new demographics, and opened with the boisterous statement: "France is now the most dynamic country in the old continent in Europe because it possesses the largest number of young people."[32]

Yet, going hand in hand with this hopeful discourse was an anxious one on the moral corruption of youth and the national decline it was bond to cause. The media, feeding on such a fear, featured sensational articles that told stories of violent crimes committed by youngsters who feared neither god nor man.[33] In the 1950s, the *blousons noirs*, thus called because they wore Marlon Brando-like leather jackets and listened to rock-and-roll music, came to embody "the worst" of this unruly youth. The summer of 1959, the year when the self-congratulatory study *The Young Face of France* was published, was actually marked by a series of violent crimes and gang fights that led the media to talk about the "Summer of the blousons noirs."[34]

[31] On this positive discourse on the new and youth, see Richard Ivan Jobs, *Riding the New Wave: Youth and the Rejuvenation of France after the Second World War* (Stanford: Stanford University Press, 2007), 2.
[32] Centre de Diffusion Française, *The Young Face of France* (Paris: La Documentation Française, 1959), 3. The book covers French youth in all its different aspects of, from the school system and the *colonies de vacances* (summer camps) to military service and sexuality.
[33] See the chapter "Rehabilitating Delinquent France" in Jobs, *Riding the New Wave*, 141–84.
[34] Despite their postive tone, the authors of *The Young Face of France* admitted that "The most serious youth problem in France, as elsewhere, is that of juvenile delinquency." Yet,

Despite all the discourses on youth, be they positive or negative, actual young people were rather invisible in French society. As Arthur Marwick explained in his studies of the Sixties, very few in France realised that the younger generation was different. Born at the end or after the War, in a time of economic prosperity and radical transformation, they had different models, values, and aspirations. Yet, when adults or officials talked about the "Young Face of France," they used timeless concepts and old ideas with which they felt comfortable but that did not reflect the actual experience of the Sixties youth.[35] The Biennale de Paris perfectly exemplifies the patronising way in which France dealt with the younger generations by providing them with visibility and recognition, but within the confine of a space clearly earmarked for the young and controlled by their elders. The incomprehension of the adults and silencing of the youth was actually a common theme in books and movies of the time, and would become a main topic of the posters of May 1968, such as the famous "Sois Jeune et Tais Toi" (Be Young and Shut Up; Figure 2.1.).

By 1964, however, it was no longer possible to ignore the existence of a growing youth. By then, 33 percent of the French population was under twenty, and nineteen million under twenty-five.[36] As the demographical weight of these Baby Boomers increased, their values became more and more visible, like what happened on 22 June 1963, when the youth magazine *Salut les Copains* organised a concert Place de la Nation. *Salut les copains* had started in 1959 as a weekly radio programme that played American, British, and French pop music. Very successful, the show was turned into a daily programme and a magazine. *Salut les copains* provided French youth with a space of their own where they could listen to their

they quickly minimized its importance, noting: "Recently, however, there has been a marked downward trend." (Centre de Diffusion Française, *The Young Face of France*, 38). On the blousons noirs and the discourses that surrounded them, see Drew M. Fedorka, "Le Temps des Copains: Youth and the Making of Modern France in the Era of Decolonization, 1958–1968" (M.A., University of Central Florida, 2015).

[35] See the chapter entitled "Blousons Noirs, Copains, Vitelloni: Youth in France and Italy" in Marwick, *The Sixties*, 95–111. For more on the specificity of the Sixties youth, see also Jean-François Sirinelli, "La France des "Sixties" revisitée," *Vingtième Siècle. Revue d'histoire* No. 69 (January–March 2001): 111–24; Jean-François Sirinelli, "Des « copains » aux « camarades » ? Les baby-boomers français dans les années 1960," *Revue Historique* 305, no. 2 (April 2003).

[36] Marwick, *The Sixties*, 99.

music and discuss the topics that interested them, outside the patronising control of their elders. The concert of June 1963 was intended to celebrate the one-year anniversary of the magazine. Organisers expected maybe 15,000 fans—but some 300,000 showed up that night. This was an astonishing event that broadcasted the mounting importance of French youth, and consequently generated much anti-youth propaganda.[37]

In response to this event, sociologist Edgar Morin published a series of articles in the newspaper *Le Monde*, in which he described the appearance of adolescence as a new age class within post-war capitalist societies. He argued that adolescence appeared because the transition from childhood to adulthood was henceforth happening gradually over several years, thereby leading to this transition period of adolescence. Morin then proceeded to analyse this new age class, which he christened the Yé-Yé generation, in reference to the "yeah! yeah!" sound often heard in British or American music. Beyond the cultural and economic differences that divided them, Morin posited that the Yé-Yé adolescents were united by common styles, belongings, language and heroes. He also evaluated the role of the mass media in making "adolescence" into a specific social class, promoting juvenile values through society as a whole, and ultimately giving a new face to France.[38]

Following Morin, people started to pay closer attention to these adolescents that would soon be full adults and, subsequently, in charge of the country. In April 1964, for instance, the popular magazine *Paris-Match* published two long articles emphatically titled "Ils nous gouverneront demain" (They will rule us tomorrow) on this new generation, its values and desires.[39] The author, Jean Farran, introduced his survey with the following equally dramatic statement:

[37] For more information on this event and the history of *Salut les copains*, see Chris Tinker, "Shaping Youth in Salut les copains," *Modern & Contemporary France* 15, no. 3 (2007): 293–308; Fedorka, "Le Temps des Copains."

[38] These articles were originally published in *Le Monde* on July 6 and 7, 1964 and were reprinted in Edgar Morin, "Salut les copains," in *La sociologie* (Paris: Le Seuil, 1994), 399–407.

[39] Jean Farran, "Ils nous gouverneront demain," *Paris-Match*, no. 782 (4 April 1964): 3–7; Jean Farran, "Cette jeuness qui nous gouvernera demain II," *Paris-Match*, no. 783 (11 April 11, 1964): 3–7.

> Today, five million of French people are between sixteen and twenty-four years-old. In 1980 they will be the leaders of the Nation. They were born and are living in a fast-changing world. They are a new race of Frenchman that their elders do no longer understand. What is their vision of the world? What importance do they attach to love, money, politics, faith? To what kind of new morality are they giving birth? Answering these questions: it is to shed light on our own future.[40]

The Younger generation was taking over, and France was finally and ineluctably changing face. Beyond the triumph of youth, it was the triumph of urbanisation, modernisation, and popular culture. Youth was simply the standard bearer for all these transformations which threatened traditional French values, and were building a new country, even though most structural and institutional changes would have to wait until the explosion of May 1968 to take place.

Conclusion

France's response to Rauschenberg's receiving the Grand Prize of Painting in Venice needs to be read in this particular generationally biased context. It was upsetting to many, because it tapped into a larger social crisis, when the mature and established generation was then feeling particularly overwhelmed by the arrival of a younger one. Clutching on to the ancestral French values, they attempted to resist the decline they feared their country was bound to undergo. It was not merely anti-Americanism and chauvinism. Such feelings were most certainly there, but it was more complicated than that. French critics could fully support American artists, such as Alexander Calder or Mark Tobey, receiving Prizes in Venice, because they were established artists representing traditional artistic values. Rauschenberg, on the other hand, was too young, too popular. In their eyes, he was to painting what the Beatles and Johnny Hallyday were to music—even if one did not dislike listening to them on the radio, one could not regard them as serious musicians. Tellingly, in their reviews of

[40] Farran, "Ils nous gouverneront demain," 3.

the Salon de Mai and Venice Biennale, many French critics made reference to the Yé-Yé when discussing Pop art.[41]

Commenting on Rauschenberg's victory in the pages of *Combat*, Alain Bosquet gave vent to his indignation at seeing some silly youngsters get rewarded for disregarding the most sacred values of Western culture: "The choice of Rauschenberg is an attack against the dignity of artistic creation: it is an admission that the painting can disappear without harm, forever." For Bosquet, the problem was not that Rauschenberg and his colleagues were creating "at the random of a spineless imagination, exchangeable objects," but that the very curators and jurors whose mission was to protect art, were surrendering to the fad of novelty and accepting, even encouraging such immature practices. Art was being betrayed from within, hence the urgency with which Bosquet called artists to resist under the banner of the great modern masters that were still alive. He declared: "We must save painting, be it representational or not. Painters must realise what threatens them. [...] Picasso, Max Ernest, Kokoschka, Miro, Chagall, Tamayo, Pignon, Matta, Lam, Vasarely, wherever you are, defend yourselves from the barbarians."[42]

Reflecting on Bosquet's and others' response to the Venice Biennale, José Pierre mused on the profound crisis of values the Western World was undergoing and of which these events were symptomatic:

> Is painting condemned? – questioned Mr. Bosquet. Not by Pop art, in any case. Unlike Nouveau Réalisme – real cancer that one, although born within the school of Paris – Pop has never banished neither painting nor its support, and on the contrary it contributed to restore its essential importance to the image.
>
> Then, it is maybe necessary to agree that Pop-art is the signal of a general crisis of modern sensibility, corresponding to this crucial moment when objects invented to serve us begin speaking more loudly than us, where the automobile,

[41] See among others, Marc Albert-Levin, "Le XXe Salon de Mai ouvert au Yé-Yé pictural," *Cimaise*, no. 68 (April–May–June 1964): 68–73; Guy Dornand, "Le Luna Park de Mai," *Libération*, no. 6147 (June 4, 1964); Jean-Albert Cartier, "La Biennale de Venise livré aux "Yé-Yé"," *Combat*, no. 6229 (June 23, 1964): 9.

[42] Alain Bosquet, "Trahison à Venise," *Combat* (June 23, 1964): 1.

> the television, the newspaper, the jukebox, the can box succeeded in colonizing our personality, in replacing it almost completely.[43]

Placing Rauschenberg's success at the Venice Biennale in its larger curatorial and cultural context allows us to refine our understanding of France's response to this event and see, beyond the official narrative of triumph and anti-Americanism, the crisis of values that was shaking Western Europe in 1964. The power structures of the international art world were indeed being reshuffled during this strategic year, but this should not be reduced to a simple shift from Paris to New York.[44] More profoundly, in the era of Pop we see the emergence of a new cultural environment, which triggered new curatorial practices and new art historical discourses. The values of the Western art worlds were changing, as novelty and youth became more important than tradition and historical continuity, even in museum circles, and art institutions saw their mission to prospect and recognise new talent, instead of retrospectively consecrating past achievements.

Bibliography

Primary sources

Albert-Levin, Marc. "Le XXe Salon de Mai ouvert au Yé-Yé pictural." *Cimaise*, no. 68 (April–May–June 1964): 68–73.

Association Française d'Action Artistique. *La France à Venise: le pavillon français de 1948 à 1988*. Rome: Edizioni Carte Segrete, 1990.

Beeren, Wim, ed. *Nieuwe Realisten*. The Hague: Haags Gemeentemuseum, 1964.

Bosquet, Alain. "Trahison à Venise." *Combat* (June 23, 1964).

Cabanne, Pierre. "A Venise. L'Amérique proclame la fin de l'Ecole de Paris et lance le Pop'Art pour coloniser l'Europe." *Arts*, no. 968 (24–30 June 1964): 16.

Cartier, Jean-Albert. "La Biennale de Venise livré aux 'Yé-Yé.'" *Combat*, no. 6229 (23 June 1964): 9.

Centre de Diffusion Française. *The Young Face of France*. Paris: La Documentation Française, 1959.

[43] José Pierre, "Les ravudeuses contre le Pop," *Combat* (July 1964).

[44] For more on the geopolitics of the Western art worlds in that period, see Dossin, *The Rise and Fall of American Art*.

Diehl, Gaston. "Vingt années d'efforts en commun," in *XXe Salon de Mai.* unpaged. Paris: Musée d'art moderne de la ville de Paris, 1964.

Dornand, Guy. "Le Luna Park de Mai." *Libération*, no. 6147 (4 June 1964).

Dypréau, Jean, ed. *Pop Art, Nouveau Réalisme, etc.* Brussels Palais des Beaux-Arts, 1965.

Farran, Jean. "Cette jeuness qui nous gouvernera demain II." *Paris-Match*, no. 783 (11 April 1964): 3–7.

—. "Ils nous gouverneront demain." *Paris-Match*, no. 782 (4 April 1964): 3–7.

Geirlandt, Karel J. "Figuration and Disfiguration," in *Figuratie Defiguratie. De Menselijke Figuur Sedert Picasso.* XLVI–XLVII. Ghent: Museum Voor Schone Kunsten, 1964.

Hofmann, Werner, ed. *Neue Realisten & Pop Art.* West Berlin: Akademie der Künst, 1964.

—. ed. *Pop, etc.* Vienna: Museum des 20. Jahrhunderts, 1964.

Pierre, José. "Les ravudeuses contre le Pop." *Combat* (July 1964).

Wescher, Herta. "Pauvre Ecole de Paris." *Cimaise*, Spring 1964, 60–67.

Secondary sources

Becker, Christoph, and Annette Lagler, eds. *Biennale Venedig: Der Deutsche Beitrag (1895–1995).* Stuttgart: Institut für Auslandsbeziehungen/Cantz Verlag, 1995.

Bigel, Clémence. "Le Pop'Art à Paris: une histoire de la réception critique des avant-gardes américaines entre 1959 et 1978." Master, Université Paris 1 – Panthéon-Sorbonne, 2013.

Charle, Christophe. *Discordance des temps. Une brève histoire de la modernité.* Paris: Armand Colin, 2011.

—. "Spatial Translation and Temporal Discordance: Modes of Cultural Circulation and Internationalization in Europe (second half of the nineteenth and first half of the twentieth century)," in *Circulations in the Global History of Art*, edited by Thomas DaCosta Kaufmann, Catherine Dossin and Béatrice Joyeux-Prunel. 113–32. Burlington, VT: Ashgate, 2015.

Dossin, Catherine. "Mark Rothko, the Long Unsung Hero of American Art." In *Mark Rothko. Obrazy z National Gallery of Art w Waszyngtonie*, edited by Marek Bartelik. 101–12. Warsaw: National Museum of Warsaw, 2013.

—. "*Pop Art, Nouveau Réalisme, etc.* Comment Paris perdit le pouvoir de nommer les nouvelles tendances," in *Le nom de l'art*, edited by Vanessa Theodoropoulou and Katia Schneller. 49–62. Paris: Publications de la Sorbonne, 2013.

—. *The Rise and Fall of American Art, 1940s–1980s: A Geopolitics of Western Art Worlds.* Burlington, VT: Ashgate, 2015.

—. "To Drip or to Pop? The European Triumph of American Art." *The Artl@s Bulletin* 3, no. 1 (Spring 2014): 79–103.

Dossin, Catherine, Béatrice Joyeux-Prunel, and Sorin A. Matei. "Spatial (Digital) History: A Total History? The ARTL@S Project." *Visual Resources: Digital Art History Special Issue* (Spring 2013): 47–58.

Duran, Adrian R. *Painting, Politics, and the New Front of Cold War Italy*. Burlington, VT: Ashgate, 2013.

Fedorka, Drew M. "Le Temps des Copains: Youth and the Making of Modern France in the Era of Decolonization, 1958–1968." M.A., University of Central Florida, 2015.

Gloor, Lukas. *Die Geschichte der Basler Kunstvereins und der Kunsthalle Basel, 1839–1988*. Basel: Kunsthalle Basel, 1989.

"Gran Premi dal 1938 al 2003," in *Storia della Biennale die Venezia, 1895–2003*, edited by Enzo di Martino. 129–30. Venice: Papiro Arte, 2003.

Ikegami, Hiroko. *The Great Migrator: Robert Rauschenberg and the Global Rise of American Art*. Cambridge: The MIT Press 2010.

Jobs, Richard Ivan. *Riding the New Wave: Youth and the Rejuvenation of France after the Second World War*. Stanford: Stanford University Press, 2007.

Marwick, Arthur. *The Sixties: Cultural Revolution in Britain, France, Italy and the United States, c.1958–c.1974*. Oxford, New York: Oxford University Press, 1998.

Morin, Edgar. "Salut les copains." In *La sociologie*. 399–407. Paris: Le Seuil, 1994.

Perier, Henry. *Pierre Restany, l'Alchimiste de l'art*. Paris: Cercle d'Art, 1998.

"Prize winners ar the XXXII Venice Biennale." *Art International*, 25 September 1964, 44.

Sirinelli, Jean-François. "Des « copains » aux « camarades » ? Les baby-boomers français dans les années 1960." *Revue Historique* 305, no. 2 (April 2003): 327–43.

—. "La France des 'Sixties' revisitée." *Vingtième Siècle. Revue d'histoire* No. 69 (January–March 2001): 111–24.

Taylor, Brandon. "The Rauschenberg Retrospective in 1964." In *The Whitechapel Art Gallery Centenary Review*. 71–75. London Whitechapel Art Gallery, 2001.

Tinker, Chris. "Shaping Youth in Salut les copains." *Modern & Contemporary France* 15, no. 3 (2007): 293–308.

Illustrations

Table 1: Percentage of artworks featured in the shows by artists' age range in 1964.

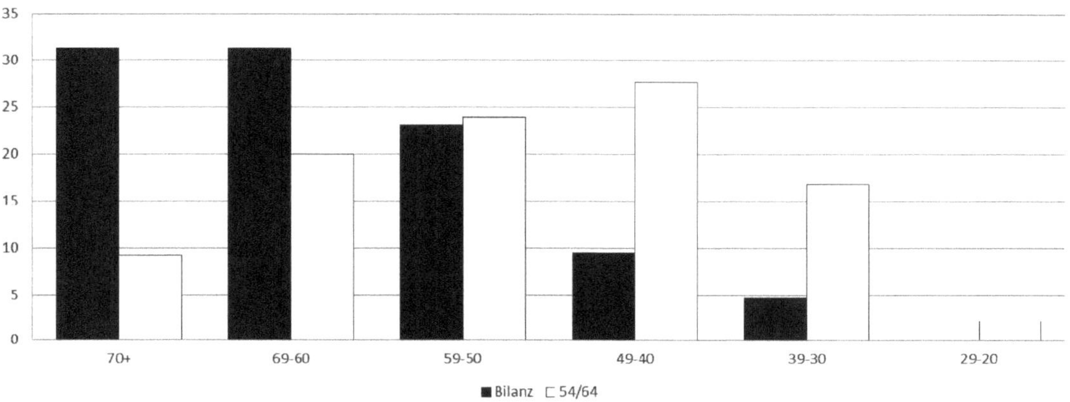

Table 2: Percentage of artworks featured in the shows by artists' residence in 1964.

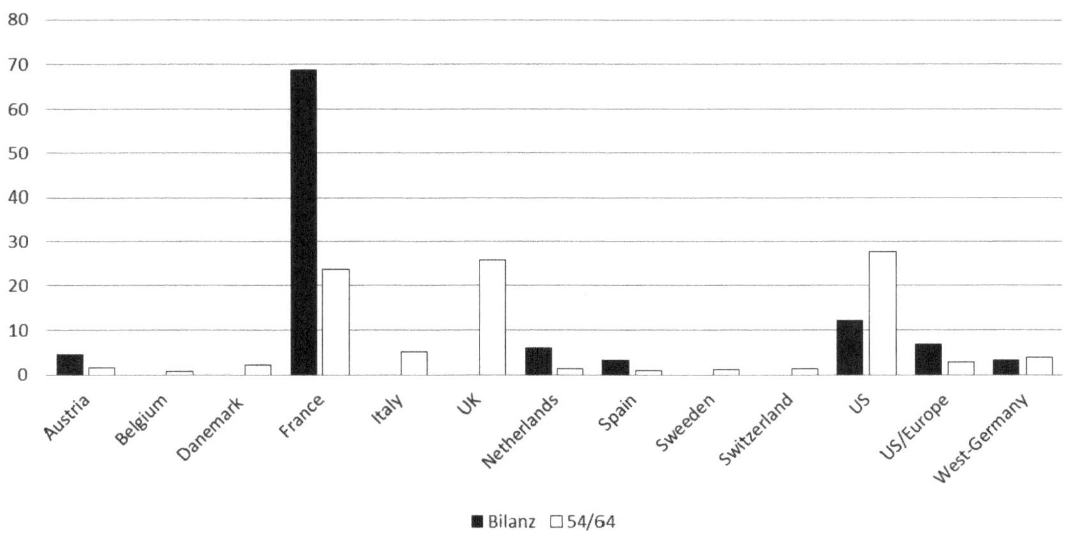

Table 3: Percentage of artworks featured in the shows by artists' residence in 1964. Note that only major countries of residency that accounted for a significant number of artists are represented in this graph.

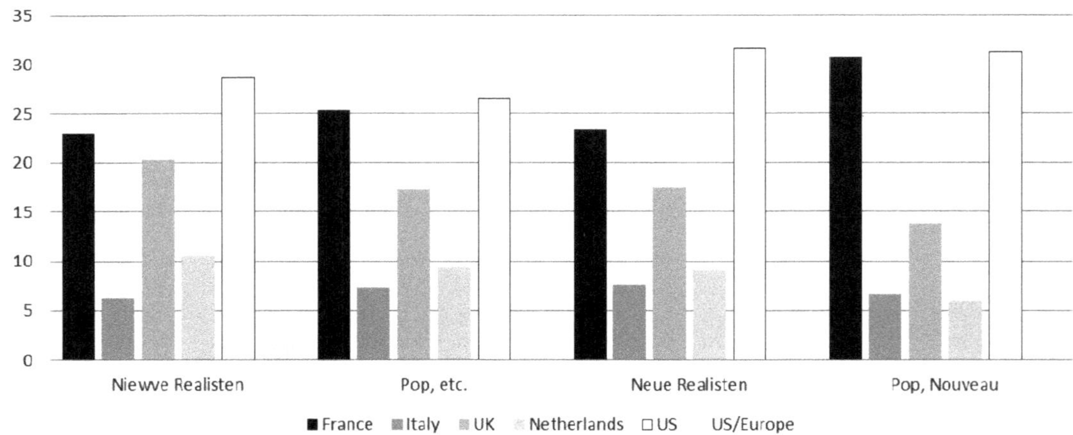

Table 4: Percentage of artworks featured in the shows by artists' age range in 1964

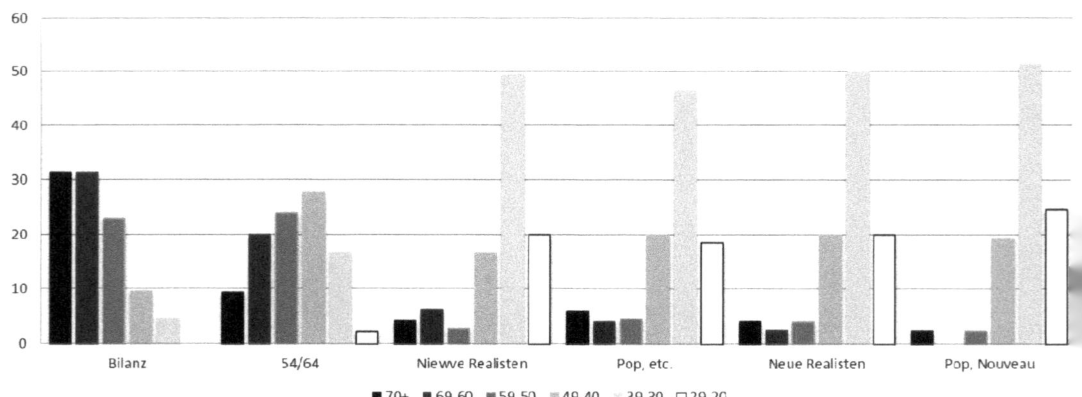

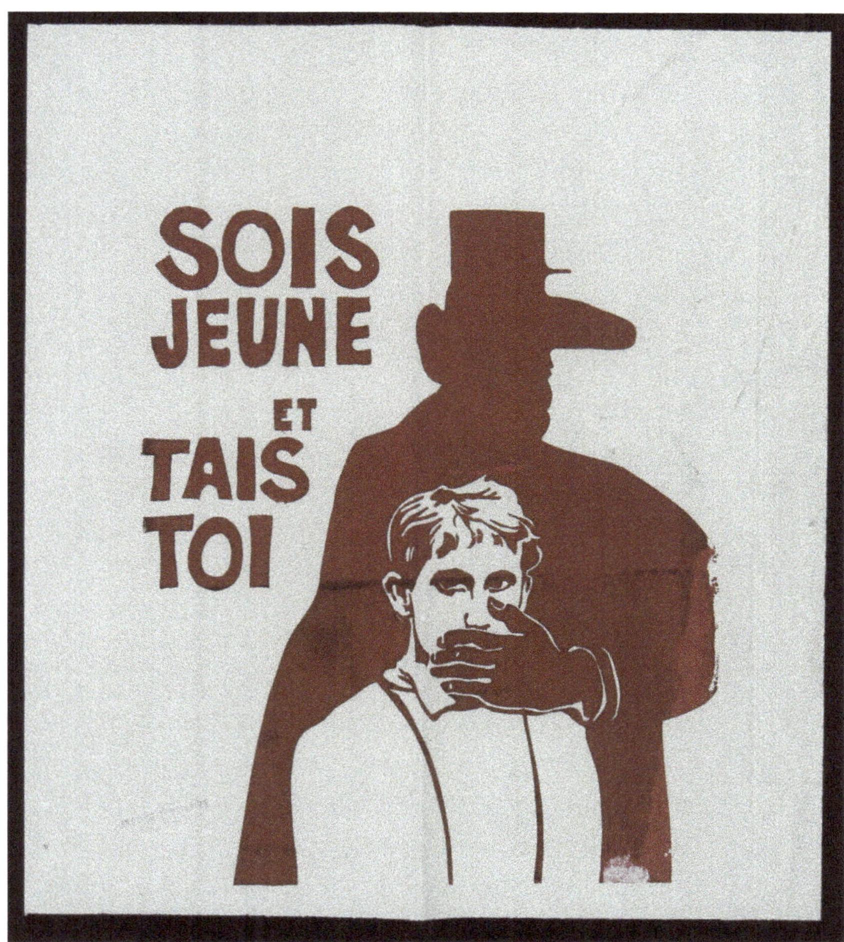

Figure 2.1: *Sois jeune et tais toi.* Poster realized by the Atelier populaire of the Ecole des Beaux-Arts in 1968. Serigraphy, 96 x 76 cm. Copyright: public domain. Source: Bibliothèque nationale de France, ENT QB-1 (1968/11)-FT6

3
The "New York Connection"
Pontus Hultén's Curatorial Agenda in the 1960s[1]

Hiroko Ikegami

[1] This chapter is based on chapter three in Hiroko Ikegami, *The Great Migrator: Robert Rauschenberg and the Global Rise of American Art*, Cambridge, Mass.: The MIT Press, 2010. I would like to thank Stefan Ståhle of the Moderna Museet, who secured all the necessary images related to the museum for the MIT book.

"Why is *Monogram* in Stockholm?" This simple question was the beginning. For a graduate student whose dissertation topic was Robert Rauschenberg, it seemed very curious that *Monogram* (Figure 3.1), arguably the most famous work by the artist, is not in the collection of the Museum of Modern Art, New York or any other representative museums in the United States, but in the collection of the Moderna Museet in Stockholm. The question caused me to fly to Sweden in March 2004 in order to conduct research at the museum, which has owned the work since 1965. In fact, I was quite nervous about this visit: I came all the way from New York out of naïve curiosity; what if I didn't find anything? As I approached the museum entrance, though, the sight of its entrance astonished me: The museum's logo was based on the handwriting of none other than Rauschenberg (Figure 3.2). I found this utterly puzzling: Why would a *national* museum of modern art in Sweden present an *American* artist's handwriting as its public identity? Even before setting foot in the museum building, I knew therefore that I was already onto something very important.

A key figure for these questions is Pontus Hultén, who became a curator of the Moderna Museet in 1959 and its director in 1963 (Figure 3.3).[2]

[2] For the history of the museum, see Anna Tellgren, ed., *The History Book. On Moderna Museet 1958–2008*, Stockholm-Göttingen: Moderna Museet, Steidl, 2008; and Annika

He built a special bond with Rauschenberg and the New York art scene in the 1960s, which in retrospect he called the "New York connection" in 1983.[3] Granted, his legendary directorship of the museum in the 1960s was already well-known when I started my research. As I explored the museum's archives, however, I uncovered fascinating materials that were little known outside of the Nordic countries about how Hultén's curatorial agenda not only animated the local art scene but also created a serious conflict in it—especially in the era of Vietnam War, which was responsible for the increased anti-American feelings among the Swedish citizens. This chapter will discuss how this shift in cultural climate affected the reception of *Monogram* in Stockholm, and will compare this case with that of Tokyo—another marginal, yet important, site on the international art scene, where many artists produced Pop-inspired works during the 1960s. By doing so, I will examine the challenge that any peripheral cities such as Stockholm and Tokyo had to face in order to strike a fine balance between their transnational ambition and localism.

Pontus Hultén and his "New York Connection"

First, let us see how Hultén developed his connection with the New York art scene. As a curator of the Moderna Museet, he visited New York for the first time in 1959, after he served as a curator for the Swedish exhibits at the Bienal de São Paulo. Among many artists he met in the city, Rauschenberg was special. In his studio, Hultén saw and fell in love with *Monogram*, which had just been completed after five years of trial and error. Despite the lack of funding, Hultén immediately decided to purchase it for the museum, and asked the artist to reserve it until the museum secured sufficient funds for its acquisition. Another important event was that Hultén reestablished contact with Billy Klüver, a Swedish engineer at the Bell Laboratory, whom he had known in the engineer's student days in Stockholm. The importance of Klüver as a mediator

Öhrner, "The Moderna Museet in Stockholm: The Institution and the Avant-Garde," in Tania Ørum and Jesper Olsson, eds., *A Cultural History of the Avant-Garde in the Nordic Countries 1950–1975*, Leiden: Brill Academic Publishers, 2016, pp. 112–121.

[3] Pontus Hultén, "Fem fragment ur Moderna Museet's historia," in Olle Granath and Monica Nieckels, eds., *Moderna Museet 1958–1983*, exh. cat., Stockholm: Moderna Museet Press, 1983, p. 54.

cannot be overstressed, as he introduced a number of Neo-Dada and Pop artists to Hultén and started acting as the museum's representative in New York from then on.

Aware of the marginal location of Stockholm within the modern art scene, Hultén planned to import the New York avant-garde in order to put his museum on the global art map. An important beginning was the 1961 exhibition *Movements in Art* (Rörelse i konsten), a large survey show of kinetic art that Hultén organised in collaboration with the Stedelijk Museum Amsterdam and with individuals such as Klüver, Willem Sandberg, Jean Tinguely, Carlo Derkert, and Daniel Spoerri. Although American art was not the main focus the show, Hultén invited up-and-coming American artists such as Rauschenberg and Alan Kaprow to create works and collaborate with European artists such as Tinguely and Niki de Saint-Phalle. The spirit of the exhibition was truly international and collaborative, as recalled by the critic Ulf Linde, who created the replica of Duchamp's *Large Glass* for the exhibition with the Swedish artist Per Olof Ultvedt.[4] This was a heroic beginning, and Hultén wanted to bring more American artworks and artists to the Swedish capital.

As mentioned before, Hultén called this curatorial agenda the "New York connection," which he established through organising a series of ambitious exhibitions such as *4 Americans* (4 Amerikanare): *Alfred Leslie, Jasper Johns, Robert Rauschenberg, Richard Stankiewicz* in 1962, a Jackson Pollock retrospective in 1963, *American Pop Art: 106 Forms of Love and Despair* (Amerikansk pop-konst: 106 former av kärlek och förtvivan) in 1964, a Claes Oldenburg show in 1966, and an Andy Warhol show in 1968, as well as other related exhibitions and events. It is important to note Hultén did not bring pre-packaged exhibitions from American institutions but organised most of these exhibitions on his own curatorial initiatives, which was very rare at the time. Hultén had his own team to realise his agenda. In New York, he had the support of Billy Klüver and Leo Castelli Gallery, which represented many Neo-Dada and Pop artists. In Paris, Ileana Sonnabend, the former wife of Castelli, helped him to secure a

[4] Ulf Linde, interview by the author, 12 March 2004, Stockholm.

number of important American Pop artworks for his shows, as she was trying to engineer a European market for American art.[5]

With their support, the Moderna Museet circulated many of these American art exhibitions to other European museums such as the Stedelijk Museum Amsterdam and the Louisiana Museum in Denmark. Hultén arranged the circulation, partly because he wanted to share the exhibition cost with other museums, but largely because he found a lively interest in American art among the museum directors in other regional cities. By responding to the general need for American art in Europe, the Moderna Museet functioned as an overseas clearinghouse of the New York avant-garde, which boosted the museum's international reputation.

Among others, *4 Americans* of 1962 is noteworthy, as it was the first museum exhibition in Europe to focus on post-Abstract Expressionist American art. Although Hultén had not secured the funding to purchase *Monogram*, this became the first occasion for the work to be shown in Stockholm, along with other representative works by Rauschenberg such as *Bed* (1955), *Odalisk* (1955–58), and *Allegory* (1959–60). In the foreword to the exhibition catalogue, Hultén wrote as follows:

> Artists used to go to Paris to learn to paint and never left the city entirely. But this is not the case anymore [...] After World War II, the greatest adventures in visual arts have played themselves out in America, the most interesting painting coming out of New York. The generation of Pollock, Kline, de Kooning, is apparently only the beginning. The artistic activity in New York has an enthusiasm that has an inspiring effect on European art.[6]

Today, this sounds like the familiar, America-centric narrative typically found in art history textbooks. In 1962, however, it was a daring statement for any European, or even an American institution, to make. When practically the same statement was made by Alan Solomon as commissioner for the American Pavilion at the 1964 Venice Biennale, it caused a huge international scandal.[7]

[5] For the marketing of postwar American art in Europe, see Ikegami 2010, pp. 17–55.
[6] Pontus Hultén, "Preface," in *4 amerikanare: Alfred Lesilie, Jasper Johns, Robert Rauschenberg, Richard Stankiewicz*, exh. cat., Stockholm: Moderna Museet, 1962, p. 5.
[7] See Ikegami 2010, pp. 51–54, 97–99.

What propelled Hultén's programme were the cartographic dynamics of modern art. The benefit seemed mutual: whereas New York needed another city's support in order to replace Paris as a major centre of world art, a marginal city such as Stockholm needed to take advantage of its connection with a central force in order to differentiate itself from other minor cities. As Patrik Andersson argued, it was precisely Stockholm's marginality—or Hultén's strategic awareness of it—that paradoxically enabled the Moderna Museet to play a critical role in the centralisation of American art.[8] In other words, Hultén secured a place for his museum on the global art map by consciously and cleverly Americanising the Stockholm art scene.

Of the four American artists in the exhibition, Rauschenberg caused the biggest stir among the local artists. As Hultén wrote to an art journalist Calvin Tomkins in 1963:

> Of course, Rauschenberg was the most shocking of the 4 Americans. People came to the museum only to see the *Bed* and the *Goat* [i.e., *Monogram*] and when they had seen those they left. [...] Rauschenberg has at the moment a certain influence on young Swedish art. If one is asking a young painter under 30 which artist impresses him the most, you would very often get the name of Rauschenberg.[9]

Not everyone was happy about this sudden flow of American art into Sweden, though. The critic Ulf Linde observed, for instance, that *4 Americans* differed from *Movements in Art* because the exhibition focused on postwar American art so much that it felt like a promotional campaign. As far as Linde was concerned, the truly collaborative and international spirit that had characterised *Movements in Art* was already gone.[10]

Attracting about 28,000 viewers, *4 Americans* brought about both positive and negative responses from the public.[11] The press reluctantly acknowledged the rise of New York art, although their responses varied

[8] Patrik Andersson, *Euro-Pop: The Mechanical Bride Stripped Bare in Stockholm, Even*, (diss.), Vancouver: University of British Columbia, 2001, p. 2.
[9] Pontus Hultén to Calvin Tomkins, 2 August 1963, Calvin Tomkins Papers, IV.C.23. Museum of Modern Art Archives, New York.
[10] Ulf Linde, interview by the author, 12 March 2004, Stockholm.
[11] Kathryn Boyer et al., "From the Editorial Board," in *Konsthistorisk tidskrift* 76, Nos. 1–2, 2007, p. 3.

from general scepticism to hysterical antagonism. One reviewer ridiculed the show as "pretentious presentations" that had an "air of Zen-Buddhist loftiness, rising above both logic and rational contexts,"[12] while another one called the exhibition a "new shock-exhibit" and warned Swedish readers, "Do not flirt with mental illness" because "this kind of art is dangerous!"[13]

Not surprisingly, *Monogram* became the literal "scapegoat" for these unsympathetic voices. The most eye-catching work in the exhibition, it was constantly reproduced in the newspapers, representing the "shock" value of the new American art. One art history professor at Lund University even mistook the stuffed Angora goat for a live one, and called for a boycott of the whole show.[14] Another reviewer referred to *Monogram* as specifically incompatible with the Swedish sensibility:

> Faced with the most shocking and unsettling work in the grim collection—a stuffed goat from an old textile-factory with his coat dragging on the floor, beautiful horns and a disgustingly painted snout, standing there on a painting instead of a pasture—all this is enough to make you surrealistically old-Swedish in your sensibilities. [...] The huge dimensions of the works, a typical expression of the American lifestyle, are incompatible with our own national ideas of art.[15]

Yet, another important feature of the Swedish response to *4 Americans* involved language. According to Anna Lundström, the Swedish title of the show, "4 amerikanare" means literally "four Americans," but also carries the connotation of "large American postwar cars," which indicates the Swedish perception of American culture at the time.[16] As if to reflect the larger cultural implication of the title, one review of the exhibition was titled "Amerikanare i farten" (Americans in Motion), because three of the four artists (that is, Rauschenberg, Johns, and Leslie) had been included in

[12] Per-Olov Zennström, "Amerikanare i farten," *Dagens Nyheter*, 6 April 1962.
[13] Harry Osbornson, "Konst på farliga vägar," *Smålandsposten*, 12 April 1962, p. 5.
[14] Hultén, "Fem fragment ur Moderna Museets historia," p. 40.
[15] Lars Erik Åström, "Bild och liv I USA," *Svenska Dagbladet*, 17 March 1962.
[16] Anna Lundström, "Comments on *4 Americans*," in *Konsthistorisk tidskrift* 76, Nos. 1–2, 2007, p. 113. According to Lundström, a more precise Swedish equivalent of "4 Americans" would be "4 amerikaner" rather than "4 amerikanare."

the *Movements in Art* exhibition.[17] Ulf Linde also compared its vibrant quality to American popular culture such as jazz and driving.[18]

After *4 Americans*, Hultén mounted a Jackson Pollock retrospective in 1963, and *American Pop Art* in 1964. Featuring seven representative Pop artists—Jim Dine, Roy Lichtenstein, Claes Oldenburg, James Rosenquist, George Segal, Andy Warhol, and Tom Wesselmann—*American Pop Art* was the first large-scale Pop Art exhibition in a European museum. This cemented Hultén's "New York connection" and put the name of the Moderna Museet firmly on the international art map.

Monogram and *Elgin Tie*

It is helpful at this point to take a close look at *Monogram*, the object in question. As the best-known work by Rauschenberg, *Monogram* has been the focus of controversy between what Thomas Crow called "iconophilia and iconophobia" in Rauschenberg literature.[19] The crux of the matter is a classical question concerning his work: To what extent is it appropriate or inappropriate to find "meaning" in Rauschenberg's work? On the one hand, as Alan Solomon once stated, "the goat absolutely defies any kind of rational explanation; it has no meaning, in the conventional sense."[20] Accordingly, the work has been discussed mainly in terms of the artist's defiance of the traditional meaning in a work of art, and thus treated as a postmodern icon of indeterminate multiplicity. On the other hand, the work has been repeatedly read as an icon of same-sex love, as Robert Hughes succinctly articulated the homoerotic reading of *Monogram*: "Goats are the oldest metaphors of priapic energy. This one, with its paint-smutched, thrusting head and its body stuck halfway through the encir-

[17] Zennström, 1962.
[18] Ulf Linde, quoted in Lars Widding, "Moderna Museet har blivit ett konstens Gröna Lund," *Expressen*, 25 March, 1962.
[19] Thomas E. Crow, "Rise and Fall: Theme and Idea in the Combines of Robert Rauschenberg," in Paul Schimmel, ed., *Robert Rauschenberg: Combines*, exh. cat., Los Angeles: Museum of Contemporary Art, 2005, p. 253.
[20] For instance, see Alan R. Solomon, *Robert Rauschenberg*, exh. cat., New York: Jewish Museum, 1963, not paginated.

cling tyre, is one of the few great icons of male homosexual love in modern culture: the Satyr in the Sphincter."[21]

While these two incompatible views have been a source of dispute for critics and scholars, the Stockholm audiences saw something different in *Monogram* in 1962. Like in other works in the show, they perceived the "moving" quality in this work. For instance, Linde associated the goat's horns with the handlebars of a motorbike,[22] while a newspaper article published a photograph that showed a little girl actually mounted on it. This observation is quite illuminating, since the "moving" aspect has received little attention in the preceding studies on *Monogram*. Seldom noted in the past is the fact that it is actually constructed as a kind of vehicle. With four casters attached beneath the canvas panel, one push will set it in motion.

Looking at its details, furthermore, we can see that the work includes many aspects related to spatial movement: a tire around the goat, a tennis ball, pictures of astronauts, a tightrope in the air, etc.[23] To counter such images, there are a number of references to gravity in the work: footprints, a shoe sole, and above all, the words "EXTRA HEAVY," stencilled on the canvas. These words probably refer to the story of how the artist encountered the goat at a second-hand furniture store. The owner of the store found the goat at a post office sale in an unclaimed crate, which would have borne similar stencilled words.[24] Although the stuffed goat should actually be much lighter than the real animal, its visual weight was the main challenge for the artist, who spent no fewer than five years to complete the work.

It is thus arguable that *Monogram* is roughly structured around the dialectic tension between gravity as a physical principle and the artist's challenge to such a force, which is abstract enough to contain a multivalent quality. Hultén rightly pointed out this quality in *Monogram* when he mentioned the following:

[21] Robert Hughes, *Shock of the New* (1981); reprinted, New York: Alfred A. Knopf, 1998, p. 335.
[22] Ulf Linde, interview by the author, 18 October 2004, Stockholm.
[23] Leo Steinberg noted there might be a theme of the "evolution of travel" in this work, only to dismiss it as untenable. See Leo Steinberg, *Encounters with Rauschenberg*, Houston: Menil Foundation, 2000, p. 54.
[24] See Robert Rauschenberg, interview by Barbro Schultz Lundestam and Marianne Hultman for the Swedish film program *Amerikanarna och Pontus Hultén*, 1997; transcribed by the author from the videotape held at Robert Rauschenberg Archives in New York.

> Yes, what's usually good for sculpture is not there, in the sense of equilibrium, the feeling of standing, or weight. Rather what is present is the opposite; the flying away, the taking off. Maybe that's something that's in the Combine with the goat. It seems to me that there is a lot about an absence of gravity, meaning that the elements, the parts do not appear to have a lot of matter, or be very material. It seems that he enjoys that, that they become poetic metaphors. They have no weight.[25]

The next time Rauschenberg visited Stockholm, in September 1964, three years after participating in *Movements in Art*, the acquisition of *Monogram* was actually being debated. Although Rauschenberg had held onto the piece upon Hultén's request made in 1959, his work was increasingly in high demand because of his rising reputation. This was especially the case after 20 June 1964, when Rauschenberg was announced to be the winner of the Grand Prize at that year's Venice Biennale, the first time for an American artist. The year 1964 was indeed special, as Rauschenberg joined the first world tour of the Merce Cunningham Dance Company in the same year as costume and set designer, and visited thirty cities in fourteen countries.

The Moderna Museet took this opportunity and organised *Fem New York kvällar* (Five New York Evenings) with Fylkingen, an experimental workshop of music and intermedia art, so that the company would stop in Stockholm and perform at the museum. Therefore, Hultén's strategy to use his "New York connection" to promote the museum was working just marvellously, except that he had not finalised the acquisition of *Monogram* yet. Hultén must have been consulting with Billy Klüver about the case, as Klüver actually sent a note to Hultén prior to Rauschenberg's visit. The note says, "Have spoken with Bob about *Monogram*, etc. Bob very positive about you getting something before Sandberg. <u>OK</u> Be persistent and pound on him as soon as you see him!"[26]

Dated 3 June 1964, this note indicates that Klüver talked with Rauschenberg about *Monogram* just before he departed for the world tour the

[25] Pontus Hultén and Julia Brown Turrell, "A Conversation about the Sculpture of Robert Rauschenberg," in Julia Brown Turrell, ed., *Rauschenberg: Sculpture*, exh. cat., Fort Worth: Modern Art Museum of Fort Worth, 1995, p. 34.
[26] Billy Klüver to Pontus Hultén, 3 June 1964, *Fem New York kvällar* Files, Moderna Museet Archives, Stockholm.

following day. It further indicates that there was somewhat of a competition for Rauschenberg's work among European museum directors, because Willem Sandberg was a former director of the Stedelijk Museum Amsterdam. Although Edy de Wilde had replaced Sandberg in 1963, the new director also expressed a strong desire to acquire a major piece by Rauschenberg.[27] So Hultén must have "pounded on" Rauschenberg, when the Dance Company arrived in Stockholm for *Five New York Evenings*. In fact, it was in December 1964, shortly after Rauschenberg's return to New York, that Leo Castelli Gallery sent the invoice for *Monogram* to the Moderna Museet.[28] It is therefore safe to think that the purchase of the work was settled during the artist's stay in Stockholm.

For *Five New York Evenings*, Rauschenberg created a new site-specific performance titled *Elgin Tie* (Figure 3.4), inspired by the procession on the Parthenon frieze, known as the Elgin Marbles, which he had seen in London. First, he performed a short piece entitled *Shot Put* in the dark, and then climbed to the roof of the museum and waited there. So the audience could not see the performer when the light was turned on. Rauschenberg then started descending from the ceiling on a rope while attaching various objects to it—including a mouton coat that belonged to Hultén, who told me cheerfully, "I hope he returned it!"[29] He then went into a barrel filled with water. Emerging soaking wet, the performer slipped into a pair of boots on a wagon and tied a white tie around his neck, which was the signal for a farmer to bring in a cow. The performance ended as the farmer led the cow off to the exit and an assistant pulled the wagon, on which Rauschenberg kept tying and untying his (Elgin) tie.

Although this performance might at first seem absurd and a bit fantastic, it should be noted that Rauschenberg himself "always took it very seriously,"[30] and that Hultén also recalled it was "very much prepared, and quite a complicated performance."[31] If *Elgin Tie* was a site-specific per-

[27] The Stedelijk Museum acquired *Charlene* (1954) for its collection in 1965.

[28] I found a copy of the invoice showing an amount of $15,000 at the Archives of the Robert Rauschenberg Foundation, New York.

[29] Pontus Hultén, interview by the author, 16 March, 2004, La Motte, France.

[30] Rauschenberg, interview for *Amerikanarna och Pontus Hultén*, 1997.

[31] Hultén, interview by the author, 16 March 2004, La Motte, France.

formance, it is arguable that it referred to a specific work most associated with the Moderna Museet—namely, *Monogram*. Indeed, as Ulf Linde noticed at the time of the performance, many aspects of *Elgin Tie* appear to correspond to those in *Monogram*. A cow, a barrel, and wagon wheels in the performance have their counterparts in the Combine: the goat, the tire around its torso, and the casters beneath the platform.[32] Moreover, Rauschenberg's gesture of entering the barrel can be seen as an enactment of the most iconic element in *Monogram*, mimicking the goat in a tire. Thus, *Elgin Tie* can be seen as a performed commentary on *Monogram*, the work that took him five years to complete and that had just found its new home in Stockholm at the time of the performance. In March 1965, then, *Monogram* entered the museum as a symbol of the strong connection of the local museum to the centre of world art.

Anti-American turn

According to Hultén, *Five New York Evenings* marked "the last big organised event in what had been the springtime of collaborations with the New York artists."[33] Indeed, the event and Merce Cunningham Dance Company were received with great enthusiasm in Stockholm, with the Swedish Television even broadcasting their performance at the Moderna Museet.[34] Nonetheless, the relationship between the Stockholm and the New York art worlds had already somewhat changed by the time they arrived. Hultén originally planned another large international art project in conjunction with *Five New York Evenings*. In April, he wrote to David Vaughan, a manager for the company's world tour: "The time you suggest, second week of September, is very good. We are planning to open the big collective exhibition *Dylaby II* on the 4th of September with the participation of Robert Rauschenberg, Jean Tinguely, Niki de St Phalle, P. O. Ultvedt, Claes Oldenburg, Öyvind Fahlström and others."[35]

[32] Linde, interview by the author, 12 March 2004, Stockholm.
[33] Hultén, "Fem fragment ur Moderna Museets historia," p. 56.
[34] This performance took place as a separate event from *Five New York Evenings*, without audience. I owe this information to Annika Öhrner.
[35] Pontus Hultén to David Vaughan, 27 April 1964, *Fem New York kvällar* Files, Moderna Museet Archives.

Although this exhibition would have offered an excellent backdrop for the company's performance, *Dylaby II* was not realised. As Patrik Andersson pointed out, the original *Dylaby* exhibition, held at the Stedelijk Museum Amsterdam in the summer of 1962, had created enough conflict and tension between Rauschenberg and the European artists, making any further collaboration difficult.[36] In 1966, when a similar collective exhibition project took place at the Moderna Museet, Rauschenberg was intentionally left out. During the preliminary discussion for the collaboration project called *HON – en Katedral* (SHE – A Cathedral), Tinguely and de Saint-Phalle wrote to Ultvedt in Sweden:

> de Saint-Phalle: I'm glad that you like the idea of an enormous collaboration. But there are problems [...] it would have to be an enormous castle. Jean and I both feel that this collaboration would be something sufficient in itself.
>
> Tinguely: What's the use in a large Pop hot dog? Don't you feel the four of us would be enough since the castle would become a unity. Why have an enormous hamburger next to it?
>
> de Saint-Phalle: Rauschenberg also may be unnecessary.[37]

These exchanges clearly point to the discomfort that Tinguely, de Saint-Phalle, and Ultvedt felt by the sudden international prominence of American art—especially works by Rauschenberg and the Pop artists—that left little room for their own works. It is easy to imagine that this situation put Hultén in a difficult position, torn between his strong connections to the New York art world and his friendship with the European artists.

On part of the Stockholm art scene, Ulf Linde was instrumental in shaping the anti-American turn—although it must be noted that he was not part of the leftist politics in Sweden. He had already developed a critical view of Rauschenberg in 1963, when he wrote from Stockholm to Ultvedt, who was then visiting New York: "The fact that Rauschenberg has begun working with silkscreen stuff I find upsetting. It is, after all, Andy

[36] Andersson 2001, pp. 113–116.

[37] Quoted in Andersson 2001, p. 126. Ultvedt provided Andersson with the translation of these coded letters in 1992. Letters were sent to Ultvedt from 1963 to 1966.

Warhol who has the patent on silkscreening. Is there no Restany over there to keep an eye on what artists are doing?"[38] From March to May 1965, then, Linde published a series of articles in the Swedish newspaper *Dagens Nyheter* to criticise American Pop art and in particular its promoter Alan Solomon.[39] His main critique was that the New York avant-garde, which he called "open art," was irrational, apolitical, and therefore irresponsible.

This anti-American turn in the Stockholm art scene actually coincided with a political conflict between the United States and Sweden over the war in Vietnam.[40] With the beginning of the bombing of North Vietnam in February 1965, views critical of U.S. foreign policy began appearing in the Swedish press. In July 1965, Olof Palme, then a young Minister of Transport and Communications, delivered an exceptionally harsh critique of American militarism in Vietnam, which caught the attention of Washington. After this incident, Swedish officials, especially Palme—who would become the next prime minister in 1970—took a more active approach to criticising American militarism.[41]

It is important to note that both the political and cultural debates took place in the same discursive arena in Sweden. Linde's criticism on American art and the preceding debates on the exhibitions at the Moderna Museet appeared in widely circulated newspapers, such as *Dagens Nyheter*, rather than in monthly art journals. In other words, readers of these general audience newspapers could learn about political issues and art debates in one sitting. Well-informed on the stakes in both politics and art, the Stockholm citizens could raise a collective voice against the museum's activities if they found it necessary to do so. As if to avoid such criticism, Hultén organised a series of exhibitions to re-anchor the Moderna Museet in Swedish society.

[38] Ulf Linde, quoted in Andersson, 2001, p. 129.
[39] For this critique, see Ulf Linde, "Den öppna konsten: Arvet från Mnchen," *Dagens Nyheter*, 26 March 1965, p. 4; "Den öppna konsten: Myten om den historielösa formen," *Dagens Nyheter*, 30 March 1965, p. 4; "Den öppna konsten: Den bild 'man' har," *Dagens Nyheter*, 4 April 1965, p. 4; "Den öppna konsten: Dialogue utan slut," *Dagens Nyheter*, 13 May 1965, p. 4.
[40] For this political conflict, see Fredrik Logevall, "The Swedish-American Conflict over Vietnam," *Diplomatic History* 17, No. 3, Summer 1993, pp. 421–445.
[41] Ibid., pp. 426–27.

For a starter, in the autumn of 1965 Hultén exhibited James Rosenquist's *F111*, a work unmistakably critical of the American government's military policy, and then mounted a thematic survey of modern art, *The Inner and the Outer Space* (Den inre och yttre rymden), which emphasised a geometric and monochromatic tendency with focus on such artists as Malevich, Naum Gabo, and Yves Klein. In the summer of 1966, the aforementioned *HON* (SHE), a woman-shaped cathedral, was built in the museum, followed by a solo exhibition by Oldenburg, an American Pop artist of Swedish descent. It can therefore be argued that, by stressing the European heritage of modern art, Hultén tried to strike a balance in the museum's activities.

Still, New York and Stockholm had another falling-out in 1966. By that year, Rauschenberg and Klüver had been intensely exploring the interaction between art and technology and they wanted to organise an event that would involve collaboration between artists and engineers on a large scale. Klüver proposed the idea for the Stockholm Festival, an annual art festival organised by Fylkingen. Since *Five New York Evenings* filled the entire 1964 festival, followed by Robert Morris and Yvonne Rainer as main performers in the 1965 Festival, the 1966 Festival was expected to be another collaborative project between Swedish and American artists. But the problem was that the art and technology project required a much grander budget. Although Fylkingen sent $3,000 to New York as part of the agreed-upon budget of $10,000, it refused to pay the rest when the American group demanded additional payment without explaining how the initial money was spent.[42]

Eventually, this led to the cancellation of the Stockholm Festival. In a long letter addressed to the American artists, Fylkingen criticised their unrealistic demands, which included extensive publicity in the Swedish press and a reception ceremony with King Gustav VI Adolf as a guest. Fylkingen concluded the letter, "you Americans seem to expect us in Fylkingen to pay large amounts of money just in order to create a platform for your own future work in USA, and that we have to be content with any

[42] Franklin Königsberg to Knut Wiggen (representative of Fylkingen), 11 May 1966, David Tudor Papers, Box 16, Folder 1. Special Collections at the Getty Research Institute.

crumbs of fame that may fall from your table."[43] Franklin Königsberg, the lawyer for the American group, responded with an equally harsh message: "Unlike Fylkingen, we have the courage of our convictions. We intend to try every means to make a reality of the Festival of Art and Technology."[44] The aborted 1966 Stockholm Festival then became a reality in New York in October 1966, as "Nine Evenings: Theatre and Engineering," the inaugural event for Experiments in Art and Technology (E.A.T.). Meanwhile, Fylkingen discontinued the Stockholm Festival after 1966 and stopped inviting American artists. As the Swedish-American relationship deteriorated even more, the presence of American artists in Stockholm diminished significantly after 1966.

New York collection for Stockholm

The tangled relationship between New York and Stockholm in the end resulted in a huge conflict in 1973, when Hultén engineered his last major project, *New York Collection for Stockholm*. It originally started as an E.A.T. project without any predetermined destinations. After organising a series of E.A.T. projects, Rauschenberg and Klüver came up with the idea to assemble a collection of contemporary art for a museum or for a corporation to purchase. When Klaus Kertess of the Bykert Gallery, New York, became unavailable for selecting the works, they asked Hultén to be the curator. Klüver explained the nature of the job to him:

> Bob R will work with you to make up the collection. [...] Your commission will be 10% of the net, which is what we get when costs are paid. [...] Your "duties" will be to select what the collection will contain, negotiate with the artists, set prices, sign contracts for us, find a buyer, make a catalogue if necessary, handle the press conference, set up an exhibition at Automation House if we decide it's necessary.[45]

Acquiring an important American art collection for the museum was Hultén's dream from the very beginning of his career. As soon as he was

[43] Fylkingen to the American artists, undated, David Tudor Papers, Box 16, Folder 1.
[44] Königsberg to Wiggen, 4 August 1966, David Tudor Papers, Box 16, Folder 1.
[45] Billy Klüver to Pontus Hultén, 13 November, 1971, *New York Collection for Stockholm* Files, Moderna Museet Archives, Stockholm.

involved with the project, therefore, Hultén sought ways to bring the collection to his museum.

However, the timing could not have been worse, given the increasing anti-American sentiment among the Swedish public. The Swedish-American political conflict over Vietnam was exacerbated towards the end of the 1960s, as the Swedish government began providing refuge to American draft evaders and military deserters in 1968. Moreover, when Sweden became the first nation to recognise North Vietnam in 1969, the U.S. government even considered imposing economic sanctions against Sweden. The conflict reached its peak near the end of 1972, with Palme's public speech against Operation Linebacker II, the Christmas Bombings of Hanoi. In this speech that received worldwide publicity, Palme went so far as to associate the Hanoi bombing with Guernica, which infuriated American officials.[46]

In this context, it is hardly surprising that the grand-scale migration of the *New York Collection* caused a heated debate in the press even before it arrived in Stockholm. Part of the problem was that the there was a lack of transparency concerning the project's funding. Although the collection was officially called a "gift," participating artists did receive the usual 50 percent of the sales price of their work, while their galleries waived their commission fees.[47] Accordingly, when it became known that the Swedish government would contribute one-fifth of the $1.5 million budget, Swedish artists raised a collective voice against the project. Among them was Ultvedt, who had been involved with Hultén's exhibitions in the 1960s but now felt neglected by the museum director of his own country. Their feeling was clearly stated as follows:

> We criticise the New York Collection because we find it to be limited in geography and in content. For us, the 1960's New York avant-garde is not important enough to defend another acquisition at this level. We therefore blame the museum leadership for provincial thinking, albeit "New York provincialism."[48]

[46] Logevall, 1993, pp. 440–41.

[47] To enhance the fundraising, each artist also later donated one print to a portfolio, but the prints did not sell very well.

[48] Karl Olov Björk, Margareta Carlstedt, Sten Dunér, Bror Marklund, and Per Olof Ultvedt, "Det finns en värld utanför axeln Paris–New York," *Dagens Nyheter*, 27 June 1972. Quoted

The diatribe against Hultén was intensified when the exhibition, which included Rauschenberg's *Mud Muse* along with works by Jim Dine, Frank Stella, and Donald Judd among others, opened in October 1973. Swedish artists published another critique against this exhibition, with a caricature drawn by Ultvedt. A caption reads: "Donation on a big scale, or what is happening under the table?"[49] The caricature insinuated that the Americans bribed Hultén, depicted with his trademark glasses and a bowtie, who is receiving the collection on the table while receiving something else underneath.

In this debate, *Monogram* was nothing but a scapegoat, as the Swedish artists saw it as the beginning of the whole trouble, *the* symbol of the postwar invasion of American art and culture in their country. Accordingly, they concluded their critique by this statement: "We hope that the collection will be the final monument of the period, which began with the goat with the tire."[50] This extreme reaction was partly influenced by the Swedish-American conflict over the war in Vietnam. Although most of the American artists in the collection were against the war, the anti-American sentiment in Stockholm was so strong at the time that the engineering technology used in the collection was perceived as a reflection of American military technology. In fact, this criticism was not entirely off the mark: *Mud Muse*, Rauschenberg's contribution to the New York Collection, was created with technical assistance from a company that made gun sights and sensors used in Vietnam.[51] Although this fact was probably unknown in Stockholm, its citizens regarded the American so-called "gift" with much scepticism.

In the end, the *New York Collection* became Hultén's parting gift to the Moderna Museet, as he moved to Paris to become the founding director of the Centre Georges Pompidou at the end of 1973. After his departure, the

from Marianne Hultman, "New York Collection for Stockholm," in *Teknologi för livet: Om Experiments in Art and Technology*, exh. cat., Norrköpings: Norrköpings Konstmuseum, 2004, p. 161.

[49] Bo Ahlsén, Karl Olov Björk, Margareta Carlstedt, Sten Dunér, Pär Stolpe, and Per Olof Ultvedt, "Debatten om New York Collection: 'Restlager på Moderna Museet,'" *Dagens Nyheter*, 18 November 1973.

[50] Hultman, 2004, p. 164.

[51] Calvin Tomkins, *Off the Wall: Robert Rauschenberg and the Art World of Our Time*, New York: Penguin Books, 1980, p. 287.

museum seldom mounted any American or contemporary art exhibitions, and, according to the critic Ludvig Rasmussen, "The Moderna Museet gave up its position as a centre for renewal and has never regained it."[52] This assessment, written in 1992, may be a little too harsh in retrospect, as the museum has now reestablished itself as one of the most popular museums in Europe with its ambitious exhibition programs. The conflict surrounding the New York Collection nonetheless suggests an important insight about the dynamics of cartography in modern art. Although major and minor forces complemented one another globally, the power relationship was essentially asymmetrical in the America-centric art world of the day, which was comprised of only one major centre (that is, New York) and numerous minor centres. In other words, whereas the "New York connection" was a necessary condition for Stockholm to partake of the world art scene, the "Stockholm connection," although important, was just one of many relationships that New York had in the 1960s.

Tokyo Pop and its ambivalence

It is instructive to compare the situation in Stockholm with that of Tokyo at this stage, since Tokyo was another marginal, yet important, site that aspired to have a "New York connection" in the 1960s. In fact, as the country was located in the distant Far East and lacked an internationally influential museum director such as Hultén, Tokyo was at a bigger disadvantage than Stockholm. It was geographically more difficult to travel to New York and bring American artworks to Japan. Yet, a key figure for the "New York connection" existed in Tokyo, similar to the figure of Hultén in Stockholm. The one in Tokyo was the critic Yoshiaki Tōno, who emerged as a young critic in the late 1950s. His encounter with American Neo-Dada was in fact quite similar to that of Hultén: In 1958, he served as a subcommissioner for the Japanese Pavilion at the Venice Biennale, where he was impressed by Johns's *Flag*, and travelled to New York for the first time in the following year.

[52] Ludvig Rasmussen, "Den Amerikanska konstens dekadens och den svenska konstens följdeffekter," *Paletten*, No. 209 (February 1992), p. 27.

There, Tōno saw Rauschenberg's *Monogram* at the Leo Castelli Gallery, and the dealer introduced him to Johns and Rauschenberg, who he became friends with.[53] It seems even possible Tōno and Hultén actually got to know each other on this occasion, as they started exchanging letters in the early 1960s—for instance, Tōno wrote a thank-you letter to Hultén in 1961 for having sent him a catalogue of *Movements in Art*.[54] In 1962, Hultén himself travelled to Japan, where his friend Sam Francis and Tōno showed him around, and through Tōno's coordination, in 1963 the Moderna Museet hosted an exhibition of works by Sengai, a Japanese Zen monk who lived in the eighteenth and ninteenth century and was known for splendid calligraphy, paintings, and terra-cottas.

Interestingly, Rauschenberg became a special artist in Tokyo, as he did in Stockholm. Tōno enthusiastically introduced his art in Japanese art journals, and the artist Ushio Shinohara, based on a black and white reproduction in Tōno's essay, produced a copy of Rauschenberg's *Coca-Cola Plan* and called it his own "Imitation Art" (Figure 3.5). How should this work be understood, is it a homage to the American modern master, or is it a critical parody of American Pop? It is a little bit of both, as Shinohara was aware of the overwhelming dominance of American art on the world art scene and still felt attracted to the latest modern art trend from New York.

How would this work look in the eyes of Rauschenberg, then? As a matter of fact, Rauschenberg visited Japan in November 1964, as part of the world tour of the Merce Cunningham Dance Company. Accompanied by the critic Tōno, he went to Shinohara's house to see *Imitation Art*. According to Shinohara, Rauschenberg was at first delighted by Shinohara's imitation of *Coca-Cola Plan*, but was disturbed upon learning that the Japanese artist had actually made ten of them. As Shinohara himself noted, "One imitation is philosophy, but ten of them make it produc-

[53] Joan Young with Susan Davidson, "Chronology," in Walter Hopps and Susan Davidson, eds., *Robert Rauschenberg: A Retrospective*, exh. cat., New York: Solomon R. Guggenheim Museum, p. 557.

[54] Yoshiaki Tōno to Pontus Hultén, 20 July 1961. *Rörelse i konsten* Files, Moderna Museet, Stockholm. In this letter, Tōno already suggested bringing the Sengai show to Stockholm, as the show, comprised of works in the collection of his father-in-law (Sazō Idemitsu, founder of the petroleum company and the Idemitsu Museum of Arts), would start touring in Europe in the autumn of 1961.

tion!"[55] Rauschenberg perhaps sensed that the multiple copies could turn the original—his work, that is—into a mere commodity and the target of original critique.

A documentary film entitled *Some Young People*, made in 1964 by Chiaki Nagano, captures activities of Japanese avant-garde artists as part of postwar youth culture in Japan.[56] The film shows Shinohara and his fellows strolling around Tokyo, with a huge sign of the Tokyo Olympics, along with advertisement of Coca-Cola. There are ample signs of Americanization of Japanese culture in the film—drinking Coke, wearing jeans, dancing the twist, etc. Of course, this Americanisation dates back to Japan's defeat in World War II, and the subsequent seven-year occupation by U.S. forces when these artists grew up. Such was the cultural context in which Japanese artists came in contact with American Neo-Dada and Pop, and created their own form of Pop art. Accordingly, in their work, they often clearly displayed their ambivalent feelings towards the American dominance of art and culture.

I call this phenomenon "Tokyo Pop," as most of these works were produced in Tokyo in the mid-1960s to the early 1970s, in part inspired by the international rise of American Pop art and in part responding to their own technology-mediated and consumerist mass culture.[57] In addition to Shinohara, Nobuaki Kojima, who was inspired partly by George Segal's plaster sculptures, created a *Standing Figure* with a cloth that looked like the Stars and the Stripes; Shinjirō Okamoto and Kōichi Tateishi produced paintings in a quasi-comic style with figurative iconic motifs; and Shinohara himself established his own Pop style with the *Oiran* (high courtesan) series, by combining mechanical production method with motifs taken from late-Edo Japanese woodblock prints.

However, because Pop art was understood to be almost exclusively an "American" thing at the time, these works were not really discussed as part

[55] Ushio Shinohara, interview by the author, 3 July 2003, Brooklyn, NY.

[56] For the transcription of the film, see Midori Yoshimoto, "*Some Young People*—From *Nonfiction Theater*: Transcript of a documentary film directed by Nagano Chiaki," *Review of Japanese Culture and Society*, Vol. 17, 2005, pp. 98–105.

[57] For a more detailed discussion of Tokyo Pop, see Hiroko Ikegami, "'Drink More?' 'No, Thanks!' The Spirit of Tokyo Pop," in Darsie Alexander and Bartholomew Ryan, eds., *International Pop*, exh. cat., Minneapolis: Walker Art Center, 2015, pp. 165–180.

of the international Pop art movement. Even the critic Tōno did not promote them overseas as examples of Japanese Pop art. Again, the situation was a little similar to the way Hultén seemed more enthusiastic about bringing New York artists to Stockholm than promoting Swedish artists such as Ultvedt in the United States. Also, as the global trend of Pop art waned by the late 1960s, superseded by new currents such as Mono-ha (the equivalent of post minimalism in Japan), intermedia art, and conceptualism, the artists of Tokyo Pop started looking in different directions. The loss of momentum of Pop had something to do with increasingly anti-American sentiments, caused by the renewal of the U.S.-Japan Security Treaty and the anti-Vietnam war protests. Like in Sweden and many other countries, the late 1960s saw the political turbulence in Japan.

In this situation, two graphic designers, Tadanori Yokoo and Keiichi Tanaami, made clever use of Pop style to express their critical ambivalence toward American cultural hegemony. For instance, in 1969 Yokoo designed a cover for an anti-American journal *Shūkan Anpo* (*Anpo Weekly*) (Figure 3.6). "*Anpo*" is shorthand in Japanese for the U.S.-Japan Security Treaty, and this journal was launched to challenge the renewal of the treaty. For this work, Yokoo picked out the letters "U" "S" and "A" in the name of Japan's then-Prime Minister Eisaku Satō, who was at the time criticised for being too submissive to the American government. When Yokoo did another portrait of the Prime Minister for the American magazine *Time*, its editor rejected his initial sketch for the cover, as he feared the depiction of Satō, with the Japanese National Diet Building on his head and dressed in a red-striped shirt and a blue tie, might allude too strongly to the United States' control over Japanese politics.[58] Yokoo thus used his Pop-inspired vocabularies to satirise the post-war U.S.—Japan relationship.

Works by Keiichi Tanaami also spoke for the ambivalent feelings the Japanese had for "America." One of his earliest Pop-style collages, *Comic Strip,* saliently expresses such sentiments, shaded by the horrifying U.S. air raids he experienced as a child and the subsequent massive inflow of

[58] Oral History interview with Tadanori Yokoo, by Hiroko Ikegami, 16 May 2014, the Oral History Archives of Japanese Art (www.oralarthistory.org)

American pop culture.[59] Pasted in the bottom in this collage is an image of a desolate dumpsite, reminiscent of the fire-raided Tokyo, above which hover American heroes and heroines such as Superman and Wonder Woman. Here, their acts of saving humans from evil are inseparable from mass destruction, intimating the admixture of fear and adoration Tanaami held for the United States.

Another collage, untitled and made around 1971, consists of a reproduction of Lichtenstein's *Whaam!* (1963) and cutouts of American comic-strip characters, all pasted over an aerial view of a field (Figure 3.7). While Lichtenstein cleaned up and simplified the air combat by excluding the landscape from the original comic, Tanaami put the scene back into a concrete background by adding the aerial photo of a bombed field, which the artist recollects was either German or Japanese-occupied land, attacked by U.S. planes during World War II. He also gave the bomber an aggressive face, thereby re-contextualising the fraught relationship between the attacker and the attacked. Another visual strategy Tanaami created was "mixing" vernacular motifs of Japanese culture and the modernised (that is, Americanized) lifestyle of post-war Japan. In another iconic collage also from the same year, kimono-clad Japanese women are juxtaposed with American glamorous beauties, while the TV monitor in the centre speaks for the artist's acute awareness that he lived in the age of mechanical reproduction and mass media.

Tanaami adopted this strategy to a series of experimental animation films he made in 1971. Among these, *Commercial War* is particularly noteworthy, as he incorporated images and sounds of real TV commercials into his animated imagery. Tanaami's juxtaposition of American icons such as Coca-Cola and Superman with Japanese commercial sound effects creates a defamiliarising effect, making his *Commercial* a meta-commercial, through which he reflected on mass media and consumer culture in Japan. Taken together, Tanaami's animation films, along with his collages, capture and convey the inherent ambivalence in Tokyo Pop,

[59] For Tanaami's war-time experience, see Oral History interview with Keiichi Tanaami, by Hiroko Ikegami and Yūka Miyata, 1 August 2013, the Oral History Archives of Japanese Art (www.oralarthistory.org)

providing a harsh commentary on American culture's bulldozing effect on the Japanese cultural landscape.

However, one particular question needs to be asked at this point: What does "America" mean anyway? As the critic Tōno once insightfully pointed out, America is a state found "not just over there [...] but in yourself."[60] In this sense, the works by Yokoo and Tanaami can be seen as a commentary not only on the colonising effect of U.S. art and culture, but also on Japanese people's own "internal America." However, their work was not appreciated as serious artworks at the time, because graphic designers' work was seen as commercial and therefor "one step down from art" in the Japanese art world at the time.[61] As a result, Pop-inspired works by Yokoo and Tanaami, along with those by Shinohara or other artists of Tokyo Pop, have yet to be historically examined in earnest. The attempt to situate their work in the larger framework of international spread of Pop art is just beginning, as will be mentioned in conclusion.

Monogram revived

In lieu of a conclusion, I would like to return to *Monogram*. What became of the work after Hultén's departure? As it is widely known, the work is now the most beloved object at the museum, affectionately called *geten* ("the goat") in Swedish. Following the backlash against American art, the 1990s saw a re-evaluation of Hultén's activities from the perspective of what had originally placed Stockholm on the global art scene, which probably worked in favour of *Monogram*'s reputation in the city.[62]

In fact, the work is always called upon as the museum's symbol in times of need. In 1991, it was even featured as a billboard image in a financial appeal for support for the construction of a new museum building. In the

[60] Yoshiaki Tōno and Shūji Takashina, "Zen'ei no eiko to hisan" (The Glory and misery of the avant-garde), *Kikan geijutsu*, No. 12, Winter 1970, p. 31.

[61] Tadanori Yokoo, a statement in *Kagayake 60-nendai: Sōgetsu Āto Sentā no zenkiroku* (Brilliant '60s: Complete records of the Sōgetsu Art Center), Tokyo: Film Art, 2002, p. 143.

[62] For this topic, see also Cecilia Widenheim, "A Goat-Eyes View: *Monogram* at the Moderna Museet," and Emma Stenström, "Another kind of Combine: *Monogram* and the Moderna Musset," *Konsthistorisk tidskrift* 76, Nos. 1–2, 2007, respectively pp. 40–47 and pp. 48–59.

billboard image, *Monogram* is heroically standing over Skeppsholmen, the small island on which this museum is located. Once a scapegoat symbolising American expansionism, the work has been revived as an icon of the museum. It was therefore no exaggeration when Rauschenberg once stated, "*Monogram* works very hard in Sweden, and it is a kind of national icon."[63] Thus, the new logo of the museum can be seen as another kind of "monogram," a combination of Rauschenberg's American (which translates as global) handwriting and the museum's national (and thus local) identity.[64]

In today's accelerated cultural globalisation, wherein a simple dichotomy of centre-periphery dynamics is no longer at work and each place has to assert its own local and global identity simultaneously, *Monogram* functions as the "glocal" icon of the Moderna Museet. The work's extraordinary story prompts us to rethink Rauschenberg's career and Hultén's "New York connection" in terms of current globalism in curatorial practices. As a simple matter of fact, "the era of Pop" itself is currently under re-examination from a viewpoint of world art history. In April 2015, the Walker Art Center held a large and ambitious exhibition entitled *International Pop*, while the Tate Modern opened a show called *World Goes Pop* in September of the same year. Both exhibitions, in each their own particular way, attempted to re-examine the transnational spread of Pop in a global context.

As a consulting curator for the Japanese section of Walker's *International Pop*, I have been observing this exciting moment in art history, in which we are expanding our scope of investigation beyond nation-based framework to talk across cultures. Hultén's curatorial agenda, Rauschenberg's transnational impact outside the United States, and international ambition of

[63] Rauschenberg, interview for *Amerikanarna och Pontus Hultén*, 1997.

[64] The logo was originally part of the catalogue cover designed by Rauschenberg in 1981 for *Le Moderna Museet de Stockholm à Bruxelles*, which was used again for *Moderna Museet: 1958–1983*, the twenty-fifth anniversary publication of the museum. It was then chosen to be the official trademark of "The New Identity Programme" for the museum's 2004 reopening. According to Lovisa Lönnebo, head of Communication at the Moderna Museet in 2004, the design firm Stockholm Design Lab, which was commissioned for the "New Identity Programme," came up with several designs for the new museum logo. One of them was based on Rauschenberg's handwriting and unanimously chosen for the new logotype. Lovisa Lönnebo, interview by the author, 12 October 2004, Stockholm.

Japanese artists and critics, can and should now be all examined on the same platform, which will give us an opportunity to think about curatorial practices and transnational strategies in our own age.

Bibliography

Primary sources

Interviews

Pontus Hultén, interview by the author, 16 March 2004, La Motte, France.

Ulf Linde, interview by the author, 12 March 2004, Stockholm.

Ulf Linde, interview by the author, 18 October 2004, Stockholm.

Lovisa Lönnebo, interview by the author, 12 October 2004, Stockholm.

Ushio Shinohara, interview by the author, 3 July 2003, Brooklyn, NY.

Oral History interview with Tadanori Yokoo, by Hiroko Ikegami, 16 May 2014. Oral History Archives of Japanese Art (www.oralarthistory.org)

Oral History interview with Keiichi Tanaami, by Hiroko Ikegami and Yūka Miyata 1 August 2013. Oral History Archives of Japanese Art (www.oralarthistory.org)

Archival materials

Fem New York kvällar Files, Moderna Museet Archives, Stockholm.

New York Collection for Stockholm Files, Moderna Museet Archives, Stockholm.

Rörelse i konsten Files, Moderna Museet, Stockholm.

Calvin Tomkins Papers, Museum of Modern Art Archives, New York.

David Tudor Papers, Special Collections at the Getty Research Institute, Los Angeles.

Amerikanarna och Pontus Hultén, 1997, a video program made by Barbro Schultz Lundestam and Marianne Hultman, Robert Rauschenberg Foundation Archives, New York.

Secondary sources

Ahlsén, Bo, Karl Olov Björk, Margareta Carlstedt, Sten Dunér, Pär Stolpe, and Per Olof Ultvedt, "Debatten om New York Collection: 'Restlager på Moderna Museet,'" *Dagens Nyheter*, 18 November 1973.

Andersson, Patrik, *Euro-Pop: The Mechanical Bride Stripped Bare in Stockholm, Even*, (diss.), Vancouver: University of British Columbia, 2001.

Åström, Lars Erik, "Bild och liv I USA," *Svenska Dagbladet*, 17 March 1962.

Björk, Karl Olov, Margareta Carlstedt, Sten Dunér, Bror Marklund, and Per Olof Ultvedt, "Det finns en värld utanför axeln Paris–New York," *Dagens Nyheter*, 27 June 1972.

Boyer, Kathryn et al., "From the Editorial Board," in *Konsthistorisk tidskrift* 76, Nos. 1–2, 2007, pp. 2–5.

Crow, Thomas E., "Rise and Fall: Theme and Idea in the Combines of Robert Rauschenberg," in Paul Schimmel (ed.), *Robert Rauschenberg: Combines*, exh. cat., Los Angeles: Museum of Contemporary Art, 2005, pp. 213–255.

Hopps, Walter and Susan Davidson (eds.), *Robert Rauschenberg: A Retrospective*, exh. cat., New York: Solomon R. Guggenheim Museum, 1997.

Hughes, Robert, *Shock of the New* (1981); reprinted, New York: Alfred A. Knopf, 1998.

Hultén, Pontus, (ed.), *4 amerikanare: Alfred Lesilie, Jasper Johns, Robert Rauschenberg, Richard Stankiewicz*, exh. cat., Stockholm: Moderna Museet, 1962.

Hultén, Pontus, "Fem fragment ur Moderna Museet's historia," in Olle Granath and Monica Nieckels (eds.), *Moderna Museet 1958–1983*, exh. cat., Stockholm: Moderna Museet Press, 1983, pp. 30–57.

Hultman, Marianne, (ed.), *Teknologi för livet: Om Experiments in Art and Technology*, exh. cat., Norrköpings: Norrköpings Konstmuseum, 2004.

Ikegami, Hiroko, *The Great Migrator: Robert Rauschenberg and the Global Rise of American Art*, Cambridge, Mass.: The MIT Press, 2010.

—. "'Drink More?' 'No, Thanks!' The Spirit of Tokyo Pop," in Darsie Alexander and Bartholomew Ryan (eds.), *International Pop*, exh. cat., Minneapolis: Walker Art Center, 2015, pp. 165–180.

Linde, Ulf, "Den öppna konsten: Arvet från München," *Dagens Nyheter*, 26 March 1965, p. 4.

—. "Den öppna konsten: Myten om den historielösa formen," *Dagens Nyheter*, 30 March 1965, p. 4.

—. "Den öppna konsten: Dialog utan slut," *Dagens Nyheter*, May 13, 1965, p. 4.

Logevall, Fredrik, "The Swedish-American Conflict over Vietnam," *Diplomatic History* 17, No. 3, Summer 1993, pp. 421–445.

Lundström, Anna, "Comments on *4 Americans*," in *Konsthistorisk tidskrift* 76, Nos. 1–2, 2007, pp. 112–113.

Öhrner, Annika, "The Moderna Museet in Stockholm: The Institution and the Avant-Garde," in Tania Ørum and Marianne Pin Huang (eds.), *A Cultural History of the Avant-Garde in the Nordic Countries 1950–1975*, Volume 3, Amsterdam and New York: Rodopi, forthcoming, 2016.

Osbornson, Harry, "Konst på farliga vägar," *Smålandsposten*, 12 April 1962, p. 5.

Rasmussen, Ludvig, "Den Amerikanska konstens dekadens och den svenska konstens följdeffekter," *Paletten*, No. 209, February 1992, p. 27.

Solomon, Alan R., *Robert Rauschenberg*, exh. cat., New York: Jewish Museum, 1963.

Steinberg, Leo, *Encounters with Rauschenberg*, Houston: Menil Foundation, 2000.

Stenström, Emma, "Another Kind of Combine: Monogram and the Moderna Museet," *Konsthistorisk tidskrift* 76, Nos. 1–2, 2007, pp. 48–59.

Tomkins, Calvin, *Off the Wall: Robert Rauschenberg and the Art World of Our Time*, New York: Penguin Books, 1980.

Tōno Yoshiaki and Shūji Takashina, "Zen'ei no eiko to hisan" (The Glory and misery of the avant-garde), *Kikan geijutsu*, No. 12, Winter 1970, pp. 22–39.

Turrell, Julia Brown, (ed.), *Rauschenberg: Sculpture*, exh. cat., Fort Worth: Modern Art Museum of Fort Worth, 1995.

Widding, Lars, "Moderna Museet har blivit ett konstens Gröna Lund," *Expressen*, 25 March 1962.

Yokoo Tadanori, a statement in *Kagayake 60-nendai: Sōgetsu Āto Sentā no zenkiroku* (Brilliant '60s: Complete records of the Sōgetsu Art Center), Tokyo: Film Art, 2002, p. 143.

Yoshimoto, Midori, "*Some Young People*—From *Nonfiction Theater*: Transcript of a Documentary Film Directed by Nagano Chiaki," *Review of Japanese Culture and Society*, Vol. 17, 2005, pp. 98–105.

Widenheim, Cecilia, "A Goat-Eyes View: Monogram at the Moderna Museet," *Konsthistorisk tidskrift* 76, Nos. 1–2, 2007, pp. 40–47.

Zennström, Per-Olov, "Amerikanare i farten," *Dagens Nyheter*, 6 April 1962.

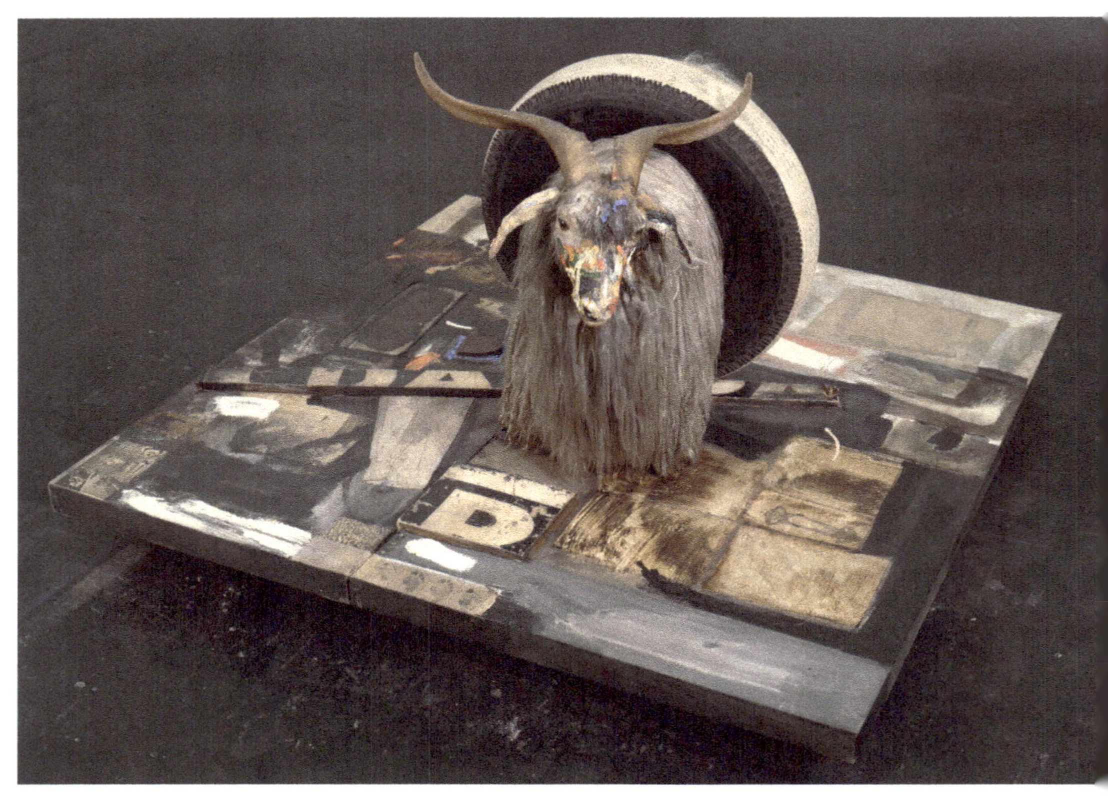

Figure 3.1: Robert Rauschenberg, *Monogram* (1955–9). Freestanding combine: oil, paper, fabric, printed paper, printed reproductions, metal, wood, rubber shoe heel, and tennis ball on canvas, with oil on Angora goat and rubber tire, on wood platform mounted on four casters 42 x 63 ¼ x 64 ½ inches (106.7 x 160.7 x 163.8 cm). Moderna Museet, Stockholm. © Estate of Robert Rauschenberg/Licensed by VAGA, New York, NY.

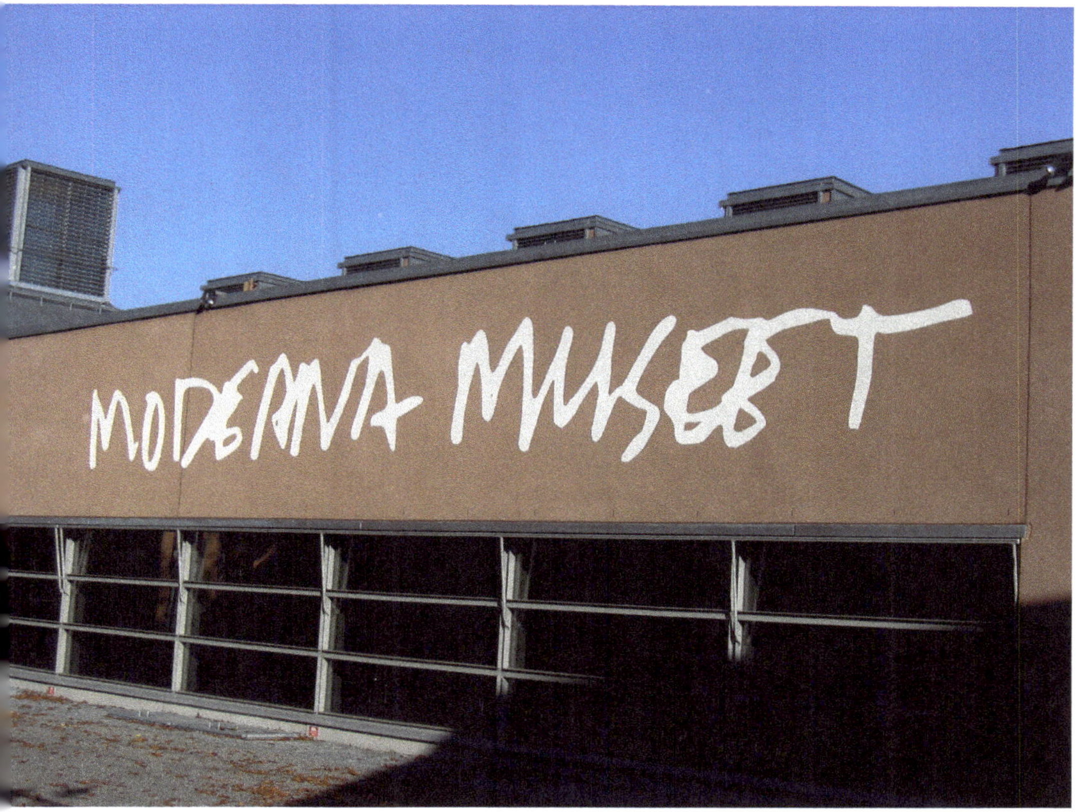

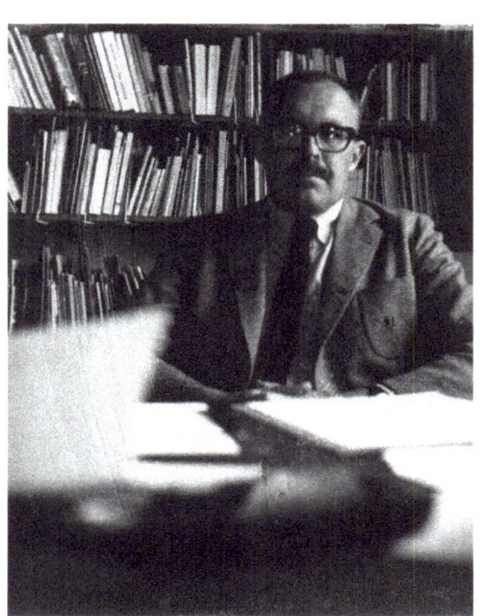

Figure 3.2: Robert Rauschenberg and Stockholm Design Lab, logotype of the Moderna Museet, in use since February 2004. Photograph: Hiroko Ikegami.

Figure 3.3: Pontus Hultén at Moderna Museet, 1958. Photograph: Moderna Museet.

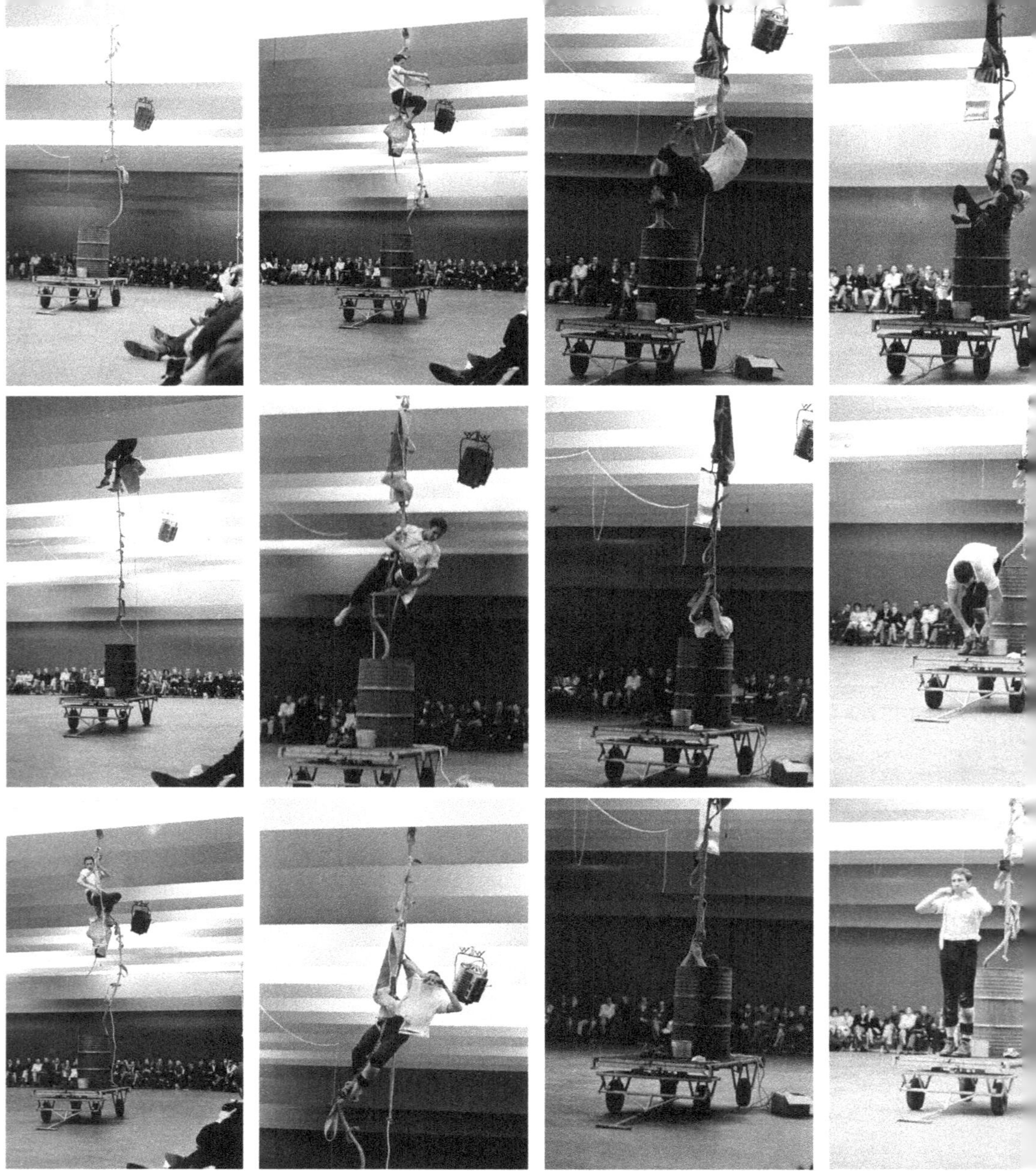

Figure 3.4: Robert Rauschenberg performing *Elgin Tie* at the Moderna Museet, 1964. Photographs by Stig T. Karlsson/Moderna Museet, Stockholm, Sweden. © Hallands konstmuseum

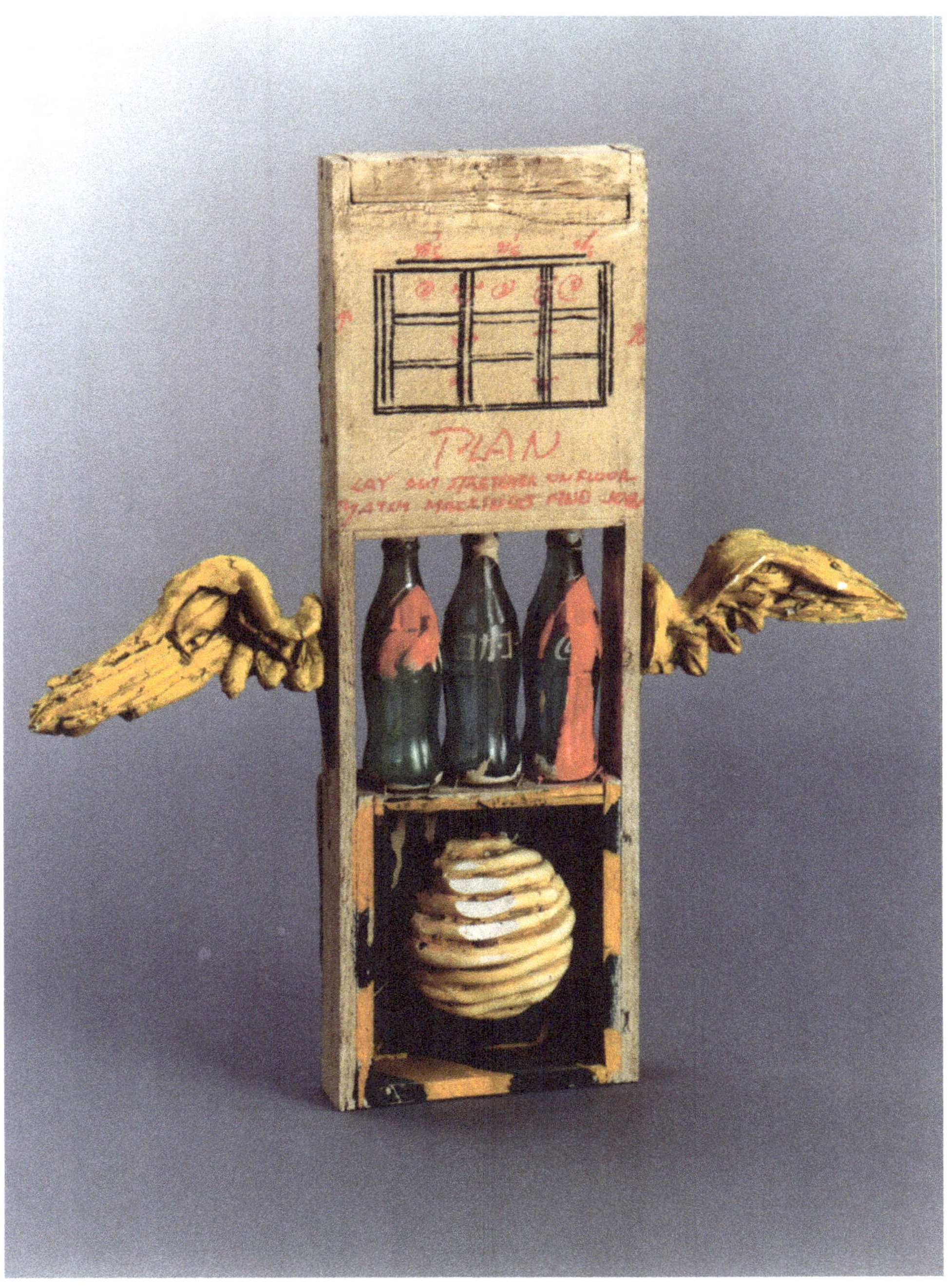

Figure 3.5: Ushio Shinohara, *Coca-Cola Plan*, 1964. Fluorescent paint, three Coca-Cola bottles, pegs, nails, and plaster wings on wood structure, 28 1/8 x 25 3/4 x 2 1/2 inches (71.5 x 65.5 x 6.5 cm). The Museum of Modern Art, Toyama, Japan.

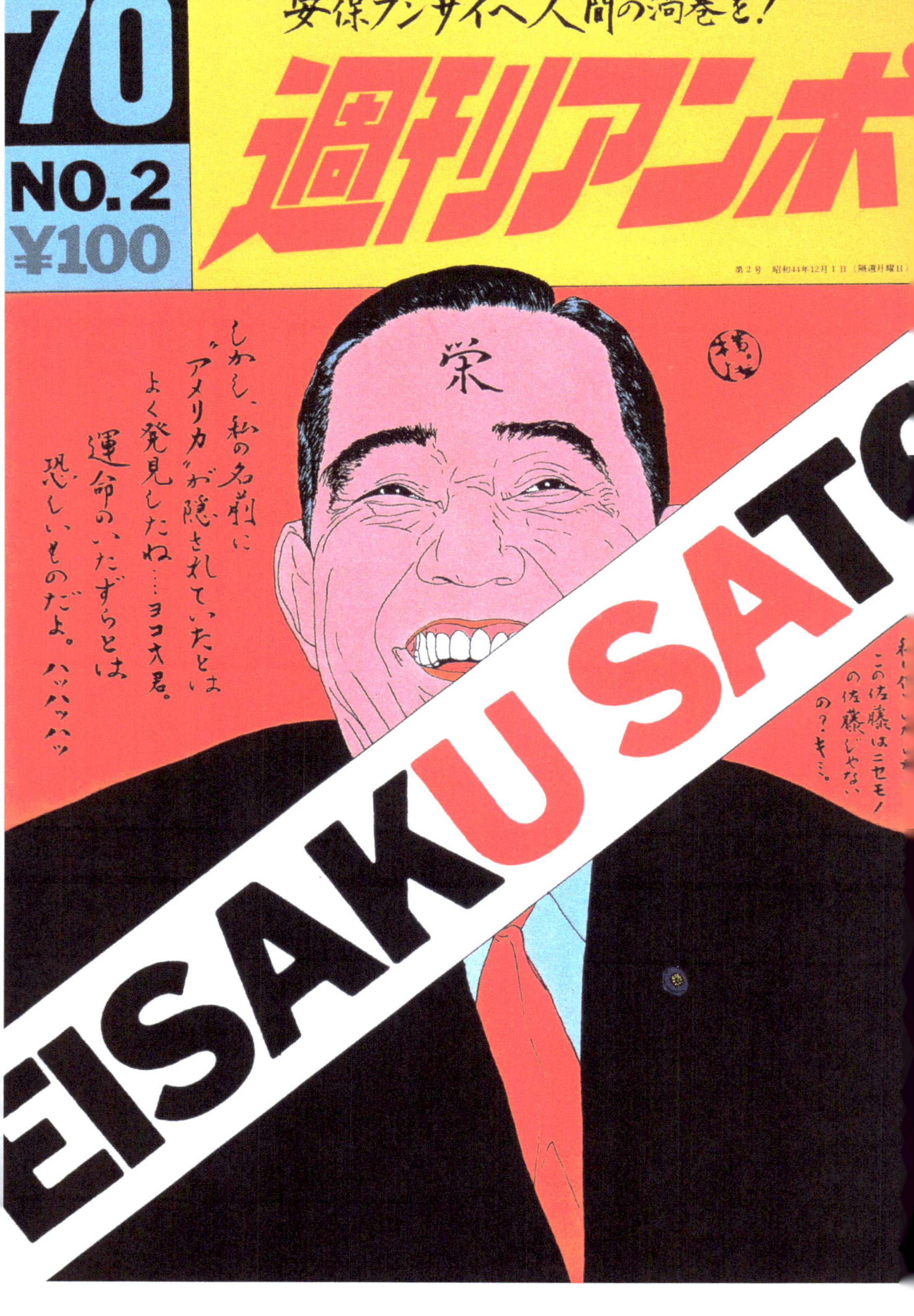

安保フンサイへ人間の渦巻を！
'70
NO.2
¥100
週刊アンポ
第2号　昭和44年12月1日（隔週月曜日）
栄
しかし、私の名前に
“アメリカ”が隠されていたとは
よく発見したね……ヨコオ君。
運命のいたずらとは
恐しいものだよ。ハッハッハッ
この佐藤はニセモノ
の佐藤じゃない
の？キミ。
EISAKU SATO

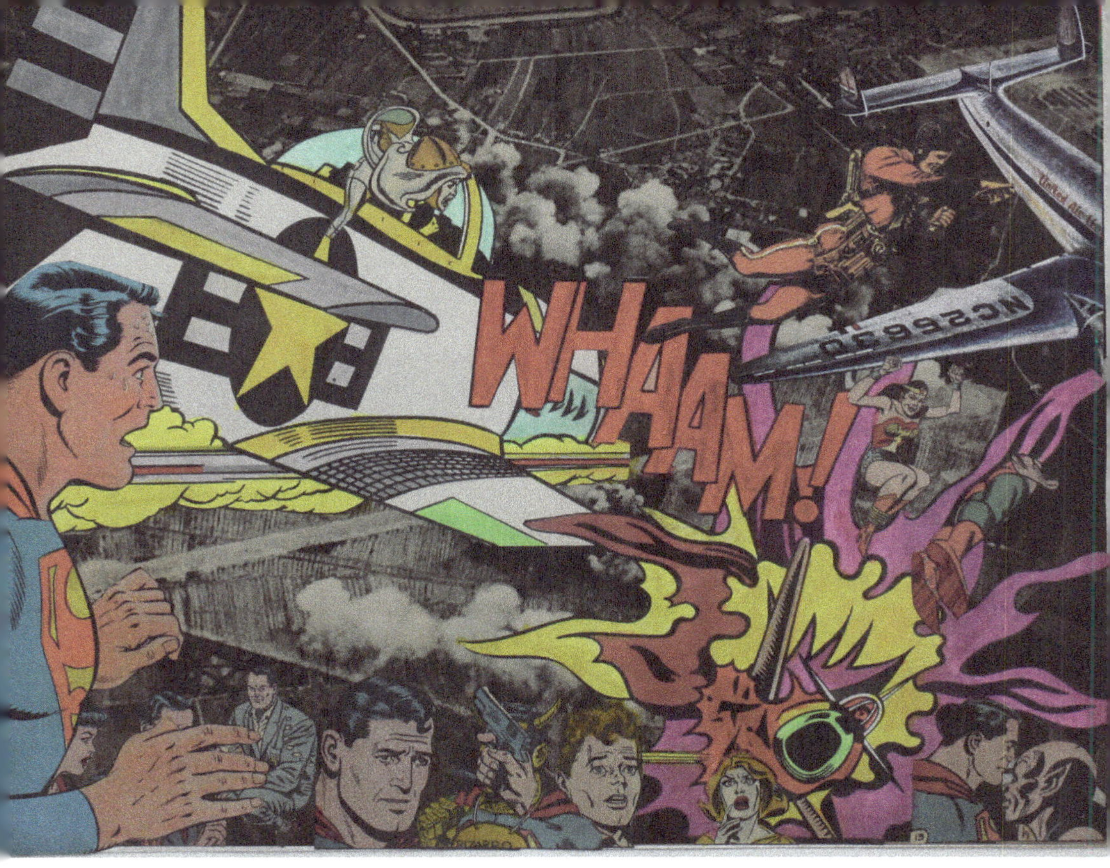

Figure 3.6 (left): Tadanori Yokoo, Cover of *Shūkan Anpo* (Weekly Anpo). 1969. 25.6 x 18.2cm offset print, paper. Artist's own collection. Courtesy of Yokoo Tadanori Museum of Contemporary Art, Kobe, Japan.

Figure 3.7: Keiichi Tanaami, *Untitled* (Collage-book 5_01). circa 1971. Ink, marker, collage on paper 27 x 35 cm. Courtesy of NANZUKA Gallery, Tokyo, Japan.

4
On the Construction of Pop Art
When American Pop Arrived in Stockholm in 1964

Annika Öhrner

It seems that there are chances that this can be made in 1964 already. We have seen a lot of the followers here and there is a risk that the whole "pop" thing will be misunderstood in Europe, if we see all the followers before we see the originals. (I would be glad if you could help us with these plans, and speak to the artists about them.)

Pontus Hultén to Richard Bellamy[1]

Art historical accounts have often relied on the idea of American pop art arriving in Europe in a sudden, almost aggressive act with immediate impact on the local milieu. It has been described as a more or less effortless conquest of the European art scene, accomplished through the power of the strong images themselves, after the pop music and the film industry had paved the way. It was and often continues to be claimed that pop art's way of bridging the gap between high and low culture, while incorporating images and symbols from American everyday life into art, as well as pop art's role in the radical redrawing of the geography of the Western art world were important factors for this influence. Authors such as Irving Sandler, Serge Guilbault, and Catherine Dossier have relied on different historical models of explanation of how America conquered Europe with

[1] Letter from Pontus Hultén of the Moderna Museet to Richard Bellamy at the Green Gallery, 23 October 1963; in the archive of the Moderna Museet, Stockholm.

pop art.[2] Intriguing as they are, they have not sufficiently accounted for the necessary *interaction* between the European parties and Manhattan art life to make this happen, nor the full impact of the coinciding strategies of several very different positions at this spatio-chronological point. The first American Pop Art show in a European Museum, Moderna Museet's *American Pop Art: 106 Forms of Love and Despair*, in early 1964, an impressive project in its aesthetic quality, impact and theoretical accurateness, even by today's standards, is one case that sheds light on some of these circumstances. This essay intends to argue that what today appears as a given, almost self-evident, the choice of both the exhibition concept and the selection of artists for the show, was in fact the result of an intense series of negotiations within a rather open discourse that wasn't settled until just before the opening.[3] With the use of close readings of archival documents and secondary sources, it presents this exhibition project as a complex of a number of coinciding transnational strategies and intentions. The individual actors were *the institution*—the Stockholm museum, Pontus Hultén, and his working partner Billy Klüver—*the market*, in this case in particular Galerie Sonnabend and Green Gallery—but also *the avant-garde*, in the guise of some artists in New York, both Swedish and American. Other important positions were found among Swedish artists and the local art press in Stockholm, already well aware of or practising new pictorial discourses and using the "pop-word". Interestingly, the very concept of pop art was actually formed during the process of realising this particular show, in the development of a discourse around "pop art" pending over the Atlantic, between New York and Stockholm, at the time.

[2] Serge Guilbault, *How New York Stole the Idea of Modern Art: Abstract Expressionism, Freedom and the Cold War*, Chicago: University of Chicago Press, 1983; Irving Sandler, *American Art of the 1960s*, New York: Harper & Row, 1988; and Catherine Dossin, *The Rise and Fall of American Art: A Geopolitics of Western Art Worlds.*, 1940s–1980s, Ashgate, 2015.

[3] Original title: *Amerikansk pop-konst: 106 former of kärlek och förtvivlan*, Moderna Museet, Stockholm, 29 February–12 April 1964. This essay has been further developed from my doctoral dissertation, which I defended at Uppsala University: *Barbro Östlihn & New York; Arts' Space and Possibilities, Stockholm: Makadam Publishers*, 2010. I quote directly from the letters, then in the Klüver-Martin Archive, New Haven and Moderna Museet, Stockholm. See also: Marianne Hultman, "Our Man in New York: An Interview with Billy Klüver on his collaboration with Moderna Museet," in Anna Tellgren (ed.), *The History Book: On Moderna Museet 1958–2008*, Stockholm: Moderna Museet 2008, pp. 233–251.

In Swedish national art history, the American Pop Art show in Stockholm in 1964, together with other early shows at the Moderna Museet such as *Movement in Art*, has been described as the starting point of a decade of *Open Art*, where anything was possible. In his chapter, the Pop art show in Stockholm is put in a slightly different perspective—and presented as the very moment of consolidation and final establishment of American pop in the historical discourse, with normative intentions as regards what "the International" could to do for "the Local."

The import of Pop Art to Stockholm

Moderna Museet and Pontus Hultén – the Institution

As opposed to many of the first American exhibition projects in Europe in the 1950s and early 1960s, the exhibitions at the Moderna Museet were not to any notable extent, the result of cooperation with official American interests.[4] From the very start, the young curator of the museum since 1959, Pontus Hultén, had an ambition to develop the museum into a stage for international art. He didn't formally become the Director until 1963, and at the time of the Pop show the following year, the Moderna Museet was still an institution under the auspices of the Nationalmuseum. The parent institution was firmly positioned in Friedrich August Stüler's impressive building, symbolically guarding the bridge that leads from the centre of the capital to Skeppsholmen Island and the Moderna Museet. It was essential for Hultén and his staff, who were relying on state funding, to create art projects with great impact and value, projects that could however not be *too* scandalised or criticised within the larger audience or among art critics.

Pontus Hultén is today closely associated with the American art scene of the early 1960s, although he had been in New York just twice before the

[4] American travelling exhibitions circulating in Europe in the 1950s and early 1960s that reached Sweden were: *Twelve contemporary American Painters and Sculptors*, Liljevalchs konsthall 1953; *American Primitive Painting*, Liljevalchs konsthall 1955; *Modern American Painting 1932–1958*, Gothenburg Museum of Art 1960 (arranged by the United States Information Service); and *ART USA NOW: The Johnson Collection of Contemporary American Painting*, at Liljevalchs konsthall in 1963. See also Francis Stonor Saunders, *The Cultural Cold War. The CIA and the World of Arts and Letters*, New York: The New Press, 2000 (original title: *Who Paid the Piper? The CIA and the Cultural Cold War*).

Pop art show in 1964: during a short term visit in the autumn of 1959 and the spring of 1963. Before leaving for the São Paulo-Biennale in 1959 and a show of the Swedish painter Olle Bærtling that he had curated, Hultén contacted the electrical engineer and researcher at Bell Telephone Laboratories, Billy Klüver, whom he knew from their youth at the student film studio in Stockholm.[5] This was the point of departure for a long and fruitful cooperation between the two, and their correspondence serves as an important source to understand the processes taking place around the museum building.[6] Billy Klüver was essential in the development of new forms of cooperation between artists and engineers, starting with helping out the French artist Jean Tinguely in constructing *Homage to New York* in the garden of the Museum of Modern Art in New York in 1961, an installation of mobile machine like sculptures. A few years later he founded *E.A.T.: Experiments in Art and Technology*, together with the artists Robert Rauschenberg and Robert Whitman, and engineer Fred Waldhauer. Klüver had his heart in Stockholm and would play a key role for the Moderna Museet in many of its early exhibitions, starting with *Movement in Art* (1961). Less known is that he was crucial for some very early pop-related exhibition projects in the U.S., which we will return to. Another important person in relation to the work with the international projects at the Moderna Museet, though with a lower profile than Hultén, was Anna-Lena Wibom, Hultén's life partner and close collaborator. As she had studied in the United States during the years 1953 to 1955, she was acquainted with the experimental film scene in Manhattan, and had a con-

[5] Letter from Pontus Hultén to Billy Klüver 7 August 1959. On Billy Klüver, see Barbro Schulz Lundestam, *Teknologi för livet. Om Experiments in Art and Technology*, Schulz: Stockholm, 2004 and Jesper Olsson, "Collaborators in Art and Technology – The Case of Billy Klüver,," in Tania Ørum and Jesper Olsson (ed.), *A Cultural History of the Avant-Garde in the Nordic Countries 1950–1975*, Leiden/Boston: Brill Rodopi, 2016, pp. 386–395.

[6] Hultén flew from São Paolo and arrived in New York on 21 September 1959. He visited museums and art collections in Philadelphia, Boston, Harvard and Washington, made studio visits together with Klüver to Sam Francis, whom Hultén knew since earlier visits in Paris, Alfred Leslie as well as Hans Richter, Naom Gabo, and Alexander Calder in Connecticut. Hans Richter showed Viking Eggeling films he owned. Hultén visited Yale University and studied the collection of the Societé Anonyme, formed by Duchamp, Man Ray, and Katherine Dreyer in 1920. He also saw (parts of) Allan Kaprow's *18 Happenings in 6 Parts*. Billy Klüver, Pontus Hultén's visit to New York 1959, undated manuscript, box 12, Klüver-Martin Archive. See also Hultman 2008, p. 235ff. For a biographical account on Pontus Hultén during these years, see f. ex. Andreas Gedin, *Pontus Hultén, Hon & Moderna*, Stockholm: Langenskiöld, 2016.

nection with to filmmakers such as Jonas and Adolfas Mekas and Robert Breer, contacts that were revitalised when the programme at Moderna Museet was constructed.[7]

In his ambition to create an international position for Moderna Museet and profile himself in the European art world, early on Hultén sought to develop curatorial concepts of a transnational character. In a letter to Billy Klüver in April 1963, he states that the contacts across the Atlantic had been what nourished the art of the century, and continues: "Listen to a proposal: Let's make a *large* exhibition here in Summer 1964, May–September, Europe-America and art in the twentieth century. Duchamp and the Armory show, etc., Mondrian, Max Ernst, leger, de Kooning, Matta, Riopelle, Tinguely, Nicki (sic), Calder, etc., etc., until the newest. Fahlström as well."[8] It is interesting that he still, one year before the actual pop show, thought of a rather broad and heterogeneous presentation of new art, when it came to the artists' national origins and artistic profiles. Although the large transatlantic exhibition drawn upon here never took place in Stockholm in the early 1960s, the exhibition concept reoccurred in Paris in the 1970s. As a result of his accomplishments in Stockholm, Hultén in 1974 became engaged in the creation of Centre Pompidou in Paris and one of his most profiling exhibition concepts was realised in the large transnational exhibitions *Paris-New York* (1977), *Paris-Berlin* (1978), and *Paris-Moscow* (1979).

Interestingly however, in contrast to this enthusiasm for American early modernism and contemporary art, other statements by Hultén bear witness to his ambivalence towards American pop. In September 1963 he summarised his impressions from his second New York visit in an article titled "About the painting in New York after Pollock, that is, ABOUT THE POP ART," in the Danish publication *Louisiana Revy*.[9] Here he refers to the established history of American art, where three or four movements or

[7] Anna-Lena Wibom studied at Stephens College in Columbia, Missouri, 1953–54 and at University of Chicago the year after, with a Fulbright scholarship, and spent of plenty spare time on Manhattan. Anna-Lena Wibom interviewed by the author 17 March 2006.

[8] Letter from P. Hultén to B. Klüver, undated, later inscription "April 1963," Klüver-Martin Archive.

[9] Hultén, K. G. [Pontus], "Om maleriet i New York efter Pollock d.v.s. OM POP-KUNSTEN", *Louisiana Revy*, nr 1, 1963, pp. 10–15.

groups could be perceived after the war in New York, beginning with abstract expressionism and ending with the pop artists who, unlike the pre-pop artists Rauschenberg and Johns, seemed to "see the position of the artist and of the art in a much more simple-minded manner." Hultén states that what he finds frightening in pop art is that it neither wants to be revolutionary nor beautiful. Instead, pop art is a matter of *desperate creation*, performed by an American generation that is unable to change its conditions of living and therefore, "in order to survive," chooses to accept it:

> Because this takes place in America, where they never have had autonomous art before, it is only natural that these artists choose America as the subject of their images. [...] But this is not seen ironically, rather in desperation, as if in an attempt to love without being loved back. They have a strong urge for self-expression and a need to be loved, but their emotions seem to be short-circuited, as if despite their efforts it is impossible to love this world of plastic and lacquered metal. Abstract expressionism is replaced by frustrated expressionism.[10]

Hultén states in his important Danish text, that the pop artist *turns away from* politics, from the problems of society, from religion and aesthetics, while turning to the soup can. In the statement he makes two important points—pop art is a way for artists to ventilate frustrated emotions and also, to distance themselves from politics and the society. This position would reoccur but in a much milder version in the marketing of the American pop art show in Stockholm the following spring and affect its reception. The statement is interesting as a mark in a process where concepts and ideas connected to pop art were still open and in flux.

The market

Pontus Hultén writes to Billy Klüver:

> Shall we do a pop-exhibition this spring? Based in Oldenburg, Rosenquist, Segal and with pieces even by Wesselman (Scull's) Lichtenstein (Leo's Washington and the Flyer at Ileana's) & Warhol (Öyvind?). Ileana is having a Segal-exhibition and thus has a good collection available in Europe. Leo would come there and I could talk with him then. Rosen-

[10] Ibid.

> quist will also come. What do you think? Pop in spring, Europe-America in autumn, that would be nice.[11]

The quote, along with several other letters from this period, illustrates the intense network with such diverse people as the art dealer Ileana Sonnabend, the Swedish king, and the Swedish ambassador in Rome.[12] The correspondence also shows that the selection of artists for the "pop-exhibition" is not set. For example, Öyvind Fahlström is mentioned as a possibility. In October 1963, Hultén had met the art dealer Ileana Sonnabend in Paris, and their cooperation in the coming months would secure several artworks for the upcoming show. Ileana Sonnabend was a partner throughout the project and also helped with negotiating pieces that she did not own herself. She did the same thing for the large exhibition at ICA in London, *The Popular Image*, which preceded the Stockholm exhibition and thereby made it easier to acquire works from New York.[13] Through the Hultén's collaboration with Green Gallery's Richard Bellamy, additional works were borrowed for the show to Stockholm.

For the art galleries it was important to establish a European market for American pop art at a moment when it had not yet been appreciated by

[11] Letter from P. Hultén to B. Klüver. Undated (probably Autumn 1963), the Klüver-Martin archive.

[12] See the extensive correspondence between Ileana Sonnabend and P. Hultén, Moderna Museet, August 1963–February 1964, Moderna Museet. The following quotation gives an impression their partnership: "I think you now can see that Rosenquist is going to be the problem- ///man nr 1 of our show. Billy writes today that we can get only three in New York, 'Tube', 'Light that won't fail No 1' (Scull), 'Spaghetti and Ford' (Hayes) and maybe 'Zone' (Tremaine). It is of course essential to have 'hommage to the American Negro' from the ICA-show. We have tried to have from Scull also the 'Portrait of Scull family' but without yes or no yet. I am very, very sorry that we are not going to have 'Capillary action'. Can really nothing be done about that? Should I ask the Swedish ambassador in Rome to intervene? The Swedish king might give Panza an order? What can I do? Could not Tate take a new one? It is essential to show now, that Rosenquist is not only a Swede but also a great artist. Maybe one of the greatest ..." Letter from P. Hultén to I. Sonnabend, 1963-12-15, Moderna Museet.

[13] See Hultén's letter to Richard Bellamy, Green Gallery, 23 October 1963. "Concerning our eventual pop-show in Stockholm a lot of things has happened. I was in Paris a week ago and spoke there to Ileana Sonnabend who now is very busy with the ICA-show in London. She told me that most of those pieces that go to London will stay in Europe for a while. She has a very beautiful Segal-show at this moment, as you know. She will later have several important 'pop'-artist shows during the winter. She thinks that important pieces of these shows can be kept in Europe and go to Stockholm." Copy in Moderna Museet.

important collectors on the upper east side of Manhattan. This was also the interest of Leo Castelli, who was powerful in this regard. Early on he was aware of the fact that American collectors did not buy new American art before it had been approved in Europe.[14] Today it is an established fact that his incomparable success in promoting art in the European market paved way for the post-war art in the U.S., a market that initially was Europe-oriented and conservative. Sonnabend's and Castelli's cooperation with the Moderna Museet to create the very first museum exhibition of Pop art in Europe was very important in that process and was crucial for securing and strengthening the whole project as such.

A pop art field emerges in the U.S.

The first years of the 1960s, saw pop art as an artistic practice and theoretical discourse emerge on Manhattan. Among early manifestations we find Claes Oldenburg's *The Store* in December 1961, where he presented objects made after consumer goods and foodstuff in a former grocery store on Lower East Side, as well as Jim Dines' one-man exhibition in January 1962 at the Martha Jackson Gallery. James Rosenquist's show at Green gallery and Roy Lichtenstein's first exhibition of painting related to comics at Leo Castelli's gallery were shown that same month. In the autumn of 1962, Andy Warhol showed paintings of Campbell's soup cans, Coca-Cola bottles, Marilyn Monroe and Elvis Presley at Castelli's. Simultaneously, the New Realists' show at the Sidney Janis Gallery, with 28 young artists, both Europeans and Americans, including Warhol, Oldenburg, Segal, Rosenquist, and Lichtenstein, and the Swedes P.O. Ultvedt and Öyvind Fahlström. In the *New York Times* Brian O'Doherty declared,

[14] Titia Hulst, "The Leo Castelli Gallery," Archives of American Art Journal, Smithsonian, 2007, pp. 14f. In a letter to Alfred H. Barr, Jr., 26 October 1955, Leo Castelli wrote: "[T]he American public itself is often reluctant to give its full appreciation and support to U.S. artists who have not yet received the European stamp of approval; and, while many new arrivals from Europe—not infrequently watered-down versions of trends which have originated in this country—shown here by our museums and galleries meet with immediate success, parallel efforts to promote American art in Europe have had, at best, a succès d'estime." Original in the Alfred Hamilton Barr papers, Museum of Modern Art (microfilm copy available at AAA, reel 218), quoted in Hulst, pp. 18f. See also Öhrner 2010, pp. 185–186, and Catherine Dossin, *The Rise and Fall of American Art, 1940s–1980s*, Taylor and Francis, 2016, pp. 164–168.

that pop art officially had arrived.[15] The plans for a pop art show at the Moderna Museet took place in this same period.

One week before the opening of the celebrated pop show at the Sidney Janis Gallery, the Philadelphia YM/YWHA (Young Men's and Young Women's Hebrew Association) launched the exhibition *Art 1963 – A New Vocabulary* (25 October to 7 November 1962), where Billy Klüver served as a counsellor to the young member of the arts council of the association, Audrey Sabol, and her co-curators Joan Kron and Acey Wolgin.[16] The exhibition was one of the first group exhibitions related to pop art. However, compared with the later canon of pop art, the selection of artists was much wider: George Brecht, Robert Breer, Jim Dine, Jasper Johns, Allan Kaprow, Marisol Escobar, Claes Oldenburg, Robert Rauschenberg, James Rosenquist, George Segal, Jean Tinguely, and Robert Watts participated. The exhibition catalogue for *Art 1963 – A New Vocabulary* was made as a kind of semantic mapping of the new phenomenon and is a very interesting document of the development of the vocabulary around pop at that moment. A column containing artists' names, as well as certain concepts in art, were presented in alphabetical order.[17] Klüver and Claes Oldenburg wrote entries that in a playful manner presented the rhetorical space "the new movement" was placed in. The label that was suggested for the new movement was *The Factualists*, a word that would survive into the catalogue of Moderna Museet's pop art show just over one year later. In Philadelphia, "Factualism" was considered an art movement of American origin, and an expression of a factual, relaxed relationship to existence. In the context of the New Realist show at the Sidney Janis Gallery, the concept reoccurred. Sidney Janis himself wrote a text for the catalogue, in which he describes "the New Realist" as a kind of folk artist who takes his

[15] Brian O'Doherty, "'Pop' goes the new art," New York Times, 4 november 1962; Harold Rosenberg, "The Art Galleries: The Game of Illusion," The New Yorker, 23 Novemver 1962. See also Irving Sandler, *American Art of the 1960s*, New York: Harper & Row, 1988, and Calvin Tomkins, *Off the Wall: A Portrait of Robert Rauschenberg* (1980), New York: Picador, 2005, pp. 168f.

[16] Billy Klüver, undated notes about *Art 1963 – A New Vocabulary*, and correspondence between Audrey Sabol and Klüver in the Klüver-Martin Archive, New Jersey. Audrey Sabrol had made contact with Billy Klüver as she approached him to buy a drawing by his friend, the Swedish artist Hans Nordenström, for *The Village Voice*.

[17] *Art 1963 – A New Vocabulary*, exh. cat., 25 October–7 November 1962.

inspiration from urban culture. Billy Klüver's use of the notion had had another connotation and referred to a certain attitude; to a "factual" approach to life as opposed to romanticism, academism, etc.[18]

After the above-mentioned gallery shows had established the idea of a new emerging art, American museum's started to take interest in pop. *Six Painters and the Object*, curated by Lawrence Alloway, was shown at the Solomon R. Guggenheim Museum in March to June 1963. The next large show was *The Popular Image* exhibition at the Washington Gallery of Modern Art in Washington, D.C. (18 April–2 June), where Klüver was involved. Alice Denney, the curator of the show, was in dialogue with him on the possibility of letting the whole show travel to Stockholm.[19] It would include all the artists that were later in the actual American Pop Show in Stockholm, that is Roy Lichtenstein, Claes Oldenburg, James Rosenquist, Georg Segal, Andy Warhol, and Tom Wesselman, as well as four other artists: George Brecht, Robert Rauschenberg, Robert Watts, and John Wesley. *The Popular Image* exhibition was accompanied by a catalogue with a text by Alan Solomon titled "The New Art," as well as of a 33.33 rpm phonograph record with interviews of the artists—produced by Billy Klüver.[20] Alice Denney and Billy Klüver produced an ambitious dance programme with new acts by choreographers, dancers, and artists somewhat in connection with the Judson Dance Theater. Rauschenberg's dance piece *Pelican* was one of them, performed with another Swedish artist, P. O. Ultvedt, the dancer Carolyn Brown, and Rauschenberg himself on roller

[18] "Today's Factual artist, and the work of these artists make up the present exhibition, belong to a new generation (age average about 30) whose reaction to Abstract Expressionism is still another manifestation in the evolution of art. [...] He is attracted to abundant everyday ideas and facts which he gathers, for example, from the street, the store counter, the amusement arcade and the home." Sidney Janis, "On the Theme of the Exhibition," *The New Realists*, New York: Sidney Janis Gallery, 1962, n.p. Janis is referring as his source for the term *The Factualists*: "Term first published in the book *Collage* by Harriet Janis and Rudi Blesh, 1962. Other titles applied to artists with this point of view: *Communists*; *Neo-Dadaists*; *Factualists*; *Artists of Pop Culture* and *Popular Realists*." The term was also present in William S. Burroughs novel *Naked Lunch* from 1959, where the Factualists are a political party in a dreamlike city called the *Interzone*.

[19] In an undated letter from Alice Denney to B. Klüver she asks whether she can include Stockholm when applying for loans to the exhibition in Washington. Klüver-Hultén archive.

[20] *The Popular Image* exhibition, Washington: The Washington Gallery of Modern Art, 1963. Alice M. Denney was responsible for the exhibition. Klüver-Martin Archive.

skates.[21] *The Popular Image* show was to influence the upcoming Stockholm project.

The avant-garde

The opening in Washington was a large event and many artists went there from Manhattan, including the Swedish artists Barbro Östlihn and Öyvind Fahlström. The couple had arrived in Manhattan in 1961, and through the intermediation of Klüver moved into Rauschenberg's former studio in 168, Front Street, a typical warehouse style building where they worked until it was demolished in 1967. They also played a part for the pop art show in Stockholm, and the selection of art works for that show.[22] Öyvind Fahlström made images and objects with references to American comics and had a rising career in New York, and Östlihn, painting large-scale images of façades in Manhattan, exhibited at galleries such as Tibor de Nagy and Cordier & Ekstrom.[23] Like Fahlström and Östlihn, James Rosenquist as well as Claes Oldenburg were of Swedish origin, and they united a close network of colleagues, all of whom were close friends with Robert Rauschenberg. At the time of the planning of the pop show in Stockholm, Claes and Pat Oldenburg also prepared his first solo exhibition, entitled *The Home*, at the Sidney Janis Gallery.[24] Klüver, Öyvind Fahlström, and Barbro Östlihn took turns to convince the couple to spare good works for the Moderna Museet, which also resulted in the *Ping Pong Table* being in

[21] Annika Öhrner, "Recalling Pelican: On P. O. Ultvedt, Robert Rauschenberg and Two 'Ballets,'" in *Rauschenberg and Sweden, Konsthistorisk tidskrift /Journal of Art History*, Routledge, 2007, Issue 76, pp. 27–39.

[22] Undated letter from B. Klüver to P. Hultén. Fahlström was in the process of leaving Cordier & Ekstrom, Inc., to start to work with Sidney Janis. In this letter, Klüver approach the matter whether his position as the museum's advisor for acquisitions could become more formalised. In another letter he writes that "Öyvind and Barbro" are "up at Janis' again to investigate different possibilities." In the letter, he reports the status in different possible acquisitions of works by Warhol, Dine, Rosenquist, Segal, Oldenburg. In other letters from this spring, there are suggestions that works by David Smith, Robert Breer and Andy Warhol should be acquired. The museum also buys Robert Rauschenberg's *Monogram*. Fahlström and Östlihn are mentioned as mediators of the purchase of *Ping Pong Table*, for instance in a letter dated 9 April 1964, where the piece finally was reserved for $2.250. The Klüver-Martin Archive.

[23] See Öhrner 2010.

[24] The exhibition took place from 7 April to 2 May 1964. Rose 1970, p. 202.

the Moderna Museet collection today. The intense work of these artists to contribute to the outcome of Moderna Museet's exhibition was one of its prerequisites.

Alan Solomon stated in his text for the catalogue of *The Popular Image* exhibition that the new art "could not have been contrived; it has followed an organic course which makes it an absolute product of its time." He underlines that the artists are not engaged politically and have no interest in cooperating in social and collective manifestations. Solomon's text would soon be published in *Art International*, and be widely spread.[25] Revised versions were published in the catalogues of *The Popular Image* at ICA, London (autumn 1963) as well as the pop art show at the Moderna Museet soon afterwards.[26] However, the very expression *Pop art* was just mentioned in passing by Solomon in the article, as one of several possible, alternative labels for the new art. Through its heavy emphasis on the determination of a development towards what art and what artist would become valid and important, it was a normative statement.

Importing pop – the exhibition and its package

In the communication from the museum about *American Pop Art - 106 Forms of Love and Despair*, pop art was framed as historically determined and autonomous. The ambivalence towards the very label of pop, was strongly reflected already in Hultén's and Klüver's correspondence in their preparations for the show: "Is it possible to find SOME OTHER NAME THAN POPOPOPOPOPOPOPOPOPOPOPOP?" Klüver writes in an undated letter, seemingly frustrated.[27] For a time Pontus Hultén calls the instigators of the movement "The Vulgarians" as in a letter to Alan Solomon in November of 1963.[28] The term had been launched by Max Kozloff in *Art International* in March of 1962, in his article "'Pop' Culture, Metaphysical Disgust, and the New Vulgarians," and it had also been at

[25] Alan R. Solomon, "The New Art," *Art International* VII/7, 25 September 25 1963, pp. 17–41.
[26] *The Popular Image*, Institute of Contemporary Art, London, 24 October–23 November, 1963.
[27] Letter from B. Klüver to P. Hultén, Moderna Museet.
[28] Letter from P. Hultén to A. Solomon, 1963-11-11. Moderna Museet.

play in Klüver's encyclopaedic travesty in Philadelphia later in 1962.[29] Kozloff's choice of label was pejorative and presented in a text that is nothing less than a treacherous attack on the new phenomena. Therefore, in November 1963, Billy Klüver questions the use of the term *vulgarians* in Stockholm, which Pontus Hultén appears to have picked up:

> About pop – PLEASE dear Pontus not the Vulgarians. No, no, please – Why not "New American art", please? The vulgarians does not work. The pop comes in anyway, so that one can vomit – "New American art." Please something like that.[30]

Soon thereafter, in a letter to Leo Castelli, Hultén does call the show "New American Art."[31] The pop art exhibition at Moderna Museet in Stockholm opened on 29 February 1964. Being the first exhibition ever in a European museum of American pop, the name of the show as well as its content had by that point been negotiated over a period of time, and the result was the somewhat odd title *American Pop Art: 106 Forms of Love and Despair* and a listing of seven core artists.

As much as the preparation of the show, as we have seen, had been one of negotiations regarding concept and content, the exhibition itself was framed as a matter of fact, or rather as a confrontation. It was launched, as for an example, in the Moderna Museets Vänner's ("The Friends of the Moderna Museet") *Bulletinen*, in a note formed as a telegram: "SWEDEN NEXT TO BE CONQUERED STOP ATTACK ON MUSEUM OF MODERN ART IN STOCKHOLM FEBRUARY 29TH STOP YOU'LL GET TO KNOW WHAT POP IS."[32] The same tendency is found when studying the presentation and lay-out of the show itself.

The architecture of the former military training hall in which Moderna Museet was housed in the centre of Stockholm was open and light, with free standing walls dividing the space, and light flooded in through large

[29] Max Kozloff, "Pop' Culture, Metaphysical Disgust, and the New Vulgarians," *Art International* (1962), Steven Henry Madoff (ed.), *Pop Art. A critical history*, Berkeley: University of California Press, 1997, p. 29–32.

[30] Letter from B. Klüver to P. Hultén 1963-11-20. Moderna Museet. Klüver pended between English and Swedish in his letters to Hultén.

[31] Letter from P. Hultén to L. Castelli, 1963-11-28. Moderna Museet.

[32] *Meddelande till Moderna Museets vänner*, no. 10, February 1964, p. 11.

windows[33] (Figure 4.1–4.9). The visitors walked on a plain wooden floor. George Segal's sculptures were presented without sockets; the figures were at eye level with the viewers. Audiences were greeted at the entrance by his *Man on a Bicycle* (1961), which was placed in front of James Rosenquist's *Capillary Action No 11*, a painting with a free standing object, a tree, in front. Segal's *Woman Painting Her Fingernails* (1961), featuring a female figure in a restaurant booth, had been fittingly installed by a window. *Gottlieb's Wishing Well* (1963), Segal's sculpture of a man playing pinball, was placed nearby, and the two installations together created an American diner setting. The two white plaster figures in *Lovers on a Bench* (1962) were placed in the centre of the room. From their bench they were viewing large size works such as Tom Wesselman's *Great American Nude No. 44* (1961) and Andy Warhol's large painting *Marilyn in Color* (1962). Oldenburg's *Soft Good Humor*—one of the minor versions of the piece of furred popsicles—rested in front of his *U.S. Flag Fragment (Flag with Four Stars)* as well as *Roast*, both from 1961. Oldenburg's *The Bride* (1961) towered in the room as a shapeless and threatening figure. Jim Dine's *Black Tools in a Landscape* (1962), a painting with real carpenter's tools heavily painted with thick, black colour, and some other of his paintings was presented. Roy Lichtenstein's *Hot Dog* (1962) and the large *Okay, Hot Shot, Okay* (1961), a comic strip with a military pilot, were facing the visitors as they walked into the space, while *Hopeless* (1963) with a weeping woman, and the graphically reduced *Radio* (1962) were hung on a perpendicular wall. The three paintings had recently been on show in Ileana Sonnabend's Lichtenstein exhibition in the spring of 1963. That gallery had also provided loans of a mixed series of Andy Warhol works, including the *Torn Campbell's Soup Can* (1962) and other versions of the famous Can. The audience was also confronted with Warhol's Marilyns, for example the huge *Marilyn in Color* (1962), and other large images

[33] The reconstruction is made on the basis of photographic documentation in "Moderna Museets Fotoalbum," Moderna Museet, as well as the exhibition catalogue, *Amerikansk popkonst: 106 former av kärlek och förtvivlan*, Stockholm: Moderna Museet 1964. The exhibition's working committee and catalogue editorial, contained of Carlo Derkert, K.G. (Pontus) Hultén, Billy Klüver, Louise O'Konnor and Anna-Lena Wibom. The exhibition later travelled to Louisiana outside Copenhagen, and Stedelijk Museum, Amsterdam.

featuring motifs from American media and popular culture, for example *Blue Electric Chair* (1963) and *Green Coca-Cola Bottles* (1963).

Okay, Hot Dog, Okay could be seen, via its provocative approach, together with Lichtenstein's *Finger Pointing*, an image appropriated from early military campaign that was put on the cover of the catalogue and on the exhibition poster, as meta pieces for the exhibition as a whole; a show that was utterly scenically installed, with consciously arranged directions of gaze in-between the viewers and the pieces, and well defined relationships between objects in the foreground and larger paintings in the background.[34] The installation photos testify about an exhibition designed to capture the visitor, inviting him or her to share the space with the objects.

The catalogue had a hybrid modern design, with pages in different colours as well as colour reproductions pasted in by hand. The main essay was written by Alan Solomon and followed by shorter contributions on the individual artists.[35] Thus, the show was carefully packaged for the Swedish public, concerned with introducing pop art properly and in line with its acquired intentions. In the catalogue, there was a short text by Fahlström in the form of a telegram from New York: "Pop Art did not start with Schwitters" the telegram started and ended, "Pop art started with Johns, who began with Rauschenberg [...] every day was equal to Americana. STOP THE POINT HAS BEEN LOST THE NEW IS NOT AMERICANA ART BUT LIFE ART."[36] Fahlström might have feared that criticism against American mass culture would also be directed against the

[34] For a discussion on how Lichtenstein, as here, deliberately exaggerated the stereotypes of the masculine and feminine in the original, see Cécile Whiting, "Lichtenstein's Borrowed Spots," in the author's *A Taste for Pop*, Cambridge University Press, 1997, p. 100–145.

[35] The catalogue consisted of Pontus Hultén's preface, followed by the article "The New American Art" by Alan Solomon, and two short texts by Öyvind Fahlström and Billy Klüver respectively. The artists were presented successively, with texts written by Öyvind Fahlström (on Jim Dine), Alain Jouffroy (on Roy Lichtenstein), Claes Oldenburg (on himself), Chell Buffington (on James Rosenqvist), George Geldzahler (Andy Warhol) and an unsigned note about Tom Wesselman. Nils-Hugo Geber wrote about the extensive film programme in connection to the exhibition. Billy Klüver discusses the choice of authors for the catalogue in a letter: "Geldzahler, Solomon, Steinberg—each good in his way, doesn't matter. Geldzahler is most in, after him Solomon, after him Steinberg" Letter from B. Klûver to P. Hultén, Moderna Museet's archive, file for "Önskemuseet." Hultén later confirms the commission to Solomon, while telling him the title "the vulgarians" is under consideration. P. Hultén in letter to A. Solomon, 11/11/1963, copy. Moderna Museet

[36] Öyvind Fahlström, in *Amerikansk pop-konst: 106 former av kärlek och förtvivlan*, p. 24.

exhibition, a fear that was probably not completely unfounded. Three days before the opening of the Moderna Museet's pop art exhibition, Swedish National Radio broadcast a lecture called "Mass Culture is Dangerous," by Theodor Adorno.[37] In it Adorno describes the deadlineness of the cultural industry and says that the mass culture was the genuine culture of the people. Unsurprisingly the theme would reoccur in parts of the reviews of the exhibition.

Pontus Hultén's preface to the catalogue argues vehemently against any understanding of pop art as an ironic treatment of mass culture. The pop artists have no social awareness and no political intentions.[38] Despite the fact that they turn from politics, as well as aesthetics, Hultén think that he they "despare in face of the realities of the world." We saw earlier that Hultén regarded pop art as strong, frustrated, emotional reactions of love to a "world of plastic and metal." After having negotiated several alternative labels, the subtitle of the final title was designed to put forward these emotions—the exhibition shows "106 Forms of Love and Despair." The position that Hultén takes towards pop art reflects Alan Solomon's article.[39] His own development in regards to the new art in New York slowly developed towards a more positive one, which is also consistent as he is now presenting it in his own museum.

The Swedish situation

In early 1963, Pop art, as a notion and a concept, was already familiar among Swedish artists and critics via international art journals, not the least *Art International.* Certainly, pop-related works such as Barbro Östlihn's New York paintings had not yet been exhibited in Sweden, but Öyvind Fahlström's art had been disseminated and, in particular through his use of comic strips, associated with pop. In the spring of 1963, one year before the large American pop show, a show simply called *POP* was presented at Galleri Observatorium—an independent, non-commercial gallery. The curator, Ludvig Rasmusson, presented international pop art

[37] Most likely it is "Résumé über die Kulturindustrie," a lecture Adorno had broadcast on German radio on 28 March and 4 April the previous year

[38] Pontus Hultén, "Förord," in *Amerikansk pop-konst: 106 former av kärlek och förtvivlan*, p. 23.

[39] Hultén in *Amerikansk Pop-konst: 106 former av kärlek och förtvivlan*, p. 16.

further through an article in the journal *Rondo*, where he claimed that themes from popular culture defined pop art.[40] This definition allowed him to include Swedish artists under the heading of pop art, even if, as he writes, none of them is a "full time popper." Lars Hillersberg is described as the "until now most typical pop artist," and Öyvind Fahlström as "the most famous." What is important to mention here is that the concept of pop art seems to have been used inclusively and concerned image strategies, rather than the work of iconic (American) artists.

We will never know if *POP* was the exhibition Hultén had in mind when talking about Swedish followers of pop in the opening quotation of this chapter, but it could very well have been the case. In his letter to Green Gallery, he emphasises the importance to hasten the exposure of American pop artists ("the originals"), so that pop art will be properly understood in Sweden.

In the spring of 1964, a film called *Stockholm à l'heure du Pop* was produced by the Belgian artist Olivier Herdies who wrote the script and, at that time, had lived in Sweden for almost thirty years.[41] The film, 33 minutes long, starts with long shots from urban life in Stockholm, the Swedish capital that had some 800,000 inhabitants at the time. The camera rests on the green underground trains, on people walking the street, and super good looking blonde girls. This is followed by cuts from the American pop art show at Moderna Museet, unlabelled, as well as by several images from the local art scene at local art galleries. The film displays a Swedish art scene with pop art expressions of its own, while pop art is interpreted as an artistic attitude rather than art by an established and well-defined group of American artists.

American Pop received wide exposure in Swedish press following the 1964 exhibition, which was more than a year before the American offensive in Vietnam that would strongly affect the Swedish cultural climate,

[40] Ludvig Rasmusson, "Pop," *Rondo*, 1963, No. 2, pp. 25–32. The Swedish artists Rasmusson refers to are partly other than those in the exhibition: Dick Bengtsson, Erik Dietman, Öyvind Fahlström, Jarl Hammarberg, Lars Hillersberg, Sven Höglund, Jack Nelson, Hans Munch-Nisted, Ulf Rahmberg, Carl Fredrik Reuterswärd, P. O. Ultvedt, and Göran Östergren.

[41] Olivier Herdies, *Stockholm à l'heure du pop* (Swedish title: *När popen kom till stan*), 1964, 16 mm, colour, 33 min. Reference Archive at the Filmform – the art film and video archive, Filmform Foundation, Stockholm.

resulting in a more negative image of American culture—as well as of Moderna Museet's international work. When the pop show opened in 1964, it served as the basis for in-depth cultural criticism and discussions in several articles and journals. The attention in the news was extensive; in the newspapers, TV, radio, pop art in general and the Moderna exhibition in particular were discussed and debated.

The critic Ulf Linde's defence of pop art in a television report of the exhibition—by pointing out patterns of abstraction on the surface of the image—was rather half-hearted, which the interviewer picked up on.[42] The dialogue in the report was a version of a recurring theme in the Swedish context: *pop art is poorly executed, if seen as painting.* When Ulf Linde published four articles on pop art in *Dagens Nyheter* one year later, he formulated his critique in a more elaborate, theoretical manner. He argued that pop art lacked the capacity to create something new, something that was not already formulated in Arnold Schönberg, Wassily Kandinsky or Kurt Schwitters.[43] Alas, the neo-avant-garde did not measure up to the "real avant-garde."

Torsten Bergmark was the most prominent art critic in the largest Swedish daily paper, *Dagens Nyheter*. He made a rather in-depth introduction to pop art, based on American art press and interviews with the pop artists in *Art News*, among other sources.[44] The most interesting aspect of pop art is, according to Bergmark, the very occupation of "this vulgar material, the ugliest and worst side of Americanism." His objection against pop art targets its inner logic. Instead of elevating images from popular culture—"such as amateur painting, illustrations in weekly magazines and comics"—to art, the artists integrate the images in their own style, extending them with things considered vulgar or banal from the standpoint of high culture. In his second, extensive text on the American art show at the Moderna Museet, Bergmark examined the exhibition

[42] *Aktuellt*, Swedish television, 1964-02-27.

[43] Ulf Linde, "Fyra artiklar" (1965), *Efter hand: Texter 1950–1985*, Stockholm: Bonniers 1985, pp. 522–541. The articles were originally published in *Dagens Nyheter* on 26 March, 30 March, and 4 April 1965, and later collected in Ulf Linde, *Fyra artiklar*, BLM-biblioteket, Stockholm: Bonniers, 1965.

[44] The source is stated in Torsten Bergmark, "Pop – den amerikanska drömmen," *Dagens Nyheter*, 25 February 1964.

itself.[45] In it his contention is that the pop artists does not measure up to the proper standards expected of painters; they are failing as a result of the dullness of the work. Pop seems "in many of its forms be a relevant expression for the taste and the desires of the audience that is supporting it financially." The art critic Torsten Ekbom would criticises Bergmark's position, stating that arguments against pop art seems to be against the mass culture that pop art depicts rather than the works of art.[46] He compares this attitude to Adorno's lecture, which presented a fundamental divide between high and low culture. Pop art's simple formalism and its trivial subject matter are conscious choices that open up the following question to the viewer: "To what extent should we accept mass culture?"[47] When approaching the pop art exhibition, the antagonists Linde and Bergmark were united in a formalistic based critique of the artistic quality of the art works.

Andreas Huyssen, in his notable 1975 essay, offered an interpretation of how American pop art was understood in West Germany in relation to American popular culture in general.[48] Interestingly, the youth movement in Germany read American pop art as a protest and a criticism of the affluent society, rather than a distanced approval of it. This was most probably the result of the extensive exposure to American culture, as well as a spirit of strong cultural criticism following the tradition of Adorno in Germany. The Swedish criticism ten years earlier, had quite a different notion of the art that was shown in Stockholm in 1964, discussing painterly qualities and ethical content. However, the emphasis on the non-commitment towards social reality among the artists had already been made in Hultén's early texts on pop. His early ambivalence, which was slowly turned into enthusiasm in the marketing of the show, still shone through and was noticed by parts of the audience.

[45] Torsten Bergmark, "Svitsch-bang på Moderna Museet," *Dagens Nyheter*, 29 February 1964.
[46] Torsten Bergmark, "Rum och realitet," *Dagens Nyheter*, 26 April 1964.
[47] Torsten Ekbom, "Popkonsten och masskulturen," *Dagens Nyheter*, 10 April 1964.
[48] Andreas Huyssen, "The Cultural Politics of Pop," *After the Great Divide: Modernism, Mass Culture, Postmodernism*, Bloomington: Indiana University Press, 1987, pp. 141–159, first published in *New German Critique*, 4, (Winter 1975), pp. 77–98.

Pop art institutionalised

Lucy Lippard acknowledges five "hard core pop artists" in the first book on pop art, her *Pop Art* (1966)—and a couple of additional ones on the American West Coast and in Great Britain.[49] These artists are painting "hard-edge" and use professional techniques to produce their popular, figurative paintings.[50] The fact that many artists from both sides of the Atlantic painted in a similar manner was acknowledged in Lippard's book; U.S.-based female painters, such as Rosalynn Drexler, Idelle Weber, and Marisol Escobar were also mentioned, as were Europeans like Niki de Saint Phalle. Recent research, such the one presented in this anthology, has of course acknowledged a much wider outreach of pop-related pictorial concepts in Europe and beyond.[51]

The version of American pop art presented at the Moderna Museet was "owned" by a certain circle, namely Lippard's "New York Five," with the addition of Dine and Segal. The title, the conceptual frame of the show, and the selection were not fixed until the last minute, and different constellations of artists had been discussed along the way. Thus, seen from a transnational perspective, Moderna Museet's pop art exhibition is early in the process of establishment of American Pop in Europe and the first museum to exhibit it in Europe. Nationally, in historical handbooks of the 1960s, it has been categorised as part of a group of shows that were a starting point for a new and open art practice.

However, if one understands the Stockholm pop exhibition in 1964 as a step in the development of a discourse around pop art, one that was based on transnational strategies of different figures, a different image emerges. Constance W. Glenn has read the development of pop art through ten important exhibitions, from an early prologue in 1960, to the moment that

[49] Lucy Lippard, *Pop Art*, London: Thames & Hudson, 1966, p. 69. Hal Foster has in recent overviews over pop credited British artists from the Independent group, Hamilton and Paolozzi, and the next British generation (Peter Blake, Derek Boshier, Pauline Boty, Patrick Caulfield, David Hockney, Allen Jones, R.B. Kitaj, Richard Smith, and Joe Tilson) as well as the New York-artists Allan D'Arcangelo, Jim Dine, Robert Indiana, Roy Lichtenstein, Claes Oldenburg, Mel Ramos, James Rosenquist, Andy Warhol, John Wesley, and Tom Wesselman. Hal Foster, Pop, London: Phaidon, 2005, p. 17.

[50] Ibid., p. 69.

[51] See e.g. *International Pop*, produced by Walker Art Center, Minneapolis and *The Ey Exhibition, The World Goes Pop*, Tate Gallery, London, both in 2015.

finally secured the international breakthrough of pop art.[52] Glenn describes the 1964 Moderna Museet exhibition as a *summary* and as the last in the line of the ten "high" pop shows. This show was:

> The final exhibition, the Postscript, stands for summation, broad consensus and the end of the magical period when American Pop Art seemed neatly definable and readily accessible.[53]

Thus, seen in an American context, the Moderna Museet's pop art show was in fact a proof that a canon had been established.[54] The canon of artists that were included in the show, that had until the opening been sized down step by step as we have seen through the pop show in the U.S. that Klüver was involved in, would from then on be repeated in the art historical narratives.[55] Pop art is here not a notion of a certain artistic style or pictorial concept but the launch of a core group of artists who until today have had a dominant position in art history. When the Moderna Museet introduced the new avant-garde, female artists were glaringly absent, as were Swedish and other non-American artists who used a pop art language. In Manhattan, there were several female artists with similar visual

[52] Constance W. Glenn, "American Pop Art: Inventing the Myth," in Marco Livingstone (red.), *Pop* Art, exh. cat., London: Royal Academy of Arts & Weidenfeld & Nicholson, 1991, p. 32.

[53] Ibid, p. 39.

[54] The exhibition history of pop can be described in different ways. Susan J. Cooke's chronology of pop exhibitions and performances lists American exhibitions exclusively. Susan J. Cooke, "Chronology," in Barbara Haskell (red.), *Blam! The Explosion of Pop, Minimalism, and Performance 1958–1964*, New York & London: Whitney Museum of American Art & W.W. Norton 1984, pp. 137–148. In his list of "[t]he key group exhibitions Hal Foster counts "*New Painting of Common Objects*, Pasadena Art Museum, 1962; *The Popular Image*, ICA, London, 1963; *Six Painters and the Object*, Guggenheim Museum, New York, 1963; and *The New Generation: 1964*, London: Whitechapel Art Gallery, 1964, and later exhibitions. *Art 1963 – A New Vocabulary*, Philadelphia 1962 and the Moderna Museet's presentation in 1964, are not included. Foster 2005, p. 40, note 6.

[55] Patrik Lars Andersson has analysed the way some European artists felt that they needed to distance themselves from the American pop art discourse, for example Niki de Saint Phalle, Jean Tinguely, and Per Olof Ultvedt, and the art critic Ulf Linde. Patrik Lars Andersson, *Euro-Pop: The Mechanical Bride Stripped Bare in Stockholm*, Even (diss.), Vancouver: University of British Columbia, 2001, p. 82–142.

interests and sensibilities as the established names who did not come to Stockholm.[56]

In the Swedish art scene, we meet a complicated situation where, according to the art historical tradition, the pop art show at Moderna Museet in 1964 had a vital function to expand the concept of art, and the fixed separation of high and low culture. However, the very same exhibition can be seen in an oppositional way, as presenting a reduced, established and openly *normative* concept that excluded alternative selections during the process of consolidation—for example local versions of pop and female artists, both local and American. Barbro Östlihn's art could, for example, not be more "right" with its pop art vocabulary and its close connection to the artists of "The New York Five."

The 1964 show in Stockholm was not produced, as is very clear from the quotation of Hultén in the beginning of this essay, simply in order to *present* American pop art for a European or a Swedish audience, but rather to set up a model. It was produced as a result of the strategies of a number of interests both in Sweden and on the New York art scene, and to establish international art on the North European scene.

Bibliography

Andersson, Patrik Lars, *Euro-Pop: The Mechanical Bride Stripped Bare in Stockholm*, Even (diss.), Vancouver: University of British Columbia, 2001.

"*Amerikansk pop-konst: 106 former av kärlek och förtvivlan*", exh. cat., Stockholm: Moderna Museet, 1964.

Art 1963 - A New Vocabulary, exh. cat., YMCA Philadelphia 25 October–7 November 1962.

Bergmark, Torsten, "Pop - den amerikanska drömmen," *Dagens Nyheter,* 25 February 1964.

—. "*Svitsch-bang på Moderna Museet,*" *Dagens Nyheter*, 29 February 1964.

—. "Rum och realitet," *Dagens Nyheter*, 26 April 1964.

[56] For a historiographical study of their exclusion, see Kalliopi Minioudaki, "Pop Ladies and Bad Girls: Axell, Pauline Boty and Rosalynn Drexler," *Oxford Art Journal*, 30 March 2007, pp. 402–430.

Cooke, Susan J., "Chronology," in Barbara Haskell (red.), *Blam! The Explosion of Pop, Minimalism, and Performance 1958–1964*, New York & London: Whitney Museum of American Art and W.W. Norton 1984.

Dossin, Catherine, *The Rise and Fall of American Art: A Geopolitics of Western Art Worlds*, 1940s–1980s, Ashgate, 2015.

—. *The Rise and Fall of American Art*, 1940s–1980s, Taylor and Francis, 2016.

Gedin, Anderas, *Pontus Hultén, Hon & Moderna*, Stockholm: Langenskiöld, 2016

Glenn, Constance W. "American Pop Art: Inventing the Myth," in Marco Livingstone (red.), *Pop* Art, exh. cat., London: Royal Academy of Arts & Weidenfeld & Nicholson, 1991.

Guilbault, Serge, How New York Stole the Idea of Modern Art: Abstract Expressionism, Freedom and the Cold War, Chicago: University of Chicago Press, 1983.

Ekbom, Torsten, "Popkonsten och masskulturen," *Dagens Nyheter*, 10 April 1964.

Foster, Hal, *Pop*, London: Phaidon, 2005.

Hulst, Titia, "The Leo Castelli Gallery," *Archives of American Art Journal*, Smithsonian, 2007, pp. 14f.

Hultman, Marianne, "Our Man in New York: An Interview with Billy Klüver on his collaboration with Moderna Museet," in Anna Tellgren (ed.), *The History Book: On Moderna Museet 1958-2008*, Stockholm: Moderna Museet 2008.

Huyssen, Andreas, "The Cultural Politics of Pop," *After the Great Divide: Modernism, Mass Culture, Postmodernism*, Bloomington: Indiana University Press, 1987.

Janis, Sidney, "On the Theme of the Exhibition," *The New Realists*, New York: Sidney Janis Gallery, 1962.

Kozloff, Max, "Pop' Culture, Metaphysical Disgust, and the New Vulgarians," in Steven Henry Madoff (ed.), *Pop Art.*

Linde, Ulf, *Fyra artiklar*, BLM-biblioteket, Stockholm: Bonniers, 1965.

Lippard, Lucy, *Pop Art*, London: Thames & Hudson, 1966.

Schulz Lundestam, Barbro, Teknologi för livet: Om Experiments in Art and Technology, Schulz: Stockholm, 2004.

Meddelande till Moderna Museets vänner, No. 10, February 1964.

Minioudaki, Kalliopi, "Pop Ladies and Bad Girls: Axell, Pauline Boty and Rosalynn Drexler," *Oxford Art Journal*, 30 March 2007, pp. 402–430.

O'Doherty, Brian, "'Pop' Poes the New Art," *New York Times*, 4 November 1962.

Öhrner, Annika, *Barbro Östlihn och New York. Konstens rum och möjligheter*, Stockholm: Makadam Publishers, 2010.

—. "Recalling Pelican: On P.O. Ultvedt, Robert Rauschenberg and Two 'Ballets,'" in *Konsthistorisk tidskrift /Journal of Art History*, Special issue Rauschenberg and Sweden, No. 76, Routledge, 2007, pp. 27–39.

Olsson, Jesper, "Collaborators in Art and Technology: The Case of Billy Klüver," in Tania Ørum and Jesper Olsson (eds.), *A Cultural History of the Avant-Garde in the Nordic Countries 1950–1975*, Leiden and Boston: Brill Rodopi, 2016.

Rasmusson, Ludvig, "Pop," *Rondo*, No. 2, 1963.

Rosenberg, Harold, "The Art Galleries: The Game of Illusion," *The New Yorker*, 23 November 1962.

Sandler, Irving, *American Art of the 1960s*, New York: Harper & Row, 1988.

Solomon, Alan R., "The New Art," *Art International*, VII/7, 25 September 25 1963.

Stonor Saunders, Francis, The Cultural Cold War: The CIA and the World of Arts and Letters, New York: The New Press, 2000.

Tomkins, Calvin, Off the Wall: A Portrait of Robert Rauschenberg, New York: Picador, 2005.

Whiting, Cécile, "Lichtenstein's Borrowed Spots," in Cécile Whiting, *A Taste for Pop*, Cambridge: Cambridge University Press, 1997.

Unpublished materials (letters, notes, interviews)

Alice Denney, letter to Billy Klüver, undated, Klüver-Hultén archive.

Pontus Hultén, Letter to Richard Bellamy, 23 October 1963, Moderna Museet, Stockholm.

—. Letter to L. Castelli, 28 November 1963. Moderna Museet.

—. Letter to Billy Klüver, 7 August 1959.

—. Letter to Billy Klüver, undated, later inscription "April 1963," Klüver-Martin archive.

—. Letter to B. Klüver, Undated (probably Autumn 1963), Klüver-Martin archive.

—. Letter to I. Sonnabend, 15 december 1963, Moderna Museet.

—. Letter to A. Solomon, 11 November 1963. Moderna Museet.

Billy Klüver, Letter to P. Hultén, undated.

—. Letter to P. Hultén, Moderna Museet.

—. Letter to P. Hultén, Moderna Museet's archive, file for "Önskemuseet."

—. Letter to P. Hultén, 20 November 1963. Moderna Museet.

—. "Pontus Hultén's visit to New York 1959," undated manuscript, box 12, Klüver-Martin Archive.

—. Notes about *Art 1963: A New Vocabulary*, undated.

Annika Öhrner, Interview with Anna-Lena Wibom, 17 March 2006.

Audrey Sabol and Billy Klüver, Correspondence, in the Klüver-Martin Archive.

Letter dated 9 April 1964, The Klüver-Martin Archive.

Film and television

Olivier Herdies, *Stockholm à l'heure du pop* (Swedish title: *När popen kom till stan*), 1964, 16 mm, colour, 33 min., Reference Archive at Filmform: TheArt Film and Video Archive, Filmform Foundation, Stockholm.

Aktuellt, Swedish Television, 27 February.

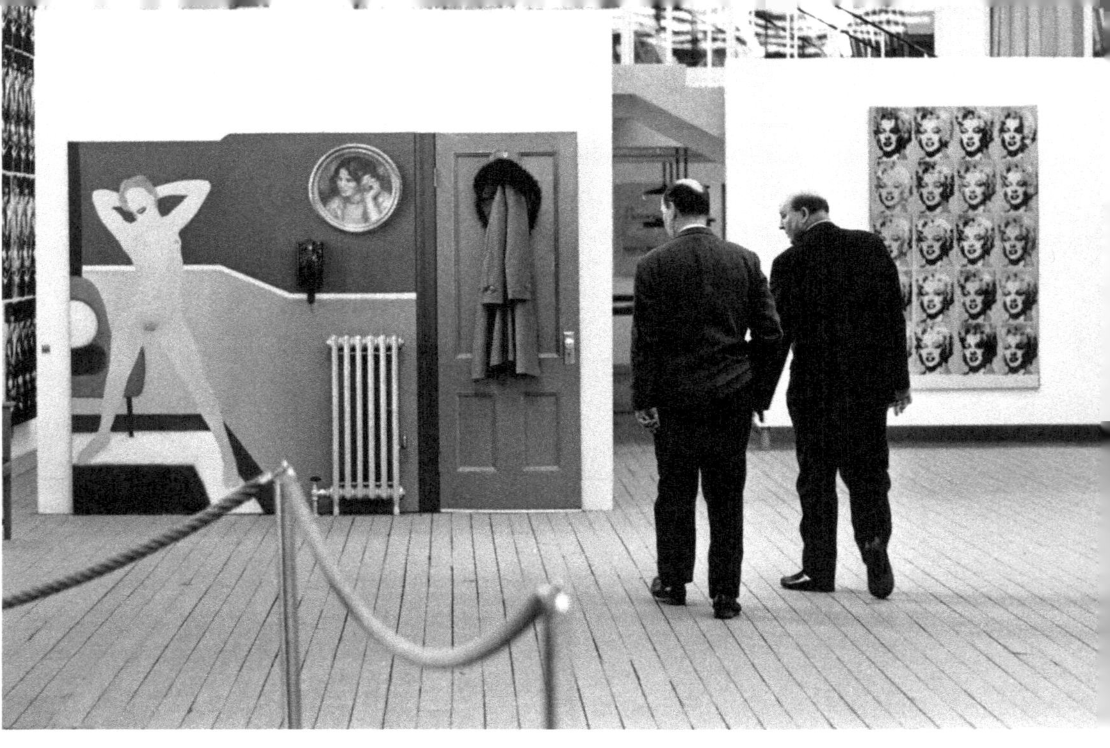

Figure 4.1: Visitors in *American Pop Art: 106 Forms of Love and Despair*, Moderna Museet, (February 29th – April 12th, 1964) contemplating on Tom Wesselman's, *Great American Nude No 44*, 1963. Andy Warhol, Marilyns in color, 1962.

Figure 4.2 (right): Visitors in *American Pop Art: 106 Forms of Love and Despair*, Moderna Museet, 1964. George Segal, *Gottlieb's Wishing Well*, 1963.

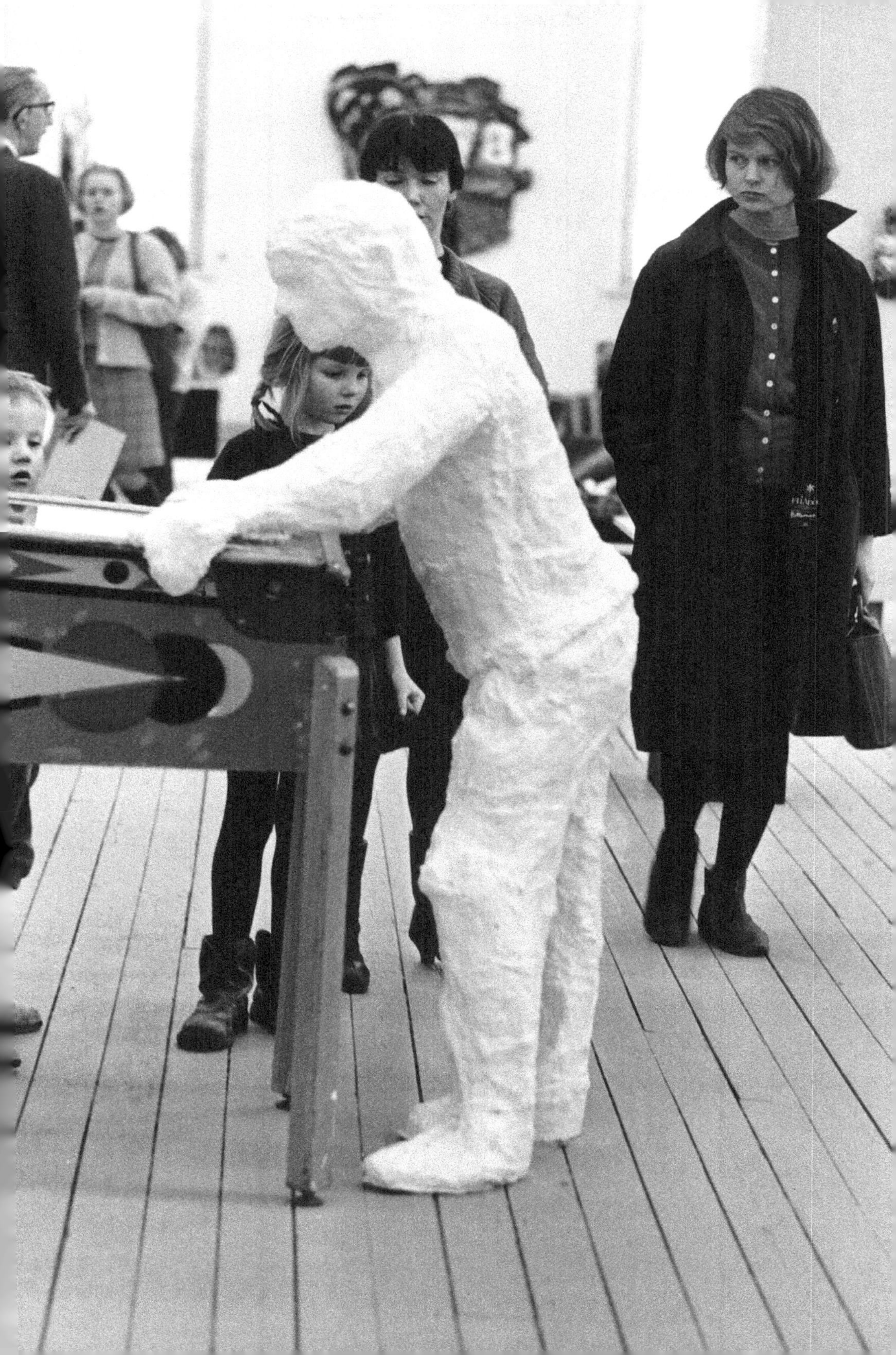

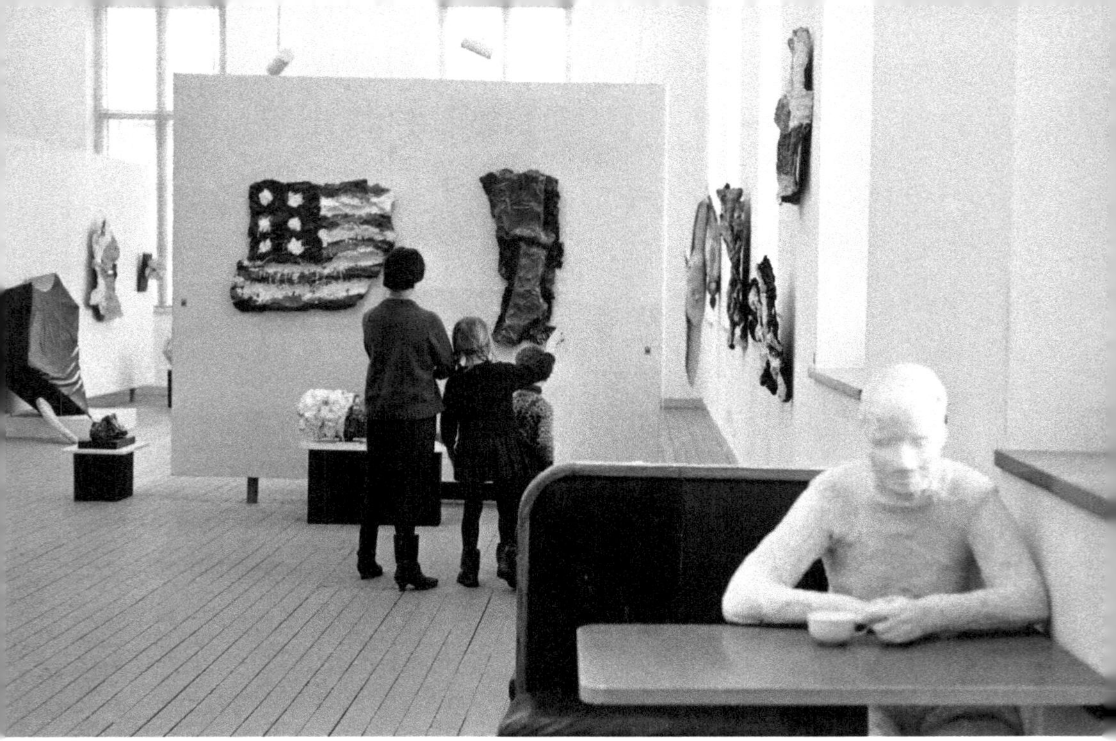

Figure 4.3: George Segal, *Woman in Restaurant Booth*, 1961. Pieces by Claes Oldenburg, in front *Ice Cream Cone,* 1962, a loan from Ileana Sonnabend.

Figure 4.4: *American Pop Art: 106 Forms of Love and Despair*, Moderna Museet, 1964.

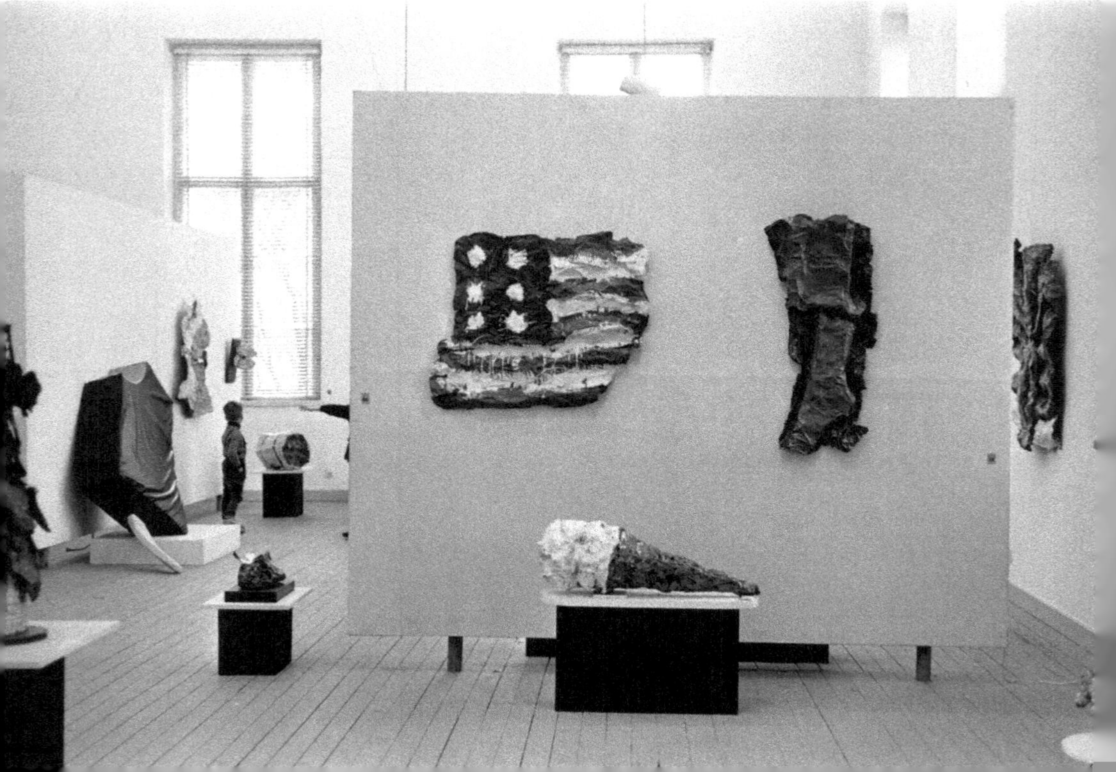

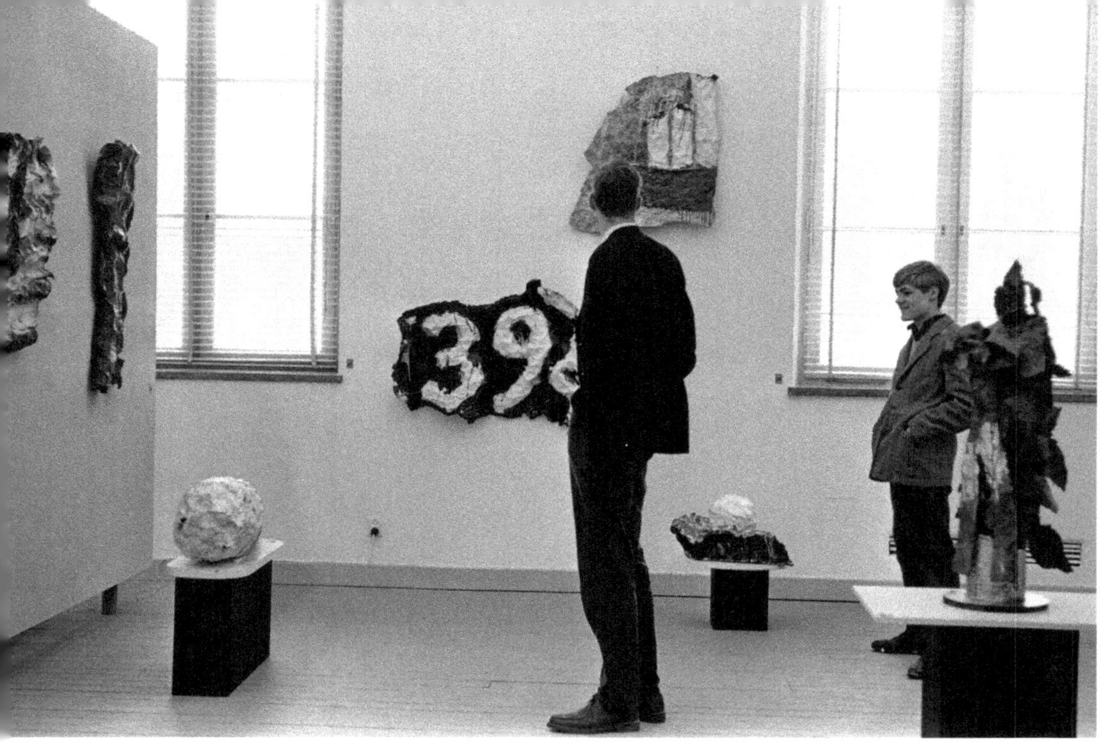

Figure 4.5: *American Pop Art: 106 Forms of Love and Despair*, Moderna Museet, 1964. Works by Claes Oldenburg.

Figure 4.6: George Segal, *Man on a Bicycle*, 1961 and James Rosenquist, *Capillary Action No 11*, 1963.

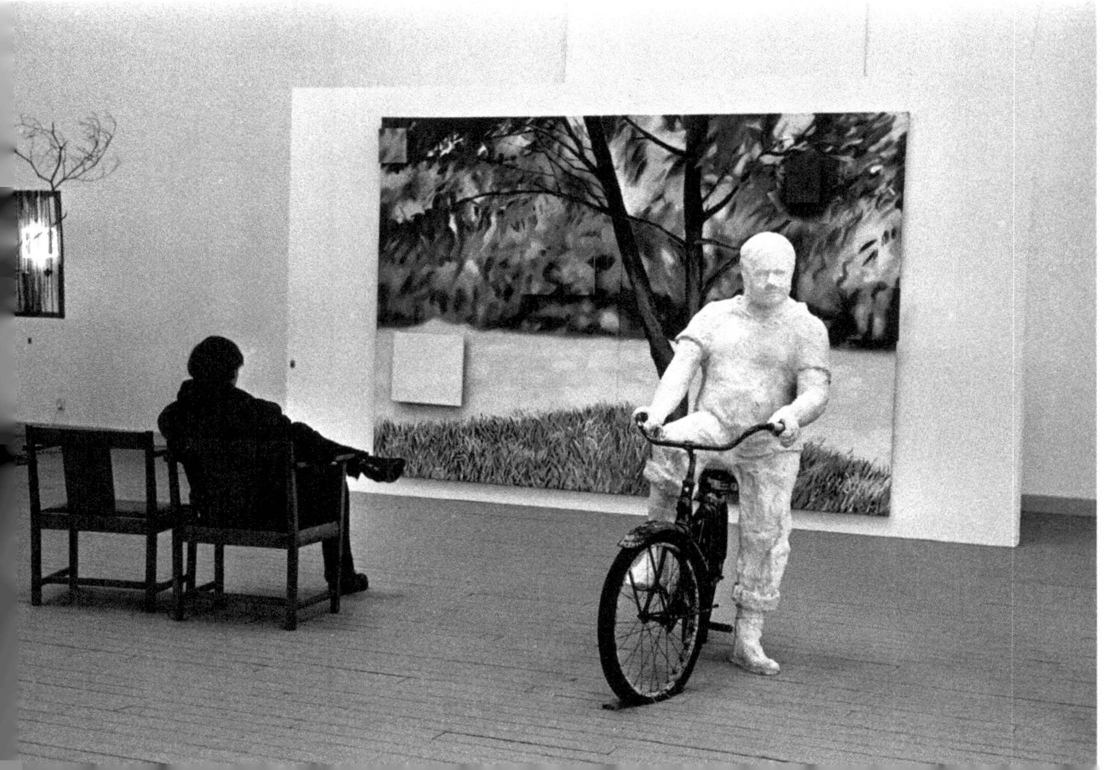

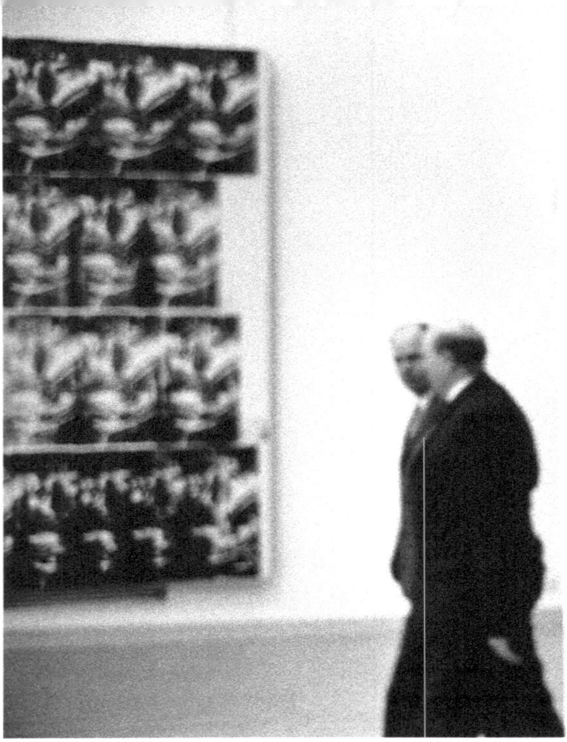

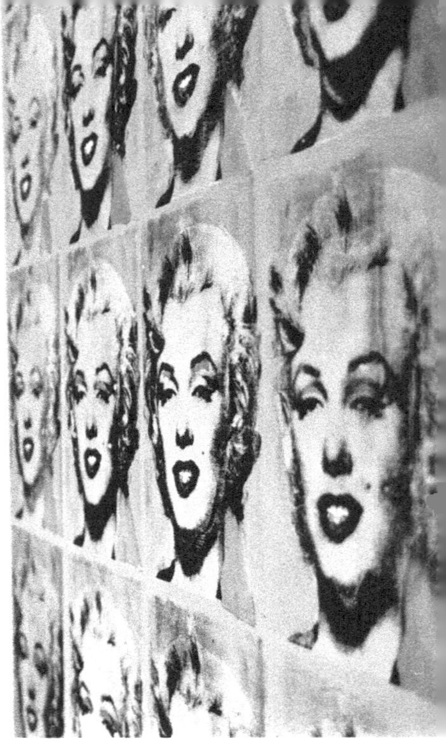

Figure 4.7 and 4.8: *American Pop Art: 106 Forms of Love and Despair*, Moderna Museet, 1964.

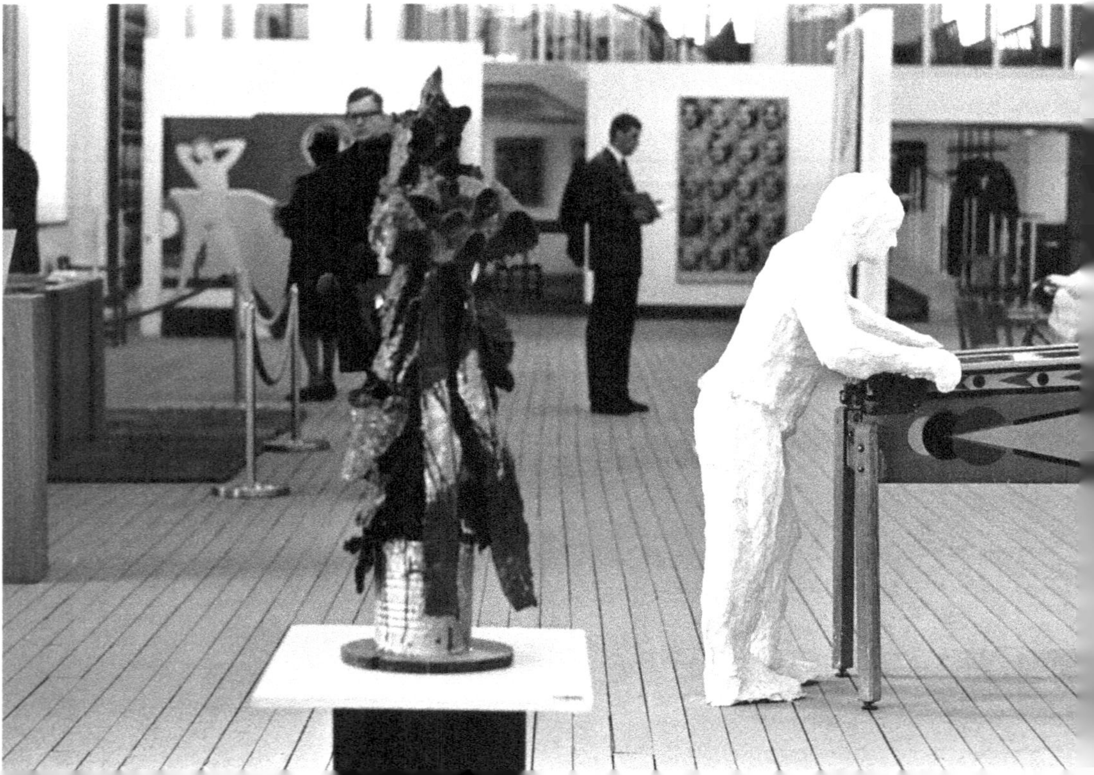

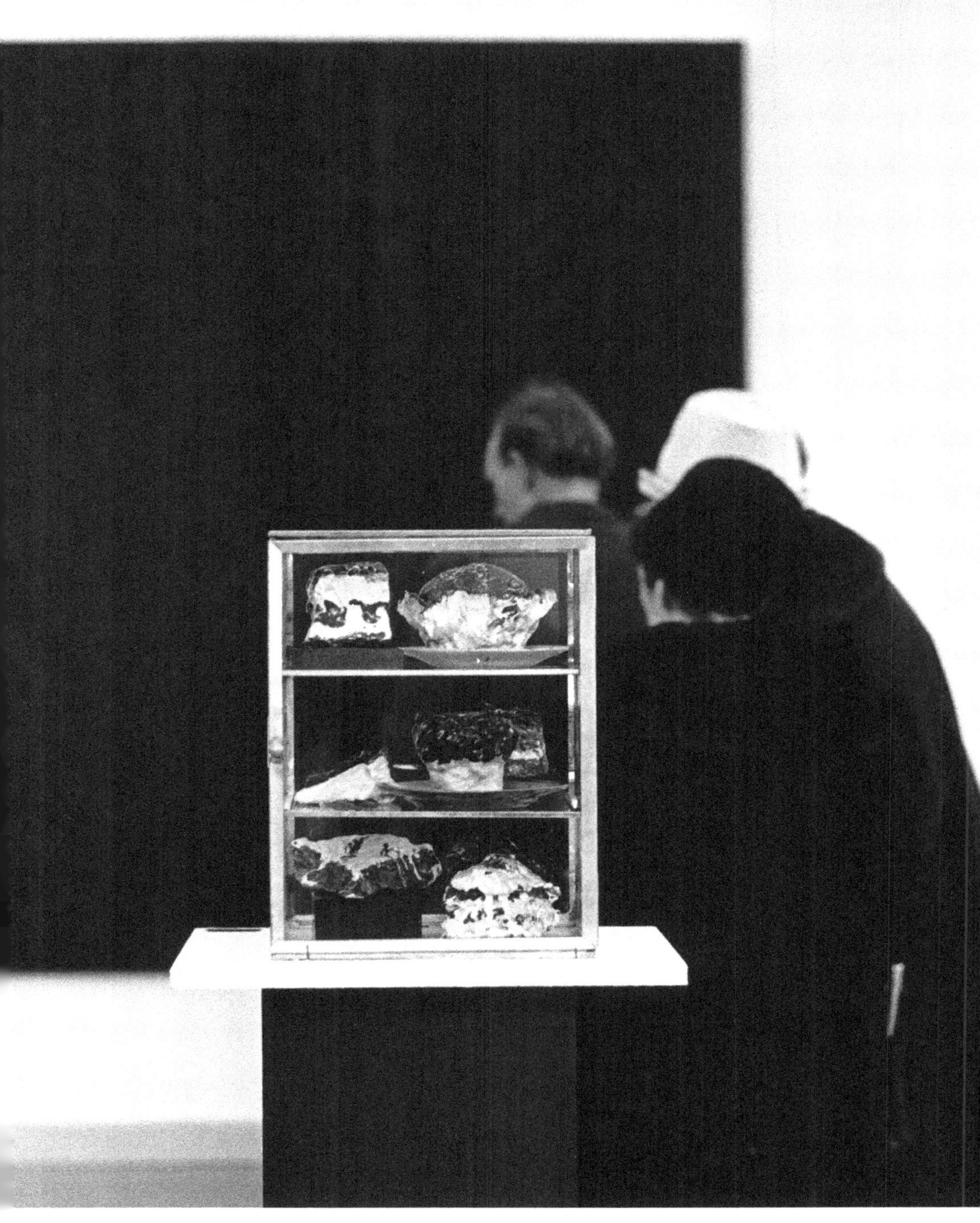

Figure 4.9: Claes Oldenburg, *Pastry Case*, 1961. *American Pop Art: 106 Forms of Love and Despair*, Moderna Museet, 1964.

All images from Moderna Museet. © Stig T Karlsson/Malmö Museer.

5
Pop Art at the Frontline of the Cold War
René Block's "Capitalist Realism" in 1960s West Berlin

Hannah Abdullah

On the 21st of November 1964 the first Pop Art exhibition in Germany, *New Realists & Pop Art*, opened at the Akademie der Künste in West Berlin with a "scandal." Protesting the absence of German artists from the show, the young gallerist René Block had initiated a spectacle. The newspaper *Der Tagesspiegel* reports on the events of the afternoon: "There were two young people wearing gasmasks, handing out flyers and carrying posters that quizzed visitors on how many German realists were missing from the show."[1] One of the protestors who Block had commissioned to stand by the Academy's entrance had a poster strapped to his back that advertised "new German realists at Gallery Block."[2] On his front, he wore a poster for Gerhard Richter's first solo-exhibition at Gallery Block and in West Berlin, *Images of Capitalist Realism.*

Block's protest was neither an outpouring of nationalist sentiments, nor was it directed against the artistic positions on display at the Akademie der

[1] Heinz Ohff, "Eine liberale Generation? Ausstellung von Gerhard Richter," in Eckhard Haack and Lothar C. Poll (eds.), *Schreiben für die Kunst. Lesebuch Heinz Off – Kunstkritik, Literatur, Feuilleton,* Berlin: InfoPress, 2007, p. 99.

[2] Gerhard Richter, "Brief an Heiner Friedrich, 23.11.1964," in Dietmar Elger and Hans-Ulrich Obrist (eds.), *Gerhard Richter: Text 1961 bis 2007 – Schriften, Interviews, Briefe,* Cologne: Buchhandlung Walther König, 2008, p. 26.

Künste. As *Der Tagesspiegel* observed, the spectacle was very much "in keeping with the Pop Art style."[3] Rather, Block, who had opened his gallery in Berlin-Schöneberg two months earlier at the age of twenty-two, was developing a gallery programme that represented artists of his generation working in the Federal Republic of Germany. Considering his gallery "a sort of correcting tool [...] that I [Block] wanted to use for this generation of German artists,"[4] he was calling for a broader perspective on pop and the new realism of the early 1960s that looked beyond the international art centres New York, London and Paris to include its manifestations in Germany.[5] With his gallery's inaugural exhibition *Neodada, Pop, Decollage, Capitalist Realism* one month earlier (16 September–5 November, 1964), Block had provided a first overview of parallel developments in West Germany. The show included ten artists, among them Gerhard Richter, Konrad Lueg, and Sigmar Polke from Düsseldorf, and K.P. Brehmer, Karl Horst Hödicke and Wolf Vostell, who were—or would soon be—based in West Berlin.

Whilst the labels "neodada," "pop" and "décollage" were internationally used to describe the new realist trends, "capitalist realism" was a slogan that had been coined by Richter one year earlier to promote the German version of Pop Art that he was developing alongside Lueg and Polke in Düsseldorf, including the happening *Living with Pop: A Demonstration for Capitalist Realism* at the Berges furniture store.[6] In its original Düsseldorf context the slogan capitalist realism was thus established as part of the pop vocabulary.[7] Eager to associate his work with the recently successful U.S.-American Pop Artists, Richter launched a pop gesture at home that thematised the increasingly Americanised domestic culture of the post-

[3] Ohff, 2007, p. 99.

[4] Block in Günter Herzog, "René Block im Gespräch mit Günter Herzog am 25.11.2008," *sediment*, 16, 2009, p. 11.

[5] Earlier versions of the exhibition *New Realists & Pop Art* at the Gemeentemuseum in Den Haag, where the title was *New Realism* (24 June–30 August 1964), and at the Museum des 20 Jahrhunderts in Vienna, where the title was *Pop Etc: Exhibition of Pop Art*, included local artistic positions.

[6] Gerhard Richter, "Brief an die Neue Deutsche Wochenschau 29.4.1963," Elger and Obrist, 2008, pp. 16–17.

[7] Jürgen Harten, "Der romantische Wille zur Macht," in Harten (ed.), *Gerhard Richter: Bilder 1962–1985*, exh. cat., Städtische Kunstalle Düsseldorf (18 January–13 March 1986), Cologne: DuMont, 1986, p. 16.

war West German *Wohlstandsgesellschaft* [affluent society]. In keeping with the blasé attitude of his American colleagues, he saw the slogan's political references to Socialist Realism as nothing more than a playful provocation, which he "could use [...] without taking it too seriously."[8] However, when Block adapted the term for the inaugural exhibition of his West Berlin gallery it took on a very different life and meaning. Block had no intention of aligning the new realism he supported with the blasé attitude of American Pop Art. Instead, he considered it a new art form that could effectively contribute to the positive transformation of the everyday social reality it portrayed. By capitalising the ironic catchphrase, he turned it into a label for a politically and socially engaged avant-garde that included, according to his definition, not only the Düsseldorf group but also the artists Brehmer, Hödicke and Vostell with their more overtly political work.

Block's curatorial programme for a political realism is clearly spelled out in his book, *Die Grafik des Kapitalistischen Realismus* (*The Graphics of Capitalist Realism*) from 1971, in which he tells the story of the beginning and end of the Capitalist Realism that he established in West Berlin during the 1960s.[9] What is perhaps most striking about the book is that whilst its frontispiece is an illustration of Richard Hamilton's classic pop collage *Just What Is it That Makes Today's Homes So Different, So Appealing?* (1956), the images and texts that follow broaden the history of 1960s Pop Art to socialist Eastern Europe. In a fourteen-page image sequence, Block compares the works of his artists with those of the official artists of the Soviet Union and the German Democratic Republic (GDR). Unlike Richter, who downplayed the parallels between his concept of "capitalist realism" and Socialist Realism, Block looked across the Berlin Wall to politically charge the new artistic movement that he had proclaimed. The question that arises when confronted with Block's book is, whether he was seriously proposing a western parallel or alternative to East Bloc Socialist Realism; and,

[8] Richter in Coosje van Bruggen, "Gerhard Richter: Painting as a Moral Act," *Art Forum*, May 1985, p. 84

[9] René Block, *Die Grafik des Kapitalistischen Realismus:* Berlin: Edition René Block, 1971. The publication appeared in an edition of 3000. Of these, 120 copies contained original graphic works by the artists, see Stefan Strsembski, *Kapitalistischer Realismus: Objekt und Kritik in der Kunst der 60er Jahre,* Hamburg: Verlag Dr. Kovac, 2010, p. 116.

if so, what this proposition entailed artistically and politically. In the following I will address this question by looking specifically at how Block's location in West Berlin affected his curatorial practice as well as the central role graphic art played in his Capitalist Realist gallery program.

"*Wüste Westberlin*" – Desert West Berlin

In stark contrast to today's Berlin, the West Berlin of the early 1960s was a cultural desert that hardly offered any spaces for young, emerging artists to exhibit.[10] The former German capital was still recovering from the physical destruction of World War II and the eradication of its cultural and intellectual elite by the Nazis. From being one of the world's leading art centres during the Weimar period, it had moved to the periphery and insignificance. Its geographical and economic situation as an island surrounded by socialist East Germany, kept alive by subsidies, had made it an isolated outpost of the new Federal Republic and its efforts to catch up with the economic and cultural development of the western ally countries. The Rhineland cities Düsseldorf and Cologne—both within easy reach of Paris—had become the new artistic centres of the Federal Republic. One of the first attempts to reinvigorate West Berlin's contemporary art scene was the postwar reopening of the earlier-mentioned Akademie der Künste in 1954. Together with the Haus am Waldsee in Berlin-Zehlendorf, it was the only public institution in the city that informed about contemporary artistic trends in and outside of Berlin. Other public institutions dedicated to contemporary art, such as the Neue Nationalgalerie, the Neuer Berliner Kunstverein (NBK) and the Neue Gesellschaft für Bildende Kunst (NGBK), did not open up until 1968/69.[11]

But the exceptional situation of Berlin exerted a strong attraction on young creative and politically minded people. Although unproductive and poor, the city had "a certain sparkle" and was "full of people who—in dark

[10] See the documentary film *Wüste Westberlin* (*Desert West Berlin*), director Helmut Wietz, Germany, 1995.

[11] For a structural analysis of art institutions in West Berlin in the early 1970s, see Christos M. Joachimides, "Versuch einer Sturkturanalyse der Situation der Bildenden Kunst in Berlin," in *Szene Berlin, Mai '72*, exh. cat., Würtembergischer Kunstverein (26 May–18 June 1972), Stuttgart 1972, n.p.

side streets—energetically dreamt of a life that the Federal Republic did not know."[12] Whilst the city's demilitarisation attracted draft resisters, the cutback in economic activity led to a drop in rents that drew artists looking for studios in central locations. In an essay on the West Berlin art scene of the period, Christos M. Joachimides observes, that the city gradually became "a sort of haven for all sorts of restless 'fugitives' to circulate and propagate their imaginative, utopian, political, anarchic, and mystic propositions."[13] The artists who moved to Berlin did not expect a quick career or a flourishing market, but instead "a lot of space and time for a 'different life'."[14] The latter slogan soon replaced the call for "a different art" from the 1950s and translated into the demand to end the post-war escape into abstraction and to engage with reality.[15] For young artists working in the city, such as Karl Horst Hödicke—who was later represented by Block –, abstract art coming out of the Rhineland, including ZERO and Tachism, had "nothing to do with Berlin, where the rubble was still lying on the streets, whilst the Rhineland had already been redesigned in the style of Knoll international."[16] Like Hödicke, many artists based in West Berlin felt a strong urge to address the memory of the Nazi past and the tensions of the Cold War, which could be felt acutely in the city.

A handful of galleries that were founded in the year 1963/64 provided the public platform for these new artistic impulses. The individuals who ran these grassroots spaces did not only take on the role of gallerists and dealers, but they also actively shaped the city's artistic discourse. As Joachimides observes:

[12] Richard Hey, "West-Berliner Exil," *Frankfurter Rundschau*, 7 April 1984.

[13] Christos M. Joachimides, "The Strain of Reality: West Berlin and the Visual Arts, 1963–78," in *13°E: Eleven Artists Working in Berlin*, exh. cat., Whitechapel Gallery (10 November–22 December 1978), London: Whitechapel Gallery, 1978, p. 7.

[14] Eckhardt Gillen, "Gruppenbild ohne Dame," Gillen (ed.), *Grossgörschen 35: Aufbruch zur Kunststadt Berlin 1964*, exh. cat., Haus am Kleist Park (6 June–10 August 2014), Berlin: Kunststiftung Poll, 2014, p. 10.

[15] Although individual artists based in West Berlin, such as Hann Trier and Fred Thieler, counted among the better-known post-war German artists that turned to abstraction in the 1950s, the style never sparked a larger movement among the city's artists who were still attached to the legacy of Expressionism.

[16] Hödicke quoted in Gillen, 2014, p. 10.

> In all these galleries, discussions about art took place which emphatically contradicted all that then counted as art in Berlin [...] An atmosphere of conspiracy and of preparation for an "attack" on established cultural values prevailed. The shared experience of the "conspiracy" between the artists and their promoters, the gallery-owners, created that personal bond of friendship that overrode their different roles and made both "accomplices" in a new artistic understanding.[17]

The first of the new galleries to open was Gallery Werner & Katz on Kurfürstendamm in October 1963. Its inaugural exhibition was a solo-exhibition by Georg Baselitz that showed the paintings *The Big Night Down The Drain* (1962–63) and *Naked Man* (1962). Baselitz's attack on the generation of the "fascist father" through the display of genitals and other vulgarities was the prelude to the politicisation of this generational conflict in the following years.[18] A driving force in this process was Gallery Block, which opened in the subsequent year.[19] Block himself had moved to West Berlin in 1962 after studying glass painting at the Werkschule in Krefeld, where he first met K.P. Brehmer.[20] Giving expression to the social-political ambitiousness of his gallery programme, he declared his gallery a "*moralische Anstalt*" ("moral institution") that critically reflected German history and the functioning of late capitalist society.[21] Soon Gallery Block became the meeting point for those who wanted to revive Berlin's Dada heritage, including its conceptual, actionist and agitational approaches, attracting not only artists from West Berlin, but also others parts of the Federal Republic.

[17] Joachimides, 1978, p. 7.

[18] Tom Holert, "Bei sich, über allem: Der symptomatische Baselitz," *Texte zur Kunst*, 9 (March), 1993, pp. 87–102.

[19] Other important West Berlin galleries from this period were Christian Chruxin's Situation 60 Galerie for visual poetry in Berlin-Schöneberg and Dieter Ruckhaberle's Freie Galerie on Kurfürstenstrasse, both of which opened in 1963, as well as the Berlin-Kreuzberg artist-cooperative Großgörschen 35 which opened in July 1964.

[20] Following the completion of his degree, Block debated whether to move to Paris or Amsterdam. Eventually he accepted Brehmer's invitation to join him on a trip to Berlin and stayed in the city to live there. See René Block, "Die frühen Jahre: René Block," *Kunstforum*, 104, 1989, p. 254.

[21] Block, 1971, p. 15.

A gallery as "Moral Institution"

For Block, the decision to focus his exhibition programme on contemporary art from Germany came with the moral responsibility to confront Germany's problematic past and present: National Socialism and the Holocaust, and the country's post-war division. In September 1965, on the occasion of his gallery's first anniversary, he showed the group exhibition *Hommage à Berlin: Paintings, Drawings, Prints* (Figure 5.1) which constituted "an important early stimulus for social involvement in the arts."[22] Critics discussed the show as "cheeky, funny, and then again very serious."[23] The newspaper *Die Welt* considered it "not a declaration of love to Berlin, […] but rather a stock-taking" of the city's situation at the frontline of the Cold War.[24] In his opening speech, the poet Peter Otto Chotjewitz described the show as deconstructing "prejudices, clichés and wrong impressions" about the city.[25] In contrast to the many contemporary documentaries about the Berlin Wall, which intended to arouse sentiments of "sorrow and disgust," the artworks on display posed the crucial question of "complicity and guilt."

Amongst the fourteen artists in the exhibition was also the group of six that Block later unified under the label Capitalist Realism. However, when one examines the group's contributions, a contrast emerges between the "harmless clichés or random motifs" of the three Düsseldorf artists, Konrad Lueg, Sigmar Polke and Gerhard Richter, and the aggressive visualisations of Cold War military violence by Wolf Vostell and K.P. Brehmer.[26] Lueg's *Gummi-Bild* (1965), a grid of gummy bears that invokes Berlin's coat of arms, and Polke's "raster dot" representation of a jelly doughnut, *Berliner* (1965), humorously reduce the city to objects of consumer culture. Although Richter's contribution departs from Lueg and Polke's more conventional pop idiom, his photo-paintings *Rococo Table* (1965) and *Small Car Park* (1965) also rely on objects of material culture

[22] Joachimides, 1978, p. 19.
[23] Heinz Ohff, "Liebeslied an eine spröde Geliebte," *Der Tagesspiegel*, 6097, 1965, p. 5.
[24] Quoted in Björn Egging, *Von Pop zu Politik: Studien zur Entwicklung der politisch engagierten Kunst KP Brehmers*, PhD Thesis, Universität Hamburg, 2003, p. 61 (http://ediss.sub.uni-hamburg.de/volltexte/2004/2236/pdf/Dissertation.pdf).
[25] Ibid.
[26] Björn Egging, "Einführung," in Egging (ed.), *Kapitalistischer Realismus: Grafik aus der Sammlung Block*, Bielefeld: Kerber Art, 2010, p. 15.

to play at Berlin's political-historical geography. Whilst the first painting shows a table from Charlottenburg Castle, the only royal residence in Berlin to survive the bombings of 1945, the second shows a row of cars parked by the city's Victory Column. Originally erected at Platz der Republik as a monument to Germany's victory in the Franco-Prussian war in 1873, the Nazis relocated the monument to its present site at Großer Stern (a major intersection on the city's East–West axes) in 1939. Yet, in Richter's painting, the monument is barely visible and appears more as a chance background in a snapshot of the latest innovations in the German car industry.

In contrast to the humorous and highly subtle works of the Düsseldorf artists, Vostell's collage *Hommage à Peter Fechter*, a critical commentary on the victims of the Berlin Wall border guards, added "a somber tone" to the show, as critic Heinz Ohff put it.[27] Similarly, Brehmer's piece, which doubled the exhibition title and which is part of his postcard series *Ansichtskarten* (1965), directly referenced the political situation of the divided city. The work consists of three postcards designed in the colours of the German flag: the first shows the checkpoint at Brandenburg Gate before the construction of the Wall; the second is titled "Shoot at Berlin Clichés" and shows a rifle case and eight targets that are covered with photographs of barbed wire, a policeman, a man shot dead, and other symbols of Cold War violence and politics; the third is a picture of an unknown soldier in a loophole pointing his gun.

Block's own vision of his gallery as a "moral institution" was no doubt closer to Vostell and Brehmer's more overtly political art. Two years after *Hommage à Berlin*, he organised the group show *Hommage à Lidice*, in which he did not only address Germany's troubled Nazi past and the question of collective guilt, but he also tried to initiate a cultural dialogue between Cold War eastern and western Europe. On the occasion of the twenty-fifth anniversary of the massacre of Lidice by Nazi troops, Block called upon his artists to donate works for a planned museum in the reconstructed town. The twenty-one works that were assembled (among them Richter's *Uncle Rudi*, 1965) were first exhibited at Gallery Block in West Berlin (22 October–19 November, 1967) and then in July 1968 at

[27] Heinz Ohff, 1965, p. 5.

Gallery Spála in Prague. Block used the window of opportunity that had opened with the Prague Spring and the political liberalisation of Czechoslovakia to transport the works to Prague in his Volkswagen minibus. However, during the violent crushing of the reform movement by Warsaw Pact troops and the political unrest that followed, the artworks went missing.[28]

The Graphics of Capitalist Realism (1971)

During the first four years of his gallery programme, Block only used the label Capitalist Realism for the works of Gerhard Richter, Sigmar Polke and Konrad Lueg. By 1968 this had changed.[29] With the expansion of the label to include the art of K.P. Brehmer, Karl Horst Hödicke and Wolf Vostell, Block gave it a more political direction than in its original Düsseldorf context. For the cover image of his book *The Graphics of Capitalist Realism* (1971), he chose Vostell's "object-graphic" *B52* (1968, Figure 5.2),[30] which is part of an anti-war series of prints that Vostell produced following his New York happening-manifesto from March 1966, in which he called upon American troops to drop western consumer goods, not bombs, on Vietnam:

> Chicken, shoe laces, chewing-gum, tomato paste, hamburgers, bagels, Coca Cola, safety pins, Beatles records, popcorn, cream pie, screwdrivers, rubbers, 4711, bras, sock holders, Kleenex, Polaroid cameras, zippers, jam, New-York-Times-Weekend editions, lipsticks [...].[31]

[28] It was only in 1996, when Block returned to the Czech Republic, that the works were recovered and officially handed over to the city of Lidice. The collection of works donated was expanded by 32 contributions from contemporary artists. See René Block, "Auf einer Reise nach Prag am 19. Januar 1997," in *Pro Lidice. 52 Künstler aus Deutschland*, exh. cat., České Muzeum Výtvarných Umění (9 March–6 April 1997), Prague: České Muzeum Výtvarných Umění, 1997, n.p.

[29] For a history of Block's use of the label Capitalist Realism, see Strsembski, 2010, pp. 83–128.

[30] Vostell defined his collages of prints and objects as "*Objektgrafiken*."

[31] Quoted in Block, 1971, p. 21.

Vostell understood art primarily "as an instrument for social change and consciousness development."[32] Considering the "artistic treatment of destruction" an answer to the question of the social role of art, he had a preference for gruesome images that shocked the viewer and that dealt with the victims of war, executions and weapons.[33] Whilst the subtle irony of *B52* is unusual for Vostell's generally more antagonistic work, it reflects Block's ambiguous approach to the question of a political realism in his 1971 book.

Reviewing the book for the newspaper *Der Tagesspeigel*, the critic Heinz Ohff celebrated it as "one of the most idiosyncratic and insightful publications in the otherwise so banal art-book scene."[34] What made the book so original was its combination of scholarly art-historical documentation and provocative political content. One third of the book is taken up by a comprehensive catalogue raisonné of the print-works of six artists who Block had exhibited since the opening of his gallery in 1964: Lueg, Polke, Richter, Brehmer, Hödicke and Vostell. Compiled by the Hamburg-based art historian and graphic art connoisseur Carl Vogel, the catalogue contains detailed information on printing techniques and editions. By contrast, the book's introductory section, written by Block, is a retrospective manifesto for the critical realism these artists formulated. For Block, the book constituted "the final stroke to one chapter of a specific artistic uprising."[35]

Written in a tone that swings between a revolutionary programme for a political art and capitulation to the realities of advanced capitalism, the book opens with a two-page declaratory statement by Block that is titled *Mein letztes Wort (ich will hier nicht klären warum)*, "*My Last Word (here I don't want to explain why)*"; the latter phrase is repeated throughout the statement. The text recounts Block's discovery and support of the new artistic movement, which he identifies as "a period in mid-60s-art, to

[32] Hubertus Butin, "René Block and the 'Graphics of Capitalist Realism'," in Bernd Slutzky (ed.), *Grafik des Kapitalistischen Realismus,* Frankfurt: Galerie Bernd Slutzky, 1992, p. 38.
[33] Vostell quoted in "Von der Collage zur Assemblage," *Art Since Mid-Century: The New Internationalism, Vol. 2: Figurative Art,* Greenwich, Conn.: New York Graphic Society, 1977, p 323.
[34] Heinz Ohff, "Sich treu bleiben!," *Der Tagespiegel*, 20 February 1972.
[35] René Block, "Nachwort," in Egging (ed.), 2010, p. 33.

which I [Block] will continue to feel deeply committed."[36] What originally drew Block to the six artists featured in the book, was their concern with the contemporary social-political condition:

> I was fascinated by the ability of these artists to reveal the context, the political everyday, the social situation and its critique (yes and no) in their realist representations of objects.[37]

However, the dialectical presentation of reality that Block ascribes to the artists is coloured by his own political ideals. Whilst these seem to coincide with the politically charged art of Vostell and Brehmer (who abbreviated his first name Klaus Peter as K.P., alluding to the spelling of the Communist Party in German),[38] they are somewhat out-of-kilter with the work of the three Düsseldorfers. Block presents the pop idiom of the latter not as an ironic commentary on post-war consumer society, but as a western brand of socialist art that is made for the working classes. Whilst he introduces Lueg as "us[ing] the graphic forms of advertising to develop an understandable pictorial language," he suggests that Richter and Polke's paintings of family photographs and magazine images reflect "the world of the more-or-less working masses."[39]

The affinity between Block's position and that of Vostell and Brehmer was both the result of political like-mindedness and friendships that went back to the time before Block moved to West Berlin from the Rhineland.[40] Especially Vostell, who was ten years older than Block (and with Beuys, the central artistic figure in his gallery programme, already having attained an international standing), strongly influenced him.[41] But it was not only the influence of his immediate confidants that determined Block's political take on the new realism he was presenting in his gallery. His location in West Berlin and the proximity to the Berlin Wall and GDR also played a central role in the development of his curatorial practice and programming.

[36] Block, 1971, p. 30.
[37] Ibid.
[38] Egging, 2003, p. 3, Footnote 6.
[39] Block, 1971, p. 15.
[40] After meeting K.P. Brehmer at the Krefelder Werkschule in 1959 (see above), Block met Wolf Vostell around 1960 at art events in Düsseldorf (Strembski, 2010, p. 85).
[41] Strembski, 2010, p. 86.

By 1971, when Block published his book *The Graphics of Capitalist Realism*, the city's contemporary art scene was becoming more established and regaining international recognition. No longer under pressure to "catch up" with developments in the western art world, some of its leading figures began to look eastwards towards the other Berlin and Germany, which "constituted a reservoir of ideas and projection-screen."[42] Whilst a large part of the West German leftist intelligentsia projected their ideals onto the GDR, "as an example of a workable alternative to the comprised culture of capitalism,"[43] some, including Block, dreamt of a better "capitalist socialism" in the West.[44] With his Capitalist Realist curatorial program, Block did not, like Richter, sidestep the comparison with Socialist Realism, but he addressed it head-on. Halfway through his statement *My Last Word,* Block inserted a fourteen-page image sequence that compares his artists' works with those of official artists from the GDR and Soviet Union. The works from East and West are paired on double-pages and according to a number of themes: coming-to-terms-with the Nazi past (Willi Sitte, *Survivors,* 1963, and Brehmer, *Example of Coming-To-Terms-With the Past, Hitler Overprint*, 1967/69); the Vietnam War (Frank Zander, *Mr. Smith in Vietnam* [five panels: *Mr. Smith Marks Bombs, The Smiths in Action*, *Mr. Smith*, *Mr. Smith Leaves a Foreign Country*, *Death in the Sea*], ? and Vostell, *B52* [serigraph], 1968); sports (Willi Sitte, *High Diving*, 1964 and Richter, *Diving*, 1965; Harry Blume, *Peace Cyclists*, 1963, and Lueg, *Boxer*, 1964); the collective (Janis Osis, *We*, 1964, and Polke, *Crowd II,* 1969); and male camaraderie and strength (Paul Pedak, *Conquerors of Winter*, 1963, and Richter, *Sailors*, 1966).

As Stefan Strsembski has observed, the comparative method of presentation that Block used for the image-sequence is part of the standard repertoire of art publishing and art historical scholarship since classical modernism, when it was first systematised by the formalist art historian

[42] Lothar C. Poll, "Die Krokodile waren wider da," in Gillen, 2014, p. 5.
[43] Debbie Lewer, "Introduction: Art and Cultural Politics in the German Democratic Republic," *Art in Translation*, 5 (3), p. 6. For a more detailed discussion of the relationship of West German leftist intellectuals to the GDR, see Andreas Huyssen, "After the Wall: The Failure of German Intellectuals," *New German Critique*, 52, Special Issue on the German Unification, 1991, pp. 109–143.
[44] Block in an interview with the author, 28 July 2014.

Heinrich Wölfflin.[45] Block enhanced the didactic effect of this form of presentation by placing extracts from writings and treatise on the social-political role of art under the illustrations as captions. Some quotes are by the featured artists and others by historical figures from the left and right: Berthold Brecht, Walter Ulbricht, Wilhelm II (the last German Kaiser), Heinrich Mann, Carlo Schermann, Ernesto Che Guevara, and an extract from the Second Bitterfeld Conference of 1964, during which East German artists and cultural officials redefined the role of art in socialism. It is hard to tell whether the didacticism of Block's comparative presentation and its echoing of the moralising rhetoric of GDR cultural politics, was meant seriously, or, whether it was merely an iconic gesture that was in part also driven by the aesthetic pleasure of arranging images.

The book no doubt constituted a provocation at the time of its publication. Although West Germany's chancellor Willy Brand had embarked on a new "*Ostpolitik*" (the foreign policy of detente with the communist bloc) that was geared towards normalising relations with the GDR under the slogan "change through rapprochement" in 1969, a strong cultural and ideological divide between the two Germanies prevailed. Still in 1973, two years after the publication of Block's book, the inclusion of artists from the GDR at *documenta* 6 in Kassel caused a storm of public protest in the Federal Republic.[46] Especially artists who had fled the GDR, including Georg Baselitz and Markus Lüpertz, refused to exhibit alongside East German official artists who were supported by the Socialist Unity Party (SED) regime. When considering these Cold War tension and the cultural trench warfare between East and West Germany, the artistic and political motivations behind Block's comparison of Capitalist and Socialist Realism become all the more significant. Was he trying to survey a common political-artistic project that unified artists in East and West? Or, was he, as Ohff asked in his review of the book, trying to elevate one form of realism over another: "what could be more social-critical and socialist: the 'socialist' or this 'capitalist' representation of reality?"[47]

[45] Strsembski, 2010, p. 119

[46] The East German artists included in *documenta 6* were the painters Bernhard Heisig, Werner Tübke, Wolfgang Mattheuer and Willi Sitte, and the sculptors Fritz Cremer and Jo Jastram.

[47] Ohff, 1972.

Steeped in ambivalence through the repetition of the phrase "here I don't want to explain why," Block's statement *My Last Word* provides no clear answers to these questions. Yet, the pairing of works from East and West by themes such as the Vietnam War and Nazi violence, suggests an attempt to highlight a shared German-German political art and a common effort to deal with the country's troubled past. The art historian Eckhart Gillen, a proponent of this interpretation, has argued that Block's direct confrontation of Capitalist Realism with its socialist counterpart constituted "a plea to his artists not to loose sight of their political commitment."[48] Indeed, this reading seems plausible when considering Block's final remark in *My Last Word*: "[T]oday I [Block] realise that, if Capitalist Realism had taken its 'partisanship' with the masses truly serious, it would have had to become a socialist Realism."[49] This sense of surrender is further enhanced by Block description of his artists' work at the time of writing:

> Since 1968 Konrad Lueg doesn't produce anymore (here I don't want to explain why). Polke and Hödicke mainly engage with aesthetic processes (here I don't want to explain why), Richter escapes into "fine arts" (here I don't want to explain why), Vostell publishes ideas and increasingly less includes the audience in his work (here I don't want to explain why), Brehmer dreams of a life as a functionary.[50]

That said, when Block's pairings of works from East and West are examined more closely, the impression of unity-by-theme is broken up by a noticeable difference in style. The academism of the works from the East Bloc (painting on canvas, expressionist brushstrokes, naturalism, and narrative history painting) appears starkly conservative and out-dated when seen next to the innovative visual languages of the western-based artists, who in varying ways engage with the iconography and techniques of reproduction of the modern mass media. This aesthetic difference between the works from East and West is further accentuated by the fact that Block's book, as the title suggests, is dedicated to graphic art. He presents

[48] Eckhart Gillen, "Is Capitalist Realism in Fact a Socialist Realism?," in *Living with Pop: A Restrospective of Capitalist Realism*, exh. cat., Kunsthalle Düsseldorf (21 July–29 September 2013), Cologne: Buchhandlung Walther König, 2013, p. 143.
[49] Block, 1971, p. 30.
[50] Ibid.

the medium not only in terms of its formal and technological innovations, but also in terms of its contemporary political significance.

Graphic arts and the democratisation of art

It was surely no coincidence that Block, one of the pioneers of editioned and multiple art in the 1960s, chose to dedicate his gallery's first catalogue raisonné to graphic art.[51] Already in 1968 he had published the editioned print portfolio *The Graphics of Capitalist Realism*, which contained one print by each of the six artists who also featured in the later book of the same name.[52] By including a reproduction of the portfolio in the 1971 book (as a kind of visual prologue), Block established the two projects as a sequel. An ironic adaptation of a brandy advertisement that he included in both, the portfolio and the book, playfully addresses controversies around contemporary graphic art and the refusal of the traditional art establishment to recognise the artistic adaptation of photomechanical printing techniques as relevant and eligible (Figure 5.3). The image shows an elegantly dressed man marvelling at a collection of duelling swords in an aristocratic residence. The caption reads: "A touch of Mastery…The Graphics of Capitalist Realism." In small print, the graphic art of Capitalist Realism is ironically advertised by reference to traditional criteria of artistic value and quality, including "beauty," "originality," "master piece," and "connoisseurship."

The two projects, published under the title *The Graphics of Capitalist Realism*, are examples of the close link between innovations in editioned art around 1968 and the cultural intelligentsia's search for a new relationship between art and society. As Hubertus Butin has suggested, on a

[51] Prior to opening his gallery, Block was director of the graphic cabinet of the Freie Galerie of Dieter Ruckhaberle, see Günter Herzog, "Ganz am Anfang/ How it all began," *sediment*, 7, 2004, p. 16.

[52] The portfolio was printed in an edition of 80 and 40 additional sheets were circulated *hors de commerce*. Other important editioned works that Block presented in the following years were *Rollschrank En Bloc*, 1969/70, which contained objects by 18 artists and was distributed in an edition of 20; *Weekend*, 1971/72, a suitcase that contained one ready-made and eighteen graphic works by seven artists, distributed in an edition of 25; and Richard Hamilton's *The Critic Laughs*, 1971, which Block produced in close collaboration with the artist, see René Block, "Notes as to Purpose, Set-up and Selection of the Exhibition," in Block (ed.), *Multiples: An Attempt to Present the Development of the Object Edition*, exh. cat., Neuer Berliner Kunstverein (8 May–15 June 1974), Berlin: Neuer Berliner Kunstverein 1974, pp. 10-24.

political level editioned art corresponded with the call for the democratisation of art, which the West German left understood in terms of Walter Benjamin's essay *The Work of Art in the Age of Mechanical Reproduction*, as the reproduction of works to increase their dissemination and impact.[53] In Block's gallery, no artist was more concerned with the democratisation of art through techniques of reproduction than K.P. Brehmer, whose prints take up almost half the catalogue raissonné included in *The Graphics of Capitalist Realism* (1971). By experimenting with the visual language of the mass media and mass media formats, such as postcards and posters, Brehmer hoped to formulate a new category of work: the "original in mass reproduction."[54] The photomechanical printing techniques that he began to use following his return to his hometown West Berlin in 1964 permitted the endless reproduction of works and turned the distinction between the original and its copy into a matter of mere definition. Brehmer's undermining of this distinction probably reached its peak in a sales-portfolio of his work published and distributed by Gallery Block in 1967.[55] Besides the price list, the portfolio contained promotional images of the sheets and postcards that could be ordered. However, the reproductions used for promotional purposes were from the same print run as the "original" artworks; a trick that facilitated a conceptual play with the notion of originality whilst also substantially reducing the work's production costs.

Whereas some advocates of multiple art, such as Daniel Spoerri at Multiplication d'Art Transformable (MAT) in Paris, produced series consisting of unique works that entailed minimal variations, the above is one example of how Block strictly adhered to the principle of serial production and the creation of identical works in his gallery program.[56] The goal underlying this principled position was to challenge the economics of the art market and to democratise art in a way that was only possible in the

[53] Butin, 1992, p. 34. On the rediscovery of Walter Benjamin's writings in 1960s West Germany and how Marxist readings of Benjamin influenced the West German reception of Pop Art, see Andreas Huyssen, "The Cultural Politics of Pop: Reception and Critique of US Pop Art in the Federal Republic of Germany," *New German Critique*, 4, 1975, pp. 77-97.

[54] Egging, 2003, pp. 45-61.

[55] Egging, 2003, p. 57.

[56] Butin, 1992, p. 34.

capitalist system. By supporting innovative experiments in editioned formats, Block strove towards the large-scale dissemination of artistic work that was financially affordable. In fact, one could argue that Block's Capitalist Realist gallery programme was not limited to the art he presented, but that it extended to his very own mode of running and managing his gallery.

Yet, at the same time, when examining Block's support of editioned formats it is important not to overlook that by the late 1960s the slogan "art for everybody" did not only stand for social commitment, but that it was also closely intertwined with the expansion of the contemporary art market.[57] In the same year that Block prepared the print portfolio *The Graphics of Capitalist Realism* (1968), he became a member of the group Progressive German Art Dealers (*Verein progressiver deutscher Kunsthändler*), which founded the world's first contemporary art fair in Cologne in 1967—the *Kölner Kunstmarkt*—presenting contemporary art as a commodity and attracting new groups and classes of buyers.[58] For Block, the fair offered a chance to connect with buyers and collectors interested in his gallery programme from across Germany, especially the more affluent Rhineland. Already the first year that he participated, his sales exceeded the total volume of sales he had made in West Berlin since opening his gallery.[59] Considering the financial interests that underpinned Block's promotion of editioned art, Butin has gone as far as to suggested, that Block's experience of the commercial presentation of art and the large numbers of buyers at the *Kölner Kunstmarkt* might have played a role in his conception of the print portfolio from 1968.[60]

But it is too easy to reduce Block's support of graphic art purely to financial interests. As his book from 1971 shows, he clearly saw a political significance in the new developments in this artistic field. Underlying his comparison of Capitalist Realism with East Bloc Socialist Realism seems to

[57] See Butin 1992, p. 34 and Roland Scotti, "Der Verstellte Blick: Zur Situation und Rezeption der westdeutschen Kunst der 60er Jahre," in Richard W. Gassen and Roland Scotti (eds.), *Von Pop bis Polit: Kunst der 60er Jahre in des Bundesrepublik*, exh. cat., Wilhelm-Hack Museum (4 March–9 June 1966), Ludwigshafen: Wilhelm-Hack-Museum, 1996, p. 22.
[58] Block, 1989, p. 254.
[59] Ibid.
[60] Butin, 1992, p. 34

have been the intention to endorse contemporary experiments in graphic art as a fresh and promising path for politically and socially engaged art. Block's scepticism towards Socialist Realism as a progressive art form comes to the fore in the final East-West pairing of artworks: Paul Pedak's *Conquerors of Winter* (1963) and Gerhard Richter's *Sailors* (1966). Under the image of Pedak's painting of an all-male socialist workers brigade bravely attempting to maintain state declared productivity levels during one of Europe's coldest winters, stands a quote from Che Guevara that questions the revolutionary nature of Socialist Realism by pointing towards its roots in bourgeois culture and the conservative aesthetic forms of nineteenth-century realism. Positioned under the East German painter's work, the quote also acts as a critical commentary on the cultural politics of the GDR of the 1960s, where dogmatic formulas that prescribed a return to classical modernism and a focus on the SED's ideological messages had stifled all experimental developments in the visual arts.[61]

These doubts about Socialist Realism as art historically and politically significant are cemented further by the contrast with Richter's photo-painting *Sailors*. Although Richter like his colleague from the East still paints, his early photo-paintings incorporate the consciousness of the contemporary crisis of painting: the purported end of painting, and—more specifically—the continuing challenge to painting posed by photography, which resumed momentum in the 1960s.[62] Richter's famous quote about the de-subjectification of artistic creation, which accompanies the illustration of *Sailors*, emphasises that his photo-paintings do not only "look" like photographs but that they are also produced by a similar mechanised mode of production: "Paintings have to be made according to a recipe. The making has to happen without subjective involvement, just like hammering stones or painting façades."[63] The fact that Block included Richter's photo-paintings in a book about graphic art suggests that he recognised their relevance for the contemporary discourse on photography and other editioned art. Like Wolf Vostell's collages of newspaper images or Sigmar Polke's raster dot works, Richter's early photo-paintings

[61] Ulrike Goeschen, "From Socialist Realism to Art in Socialism: The Reception of Modernism as Instigating Force in the Development of Art in the GDR," *Third Text*, 23 (1), 2009, p. 47.
[62] Peter Osborne, "Painting Negation: Gerhard Richter's Negatives," *October*, 62, 1992, p. 104.
[63] Richter quoted in Block, 1971, p. 29.

interrogate the photographic image as a "cultural form," reflecting critically on the strategies and mechanisms of the mass media and how they shape peoples' consciousness.

The political ambitiousness of Block's curatorial programme was no doubt characteristic of the spirit of revolt that prevailed in 1960s West Berlin and the Federal Republic more generally. By 1976, when Block published the second volume of the catalogue raisonné of his artists' graphic works, the revolutionary potential he saw in graphic and editioned art still a few years earlier had evaporated.[64] The label Capitalist Realism is omitted from the title and all political references are removed. Instead of opening with a manifesto, the catalogue's second volume opens with a lexicological essay on printing techniques. Block's ideal of a better "capitalist socialism" in the West and a "democratic" art market, had been overridden by the professionalisation of the art business and the return of the aura of the unique artwork and its creator. Anticipating his gallerist's capitulation, Brehmer had already questioned the effectiveness of techniques of mass reproduction for the democratisation of art in 1971, when he observed: "We are absolutely wrong, if we assume that in our situation we can achieve something like popularity [*Volkstümlichkeit*] through mass editions."[65] Instead, he argued that the engagement of the "common people" still depended on a content that appealed to popular taste. Perhaps it was also this recognition which led Block to his final remark in *My Last Word*: "[I]f Capitalist Realism had taken its 'partisanship' with the masses truly serious, it would have had to become a socialist Realism."[66]

Epilogue
politics and pop – Block & Richter

Remembering the publication of *The Graphics of Capitalist Realism* in 2010, Block recalls how his artists were eagerly awaiting the book: "the unconventional content and format of the volume [...] had led to their

[64] René Block, *KP Brehmer, KH Hödicke, Sigmar Polke, Gerhard Richter, Wolf Vostell: Werkverzeichnis der Druckgrafik, Band II, September 1971 bis Mai 1976*, Berlin: Edition Block, 1976.
[65] Quoted in Egging 2003, p. 58.
[66] See note 50.

unconditional support and enthusiasm."[67] In a letter from 1971, Gerhard Richter congratulates his gallerist: "You made a great book! The first art book one can read with unblemished joy!"[68] When considering Richter's often-stated disapproval of Block's political remodelling of his concept of capitalist realism, his positive response to the book comes as a surprise. As his biographer Dietmar Elger writes: "Richter was opposed to Block's constant reanimation of Capitalist Realism, especially under this ideological program."[69] For Richter, the term was an ironic catch phrase that he did not intend to fill with any concrete political messages let alone program: "I really only wanted this for the demonstration at the Berges furniture store. It's not good to be associated with such a label."[70]

Having experienced the subordination of art to the political propaganda apparatus of the GDR, Richter had become wary of any flirtations between art and politics since defecting to West Germany in 1961. Susanne Küper has argued that for Richter capitalist realism was only the subject of his art, never a political artistic movement: "I never thought that I am doing 'capitalist realism,' not even at the time when we did the happening at the furniture store."[71] Exemplary of this apolitical attitude is Richter's screenprint *Hotel Diana* (1967) from the 1968 portfolio *The Graphics of Capitalist Realism*. The photograph shows Richter and Polke lying in bed in a hotel room in Antwerp the morning after the opening night of Richter's solo show at the gallery Wide White Space in October 1967.[72] Examined in the context of the 1968 portfolio, the image clearly undermines the social-political ambitiousness of Block's project. The same portfolio also included Wolf Vostell's screenprint *Starfighter* (1967), which was inspired by the public scandal around the Starfighter aircraft (notorious for its frequent crashes), during which high-ranking German government officials were accused of having been bribed by the plane's American manufacturer. The close-up of the violent war machine that is

[67] Block, 2010, p. 33.
[68] Richter in an undated letter to Block, Edition Block, Archive.
[69] Elger, 2002, p. 96–97.
[70] Richter quoted in Elger, 2008, p. 96–97.
[71] Richter quoted in Susanne Küper, "Konrad Lueg und Gerhard Richter: 'Leben mit Pop – Eine Demonstration für den Kapitalistischen realismus," *Wallraf-Richartz-Jahrhuch*, 8, 1992, p. 304.
[72] Elger, 2008, p. 142

endlessly replicated was not only a biting critique of the German military establishment but also of German rearmament.[73] Whereas Vostell appears here as the artist-agitator who engages in political debate and aims for the transformation of society, Richter's *Hotel Diana* subverts this image by portraying the contemporary artist as a foolish clown withdrawn from the public realm.

So why was it that Richter reacted so enthusiastically to Block's book? The catalogue for Richter's first retrospective, *Gerhard Richter: Bilder 1962–85*, at the Kunsthalle Düsseldorf in 1986, provides some answers.[74] In the catalogue's introductory essay by Jürgen Harten, two of Richter's works are presented next to each other. The first is from his Socialist Realist period, a wall painting at the SED's party offices in Dresden from 1958. The second is a photograph of his performance *Volker Bradke* at Gallery Schmela in Düsseldorf in 1966, generally considered the final piece of his capitalist realist period.[75] Similar to Block's East-West pairings in *The Graphics of Capitalist Realism* (1971), the two images are thematically linked through the subject of the flag. The wall painting shows a workers' political protest, in the midst of which an injured comrade hands over a waving red flag to a strongly built woman. In turn, the photograph from *Volker Bradke* shows Richter with a white flag that has the face of Bradke—an average youth and regular visitor at Düsseldorf art events—printed on it. Commenting on the catalogue's pairing of the two illustrations, Gillen has observed:

> The eye-catching arrangement of the two illustrations marks the drastic shift from a political demonstration in the space of the East German party headquarters to the depoliticised demonstration of a cult of personality involving an unknown young man in the space of a commercial art gallery.[76]

Similar to Andy Warhol's *Screen Tests* and their commentary on the media industry's arbitrary production of short-lived celebrities, Richter turned

[73] Jasmine Morehead (ed.), *Pop Impressions Europe/USA: Prints and Multiples from the Museum of Modern Art*. New York: Museum of Modern Art, 1999, p. 84.
[74] Harten (ed.), 1986.
[75] Harten (ed.), 1986, p. 17.
[76] Gillen, 2013, p. 143.

Bradke into a "star for a day" by printing his portrait on a flag and cartons, and writing his name in large letters on the gallery wall.[77]

But when considering Richter's experience of "real existing" Socialism, it is not only the western media but also the SED's propaganda apparatus that the performance ironises and criticises. By printing Bradke's head on a flag, Richter also mimicked the symbolic economy of the GDR, where flags adorned with the heads of Socialism's ideological forefathers (Marx, Engels, Lenin and Stalin) were deeply engrained in everyday life. Bradke's face, which is the face of an anti-hero and an unknown person, ironically undermines "all cultic admiration and ideological claims that usually come with such political symbolisms."[78] The presentation of the photograph from *Volker Bradke* next to the earlier wall painting enhances this critical nudge towards the GDR's propaganda machinery. It is unlikely that this editorial detail was Harten's choice alone, but Richter, who has always tightly controlled art historical interpretations of his work, probably had some say in this. In many ways, the arrangement of the images expresses an attitude that Richter articulated verbally two years later: "I have become involved with thinking and acting without the help of an ideology [...] Ideologies seduce and exploit uncertainty, legitimise war."[79]

One can only speculate, but it seems likely that Richter responded so positively to Block's book because he saw his own artistic development reflected in its unconventional format and content: his move from a moralising Socialist Realism towards a critically and ironically versed pop art, and with this his emancipation from the political dogmatism of the GDR. Although the moral imperative that underpinned Block's curatorial programme often resonated with the ideological rhetoric of GDR cultural politics, Block never went all the way to identify with the latter's dogmatism. His retrospective account of Capitalist Realism in his 1971 book, whilst suffused with concepts of a political realism and notions of the

[77] On the parallels between Richter's *Volker Bradke* and Warhol's *Screen Tests*, see Dietmar Elger (ed.), *Gerhard Richter. "Volker Bradke," 1966, 16 mm, s/w, 14:32 min*, Cologne: DuMont, 2010, pp. 26–27.
[78] Hubertus Butin, "Gerhard Richters Film *Volker Bradke* und das Prinzip der Unschärfe," in Elger (ed.), 2010, p. 27.
[79] Richter quoted in Michael Danoff, "Heterogeneity," in Terry A. Neff. (ed.), *Gerhard Richter: Paintings*. New York: Thames and Hudson, 1988, p. 21.

curator/artist-agitator, also half humorously presents these concepts as failure. By mobilising the new realist idiom to thematise pressing social and political issues in Cold War Germany, Block tried to push pop to its limits. Politics and pop coexisted in his programme of Capitalist Realism. This attitude is encapsulated in the first East-West pairing of artworks in the 1971 book, not mentioned until now: Geleiy Korshev's painting, *The Flag* (1957–60) and Edward Kienholz's famous anti-war tableaux, *The Portable War Memorial* (1968).[80] Like Block's book, Kienholz's assemblage reads from left to right: the propaganda devices (in this case, not socialist but rather capitalist) are placed on the left—"Uncle Sam of the First World War," Kate Smith singing "God Bless America," the "Marines on Mount Suribachi"—and on the right is the "business as usual" section—"with tables *ta* sit at and real Cokes to be bought from a real Coke dispenser."[81] Instead of looking towards the Pop Art of prominent figures such as Andy Warhol and Roy Lichtenstein, Block took inspiration from artists such as Kienholz and Richard Hamilton, who moved about on the margins of the international pop wave, for the formulation of his own brand of political pop in West Germany.

Bibliography

Primary references

René Block, "Die frühen Jahre: René Block," *Kunstforum*, 104, 1989, p. 254.

—. *KP Brehmer, KH Hödicke, Sigmar Polke, Gerhard Richter, Wolf Vostell: Werkverzeichnis der Druckgrafik, Band II, September 1971 bis Mai 1976,* Berlin: Edition Block, 1976.

—. *Die Grafik des Kapitalistischen Realismus,* Berlin: Edition René Block, 1971.

Coosje van Bruggen, "Gerhard Richter: Painting as a Moral Act," *Art Forum*, May 1985, p. 84

[80] Although Block never exhibited the American artist in his gallery, Kienholz began working in West Berlin in the early 1970s where he moved in the same artistic circles as Block.

[81] Kienholz, Edward, "The Portable War Memorial" (1969), in Pontus Hultén and Katja Waldén (eds.), *Edward Kienholz: 11+11 tableaux,* exh. cat., Moderna Museet (17 January–1 March 1970), Stockholm: Moderna Museet, 1970, n.p.

Günter Herzog, "René Block im Gespräch mit Günter Herzog am 25.11.2008," *sediment*, 16 (2009), p. 9–12.

Günter Herzog, "Ganz am Anfang/ How it all began," *sediment*, 7, 2004, pp. 10–17.

Richard Hey, "West-Berliner Exil," *Frankfurter Rundschau*, 7 April 1984.

Heinz Ohff, "Eine liberale Generation? Ausstellung von Gerhard Richter," in Eckhard Haack and Lothar C. Poll (eds.), *Schreiben für die Kunst: Lesebuch Heinz Off - Kunstkritik, Literatur, Feuilleton,* Berlin: InfoPress, 2007, p. 99.

—. "Sich treu bleiben!," *Der Tagespiegel*, 20 February 1972.

—. "Liebeslied an eine spröde Geliebte," *Der Tagesspiegel*, 6097, 1965, p. 5.

Secondary references

13°E: Eleven Artists Working in Berlin, exh. cat., Whitechapel Gallery (10 November–22 December 1978), London: Whitechapel Gallery, 1978, pp. 7–24.

Living with Pop: A Restrospective of Capitalist Realism, exh. cat., Kunsthalle Düsseldorf (21 July–29 September 2013), Cologne: Buchhandlung Walther König, 2013.

Pro Lidice: 52 Künstler aus Deutschland, exh. cat., České Muzeum Výtvarných Umění (9 March–6 April 1997), Prague: České Muzeum Výtvarných Umění, 1997.

Szene Berlin, Mai '72, exh. cat., Würtembergischer Kunstverein (26 May–18 June 1972), Stuttgart 1972, n.p.

René Block (ed.), *Multiples: An Attempt to Present the Development of the Object Edition,* exh. cat., Neuer Berliner Kunstverein (8 May–15 June 1974), Berlin: Neuer Berliner Kunstverein 1974.

Björn Egging (ed.), *Kapitalistischer Realismus: Grafik aus der Sammlung Block,* Bielefeld: Kerber Art, 2010.

Björn Egging, *Von Pop zu Politik: Studien zur Entwicklung der politisch engagierten Kunst KP Brehmers,* PhD Thesis, Universität Hamburg, 2003, http://ediss.sub.uni-hamburg.de/volltexte/2004/2236/pdf/Dissertation.pdf, accessed 17 October, 2015.

Dietmar Elger (ed.), *Gerhard Richter: "Volker Bradke," 1966, 16 mm, s/w, 14:32 min,* Cologne: DuMont, 2010.

Dietmar Elger and Hans-Ulrich Obrist (eds.), *Gerhard Richter: Text 1961 bis 2007 - Schriften, Interviews, Briefe,* Cologne: Buchhandlung Walther König, 2008.

Richard W. Gassen and Roland Scotti (eds.), *Von Pop bis Polit: Kunst der 60er Jahre in der Bundesrepublik,* exh. cat., Wilhelm-Hack Museum (4 March–09 June 1966), Ludwigshafen: Wilhelm-Hack-Museum, 1996.

Eckhardt Gillen (ed.), *Grossgörschen 35: Aufbruch zur Kunststadt Berlin 1964*, exh. cat., Haus am Kleistpark (6 June–10 August 2014), Berlin: Kunststiftung Poll, 2014.

Ulrike Goeschen, "From Socialist Realism to Art in Socialism: The Reception of Modernism as Instigating Force in the Development of Art in the GDR," *Third Text*, 23 (1), 2009, pp. 45–53.

Jürgen Harten (ed.), *Gerhard Richter: Bilder 1962–1985*, exh. cat., Städtische Kunstalle Düsseldorf (18 January–13 March 1986), Cologne: DuMont, 1986.

Tom Holert, "Bei sich, über allem: Der symptomatische Baselitz," *Texte zur Kunst*, 9 (March), 1993, pp. 87–102.

Pontus Hultén and Katja Waldén (eds.), *Edward Kienholz: 11+11 tableaux*, exh. cat., Moderna Museet (17 January–1 March 1970), Stockholm: Moderna Museet, 1970.

Andreas Huyssen, "After the Wall: The Failure of German Intellectuals," *New German Critique*, 52, Special Issue on the German Unification, 1991, pp. 109–143.

—. "The Cultural Politics of Pop: Reception and Critique of US Pop Art in the Federal Republic of Germany," *New German Critique*, 4, 1975, pp. 77–97.

Susanne Küper, "Konrad Lueg und Gerhard Richter: 'Leben mit Pop - Eine Demonstration für den Kapitalistischen realismus," *Wallraf-Richartz-Jahrhuch*, 8, 1992, pp. 289–306.

Debbie Lewer, "Introduction: Art and Cultural Politics in the German Democratic Republic," *Art in Translation*, 5 (3), pp. 5–14.

Jasmine Morehead (ed.), *Pop Impressions Europe/USA: Prints and Multiples from the Museum of Modern Art*. New York: Museum of Modern Art, 1999.

Terry A. Neff. (ed.), *Gerhard Richter: Paintings*, New York: Thames and Hudson, 1988.

Peter Osborne, "Painting Negation: Gerhard Richter's Negatives," *October*, 62, 1992, pp. 102–113.

Bernd Slutzky (ed.), *Grafik des Kapitalistischen Realismus*, Frankfurt: Galerie Bernd Slutzky, 1992.

Stefan Strsembski, *Kapitalistischer Realismus: Objekt und Kritik in der Kunst der 60er Jahre*, Hamburg: Verlag Dr. Kovac, 2010.

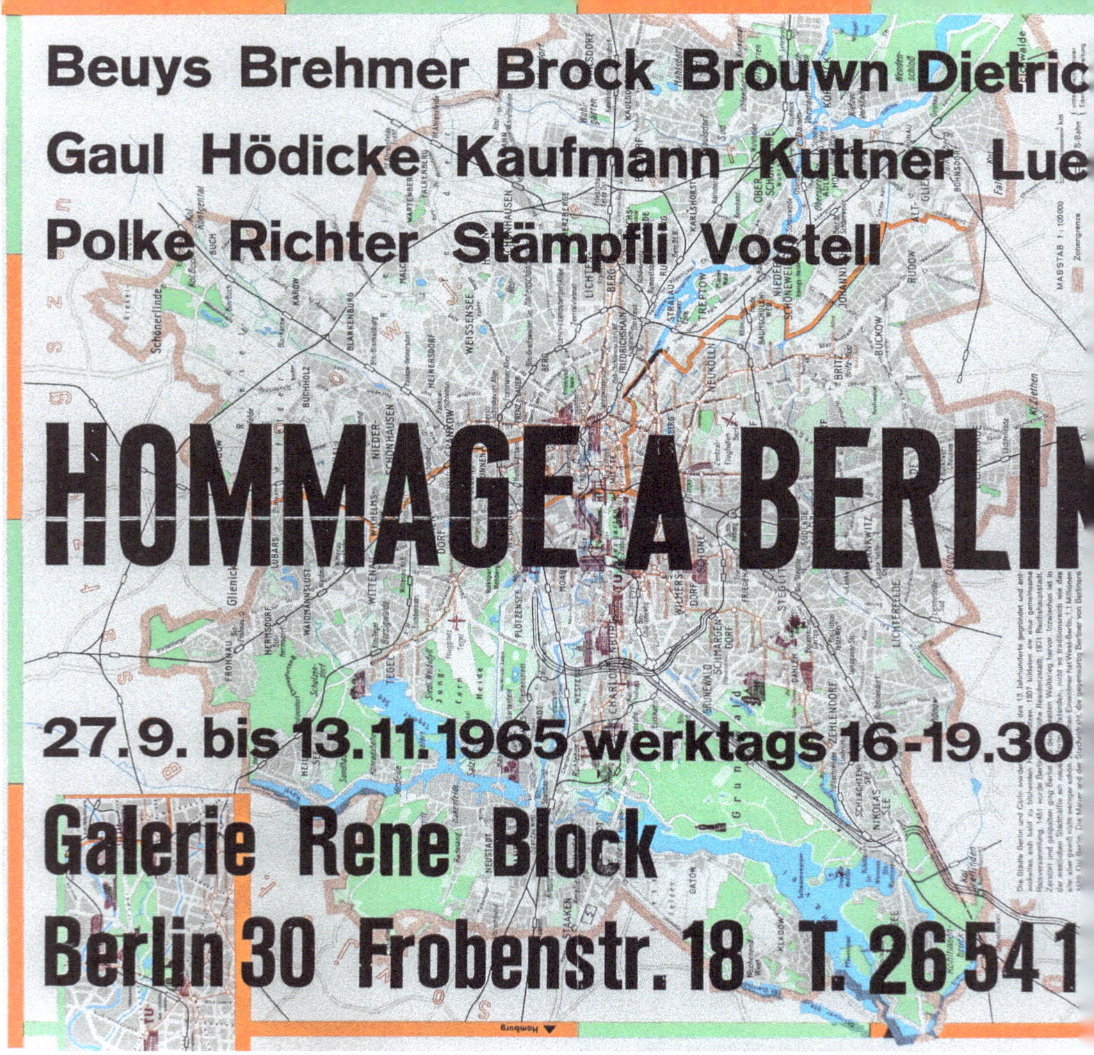

Beuys Brehmer Brock Brouwn Dietric

Gaul Hödicke Kaufmann Kuttner Lue

Polke Richter Stämpfli Vostell

HOMMAGE A BERLIN

27.9. bis 13.11.1965 werktags 16-19.30

Galerie Rene Block

Berlin 30 Frobenstr. 18 T. 26 54 1

Figure 5.1: Poster for the exhibition *Hommage à Berlin*. Paintings, Drawings, Prints, 1965 © Edition Block, Berlin.

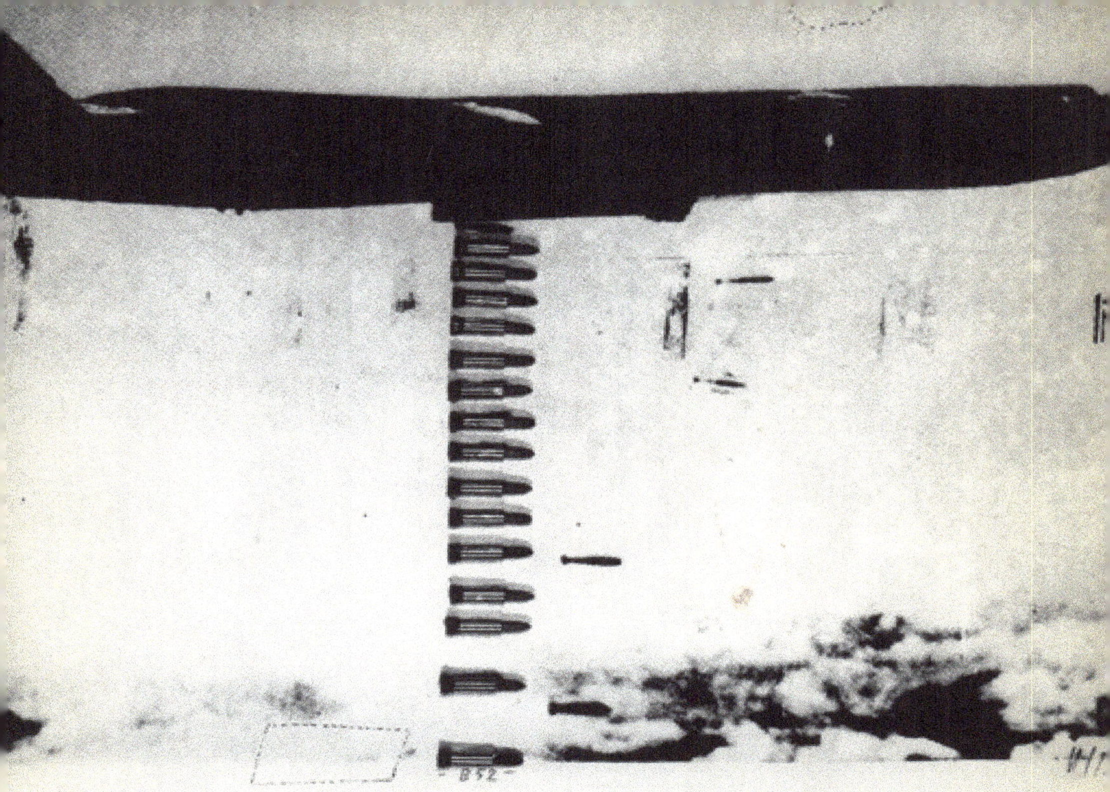

Figure 5.2: Book cover of *The Graphic Art of Capitalist Realism*, 1971 © Edition Block, Berlin.

Figure 5.3: René Block, Von Meister-hand …, part of the portfolio *The Graphic Art of Capitalist Realism*, 1968 © Edition Block, Berlin.

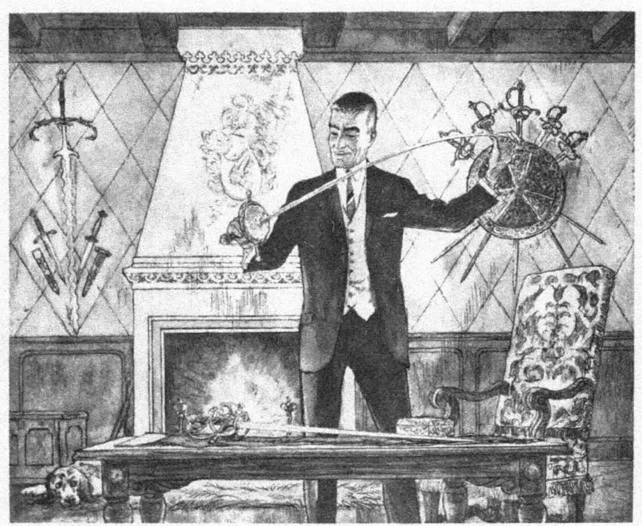

Von Meisterhand . . .

Die Meisterschaft und Kunstfertigkeit, die in den vergangenen Jahrhunderten den Waffen zugewandt wurde, wird wohl bei den Blankwaffen am deutlichsten sichtbar; also bei den Schwertern, Säbeln, Messern, Dolchen und Degen.

Leider kann der Sammler nur noch selten wahre Meisterstücke erwerben. In Museen und Fürstenhäusern hängt das meiste und schönste. Vielleicht ist es gut so . . . wer es liebt und zu suchen weiß, wird es finden. So ist es ja mit allem. Man muß lernen und entdecken wollen. Das gilt ja selbst für Essen und Trinken. Die Kennerschaft wird einem nicht in die Wiege gelegt. Der jedoch, der sie erworben hat – nun, der wird gerade die Grafik des Kapitalistischen Realismus zu würdigen wissen. Jenen Realismus, der in Städten wie Berlin, Düsseldorf und Köln von wahren Meistern bereitet, gehegt und gepflegt wird. Zur Freude der Kenner, die es immer gab und die es immer geben wird.

Grafik des Kapitalistischen Realismus

Berlin 1968 René Block im stolpeverlag

Part 2

Works, Practices, Movements

6
Öyvind Fahlström's Impure Pop in a World of Impure Cold War Politics

Sophie Cras

> It was formerly the custom in British schools, even during my own childhood, to have hanging on the wall of each class-room a large map of the world. The dominant colour was red, for this was before the Russian revolution, and red had not yet been appropriated by the communists. India, Canada, Australia, New Zealand, huge areas of the African continent running from Cairo to the Cape of Good Hope; Samoa, Burma, Malaya, Hong Kong, the West Indies, Ceylon—all coloured red. [...] Here on these maps, for the edification of British youth, was spread the British Empire in all its majesty. One-quarter of the land surface of the world, one-fifth of the human population intimately linked with or controlled by our own tiny island. It made us feel very superior. [...] Those maps, of course, no longer hang in British class-rooms. The old methods of empire have changed. Such control [...] is more indirect, less visible. A new empire, the American Empire, has replaced the British Empire as the leading imperialist power. Exercising its power in a structurally different way, but nevertheless seeking the same ends and often with the same means, it is the American Empire which today bestrides the world.[1]

These words by the British-American journalist Felix Greene appeared in a book entitled *The Ennemy*, published in 1970. They demonstrate the geographic, even cartographic dimension of the reflection on imperialism,

[1] Felix Greene, *The Ennemy: Notes on Imperialism and Revolution*, London: Jonathan Cape, 1970, p. 51, 53.

which reached its peak in leftist circles in the midst of the protests against the war in Vietnam. "The old methods of empire have changed," he writes; nowadays military, economic and political domination is less direct, "less visible," and therefore all the more pervasive and dangerous.

Öyvind Fahlström was an avid reader of Greene's writings—quoted at the centre of his *World Map* (1972) (Figure 6.1). And a contentious reader too. Since the old imperialist maps no longer hang in classrooms, how could one picture the new Empire? What kind of maps, of ingenious cartographic tools could make apparent the new structure of imperialist politics, indirect, hidden against the pretense of Aid to the Third World, or against the mask of clear-cut Cold War politics?

It has been argued that Fahlström's interest in cartography related to his own international background.[2] A naturalised Swede born in Brazil, he worked between Stockholm, Paris, New York and Italy. Not only did Fahlström travel places; he also maneuvered between categories. In the United States, he was often considered a Pop artist, due to his use of comic strips and his friendship with Rauschenberg, Oldenburg, Lichtenstein, and others.[3] There, he was reproached by critics for engaging with political subjects, and renouncing the neutral and cold approach to the source material that pop art supposedly implied.[4] In France, after being looked upon as a Surrealist in the 1950s, he was assimilated to the outwardly leftist Figuration Narrative in the 1960s, and consequently reproached for not making his political claims clear enough.[5] Never in the proper category for critics, it seems, Fahlström was nevertheless supported by renowned and respected galleries: Daniel Cordier in Paris, then Sidney Janis in New York.[6] How this artist, who connected different artistic and ideological

[2] Suely Rolnik, "Öyvind Fahlström's Changing Maps," in *Öyvind Fahlström: Another Space for Painting*, exh. cat., Barcelona: MACBA, 2001, p. 333.

[3] Pontus Hulten, "Öyvind Fahlström, citoyen du monde," in *Öyvind Fahlström*, exh. cat., Paris: Musée National d'Art Moderne, Centre Pompidou, 1980, p. 95.

[4] See for instance Hilton Kramer, "From Pop to Social Consciousness," *New York Times*, 16 March 1969, p. D21; John Canaday, "Everything's Wrong With the World, But…," *New York Times*, 15 April 1973, p. 151.

[5] José Pierre, "Les petits monstres de Leonor Fini et le vrai surréalisme," *France Observateur*, No 461, 5 March 1959, p. 20; Alain Jouffroy, "Le 'Bel Canto' d'Öyvind Fahlström," in *Öyvind Fahlström*, exh. cat., Paris: Alexander Iolas, 1975, n.p.

[6] Fahlström was put under a verbal contract by Daniel Cordier in 1958. See Bernard Blistène, "Öyvind Fahlström," in *Daniel Cordier: Le regard d'un amateur*, exh. cat., Paris: Musée

milieus, came to propose a new geographic visualisation where divisions could be traversed, condemned, or ridiculed, is the subject of this chapter.

Fahlström described his *World Map* (1972) as "a medieval type of map" where "the shapes of the countries are defined by the data about them"[7]: statistics about the economic recession in the United States meet a description of torture methods in Brazil and of peasant uprisings in West Bengal. Numerous figures, names, dates, arrows, places, and facts give the map both its overall visual unity and its accumulative character in an overabundance of information. Much of this data is directly borrowed from Felix Greene's book *The Enemy*: 5 million of children starving in India (Figure 6.1, lower-right), low life expectancy and untreated diseases in the United States; 105 million Americans living below the poverty line (Figure 6.1, upper-left).

A year before completing his *World Map*, in 1971, Fahlström had already carefully studied Felix Greene's book, and had tackled the challenge of putting into images its most conspicuous facts and figures. Immediately preceding and preparing *World Map*, Fahlström's *Notes 9* is subtitled *Reading Felix Greene's "The Enemy"* (Figure 6.2). It brings together information directly borrowed from the book: "More electricity is consumed in New York City than is generated in all the subcontinent of India"[8] (upper-centre); one finds on 5th Avenue clothes-hangers in chinchilla for $175 each and "gold-plated faucets [...] at $475 the pair"[9] (lower-centre); London's crime rate compared to Washington, D.C.'s (centre-right);[10] or massive imports of primary goods from Third World countries to industrialised nations[11] (lower-left, to be compared to Green's own table).

How to give visual form to this type of information was obviously the major problem Fahlström had to solve. He could rely on a kind of visual language he had elaborated and practiced for a while already: one inspired

National d'Art Moderne, Centre Pompidou, 1989. In 1961 he moved to New York upon receiving a scholarship, and later settled there. He became associated with the Sidney Janis Gallery in 1965.

[7] Öyvind Fahlström, "Description of five paintings" (1975), in *Öyvind Fahlström, Another Space*, p. 258.

[8] Greene, 1970, p. 136.

[9] Greene, 1970, p. 46.

[10] Greene, 1970, p. 30.

[11] Greene, 1970, p. 138.

from that of American Comics. As early as the late 1950s, he turned to Bill Elder's drawings for *MAD* as source materials to be combined through chance selection.[12] He used comic cut-outs directly or indirectly in his works from the 1960s. This long-lasting interest was reinvigorated in 1969 when, during a visit to Los Angeles, he discovered the underground comic books *ZAP* and the work of Robert Crumb.[13] He immediately appropriated his work to compose a repertory of images and forms. His *Study for Meatball Curtain* (1970, Figure 6.3) is largely a collection of motives taken from Crumb's comics. His borrowings are as deliberate and as varied as his selection of facts in Felix Greene's book. It includes striking signature figures (such as Crumb's recognisable marching man from *Keep On Truckin*, drawn in the upper-left corner), but also seemingly anecdotal elements of background, such as a wave (upper-left corner) borrowed from a page of *Head Comix* (Figure 6.4, lower-right), as well as minor characters, images which could became archetypes for societal issues like drugs (an addict shooting up extracted from Crumb's *Stoned* (1967)) or religion (Jesus carrying the cross from *Hey Boparee Bop*).

Fahlström is not simply copying comics in a "Pop" manner. A significant transformation is evident. The figures are simplified, outlined, devoid of volume and are given one single bright colour. The reason for this stylisation is not only that Fahlström was then preparing the big silhouettes of metal and Plexiglas sheets that would constitute *Meatball Curtain (for R. Crumb)* (1969), realised in cooperation with the firm *Heath and Company* in the framework of the *Project for Art and Technology*.[14] What he was in fact attempting was a transformation of these elements into pictograms that constituted a new vocabulary. In his following works, the series of *Notes* from 1970–71, direct borrowings from Crumb are more sparse than in the *Study for Meatball Curtain*. In *World Map,* though one unmistakably recognises the style of comics, no specific quotation is identifiable. Instead, Fahlström retained from his source images a few

[12] See Öyvind Fahlström, "The Comics as an Art," *Expressen*, 27 August 1954, and the work *Dr. Livingstone, I Presume* (1959).

[13] Jane Livingston, "Project for Art and Technology, Los Angeles County Museum," in Sharon Avery-Fahlström (ed.), *Öyvind Fahlström: Die Installationen*, exh. cat., Ostfildern: Cantz Verlag, 1995, p. 66.

[14] Indeed, his "Studies" for *Meatball Curtain* are dated 1970, after the completion of the work.

elementary type-forms that he then reused again and again in diverse configurations. The image of the toilet (Figure 6.3), directly borrowed from Crumb (Figure 6.4), thus underwent different hybridisations in later works. Its distinctive shape and scatological connotation were used to denounce, at times, self-destructive Washington politics (in the upper-centre of *World Map* (Figure 6.1) for example, and in *Notes 5*), the hypocrisy of international aid (in *Notes 7*), or the shameful exploitation of South America by the United States (in *Notes 3*). Likewise, a crawling figure borrowed from Crumb (Figure 6.4), once reduced to a shadow silhouette (Figure 6.3), became a recurrent figure representing oppressed people in several works. Deprived of a head (Figure 6.3), it became a symbol of mortality (like in *Word Map*, Figure 6.1 upper-centre).

The quest for pictograms, more or less standardised flat figures able to convey a meaning and to be arranged in relation to one another in order to produce a form of visual language, was an obsession for Fahlström from the very first years of his career. Deeply influenced by the Aztec hieroglyphs he discovered in Mexican codexes and other pre-Columbian manuscripts in Europe in the early 1950s, he persistently used glossaries of forms to accompany his works, and wrote extensively about his interest in what he called "signs" or "character-signs" and sometimes "hieroglyphs."[15] Fahlström considered the main challenge of art to be its "communication possibilities," its ability to affect the largest possible number of people.[16] He also recognised that "statistics and other similar kinds of data, which demand that a multitude of precise pieces of information be included, are hard to transmit."[17] Creating type-images that could work as pictograms to transmit information in a simplified, yet expressive and vivid manner, was therefore his favoured solution.

[15] See "Levande tecken." *Konstrevy*, No 2, 1961, "Letter from Fahlström to Groschwitz" (1967) and "A Game of Character" (1962), *Art and Literature*, No 3, 1964, republished in *Öyvind Fahlström, Another Space*, p. 98, p. 134 and p. 145. His interest in "character-forms" is also embedded in his early production of concrete poetry. See Öyvind Fahlström, "HÄTILA RAGULPR PÅ FÅTSKLIABEN: Manifeste pour une poésie concrete," *Odyssé*, Stockholm, Vol.1, No 2–3, 1954.

[16] "Art, Life, Society, School, Science, Technology, Economics, Etc.," in *Öyvind Fahlström, Another Space*, p. 153.

[17] "Anteckningar om gatuteater och demonstration," *Dialog*, Vol.4, No 4–5, 1968, republished in Öyvind Fahlström, *Essais Choisis*, Dijon: Les Presses du Réel, 2002, p. 203.

The facts and figures that abound in Felix Greene's book, and sometimes make the reading difficult, are not merely illustrated by Fahlström, but properly visualised. This is especially clear in *Notes 9* (Figure 6.2). In the centre-right, the size of the criminals reflects the number of crimes committed, manifesting the disproportion of the figures between London and Washington, D.C. On the left-hand side, the monetary equivalence between a military submarine and 50 hospitals is made clear by the repetition of 50 identical symbols in the space defined by the length of one submarine. In the lower-left corner, the unequal distribution of taxes between workers' wages and capitalists' dividends, shares and bonds, is represented by four character-types, each holding a different lead weight. Further right, the "poverty line" is materialised by a horizontal line, while half of the U.S. population is indicated by a vertical dotted line crossing the continent.

This arrangement of pictograms also includes a geographic dimension: while different continents are organised spatially on the surface of the paper—with India in the upper-left corner or South America in the centre—a colour code, in the lower-right corner, helps identifying the countries concerned. Blue represents the United States, purple is Western Europe, red is the communist countries and green is the Third World. This arrangement announces the spatial organisation of the *World Map*.

Fahlström's quest for a visual language, inspired by hieroglyphs, by which simple pictograms could transmit statistics and other complex economic data in an immediately understandable way, met the objectives of the then booming discipline of communicational graphics, itself indebted to the first findings of the Viennese philosopher and economist Otto Neurath.

Neurath started to elaborate his International Picture Language in the context of the democratic and leftist post-war Vienna. With the help of the designer Gerd Arntz, he created what he called Isotypes, a system of pictographic visualisation of data.[18] The first Isotypes were produced to put into images the economic statistics exhibited in the Economic and Social Museum of Vienna, directed by Neurath from 1925 to 1934.[19] Like

[18] Gerd Arntz, Ed Annink, Max Bruinsma *et al.*, *Gerd Arntz: Graphic Designer*, Rotterdam: 010 Publishers, 2010.
[19] Robert J. Leonard, "'Seeing is Believing': Otto Neurath, Graphic Art and the Social Order,", *History of Political Economy*, 1999, Vol. 31, No 5, pp. 452–478.

Fahlström's character-forms, Neurath's Isotypes are simplified, mostly monochrome silhouettes, devoid of details or specification. Neurath, like Fahlström, linked his pictograms to ancient hieroglyphs, children's drawings and comics.[20] For Neurath as well as Fahlström, the image should be able to transmit complex economic information in a more democratic way than text and should demonstrate that, in the words of Felix Greene, "facts are not quite what [people] think they are."[21]

Many of Fahlström's choices of visualisation are in fact based on the recommendations of Neurath's communicational graphics. For example, in his book *International Picture Language: The First Rules of Isotype* (1936), Neurath explained the use of one repeated pictogram to proportionally represent a quantitative data. He wrote: "A sign is representative of a certain amount of things; a greater number of signs is representative of a greater amount of things."[22] His chart representing "Automobiles produced in 1929 in America and in Europe" as compared to the workforce (Figure 6.5) is quite comparable to Fahlström's visualisation of the equivalence between a military submarine and 50 hospitals in *Notes 9* (Figure 6.2, centre-left). Neurath also shared Fahlström's idea to materialise a mathematical division by drawing an actual line—see Fahlström's "poverty line" (Figure 6.2, lower-left)—and to add distinctive accessories and clothes to distinguish between different social categories of the population (compare his examples in Figure 6.6 to Fahlström's workers and capitalists in Figure 6.2, lower-left corner). Likewise, using a colour code to distinguish different elements in a group—such as different geographical areas—is also recommended by Neurath, who made it a rule that, for the sake of clarity: "There are only seven colours for use in ISOTYPE pictures: white, blue, green, yellow, red, brown, black."[23] Rethinking cartographic conventions was actually one of Neurath's specific concerns.[24] He rejected the usual Mercator projection of world maps,

[20] See Otto Neurath, *From Hieroglyphics to Isotype: A Visual Autobiography* (1945), London: Hyphen Press, 2010.

[21] Greene, 1970, p. 23.

[22] Otto Neurath, *International Picture Language: The First Rules of Isotype*, London: Kegan Paul, Trench Trubner & Co., Ltd, 1936, p. 73–74.

[23] Neurath, 1936, p. 42.

[24] See Hisayasu Ihara, "Otto Neurath's Atlas 'Society and Economy': Design, Contents, and Context," paper delivered to the congress of the International Association of Societies of

which, he argued, distorted the surface of the continent in an unacceptable way, and worked on alternative cartographic projections which would give back to the Southern hemisphere its visual importance compared to the North. Like Fahlström, he praised the inspiring quality of pre-modern cartography, and reproduced one in his *International Picture Language* under the caption "Old military picture."[25]

It is not clear exactly how much Fahlström would have known of Otto Neurath's contribution. In the 1960s and 1970s, Neurath's work was undergoing a posthumous rediscovery, with a number of articles published in the European and American literature.[26] But more importantly, the development of communicational graphics, for public signage, road signs, airports, as well as for business communication, made Neurath's basic principles very widespread in the 1960s. Likewise, in the context of anti-imperialist politics and the rise of the Third World, the debates over the ideological impact of the Mercator projection were fierce, and several alternative projections were promoted, such as Arno Peter's projection.[27]

It is evident, nevertheless, that Fahlström's pictograms and visualisation of data differ from Neurath's as much as they relate to them. Neurath's representations are sober, neutral. They seek the dispassionate and professional look of science. Fahlström's characters are feverish, screeching, rough and approximate. They share with Crumb's drawings, in Fahlström's words, their "exuberance," "energy," "rawness" and "dumbness," as well as their "madness," and "ecstatic" quality.[28] In fact, one could even read Fahlström's figures as an implicit criticism of Neurath's Isotypes, a

Design Research (IASDR07), Hong Kong Polytechnic University, 12–15 November 2007. Online: http://isotyperevisited.org/Ihara_Society_and_Economy.pdf.

[25] Neurath, 1936, p. 107.

[26] Martin Krampen, "Signs and Symbols in Graphic Communication," *Design Quarterly*, No 62, 1965, pp. 3–31; Marie Neurath, "Otto Neurath und Isotype," *Graphic Design*, No 42, 1971, pp. 11–30. See also Robin Kinross, "On the Influence of Isotype," *Information Design Journal*, Vol. 2 , No 2, 1981, pp. 122–130.

[27] Elaborated in 1967 and published in 1973, Arno Peters's projection actually borrows from James Gall (1855).

[28] "I wanted my figures to have a sort of quality of exuberance and the energy of American life and the fatality and rawness of it and the sort of dumbness about it too and the animal-like quality which is very well depicted in Crumb's drawings, as well as the aspect of madness, the ecstatic factor." Fahlström quoted by Jane Livingston (1971) in *Öyvind Fahlström, Another Space*, p. 230.

subversion of this economic visual language already well-established in the late 1960s and serving powerful interests in the name of expertise. While Neurath had initially conceived the Isotypes in the context of the democratic, progressive Vienna circle of the 1920s, he put them at the service of Soviet propaganda in the 1930s, endorsing clearly falsified statistics.[29] Fahlström was suspicious of any kind of authoritative visual discourse; he did not claim to "educate the viewers."[30] As Robert Rauschenberg wrote in 1962, his work is about invitation, not intimation.[31]

Fahlström's own *World Map* does not claim to be truer to geographic reality than a Mercator projection; it simply contends that space is above all political. A country is not contained within its administrative borders: it should be made visible on the map wherever it exerts true power. Fahlström's map therefore rejects conventional territorial divisions in favor of interpenetrating spaces. The United States, for instance, is not restricted to North America, but inserts itself in all other continents due to its imperialist designs: in South America, where it overthrows local governments, or in South Africa, where it controls 68 percent of the automotive industry. On the map, Detroit is even relocated to the South-African continent, to show the dependency of the city's economy on American foreign policy. The colour code draws attention to these new "methods of empire," which, as Greene mentioned in the quote discussed at the beginning of this chapter, allow one country to effectively rule another country without appearing on a traditional map. Because the nations' positions on the map are not a given, parallels can be drawn and connections made, which contradict the neat divisions of Cold War geo-politics. The *World Map* brings together internments of political opponents in the United States, as well as in the USSR; it associates the ETA in Spain and the IRA in Ireland as two examples of Europe's failure to deal with its internal divisions.

In this new visualisation of data, both statistic and geographic, the indirect forms of domination that traditional maps fail to render are now

[29] Clive Chizlett, "Damned Lies and Statistics: Otto Neurath and Soviet Propaganda in the 1930s," *Visible Language*, Vol. 26, No 3–4, 1992, pp. 298–321.
[30] "Notation 1974." *Öyvind Fahlström*, Milan: Multhipla Edizioni, 1976, reproduced in *Ubi Fluxus,* exh. cat. Venice: Venice Biennale /Mazzotta, 1990, p. 54.
[31] *Öyvind Fahlström*, exh. cat., Paris: Daniel Cordier, 1962, n.p.

evident. In Fahlström's personal map, countries can dissolve into one another, elements can hybridise, and space for action exists. In a manifesto dated 1966, in a chapter entitled "Risk reforms," Fahlström wrote as an injunction to himself:

> not to take any of the existing systems for granted (capitalist, moderately socialized or thoroughly socialized). Refuse to presume that "sharpness" of the opposite systems will mellow into a worthwhile in-between. [...] The reforms mentioned below are of course not proposed with the huge, rigid warfare states like China, Russia or the U.S.A. in mind, but rather small welfare states like Sweden, groping for goals.[32]

Indeed, perhaps only a small country, relatively distant from the Cold War balance of power and even absent from the *World Map*, could become the centre of a creative political thinking.

References

Daniel Cordier, *Le regard d'un amateur*, exh. cat., Paris: Musée National d'Art Moderne, Centre Pompidou, 1989.

Öyvind Fahlström, *Essais Choisis,* Dijon: Les Presses du Réel, 2002.

Öyvind Fahlström: Another Space for Painting, exh. cat., Barcelona: MACBA, 2001

Öyvind Fahlström, exh. cat., Paris: Musée National d'Art Moderne, Centre Pompidou, 1980.

[32] Öyvind Fahlström, "Take Care of the World," in *Manifestos*, New York: Something Else Press, 1966, p. 11.

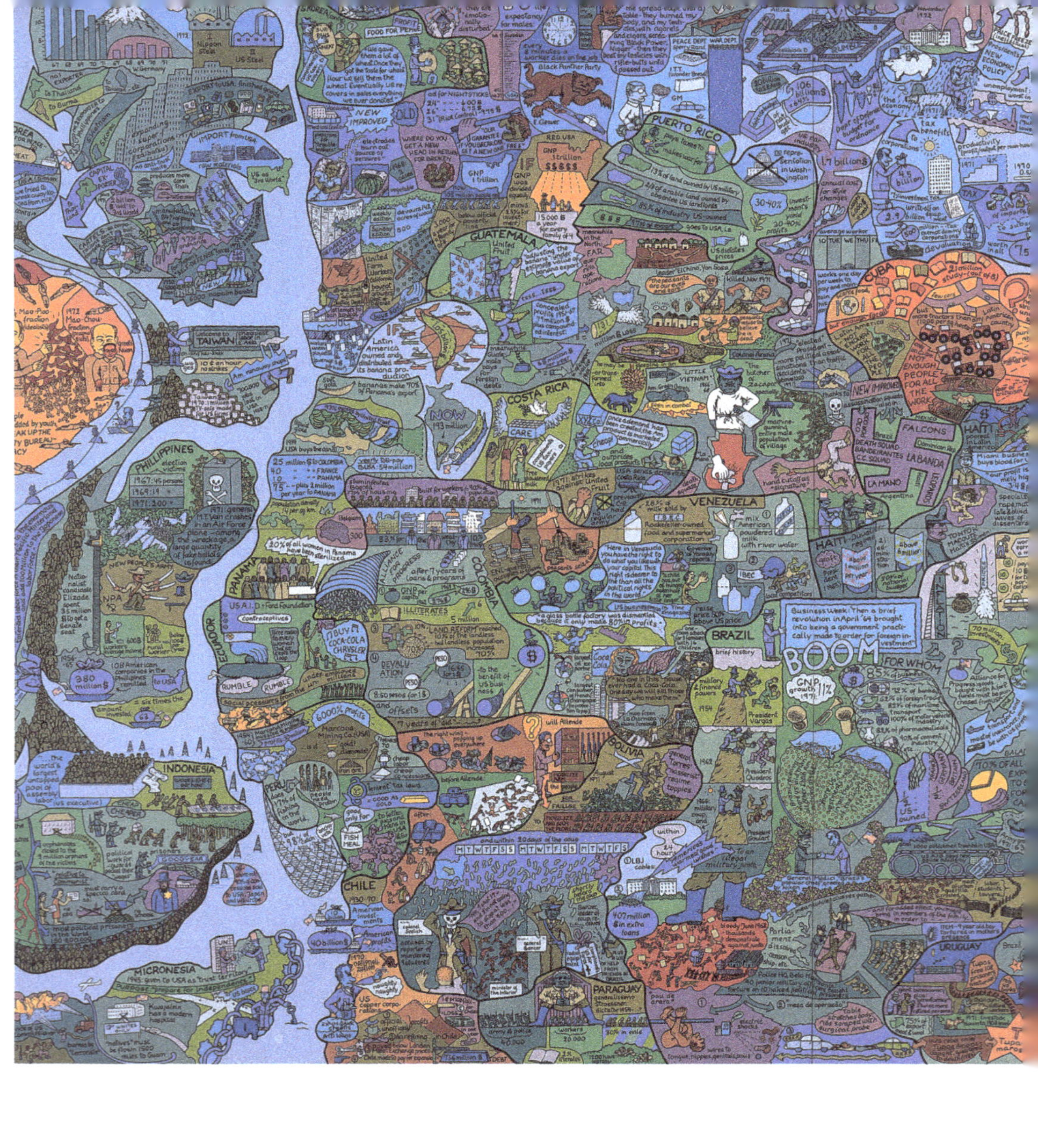
PUERTO RICO
GUATEMALA
COSTA RICA
PANAMA
COLOMBIA
ECUADOR
VENEZUELA
CUBA
HAITI
BRAZIL
BOOM
FOR WHOM
PERU
BOLIVIA
CHILE
PARAGUAY
URUGUAY
PHILIPPINES
TAIWAN
INDONESIA
MICRONESIA
FALCONS
LA BANDA
NOW
Business Week: Then a brief revolution in April '64 brought into being a government practically made to order for foreign investment.

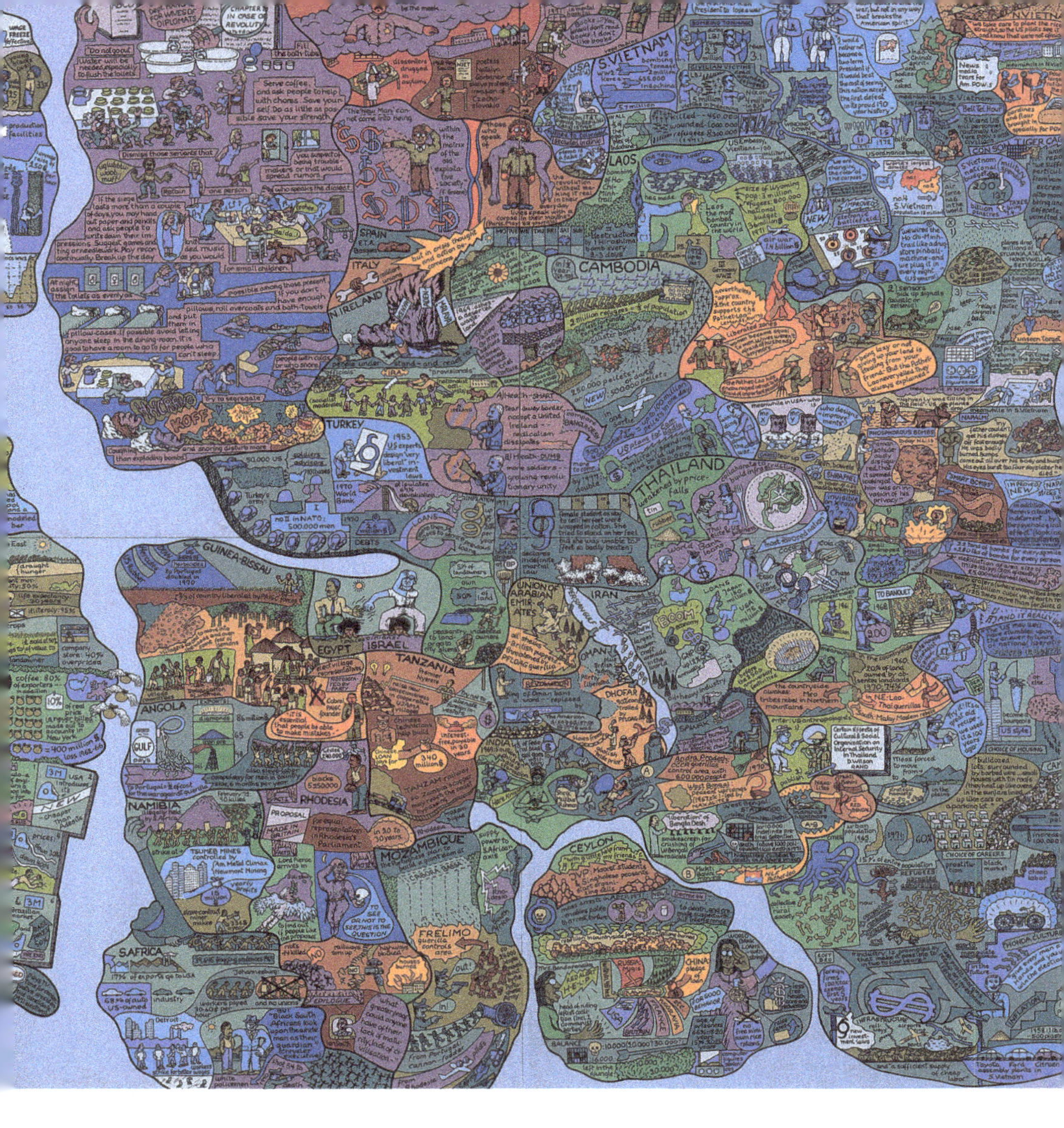

Figure 6.1: *World* Map (1972), Öyvind Fahlström. © 2016 Sharon Avery-Fahlström.

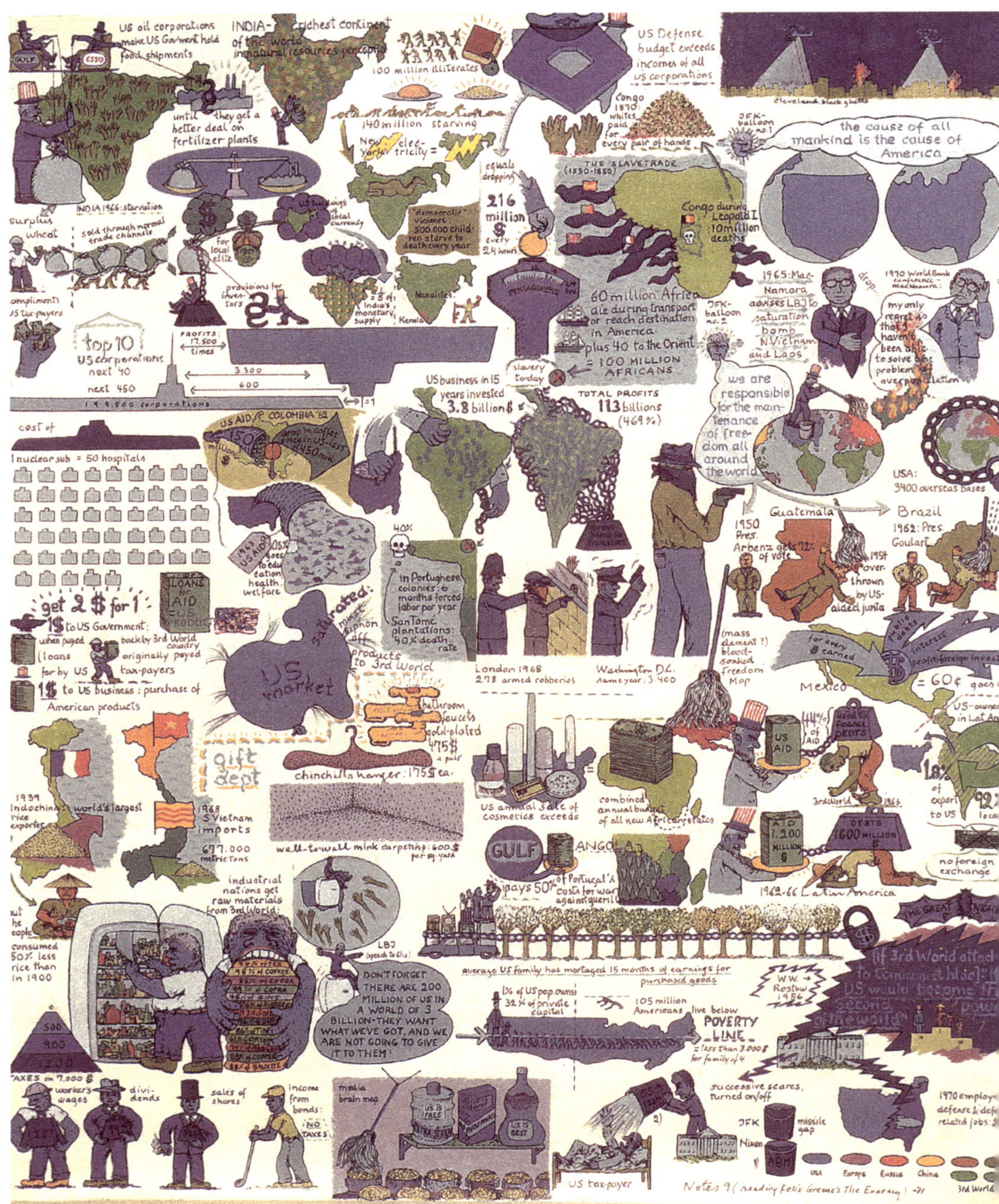
US oil corporations make US Gov'ment hold food shipments
until they get a better deal on fertilizer plants
INDIA 1966: starvation
surplus wheat
sold through normal trade channels
compliments US tax-payers
for local elite
provisions for investors
US holdings of local currency
India's monetary supply
100 million illiterates
140 million starving
New York electricity =
"democratic" violence 500.000 children starve to death every year
Naxalites
Kerala
US Defense budget exceeds incomes of all US corporations
Congo 1890: whites paid for every pair of hands
equals dropping
216 million $ every 24 hours
THE SLAVETRADE (1550-1850)
Congo during Leopold I: 10 million deaths
60 million Africans die during transport or reach destination in America
plus 40 to the Orient
= 100 MILLION AFRICANS
slavery today
JFK-balloon no. 1
the cause of all mankind is the cause of America
JFK-balloon no. 2
1965: MacNamara advises LBJ to saturation bomb N.Vietnam and Laos
1970 World Bank conference - MacNamara:
my only regret is that I haven't been able to solve the problem of overpopulation
we are responsible for the maintenance of freedom all around the world
USA: 3400 overseas bases
top 10 US corporations
next 40
next 450
PROFITS: 17.500 times
3.300
600
=1
cost of
1 nuclear sub = 50 hospitals
US AID COLOMBIA '62
150 millions $
drop in coffee prices in US - loss $450 mill.
1968 US AID
10% goes to education, health, welfare
LOANS for AID
get 2 $ for 1
1$ to US Government: when payed back by 3rd World country (loans originally payed for by US tax-payers
1$ to US business: purchase of American products
US market
saturated: must siphon off products to 3rd World
US business in 15 years invested 3.8 billion $
TOTAL PROFITS 113 billions (469%)
40%
in Portughese colonies: 6 months forced labor per year
San Tomé plantations: 40% death rate
London 1968 278 armed robberies
Washington D.C. same year: 3.400
Guatemala
1950 Pres. Arbenz gets 72% of vote
1954 over-thrown by US-aided junta
Brazil
1962: Pres. Goulart
(mass element?) blood-soaked freedom mop
for every $ earned
interest
profit
foreign invest
= 60¢ goes
Mexico
1939 Indochina world's largest rice exporter
1968 S Vietnam imports 677.000 metric tons
gift dept
bathroom faucets gold-plated 475$ a pair
chinchilla hanger: 175$ ea.
wall-to-wall mink carpeting: 600$ per sq. yard
US annual sale of cosmetics exceeds
combined annual budget of all new African states
44% of AID
used to finance DEBTS
US AID
3rd World 1965
US-owned in Lat Am
1.8% of export to US
no foreign exchange
AID 1.200 MILLION $
DEBTS 1600 MILLION $
1962-66 Latin America
GULF
ANGOLA
pays 50% of Portugal's costs for war against guerillas
industrial nations get raw materials from 3rd World:
but the people consumed 50% less rice than in 1900
LBJ (speech to GIs)
DON'T FORGET THERE ARE 200 MILLION OF US IN A WORLD OF 3 BILLION - THEY WANT WHAT WE'VE GOT, AND WE ARE NOT GOING TO GIVE IT TO THEM!
average US family has mortgaged 15 months of earnings for purchased goods
1% of US pop. owns 32% of private capital
105 million Americans live below POVERTY LINE = less than 3.000$ for family of 4
W.W. → Rostow 1956
THE GREAT NIGHT
"If 3rd World attached to Communist bloc" - US would become the second ... power of the world"
500
900
1300
TAXES on 7.000 $
worker's wages
dividends
sales of shares
income from bonds: NO TAXES
media brain mop
US IS FREE
US IS BEST
US tax-payer
successive scares, turned on/off
JFK missile gap
Nixon ABM
USA
Europe
Russia
China
3rd World
1970 employ defense & defe related jobs
Notes 9 (reading Felix Greene's The Enemy) -71

Figure 6.2: *Notes 9* (1971), Öyvind Fahlström. © 2016 Sharon Avery-Fahlström.

Figure 6.3 (following spread): *Study for Meatball Curtain* (1970). © 2016 Sharon Avery-Fahlström.

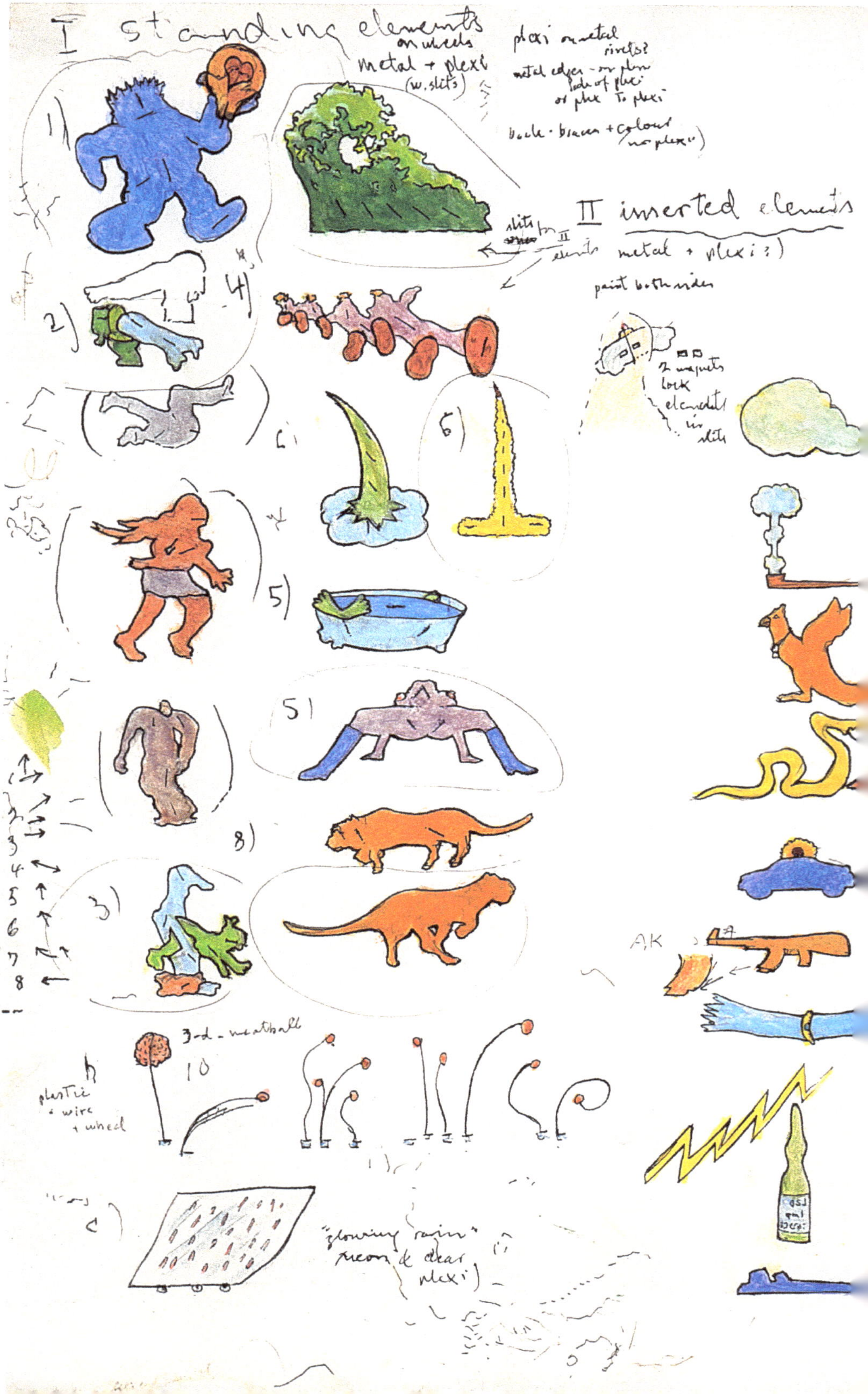

I standing elements on wheels metal + plexi (w. slits)

plexi or metal rivets? metal edges – or plexi back of plexi or plexi to plexi

back – braces + colour (no plexi)

II inserted elements

slits for II elements metal + plexi ?)

paint both sides

2 magnets lock elements in slits

1)

2)

4)

6)

5)

5)

8)

3)

1 2 3 4 5 6 7 8

AK

3-d – meatball

10

plastic + wire + wheel

"glowing rain" neon & clear plexi)

LSD

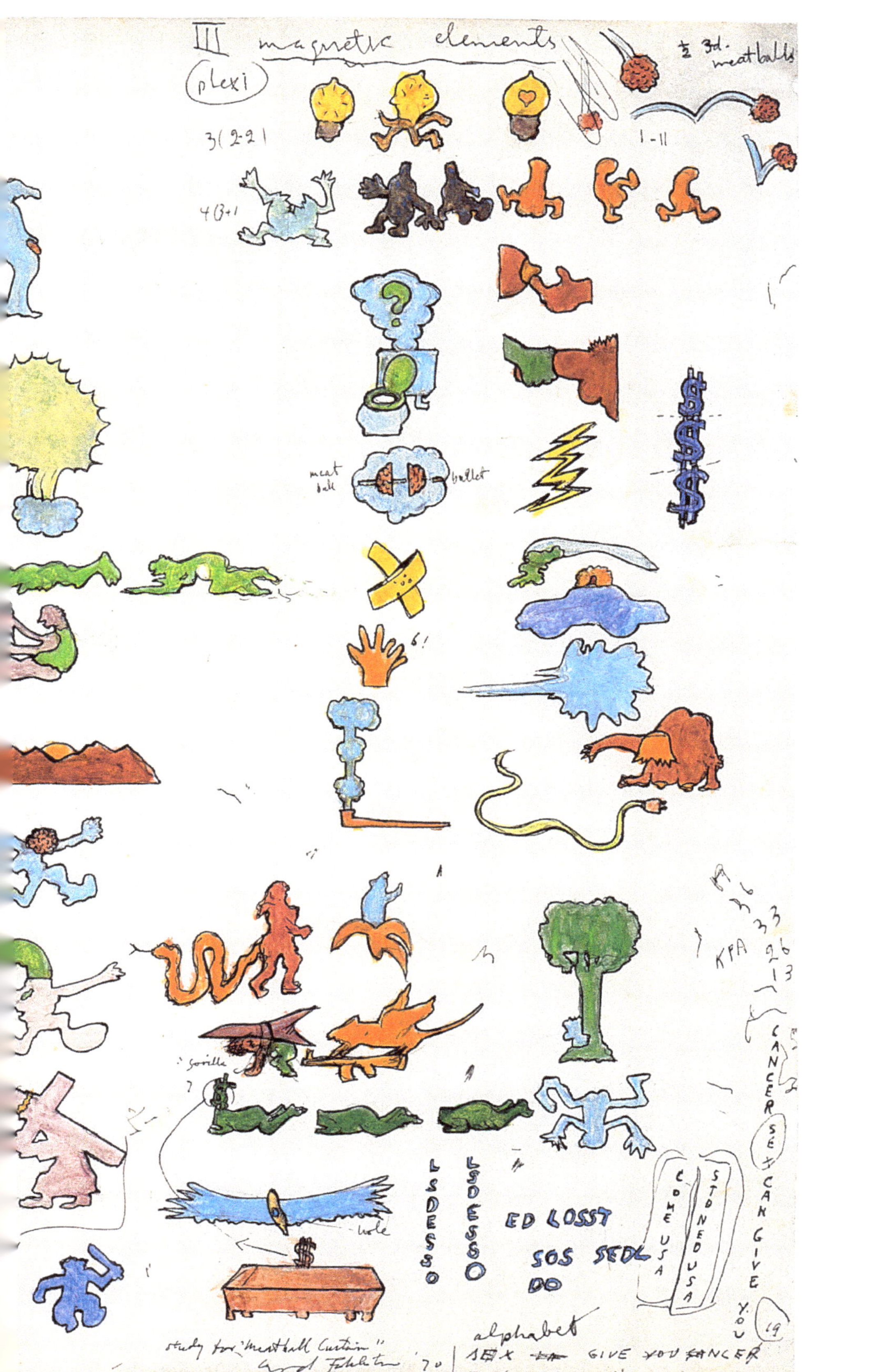

III magnetic elements
plexi
½ 3d. meatballs
meat ball
bullet
gorilla
hole
LSDESSO
LSDESSO
ED LOSST
SOS SEDL
DO
COME USA
STONED USA
CANCER
SEX CAN GIVE YOU
alphabet
SEX GIVE YOU CANCER
study for "Meatball Curtain" '70

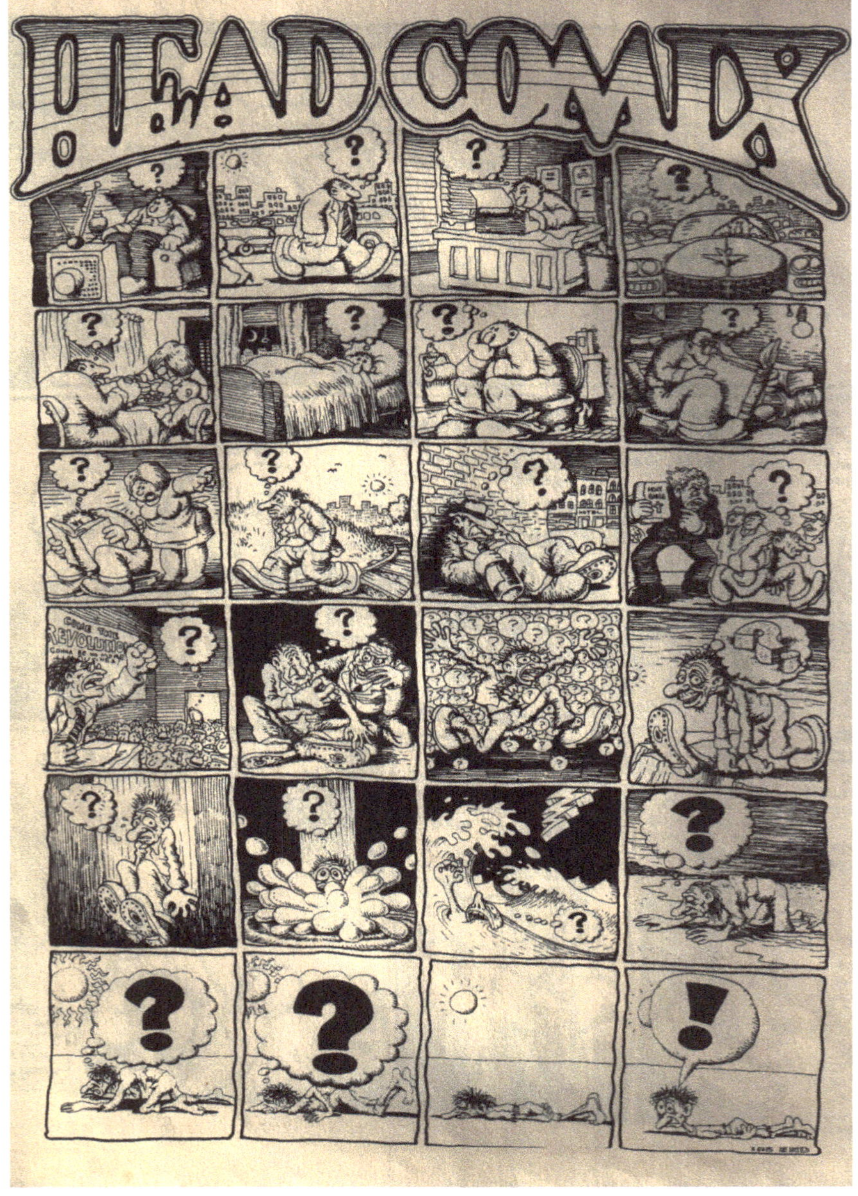

Figure 6.4: Robert Crumb, "Head Comix," 1967, republished in *R. Crumb's Head Comix*, New York, Ballantine Books, March 1970. © Robert Crumb, 1967.

Figure 6.5 (right): "Picture 33: Automobiles produced in 1929" from Otto Neurath, *International Picture Language, The First Rules of Isotype*, London: Kegan Paul, Trench Trubner & Co., Ltd, 1936, p. 93. Otto and Marie Neurath Isotype Collection, University of Reading.

Figure 6.6 (following page) "Picture 18" from Otto Neurath, International Picture Language, The First Rules of Isotype, London: Kegan Paul, Trench Trubner & Co., Ltd, 1936, p. 53. Otto and Marie Neurath Isotype Collection, University of Reading.

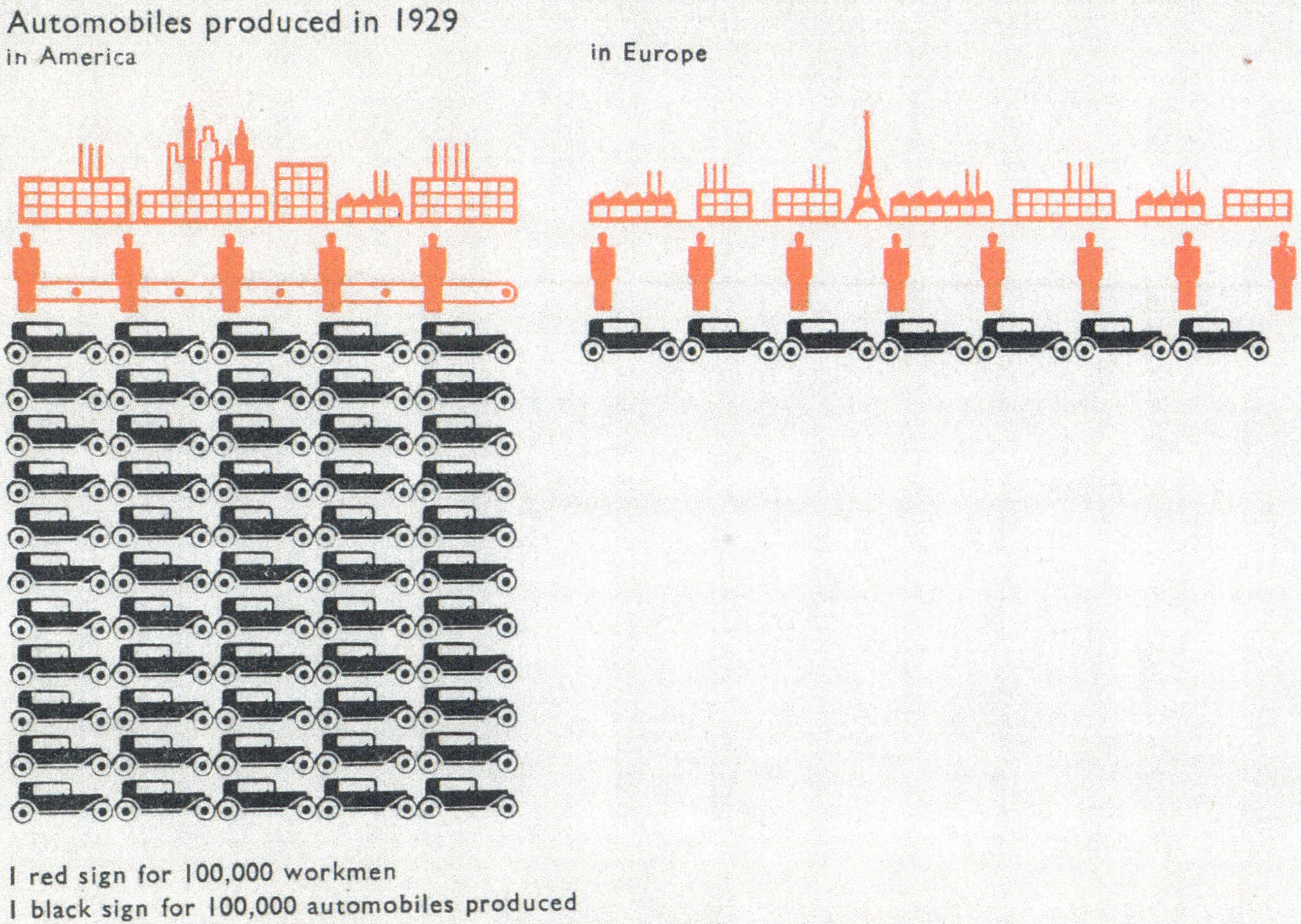

Automobiles produced in 1929

in America

in Europe

I red sign for 100,000 workmen

I black sign for 100,000 automobiles produced

PICTURE 33

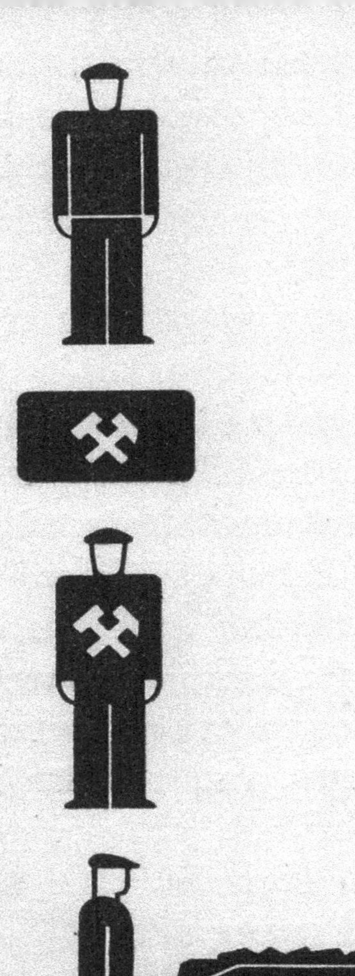

worker

coal

coal-worker

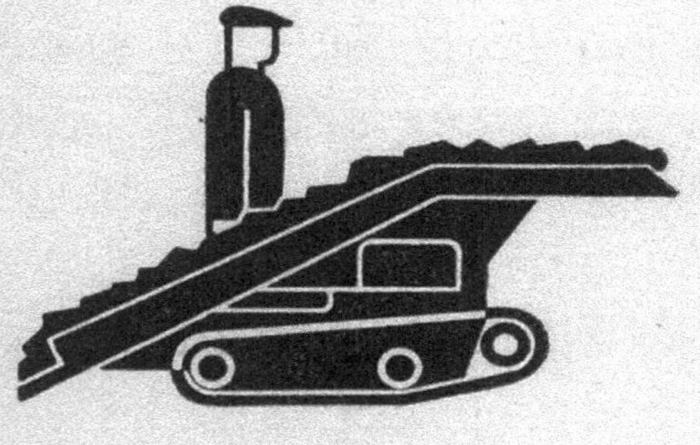

coal produced
by machine

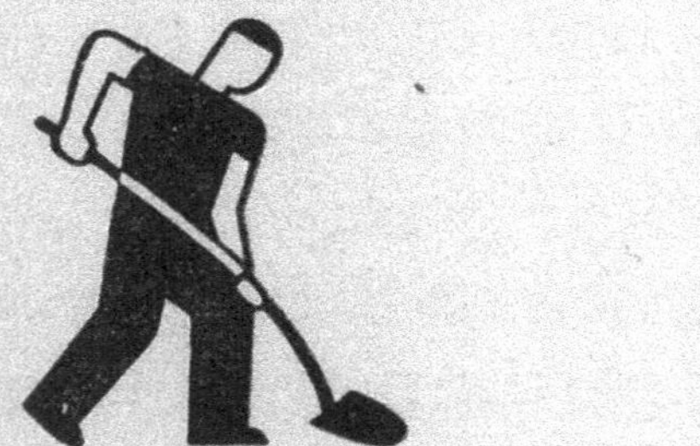

coal produced
by hand

PICTURE 18

7
AnthroPOPhagous
Political Uses of Pop Art in the Aftermath of the Brazilian Military Coup D'état of 1964

Oscar Svanelid

It has been presumed that Brazilian artists in the 1960s thought U.S. pop art to be a devaluation of art without, that is, perceiving the critical implications of that position (e.g. pop art as an attack on art as high culture). Brazilian art historian Sérgio B. Martins has recently given authorial weight to this view in his influential study *Constructing an Avant-Garde: Art in Brazil 1949–1979*. In a critical review of the Brazilian avant-garde and the realist turn that it took in the 1960s, Martins makes a brief but suggestive comment on its anti-reception of pop art. His argument is that the critical standpoint that Brazilian artists and critics took in relation to pop art showed signs of ignorance on their part.[1] Martins' claim is basically that the Brazilians did not know better than to dismiss pop art together with its commercial imagery. To explain this ignorance, Martins points to the peripheral position of the Brazilian avant-garde and its limited access to the original works of pop art. In the 1960s, the only time U.S. pop art was only shown in Brazil was when William C. Seitz curated the American pavilion at the IX São Paulo Biennial, 1967. That year Seitz had put together a selection of American artists into an extended lineage

[1] Sérgio B. Martins, *Constructing an Avant-Garde: Art in Brazil 1949–1979*, Cambridge, Mass. and London: The MIT Press, 2013, p. 106.

of pop art, from the early works of Rauschenberg and Johns, to works of Warhol, Lichtenstein, Oldenburg and others. Today we would certainly object to such all-inclusive notion of pop art, but it does not seem that this objection was raised in Brazil in the 1960s. Instead, it seems that Johns was the one who turned into the official representative of pop art in Brazil, after having been awarded the most prestigious prize at the São Paulo Art Biennial of 1967, known as the "Biennial of Pop."[2]

Martins claims, however, that the Biennial of Pop did not change much, as the Brazilian avant-garde had already made up their minds about pop art. They presumably did not see anything in pop art more than its commercial imagery, which they condemned with the anti-imperialistic spirit that spread within the Brazilian left in the aftermath of the military coup d'état in 1964. In a sweeping passage, Martins argues that this identification of pop art and commercial images happened when Brazilian artists looked at pop art in bad quality reproductions found in international art magazines that circulated within the Brazilian art world at that time. That transfer then presumably blurred every line that distinguishes pop art from ordinary commercial images. Without the capacity to make such distinction, Martins argues, the Brazilian easily dismissed pop art as "too acquiescent to consumerist society, if not an outright case of imperialistic propaganda."[3]

In these pages, I will not dispute Martins' claim that the Brazilian avant-garde refused to adapt the commercialised imagery of U.S. pop art. I argue however that Brazilian artists not only rejected pop art, but also picked it up and used it in their own practices. It is puzzling that Martins, who otherwise shows such acute understanding of the "AnthroPOPhagous" tricks played out by the Brazilian avant-garde in the 1960s, fails to distinguish the anthropophagism in their reception of pop art.[4] It is well-known today that the Brazilian modernist writer Oswald de Andrade's idea about anthropophagism (meaning cultural cannibalism) from the 1920s became actualised

[2] Martins, 2013, p.106. For further discussion about the IX São Paulo Biennial see *Wesley Duke Lee: Um salmão na corrente taciturna*, Cacilda Teixeira da Costa, São Paulo: Alameda Edusp, 2005, p.142–143.
[3] Martins, 2013, p. 106.
[4] See for example his very interesting analysis of Oiticica's AnthroPOPhagous take on the notion of constructive in Martins, 2013, pp. 51–78.

by artists and theorists in the 1960s as a means to rethink Brazilian cultural identity. An anthropophagical notion of identity can be seen to differ from that of traditional Western ontology in which identity is understood as that which remains the same across time. In contradistinction to this, Anthropophagism forms an autonomous sense of selfhood through processes of regenerations. An AnthroPOPhagous subject does not form itself by turning inwards but instead comes about through encounters with others, which, in a double movement, it both places within and without. Anthropophagites differ from cosmopolitans in that they distance themselves from others but, as philosopher Marcia Sá Cavalcante Schuback writes, for them such distancing "is already a coming close."[5]

The aim of this chapter is to rewrite the Brazilian reception of pop art in AnthroPOPhagous terms. With this, I do not suggest to make an argument for the existence of a Brazilian pop art. Instead I hold on to Martins' idea that pop art turned into the Other of the Brazilian avant-garde in the 1960s and in that way was kept at a distance. The Brazilian avant-garde never went pop, but I do think it displaced pop art into its own artistic corpus. I set out to argue this thesis via analyses of works by the Brazilian artists Waldemar Cordeiro and Hélio Oititica. My focus question through these cases will be how these artists managed to make a political use of pop art in the aftermath of the Brazilian military coup d'état of 1964?

Waldemar Cordeiro and the Popcretos

Immediately after the rise of the military dictatorship, Waldemar Cordeiro produced a series of circa two dozens of works (some of which are lost today), known as the Popcretos. When read, this term can be understood as a linguistic fusion of pop art (Pop) and *arte concreta* (-cretos). That this fusion was brought about by Cordeiro in the mid-1960s is surprising when his previous dogmatic approach to concrete art is taken into account. In the 1950s, Cordeiro lead the São Paulo-based avant-garde group; *Grupo Ruptura* that positioned itself in line with the post-Bauhaus concretism of

[5] Marcia Sá Cavalcante Schuback, *Olha a Olho: Ensaios de longe*, Rio de Janeiro: 7 Letras, 2011, p. 38. I stand as the translator of Portuguese texts if not stated otherwise.

Max Bill.[6] With the secure self-consciousness of a "true" modernist Cordeiro positioned himself in stark opposition to both the Brazilian school of figurative painters (Portinari, Segall, Di Cavalcante, Pancetti, etc.) and what he considered as a "false" form of abstract art that was developed in Rio de Janeiro at that time.[7]

During the early part of the 1960s, Cordeiro however began to question his own position but also the modernisation project of Brazil as such. An obvious reason for Cordeiro's shift is found in the breakup of Brazilian society that occurred when its utopian project of the 1950s flipped over into stagflation, political insecurity, and social uprisings in the 1960s. It was with the outspoken aim to counteract such disorder that the Brazilian military succeeded so easily with their armed, but unbloody, coup d'état in 1964. Cordeiro started making his first Popcretos at a time coeval with this military coup. In the following, I set out to question what it was in particular in pop art that Cordeiro put into use within this heated political context.

What Is the Pop of the Popcretos?

It is certainly difficult to discern what the pop of the Popcretos is simply by looking at them. They do not have that striking and colourful visuality that we are accustomed to associate with pop art. The Popcretos are also relatively small in scale, with an *in median* measure of 80x80. On the other hand, they do use mass-media images, often in the form of cut-outs from newspapers; but these images seem empty of drama. In this sense, the Popcretos add nothing to the "love and despair" list that Pontus Hultén

[6] Max Bill became the star of a generation of Brazilian modernists after his celebrated exhibitions in both São Paulo in the early 1950s, and most importantly his prestigious award received at the I São Paulo Biennial in 1951. Ronaldo Brito, *Neoconcretismo: Vértice e ruptura do projeto construtivo brasileiro*, Rio de Janeiro: Cosac & Naify Edições, 1999, p. 36. For a good discussion about Max Bill in Brazil, see Angela Lammert, "The 'Swiss Watchmaker' and the 'Jungle in Construction'—Max Bill and Modernism in Brazil or: What is Modern Art?" in Kudielka, Lammert, & Osorio (ed.*), Das Verlangen nach Form: Neoconcretismo und zeitgenössische Kunst aus Brasilien = O desejo da forma*, Berlin, Akademie der Künste, 2010, 259–269.

[7] For a good discussion of the conflict between concretist from Rio de Janeiro and São Paulo that crystallised after the *National Exhibition of Concrete Art* held in both Rio de Janeiro and São Paulo in 1956–1957; see Martins, 2013, pp. 19–31.

drew up in his seminal pop show at the Moderna Museet in Stockholm, 1965. By looking at the Popcretos, I would like to conclude that they are not pop art, nor do they pretend to be.

In fact, the very term Popcretos seems itself a bit suspicious. It was not Cordeiro who coined it but his friend and artistic colleague, the poet Augusto de Campos. When spotting these works, de Campos is quoted to have said that they have "swallowed the experience of North American pop art in a critical and anthropophagic fashion."[8] Cordeiro then applied the term Popcreto, perhaps because it was quite catchy, to this work series and also "swallowed" it into some of the works themselves.[9] But what was pop about them? There has been but a few previous attempts to answer this question. Within these accounts there is however a general agreement that Robert Rauschenberg was Cordeiro's main reference on pop art at the time. The thought of Rauschenberg as pop art certainly bends our present conception, but it seems to set it straight when it comes to explain the pop of the Popcretos. After all, the Popcretos are enactments of Combine painting as they mix colours and ready-made objects on the canvas.

The Brazilian art historian Nunes Fabrizio Vaz identifies Paris as the "contact zone" of Cordeiro and Rauschenberg. This seems plausible, as Rauschenberg started to appear in Cordeiro's writings while staying in Paris from the late spring to the autumn of 1963, which was right before he had started working on his Popcretos series.[10] However this point of transfer is, in fact, a bit more complicated than Fabrizio Vaz wants to make it appear, as it would not have been possible for Cordeiro to actually see Rauschenberg's works, since they were not exhibited in Paris during this period. Then again, I suggest that it would have been close to impossible for anyone circulating in the Parisian art world in 1963 *not* to known of Rauschenberg. Although still lacking exact information concerning Cordeiro's experiences of Rauschenberg, we know for certain that it did

[8] José Lourerio, "Poetas de Vanguarda tomam posição," *Correio da Manhã*, Rio de Janeiro, 13 March 1965.

[9] The works *Popcreto para um popcritico* (1964) and *Popcreto I* (1964) explicitly address the term Popcreto.

[10] It has been said that Cordeiro got to know of Rauschenberg after the latter's historical success at the XXXII Venice Biennial in 1964. This does not make sense, however, as Cordeiro showed his first Popcretos at an exhibition in June at *Instituto dos Arquitetos do Brasil* (IAB); at the same month, that is, as Rauschenberg won his prestigious award.

not come about after seeing the originals but from reproductions. I differ from Martins' argument that I discussed in the introduction to this chapter, since I do not think that the lack of access to original works mattered much in this case. Cordeiro was not a connoisseur of pop art, nor did he ever pretend to be one. I would like to show that what he took from pop art, or from Rauschenberg in particular, was on such general level that it could have been transferred even by the worst quality copy.

What do the Popcretos mean?

The first person to ponder what the pop in the Popcretos meant was the German philosopher Max Bense. Bense had come to know Cordeiro in the early 1960s while lecturing on modern aesthetics in Brazil. Bense's appearance on the Brazilian art scene is best seen as part of the quite intense transatlantic traffic that flowed between Brazilian art institutions and the *Hochscule für Gestaltung* in Ulm, where Bense was a professor in 1954–1958.[11] Bense did not make a trip to Brazil to visit Cordeiro in order to see his Popcretos, however. Instead, Cordeiro sent photographs of them to Bense in Stuttgart and asked him to provide his thoughts. Bense answered in a letter, which was later published in the exhibition catalogue of *Espetáculo Popcreto* that Cordeiro and Augusto de Campos organised at Galeria Atrium in São Paulo towards the end of 1964. We know from press reports that this exhibition attracted a relatively large audience, with one reporter writing about a bunch of people who were "scratching their heads" when standing in front of the Popcretos.[12]

In his analysis however, Bense did what he could to ease things up. In his interpretation, he divided the term Popcreto into pop art and concrete art. This nominal split, he then argued, is equally present within the works themselves, which stages a form of dialectics of pop art and concrete art.[13] Out of what Bense says, this dialectics sorts into a diagram that looks something like this:

[11] Bense reflected on his experience of Brazil in his book *Brasilianische Intelligenz: Eine cartesianische Reflexion*, Limes, Wiesbaden 1965.
[12] Ivo Zanini, "Muita gente coçou a cabeca na exposição 'Popcreta'," *Folha de São Paulo*, 19 December 1964.
[13] Max Bense, "Max Bense: Carta-prefácio" in Analívia Cordeiro, *Waldemar Cordeiro (CD-Rom)*, São Paulo: Galeria Brito Cimino, 2001.

POP	CONCRETE
Everyday objects (e.g. chairs)	Mathematical figures (e.g. polygons)
Banal	Ideal
Material	Platonic
Disorder	Order
Practical use	Theoretical consumption

At first, Bense's reading of the Popcretos seems quite plausible. When folding through the photographs of the Popcretos, I find both mathematical figures and everyday objects, although the mathematics is more downplayed. At the same time, I think it is important to ask "what everyday do these objects point to?" Cordeiro's everyday is not that of commercial mass-consumption. Instead there is furniture, but also different kinds of tools. However, I am not in total agreement with Bense that these tools denote practical use. Of course, the viewers could not use these tools. In that sense, they were out of the ordinary order of things. That suppression of utility, however, highlighted their being as signs for us to think about. In opposition to Bense, I suggest that these tools are for theoretical consumption; they are tools for thought, to be pondered. In that sense, they are not within the realm of the banal. Instead, they can be thought of as conveying ideas. But what ideas? I argue that this is the question that the Popcretos prompts each viewer to ask. That is also why the Popcretos should not be resolved into the closure of a diagram. In fact, I believe the news report of people scratching their heads to be closer to the function of the Popcretos than Bense's philosophical interpretation. I suggest that this enforcement of thought is what these works are really about.

Popcretos as semantical concrete art

To grasp the thinking that the Popcretos entails, I find it necessary to bracket the term Popcreto, at least for a while. Cordeiro, in fact, also used another term to designate these works which is less catchy, but perhaps closer to the point: "semantic concrete art."[14] I find this term interesting, as it shows how far Cordeiro has travelled conceptually in relation to historical concretism. His paintings from the 1950s were designed with the purpose of deepening an apprehension of form. It is clear that such form was not thought to *mean* something. Semantics thus appeared on the outside of concrete art where it lingered as nothing more than an archaic trace from old figurative art. This distance was held intact, I would argue, also in the renewed trend of concrete art that spread across Europe through the New Tendencies network in the 1960s. New Tendencies germinated from an exhibition held in Zagreb in 1961, organised by the Brazilian Almir Mavignier, who was then based in Ulm, in collaboration with the Serbian art historian Matko Meštrović. Cordeiro also came in contact with the New Tendencies in Paris during his stay there in 1963, via his close affiliation with the French *Groupe de recherche d'art visual* (GRAV), then partaking in New Tendencies. In the GRAV manifesto for "progressive abstract art," written in 1963 by François Molnar and François Morellet, it continued to hold semantics at a distance. In an ironical remark, they speak about "ill-informed art lovers" at pains to *understand* abstract art. "But," as they say, "abstract art doesn't mean anything; it's a system of signs that refer to nothing but itself."[15]

Theorised as semantic concrete art the Popcretos do indeed set out to mean something. It differs on this point from historical concrete art but also from the progressive abstract art of the New Tendencies. Keeping to Augusto de Campos' analysis that Cordeiro had "swallowed" pop art in these works, meaning seems to have been one of his most important takes. What this implies however, is that despite their name, the Popcretos are not a fusion of pop art and concrete art. Instead it seems that pop art has taken Cordeiro out of concrete art with its principles of formalist autonomy into the abyssal space of meaning production.

[14] Waldemar Cordeiro, "Semantic Concrete Art," in Rosen, 2011, pp. 202–203. Cordeiro wrote this important text in September 1964 and it was published as "Art Concret Sémantique," in *Nova tendencija 3*, exh. cat., Galerija suvremene umjetnosti, Zagreb, 1965.

[15] François Molnar and François Morellet, "For a Progressive Abstract Art," in Rosen, 2011, p. 137.

Popcretos and political meaning

It is my thesis that Cordeiro's take on pop art had political implications. But what was political about them? In her book *Waldemar Cordeiro: A ruptura como metáfora* (2002), the Brazilian art historian Helouise Costa has attempted to answer this question. It is developed in her reading of the painting *Popcreto para um popcrítico*, exhibited at Galeria Atrium in December 1964 only about six months after the military coup d'état. Costa writes:

> On top of a red ground [this painting] presents us with a hoe flanked by some photo clippings. While it is possible to identify images of mouths, noses and strands of hair within the small circles [in the red ground], a tactically situated eye stands out from this arrangement. If we make use of the interpretative liberty advocated to us by the artist and take the political imagination of this period as a reference point; we find that the possibilities of communication of the works amplifies: red = communism; hoe = agrarian reform; fragments of imprisoned bodies tortured and a centralised eye of control.[16]

Costa has a good case here. Her interpretations are underscored by historical facts; the agrarian reform was a heated subject in Brazilian politics around the time of the military coup; censorship and dictatorial control came in its wake, and so on. I would suggest, however, that Costa betrays her own premises when reading the Popcretos in the way she does. Would not an "interpretative liberty," to which she refers, mean that the signs that are encountered in these works (hoe, red ground, circles, body parts, eye) rather than point to fixed connotations open towards the unknown? I think that they do; and find it significant that beside Rauschenberg, Cordeiro also turned to Umberto Eco's notion of "the open work" around the time of making his Popcretos. Then perhaps the political aspect of these works does not lay so much in the content as in the mode of reading that they propose. I want to make clear that an important aspect of the Popcretos was that they stimulated thinking to unfix itself. That is why I think both Bense and Costa are wrong in their respective attempts to nail the meaning of these works. I argue that what is at stake in the Popcretos is an empowerment of the reader, who is called into the work in order to

[16] Helouise Costas, 2002, pp. 14–17.

think it through. The signs of the Popcretos are then not signs in and of themselves, as it still was in the progressive abstract art that was forwarded by the GRAV at this time, but rather encounters the reader as mental tools. With the help of these tools, the Popcretos are to be processed. Where this process ends up, I suggest, is not given from the outset. There is a conflict here between this form of open process that the Popcretos enacts and the return to order that was projected by the Brazilian military regime at this time. The Popcretos are filled with signs of the broken. If there is an everyday quality in these works, it is one that is breaking down. The ready-made objects shown are either worn out, disintegrating, or mechanically divided up. One gets the same sense of fragmentation when looking at the newspaper cut-outs that appear in the Popcretos, both images and words. A work titled "Jornal" (Newspaper) has multiple front pages folded into each other into a single page. This results in a semantic system of broken sentences, singular letters and gaping holes. At first, I encounter nothing here but semantic noise, absence of meaning. Then, from this noisy space, the phrase "revolução") ("Revolution, or "Revolts") suddenly appears. It thus seems that it is in the negative break-down of the system that the Popcretos locates its revolt. At the same time, it sets out to enforce a mode of reading that knows how to sustain an open semantics. This is also where they crash with the dictatorial project of a "return to order." As epitomised in the work *Contra-Mão* (Wrong Way), the Popcretos aimed to steer the mind of the Brazilian public in the opposite direction to that of the military regime, simply by showing things that defy the law of concrete and semantic unity (Figure 1).

Hélio Oiticica and Pop Art

In a diary note from 1968, the Brazilian visual artist Hélio Oiticica writes:

> For a true Brazilian culture to be created, strong and with proper character, this damn European and American heritage [Oiticica has just explicitly referenced U.S. pop art] had to be absorbed anthropophagously by the Blacks and Indians of this country, which are in fact the only thing of significance, because most Brazilian art is hybrid, intellectualized to the extreme, empty of any proper significance.

In the critical literature on Oititica much has been said about his "absorption" of constructive art into the life of the world of the Brazilian *favela* in works such as the *Parangolés* (1964) and *Tropicália* (1966).[17] On the other hand, there has been but a few inquiries into Oititica's relationship to U.S. pop art. This neglect is not without reasons. In his writings, Oititica often manifested an eagerness to distance his works from pop art. Without disagreeing that Oititica showed a critical or even hostile attitude towards pop art, I argue that he also accepted and incorporated parts of it into his works.

Oititica's anti-pop attitude is explicitly stated in his text *Esquema geral da nova objectividade* (General Scheme for a New Objectivity) that was published in connection with his seminal Tropicália-installation at the Museo de Arte Moderna in Rio de Janeiro, 1967. In this text, Oititica proclaimed the unity of the Brazilian avant-garde unlike internationalist trends such as op art and pop art. For this, he formulates a manifesto with six-points:

> 1 – general constructive will; 2 – move towards the object, as easel painting is negated and superseded; 3 – the participation of the spectator (bodily, tactile, semantic, etc.); 4 – an engagement and a position on political, social and ethical problems; 5 – tendency towards collective propositions and consequently the abolition, in the art of today, of "isms," so characteristic of the first half of the century (a tendency which can be encompassed by Mário Pedrosa's concept of "Post-Modern Art"); 6 – a revival of, and new formulations, in the concept of anti-art.[18]

Without wanting to dispute Oititica's claim in this manifesto, I would like to suggest that it also reads as a tactical move. At the time for writing this, Oititica was also reclaiming the notion of anthropophagism.[19] As previously discussed, anthropophagites does not only refuse but also strives to incorporate the other into itself so as to mutate its own selfhood. The other is thus caught in a double movement, where it is simultaneously

[17] See for example, Martins, 2013, pp. 51–78, Michael Asbury, "Hélio Couldn't Dance," in Paula Braga (ed.), *Fios Soltos: a arte de Hélio Oititica*, São Paulo: Perspectiva, pp. 52–65.
[18] Hélio Oiticica, "Esquema geral da nova objectividade" (1967) in Martins, 2013, p.63. Martins's translation.
[19] Martins, 2013, p. 51.

within and without. What we know is that Oititica placed pop art on the outside of the Brazilian avant-garde, and this is beyond dispute; I suspect that he also put it inside.

Rauschenberg and neo-concrete theory

I have located an "entry" in a diary note that Oititica wrote as early as 1963. In this note, Oititica discusses Rauschenberg and Johns and places them in relation to the work series *Bólides* (Bolides) which he had started making that year.[20] It was in the Bolides that Oititica started to make use of ready-made objects. This series changed quite a bit throughout Oititica's artistic trajectory, but the initial works limited their use of ready-mades mostly to boxes and glass bottles of various different kinds.[21] Ferreira Gullar, a leading critique of the Neo-concrete group in which Oititica participated from 1959–1961, had argued against the use of ready-mades for constructive art in his *Teoria do Não-Objeto* (Theory of the Non-Object). In Gullar's view, ready-mades, which he knew about through Duchamp and Schwitters, showed a false answer to the problem of spatial construction. What Gullar was after was a type of object that while being distinct from the traditions of painting and sculpture also distinguished itself from everyday objects. Ready-mades, I think, implied too much of the everyday to be accepted in Gullar's aesthetics; and for which Lygia Clark *Bichos* (Animals/Critters) manifested the seminal example.[22] When Oititica came to accept ready-mades into his Bólides four years after Gullar's text, while still holding on to many of its main ideas, it was not without reservations.

As mentioned, Oititica's main reference on the ready-made was the works of Rauschenberg and Johns. Oititica had not been able to see their

[20] Hélio Oiticica, "Bólides," October 29, 1963 (Arquivo Hélio Oititica/Projeto Hélio Oiticica 1816.63), 1. Oiticica had written another note of the Bolides i September 1963, where he placed it in relation to Ernst Cassier's "symbolic form." See, Hélio Oititica, "Experiência dos Bólides," September 19, 1963 (Arquivo Hélio Oititica/Projeto Hélio Oiticica 007.63), 1–2.

[21] For a throughout discussion of the development of the Bolides and their relation to Oiticicas work series Parangolés see. Irene. V. Small, *Hélio Oititica: Folding the Frame*, Chicago, The University of Chicago, 2016, chapter 3 and 4.

[22] Ferreira Gullar, "Teoria do não-objeto," in Ferreria Gullar, *Etapas da arte contemporânea: do cubismo à arte neoconcreta*, Rio de Janeiro: Revan, 1999, pp 291–292.

works in the original but instead based his observations on what he had seen from secondary sources. Of this, little is known besides that he had seen an image of Rauschenberg's *Pilgrim* (1960), of which he writes in a diary note from 1963. Oititica makes a quite absurd but interesting reading of the chair that stands attached to the canvas in Rauschenberg's *Pilgrim*, to have the appearance of a "spine" securing the traditional structure of painting (the rectangular structure of the canvas) at a moment when painting is at its closest of leaving it behind.[23] Thus rather than comprehending Rauschenberg as a free-spirited migratory bird, Oititica sees him to be stuck within the gravity field of traditional easel painting.

What Oiticica seems to suggest in his analysis of Rauschenberg is that just attaching things to the canvas does not take us very far. This form of Combine painting does not escape or even counteract its structural givens. What Oititica wants at this time, and what he later returns to speak about as properly Brazilian in his 1967 manifesto, is to supersede traditional easel painting. In opposition to Gullar's Neo-concrete aesthetics, Oititica proposes to make this transgression through the use of ready-mades. But he wants to have it the other way around from what he discerned in Rauschenberg, by bringing forth painting out of the already existing instead of bringing things into the painting. In that sense, the ready-made enters as a means to enforce a structural displacement of painting. It makes it lose the traditional grounds of the canvas or anything functioning as its structure *a priori*. When incorporating the ready-made, Oititica certainly does not transform into a pop artist, but it was in reference to pop art that he incorporated it. Through pop art, but also despite it, Oititica regenerated his practice away from his previous Neo-concrete standpoint on how to spatialise painting.

The aesthetics of the Bolides

But what about the anthropophagical "absorption" of pop art and black culture that Oititica spoke about in his retrospective diary note from 1968, quoted at the outset of this case study? When looking at the Bolides that Oititica produced in the early to mid-1960s, it is most difficult to discern

[23] Hélio Oititica, in Oiticica Filho (org.), 2011, p. 64.

such connection. As I mentioned above, the initial versions of the Bólides were made out of ready-made boxes or bottles. Oiticicas explicit purpose was to use these objects to convey an aesthetical concept.[24] To get this concept, I find it helpful to dissect the etymological meaning of the term Bolide, which comes from Greek βολίς, meaning "missile" or "flash"; Bolide is also used in astronomy to designate an exploding meteor. Likewise, the Bolides could be seen as an attempt to flash out colour and object as one. I suggest that this idea or concept should be understood in relation to Oititica's attempt to transgress the notion of painting as colour applied to a pregiven surface. Colour was meant to appear as integral to the ready-made structure of the Bolides; these were to be seen as objects of colour and not as painted things. The Bolides also stresses the involvement of the viewer. They are interactive in a perceptual sense. It is the viewer that actualises them but in this actualisation the viewer enters into a kind of creative regression. By using pigments, the Bolides brings the eye back to look at colours in their embryonic state; which is also a state of high intensity. This creative regression is also enacted through the perceptual play that the Bolides works to enact in the viewer by inviting him or her to open drawers or boxes, sneak into narrow spaces, looking closely, touching to know.

Homage to Cara de Cavalo

One Bólide, however, shows a stark contrast to the aesthetical idea found in the others. We can see this work flashing in the foreground at a photograph taken at Oititica's first solo exhibition at Galeria G-4 in Rio de Janeiro, 1966; in front of the children playing, there is another Bólide (Figure 7.2). This Bólide is titled *B33 Bólide Caixa 18, Poema-Caixa 2 – "Homenagem a Cara de Cavalo"* (B 33 Box Bolide 18, Box Poem 2 "Homage to Cara de Cavalo"). On the four sides of this box there is one and the same photograph showing a horrible image of the mutilated corpse of a black man known as Cara de Cavalo. This man gained an infamous reputation for himself after killing a police officer in Rio de Janeiro in 1964. The Brazilian public could follow the police hunt for this

[24] Oititica, 2011, p. 63.

man through an intense media coverage. When the photograph of the executed Cara de Cavalo (his body had been perforated with over 70 bullets) appeared in the press, one of which Oiticica appropriates for this work, it was framed as a police trophy; a symbol of law and order.

Oiticica's *Box Bolide 18* is then easily seen as an anomaly within his *Bolide* series. Instead of creative regression, it stands up to touch upon a heated political subject. In passing, it could be noted that such engagement with the social world made this work be received as pop art in a press review of Oiticica's exhibition at Galeria G-4. While not being in agreement here, it is certainly so that its use of media images makes it appear closer to pop art then other Bólides. The box used in this work is still a ready-made, but through the use of media images it no longer answers only to the transgression of painting. Instead of just pointing towards its own aesthetics, it uses the ready-made as a structure from where to voice a statement on a political subject.

Martins has previously discussed the political aspect of Box Bolide 18. He also looks at this work to stage a different perceptive mode then other Bolides. Instead of trying to "absorb" its viewer, Martins argues that Box Bolide 18 is "*thrown* like a bomb at the viewer's face" (Martins' emphasis).[25] To support his claim, Martins points to a photograph taken of Box Bolide 18 in 1966. On this photograph, Oiticica is seen kneeling down beside his work, looking at the viewer in danger. When staged as in this photograph, Box Bolide 18 certainly does appear to attack its viewers. Even when looking at this photograph today, I feel myself taking a step backwards, as when receiving a blow. But I get quite another feeling when I see another photograph in which I see the black girl Luiza, who was also a friend of Oiticica, looking into this box (Figure 7.3). Martins also discusses this other reception, which instead of attack seems to reflect an emotional encounter, of which he is at pains to legitimate. When Martins defines the agency of *Box Bolide 18* as aggressive, I think he overlooks something quite important. For Oiticica to flash this work open to the camera, at first he had to remove a pink net of iron hanging in front of the images of the dead Cara de Cavalo; screening them, as it were. When ordinary viewers such as Luiza encountered this work as it was exposed at

[25] Martins, 2013, p.111.

Galeria G-4, this net was not yet removed however. What they were invited to do then were to come up close to the work, kneel down beside it and look in. When doing this they were also enabled to ready that brief dedication that Oiticica had written for Cara de Cavalo, as if to a king, inscribed on a transparent plastic bag filled with yellowish pigment laying inside the box like a pillow, reading: "Here he is and here he will stay! Contemplate his heroic silence."

Rather than exploding like a bomb, *Box Bolide 18* talks about a contemplation of silence. This is a political silence, no doubt. Oiticica proposes that the reader listen to this silenced body. Through slow contemplation, Cara de Cavalo is meant to transform from a trophy of the law to a symbol of resistance. It is within these lines I suggest we are to read Oiticica's later statement, quoted above, that pop art had to be absorbed anthropophagously by the blacks of Brazil. In *Box Bolide 18*, the ready-made object functions as structure on which the inglorious reputation of the black criminal is turned around into a heroic resistance. I suggest that Oiticica wanted to establish an affective relationship between the viewer and this man. But rather than piercing out like *a punctum*. or exploding like a bomb, Box Bolide 18 sets the viewer, becoming a reader, becoming a listener, in an contemplative intimacy with the brutal encounter of Black political resistance and the military police.

Conclusion

In this text, I have argued that the Brazilian reception of U.S. pop art in the 1960s should be reformulated in AnthroPOPhagous terms. I have shown how the Brazilian artists Waldemar Cordeiro and Hélio Oiticica, while certainly distancing themselves from pop art as such (neither of them wanted to produce pop art in any strict sense), also incorporated it into their respective practices. In my perspective, pop art can be seen as having functioned as a turning point for both Cordeiro and Oiticica in the early period of the military dictatorship (1964–1968). Cordeiro picked up the idea of semantic painting from Rauschenberg and used it to stimulate antagonistic thoughts. Oiticica incorporated ready-made objects, with reference to Rauschenberg and Johns, and also started to deal with the symbolic order. In his famous work Box Bolide 18 from 1966, these elements were combined and used in order to get the Brazilian public in touch with the death of the black other. Far from seeing pop art as nothing but a devaluation of art as has previously been presumed, I have shown that these Brazilian artists transformed it into a political instrument.

References

Books

Beatriz Scigliano Carneiro, *Relâmpagos com Claror: Lygia Clark e Hélio Oititica, vida como arte*, São Paulo: Imaginário, 2004.

Branden W. Joseph, *Random Order: Robert Rauschenberg and the neo-avant-garde*, Cambridge, Mass and London, The MIT Press.

César Oititica Filho (org.), *Hélio Oiticica: Museu é o mundo*, Rio de Janeiro: Beco do Azougue, 2011.

François Molnar and François Morellet, "For a Progressive Abstract Art," in Margrit Rosen (ed.), *A Little Known Story About a Movement, a Magazine, and the Computer's Arrival in Art: New Tendencies and Bit International, 1961–1973*, Cambridge, Mass. and London: The MIT Press, 2001.

Ferreria Gullar, *Etapas da arte contemporânea: do cubismo à arte neoconcreta*, Rio de Janeiro: Revan, 1999.

Hélio Oititica, "Esquema geral da nova objectividade," in César Oititica Filho (org.), *Hélio Oiticica: Museu é o mundo*, Rio de Janeiro: Beco do Azougue, 2011.

Helouise Costas, *Waldemar Cordeiro: Ruptura como metáfora*, São Paulo: Cosac & Naify, 2002.

Hiroko Ikegami, *The Great Migrator: Robert Rauschenberg and the Global Rise of American Art*, Cambridge, Mass and London: The MIT Press, 2010.

Sérgio B. Martins, *Constructing an Avant-Garde: Art in Brazil 1949–1979*, Cambridge, Mass. and London: The MIT Press, 2013.

Marcia Sá Cavalcante Schuback, *Olha a Olho: Ensaios de longe*, Rio de Janeiro: 7Letras, 2011.

Irene. V. Small, *Hélio Oititica: Folding the Frame*, Chicago, The University of Chicago, 2016

Margrit Rosen (ed.), *A Little Known Story About a Movement, a Magazine, and the Computer's Arrival in Art: New Tendencies and Bit International, 1961–1973*, Cambridge, Mass., and London: The MIT Press, 2001.

Michael Asbury, "Hélio Couldn't Dance," in Paula Braga (org.), *Fios Soltos: A arte do Hélio Oititica*, Rio de Janeiro: Perspectiva, 2008.

Nunes Fabrizio Vaz, *Waldemar Cordeiro: da arte concreta ao "popcreto,"* Campinas, Master thesis (unpublished), 2004.

Paula Braga (org.), *Fios Soltos: A arte do Hélio Oititica*, Rio de Janeiro: Perspectiva, 2008.

Angela Lammert, "The 'Swiss Watchmaker' and the 'Jungle in Construction' – Max Bill and Modernism in Brazil or: What is Modern Art?" in Kudielka, Lammert, & Osorio (ed.), *Das Verlangen nach Form: Neoconcretismo und zeitgenössische Kunst aus Brasilien = O desejo da forma*, Berlin, Akademie der Künste, 2010

Waldemar Cordeiro, "Semantic Concrete Art" (1965), in Margrit Rosen (ed.), *A Little Known Story About a Movement, a Magazine, and the Computer's Arrival in Art: New Tendencies and Bit International, 1961–1973*, Cambridge, Mass., and London: The MIT Press, 2001.

Teixeira da Costa, Cacilda (ed.), *Aproximações do espírito pop: 1963–1968 : Waldemar Cordeiro, Antonio Dias, Wesley Duke Lee, Nelson Leirner,* Museu de Arte Moderna, São Paulo, 2003.

Periodicals

Ivo Zanini, "Muita gente coçou a cabeca na exposição 'Popcreta'," *Folha de São Paulo*, 19 Deember 1964.

José Lourerio, "Poetas de Vanguarda tomam posição," *Correio da Manhã*, Rio de Janeiro, 13 March 1965.

John Cage, "On Robert Rauschenberg, Artist, and His Work," *Silence*, Middletown, Conn., Wesleyan University Press, 1961

Digital media

Analivia Cordeiro (org.), *Waldemar Cordeiro (CD-Rom)*, São Paulo: Galeria Brito Cimino, 2001.

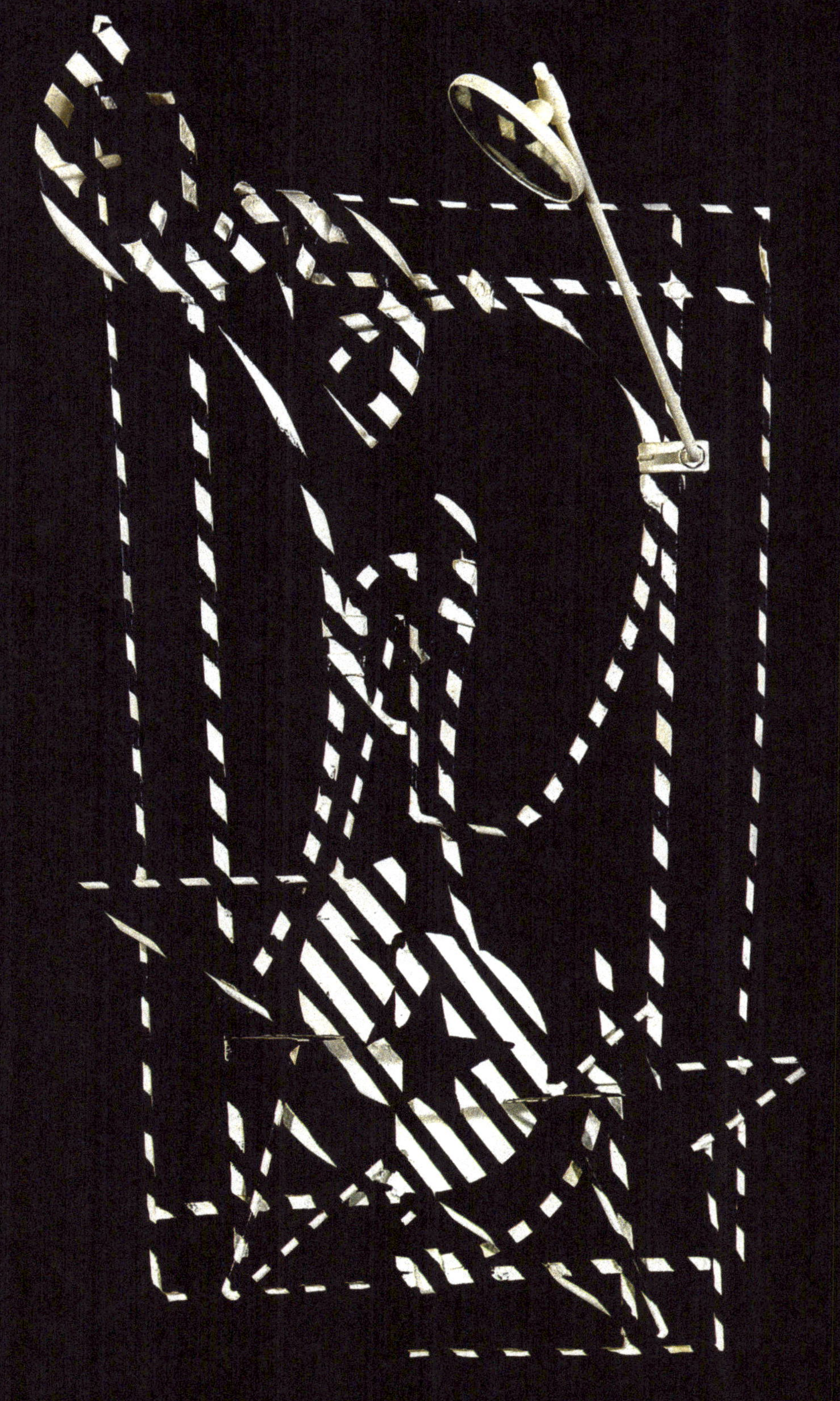

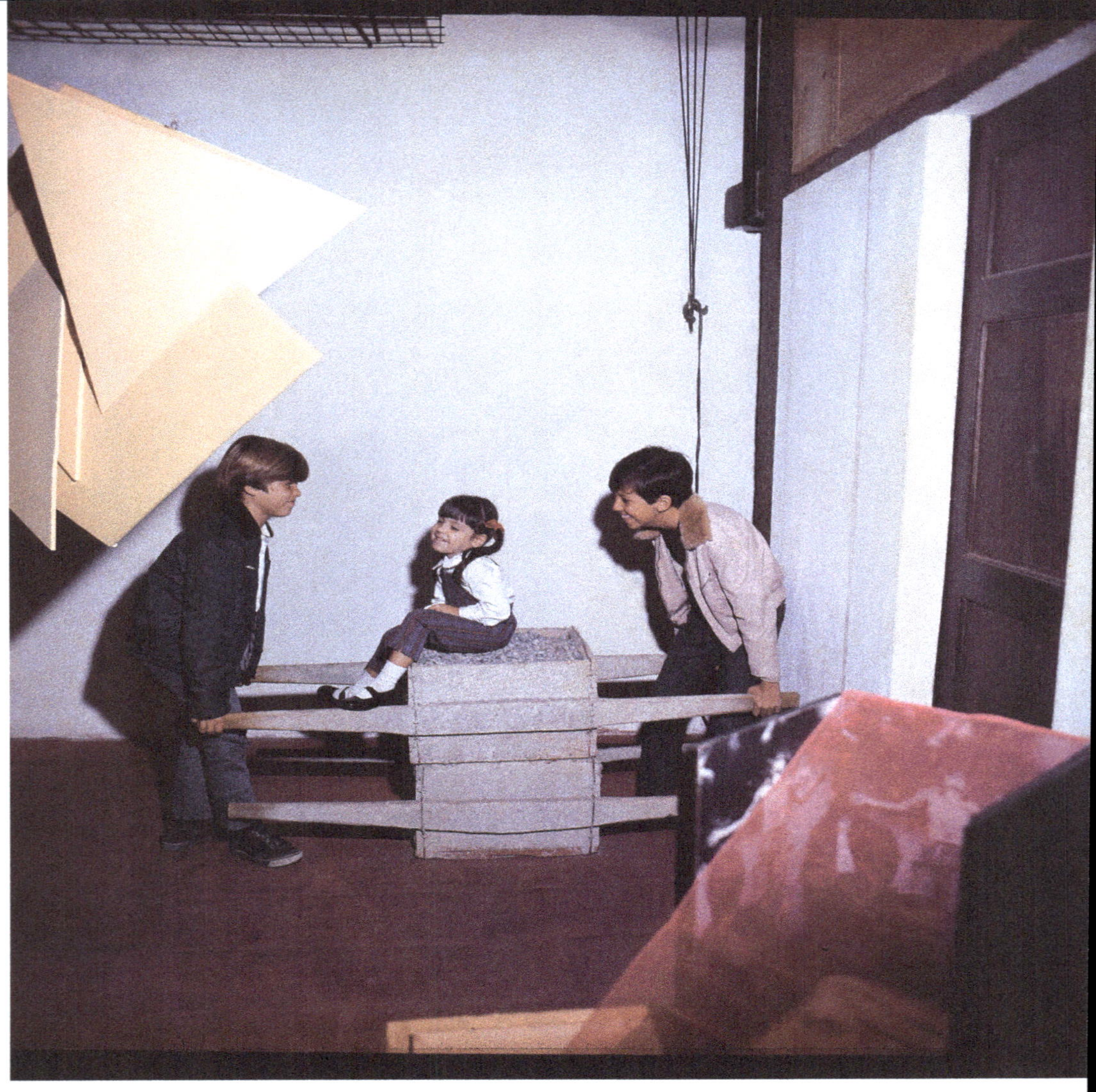

Figure 7.1 (previous page): Waldemar Cordeiro, Contra-Mão, Montage with objects in painted iron, 70 x 100, 1964. © Família Cordeiro.

Figure 7.2: Photograph from Oiticicas first solo exhibition at Galeria G-4, Rio de Janeiro, 1966. Photo: Alexandre Baratta. © César and Claudio Oiticica.

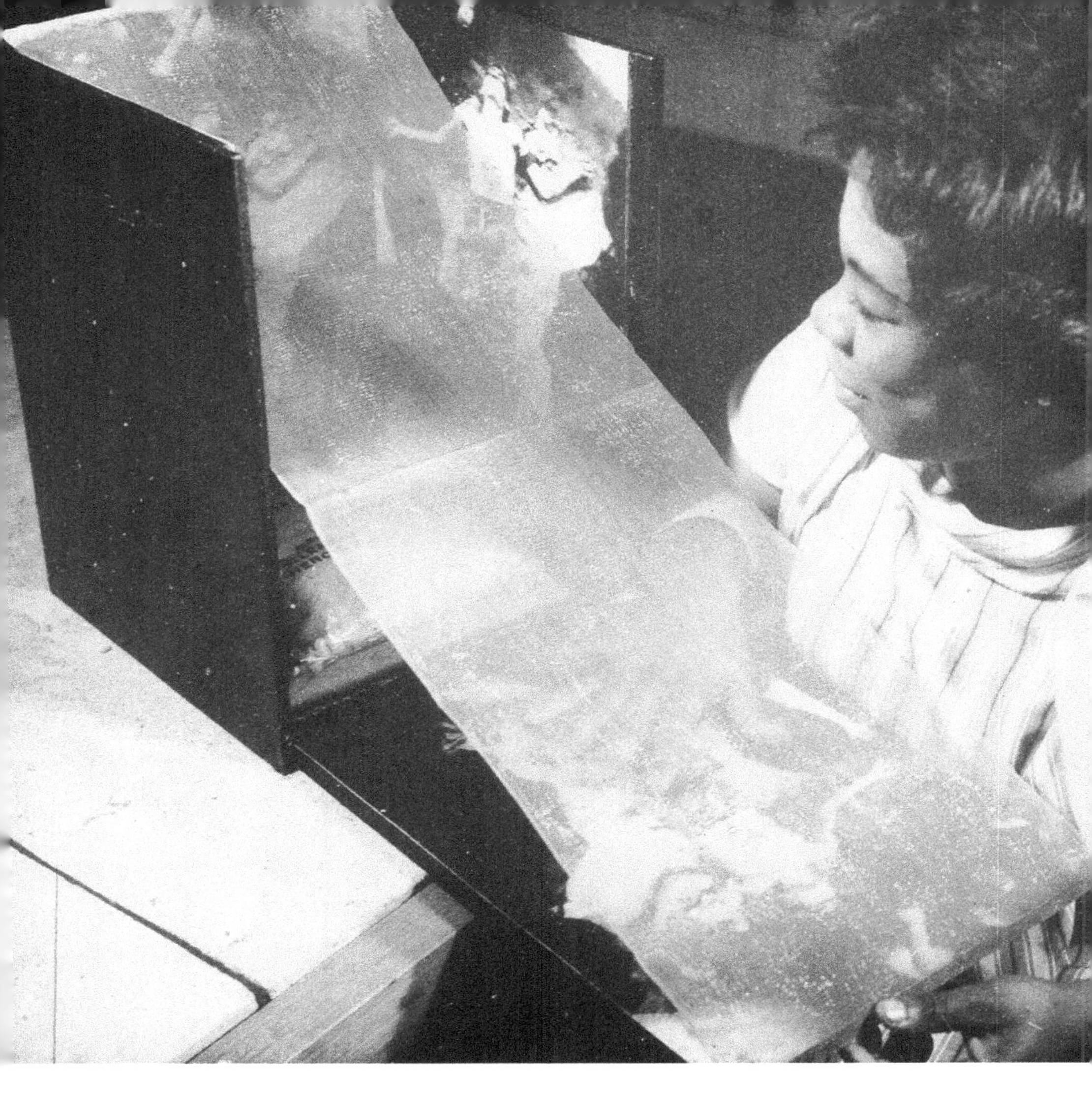

Figure 7.3: Luiza com Bólide B33 Bólide Caixa 18 – "Homenagem a Cara de Cavalo", 1966. Photo: Claudio Oiticica. © César e Claudio Oiticica.

8
Personalising the Global History of Pop Art
Alina Szapocznikow And Maria Pinińska-Bereś

Agata Jakubowska

As an art historian dealing with women artists who lived and worked in Poland, the country where art canons are not formulated, I am always excited by exhibitions that promise to challenge Western and masculine art dominancy. The feelings that accompany their reception are, however, ambiguous. It is fascinating, and sometimes frustrating, to observe which women artists on which occasions are included (or which are not) and how this influences their recognition outside Poland. It is interesting, and sometimes disappointing, to learn how their art is contextualised and (mis)understood, thanks to brilliant ideas and at times shortcomings in the historical knowledge of the local.

As far as the field that is addressed in this text is concerned—i.e. women artists and pop—I have had lately several occasions for that sort of excitements. In 2010, two exhibitions dealing with women artists and pop were organised. *Seductive Subversion: Women Pop Artists, 1958–1968* originated at the University of the Arts in Philadelphia and was later shown in three other North American cities. *Power Up: Female Pop Art* was on view in the Kunsthalle Wien. They both aimed at presenting women artists associated with pop art that mostly "have been relegated to the margins of [its] history."[1] Both attempted to break the dominance of the Anglo-American version of pop, yet they had no ambition of really globalising pop art. No works of women artists from other places, such as Eastern Europe, were shown—with one exception, a photo of Alina Szapocznikow's *Stella* (1968) was reproduced in the book accompanying the *Seductive Subversion* exhibition. As Kalliopi Minioudaki, one of its editors, explained to me, she had learned too late about the artist to include her into the exhibition and texts, yet the photo could be added.[2]

Two exhibitions were opened in 2015 whose authors had an ambition of presenting pop art from artists across the globe—*International Pop* at the Walker Art Center in Minneapolis and *The World Goes Pop* at the Tate Modern. In both cases it was underlined that in different parts of the world, popular culture stimulated artists—and the curators aim was to show multiple takes on pop art. Both exhibitions included Natalia LL with her *Consumer Art* (1972–1974), and the second also showed Maria Pinińska-Bereś' pieces *Love Machine* (1969), *Is a Woman a Human Being* (1972) (Figure 8.2), and *Screen* (1973). The *International Pop* catalogue does not offer any passages devoted to Natalia LL. The situation is different in the case of *The World Goes Pop* catalogue, as that includes a text by Kalliopi Minioudaki—an independent art historian who has been working on women of pop for a long time. In her article entitled *Feminist Eruptions in Pop Beyond Borders* she aims at "lifting geocultural and chronological borders among the women of pop," yet "with due attention to its locational specificities."

Minioudaki's text is a good example of global art history that proposes to move on our focus from binary relationships, such as West–East, centre-periphery, into a multifocal and polyphonic set of relations. This perspective is a response to the challenge posed by global connectivity to regionally based research, the latter being connected with identity formation processes, often of a nationalistic character. It advocates a transcultural overview instead of what is most often executed, in one of two types of projects. The first aims at capturing the dynamics of entanglement and cultural exchange,

[1] Sid Sachs, "Beyond the Surface: Women and Pop Art 1958–1968," in Sid Sachs (ed.), *Seductive Subversion: Women and Pop Art 1958–1968*, Kalliopi Minioudaki: Abbeville Press, 2010, p. 18.

[2] Conversation with Kalliopi Minioudaki.

illustrating the way works, people, and ideas travelled across different kinds of borders. The second is of a more comparative nature and offers a juxtaposition of similar artistic phenomena developed in different parts of the world in order to present multiple versions of global issues. Klara Kemp-Welch's project *Networking the Block* and Piotr Piotrowski's *East-European Art Seen from Global Perspective* can serve as examples of these attitudes, here in relation to East-European art.[3] Kemp-Welch concentrates on international exchange among East-European unofficial artists in the period 1968–1981; for Piotrowski, it was just a pretext to offer comparative interpretation of their art. Most of the exhibitions that inscribe themselves into global art history, as the fore-mentioned pop art show, correspond with the second type. Yet, there are not many art historians who are able and willing to undertake such a challenge to grasp particular art phenomena from the global perspective, as that requires access to a multiplicity of sources and the desire/possibility of understanding a multiplicity of social/cultural/financial/political contexts. As a result, in practice countries or regions are very often used again as geographical frames. On the level of texts, the global perspective is offered in the form of a set of locally (country or region) oriented research papers, something that is clearly visible in catalogues. Particular artists are often closed in the frame they were just about to be freed from and risk being a representative of a specific country. The field of women artist and pop is special in this regard thanks to one scholar—the aforementioned Kalliopi Minioudaki. In her text in *The World Goes Pop* exhibition catalogue, she promises "to unveil important transnational feminist affinities that in all their diversity underpin the radical intersections of women and pop across its centres and peripheries."[4] What is crucial is that in her overview of numerous artworks from different parts of the world she offers an analysis of the global phenomenon that is always, in the case of each artist and her pieces, related to the local.

[3] Klara Kemp-Welch, http://networkingthebloc.blogspot.de. Piotr Piotrowski, "The Global NETwork: An Approach to Comparative Art History," in Thomas DaCosta Kaufmann, Catherine Dossin, and Béatrice Joyeux-Prunel (eds.), *Circulations in the Global History of Art*, Ashgate, 2015, pp. 149–165.

[4] Kalliopi Minioudaki, "Feminist Eruptions in Pop: Beyond Borders," in Jessica Morgan and Flavia Frier (eds.), *The World Goes Pop*, exh. cat., Yale University Press, 2015, p. 73.

In the following, I propose a detailed analysis of works with the reference to pop art from two Polish sculptors – Alina Szapocznikow (1926–1973) and Maria Pinińska-Bereś (1931–1999). My aim is to challenge the practice of country/region-oriented analysis in a way that corresponds to Minioudaki's perspective. This is going beyond borders, yet not forgetting the local. Hardly any country has a homogenous art scene, obviously. Nor does Poland. Similarly evident is that in the case of every country we can point out numerous aspects of social, financial and political life that determine conditions of art production and reception. The artists that I am going to juxtapose here—Alina Szapocznikow and Maria Pinińska-Bereś—function as Polish artists. I will compare them, taking into account the local conditions and simultaneously pointing out differences that are the result of different career tracks and also diverse personal experiences. I will globalise the history of the Polish version of pop art, but also personalise the global history of pop.

Maria Pinińska-Bereś and Alina Szapocznikow were almost of the sam age—Szapocznikow was born in 1926 in Kalisz, Pinińska in 1931 in Poznań. Their origins strongly influenced them especially at the beginnings of their artistic careers, stronger than what is normally the case, if there is anything "normal" in this matter. Szapocznikow, being of Jewish origin, spent the Second World War mostly in ghettos and camps with her mother (her father died before the war broke out).[5] Pinińska-Bereś lost her father, who was a Polish officer; he was killed in Kharkov at the beginning of the war. Her family's safety was assured by her grandfather on her mother's side, who had an old German passport (he was born in Silesia, and before the war he studied and lived for a couple of years in Berlin).[6] After the war, Pinińska-Bereś attended the fine arts high school in Katowice and then in 1950 moved to Cracow to study at the Academy of Fine Arts; she spent the rest of her life living in that city. After being liberated from the Theresienstadt camp, Szapocznikow went with her Czech inmates to Prague. In the autumn 1945, she enrolled at the School

[5] Marek Beylin and Ferwor, *Życie Aliny Szapocznikow*, Warsaw-Cracow: Museum of Modern Art, Karakter, 2015, especially chapter 2, pp. 11–25.

[6] Piotr Korduba and Aleksandra Paradowska, *Na starym Grunwaldzie: Domy i ich mieszkańcy*, Poznań: Wydawnictwo Miejskie, 2012, Chapter: "Marcelińska 48. Ułańskie tradycje," pp. 154–159.

of Applied Arts and also started working in a stonecutting workshop. At the end of 1947, she moved to Paris and continued her formal education, but financial and health problems hindered its completion.

Thorough their whole lives, Szapocznikow and Pinińska-Bereś continued these life-tracks; that is, Szapocznikow changed life and working places quite often, while Pinińska-Bereś maintained a stabile life in Cracow. This strongly influenced their international contacts. In the 1960s and at the turn of the 1970s, that is in the period I will concentrate on, Pinińska-Bereś had hardly any exibitions, while Szapocznikow lived both in Warsaw and Paris and exhibited internationally. To illustrate difference in their position in the international art world one can compare places of solo exhibitions organised in that period. Szapocznikow held them in Paris/Warsaw (1967), Bruxelles (1968), Geneve (1971), and an exhibition in Paris 1973 after her death. Pinińska-Bereś held exhibitions in Cracow (1970), Warsaw (1973), and Lublin (1975). So far no solo exhibition of hers has been organised outside of Poland.

Being an artist based in Cracow did not necessarily result in the locality of a career, as the examples of Tadeusz Kantor, or even Pinińska-Bereś' husband Jerzy Bereś indicate. In the case of both women artists, what was crucial for their different career-tracks was, besides the above-mentioned historical conditions, their different attitude to artistic career and also personality. While Szapocznikow very actively, actually pro-actively, sought out chances and did quite a lot to take advantage of them, Pinińska-Bereś was much more resigned to her marginal position in the Cracow art milieu dominated by the strong personality of Kantor.

For many women artists in Poland, but not exclusively there, the first half of the 1960s was a crucial period in terms of artistic development, as many of them gave up previously used stylistics and turned to new forms, materials and subjects. The latter were usually connected with personal dimensions, subtly visible at that time. In the early 1960s, Pinińska-Bereś started her experiments that she herself presented as "a kind of protest against professionally and commercially legitimised sculpture-monuments."[7] At first she created *Rotundas,* which were compact concrete

[7] Maria Pinińska-Bereś, *Piwnica pod Baranami*, Cracow, 1970, a leaflet accompanying the exhibition.

forms, some of them resembling female figures. Later, she started adding linen and creating forms more directly referring to women or feminine experience. *Lady with a Bird* (1964), half-gravestone, half-woman, with a linen gown and a comb, a ring and beads merged in cement, is a good example. Then *Corsets* were created that should be understood here metaphorically as de/formative for the entire personality, not only a body. These works (from *Rotundas* to *Corsets*) are archaic in character and had hardly any reference to the present-day. They are, however, related to the artist's biography and the conditions under which she grew up, "in an ultra-Catholic family whose head, because of deaths during the war, was the patriarch, a senior formed by the 19th century."[8] What was crucial for her at that time was a combination of religion and of woman's sexuality as two elements joined in exercising control over young women.

At the turn of 1960s, Szapocznikow did abstract works, yet she soon became more interested in the representation of the female body. In 1962, still in Warsaw, she first cast fragments of her body—a leg and the lower part of her face. She explained her need for an experiment with the words "beset by the academic approach to abstraction, partly out of spite, or perhaps due to artistic exhibitionism."[9] At first, they remained studio works, as if she did not know what to do with them. She showed then, already transformed, only at her first Parisian solo exhibition in 1967. In the meantime, she created *Goldfinger* (1965) (Figure 8.4)—the first work in which one can see clear reference to popular culture that is the third consecutive James Bond film of the same title. An image photo of a nude, reclining woman, covered with gold paint that appeared on the film's poster and in its trailer must have also influenced the way Szapocznikow transformed her leg cast into a golden fetish (*Leg*, 1962–1967). In 1966, Szapocznikow started creating *Lampes-bouche*—lamps consisting of casts of mouths transformed into a lampshade. The lamps appealed to the visitors of the Galerie Florence Huston Brown in 1967. Szapocznikow

[8] Maria Pinińska-Bereś, *Gorsety i wieże*, 1994, the artist's archive. More on the early works for Pinińska-Bereś, see Agata Jakubowska, "Ambiguous Liberation: The Early Works of Maria Pinińska-Bereś," *Konsthistorisk Tidskrift/Journal of Art History*, Vol. 83, No. 2, 2014, pp. 168–182.

[9] Alina Szapocznikow, "Z Paryża pisze Alina Szapocznikow," *Współczesność*, No. 5, 1966, p. 8, trans. Anna Szyjkowska-Piotrowska

received many orders, which she sought to meet by developing a kind of serial production. She began to create *Souvenirs*, that is photos of friends and also movie stars, among others Monica Vitti, covered with polyester. The photos with their arrangement, which can be found in Szapocznikow's archive, depicting them standing on a coffee table, leave no doubt as to how she wanted them to be exhibited. She also developed an idea and undertook several more or less successful attempts to make poliuretan cushions that were formed from belly casts. Pierre Restany, the curator of her 1967 show, praised the change he had observed in the works by Szapocznikow, who

> finally managed to free herself from dramatic expressionism. The artist seemed to escape the long torment of her life, the horror of her past of war and camps: she slowly woke up to a new objective consciousness of the world.[10]

Restany stressed that it had happened thanks to her staying in Paris. Yet, in order to better understand the changes in Szapocznikow's art, it is necessary to take a closer look at the milieu she functioned it.

It is usually underlined that Szapocznikow had contacts with the new realists, yet it is in fact basically only Restany whom she was in touch with, and although he was an important figure for her, it was not her most, or at least not her only, inspiring relationship. Szapocznikow moved to Paris together with her partner—the graphic designer Roman Cieślewicz. Already in Poland he gained a high position thanks to his film and theatre posters and illustrations for magazines, for example for the very popular life style magazine *Ty i Ja* (*You and Me*). After moving to Paris he cooperated with several publishing houses and quickly managed to find work in fashion magazines, such as *Elle*, where he worked in the second half of the 1960s as an art director. The couple pursued ongoing artistic dialogue, which is visible when one compares their works from different periods. For example, Cieślewicz's poster for Moda Polska and Szapocz-

[10] Pierre Restany, "Alina Szapocznikow par Pierre Restany," in *Alina Szapocznikow*, ex. cat., Galerie Flocence Houston-Brown, Paris 1967, n.p. More on this see Anke Kempkes, "Black Drips and Dark Matter - The Luxury Cap - Concept Individuel - Quarry Desert," in Agata Jakubowska (ed.), *Alina Szapocznikow. Awkward Objects*, Warsaw: Museum of Modern Art, 2011, pp. 161–186.

nikow's sculpture *Bellissima*, both from 1959, when they still lived in Warsaw. Moda Polska (Polish Fashion) was a monopolistic state enterprise that was created to introduce new tendencies in fashion. Cieślewicz proposed a poster with a dominant bust of a woman having her head crowned with a huge rose. Szapocznikow's plaster female figure, whose corpus is bigger though reduced (without arms and cut at the level of the hips instead of the head), has an abstract form resembling flowers. Among Szapocznikow's drawing there are several sheets that present a transformation of a woman into a rose. Another comparison that I want to propose comes from the second half of the 1960s. It is when Szapocznikow transformed her leg turning it into a golden fetish, as has been said already. At that time, Cieślewicz used this motive on several occasions, for example on a cover of *Ty i Ja* (2/1968) and on a cover of one of guides from the Ultra Guide series (Gouraud editions) that he designed. Other guides featured a mouth and a breast, also extensively used by Szapocznikow at that time.

What I want to prove by these comparisons is that already in Poland, Szapocznikow might have been under the influence of the popular imaginary. In Paris, her interests found much better conditions to develop and her works became more openly related to popular culture. Firstly, this was because of the technical possibilities, which they both stressed as important when they explained their reasons for leaving Poland. Cieślewicz explained in one interview:

> I could no longer stand in Poland this huge technical and mental delay compared to what is happening in the world. [...] By this I want to say that in my profession, in which technology plays a huge role, [it is crucial to have] a possibility to compose an image without dirtiness, without stains, without dribbling [...].[11]

[11] "Roman Cieślewicz *Na maksimum wyobraźni. Rozmowa*," in *Autoportrety: O sztuce i swojej twórczości rozmawiają z Wiesławą Wierzchowską*, Warsaw: Agencja Wydawnicza Interster, 1991, p. 75.

Szapocznikow's friend, the film director Andrzej Wajda, recalls her saying that their move to Paris was "an expedition to a place where they know how to cast any required form out of coloured plastic."[12]

The latest remark is related to the second reason for her more open dialogue with popular culture—the Parisian art scene was much more favourable to the incorporation of popular motives and contemporary materials and for artists' interest in design. She met with approval she could not count on in Poland. Szapocznikow did not find understanding for her new works in her native country. What is interesting is that the opposition of expressionism and objectification, which was stressed in the above-mentioned Restany's essay, can also be found in texts devoted to pop art written by Polish art historians. For example, once Alicja Kępińska explained that

> in Poland it is hard to find objectivism that is typical for pop-art, because a strongly expressionist tendency prevails here, in which "expressing" one's own inner experiences becomes a value.[13]

The reception of Szapocznikow's 1967 exhibition, which after having been shown in Paris travelled to Warsaw, is an example of this attitude. It is symptomatic that the same lamps were titled here not *Lampe-bouche*, as in France, but *Illuminated lips*. It is clear that in the Polish version of the catalogue, the utility of these objects was pushed aside. One of the critics—Andrzej Osęka—recalled, shortly after the death of the artist, that he had been distrustful of these innovations. "I considered them to be unnecessary," he admitted.[14] These opinions are characteristic for Polish modernity, with its unflagging reluctance to popular culture.

The suspicion towards pop culture—similar to the one expressed by Polish critics—can be observed in Maria Pinińska-Bereś' attitude. Yet, it is her—not Szapocznikow—who made a direct reference to pop art as a frame of her works. Pinińska-Bereś had her first solo exhibition in 1970 in

[12] Andrzej Wajda, "*Alina Szapocznikow (1926–1973)*," in Józef Grabski (ed.), *Capturing Life: Alina Szapocznikow – Drawings and Sculptures*, Cracow-Warsaw: IRSA Fine Arts, 2004, p. 131.
[13] Alicja Kępińska, *Nowa sztuka: Sztuka polska w latach 1945–1978*, Warsaw: Wydawnictwa Artystyczne i Filmowe, 1981, p. 101.
[14] Andrzej Osęka,"Alina Szapocznikow," *Kultura*, No 12, 1973, p. 12.

a cultural club functioning also as an art gallery and called Piwnica pod Baranami. Dissatisfied with the lack of reviews she wrote one herself. In it she claimed:

> In the exhibition a spirit of freedom of pop-art joined with the high discipline of the choice of accomplishments is present [...] it [exhibition – AJ] contradicts vulgarly understood pop-art and yet it is freed from the all previous rigours [Pinińska-Bereś 1970, private archive].

The laconicism of this statement makes it hard to clearly understand precisely what Pinińska-Bereś had in mind. What she showed in the exhibition were not only the above-mentioned *Corsets,* but also new works that had clear references to the present day. A good example is *Love Machine* from 1969, as both in terms of formal elements and a message it was very much immersed in contemporaneity. It is a construction made of plywood, painted with bright colours, with mobile elements (yellow painted legs, for example) that could be seen as a loose example of psychedelic art. It resembles sex machines, pointing our attention to issues of women's sexuality being not restricted by Catholicism, which was important for her before, but rather liberated by the sexual revolution.

The appearance of this kind of formal elements and subjects is easy to understand if one takes into consideration that the Bereś family was in close contact with hippies at that time. Avant-garde artists from at least two milieus were in touch with hippies—in the Cracow Group and in the Foksal Gallery in Warsaw.[15] Many of them quickly distanced themselves from these youth groups, for different, often political reasons, yet not Bereś. Jerzy Bereś recalled:

> Hippies had an incredible charm [...]. The whole atmosphere was saturated with freedom, an idea of free love. I was almost forty then and it was a second youth. Never-ending youth. My wife [Maria Pinińska-Bereś – AJ] was a little nervous, because swarms of people kept coming to see us, sometimes very

[15] Kamil Sipowicz, *Hipisi w PRL-u*, Warsaw: Baobab, 2008.

> strange people. They hung around at nights, Bettina [their daughter – AJ] fell asleep next to them.[16]

I don't know of any statements by Maria Pinińska-Bereś regarding hippies in particular. Yet her reference in the review of her exhibition, to freedom, which she associated with pop art, is telling. It seems that in her case, freedom was related to the openness in addressing eroticism but also everyday experience. Pinińska-Bereś' references to the sexual revolution are by no means just celebratory. On the contrary. The liberation of the erotic female body is accompanied by its objectification, as is clear from the *Table* pieces.

It is here that Pinińska-Bereś and Szapocznikow meet, but comparisons of works of theirs that deal with objectification of the female body reveal that they had a completely different set of references. What they have in common is the focus on a female body, whose fragments are represented. Sometimes we even find similar motives, such as female body fragments offered for consumption. Maria Pinińska-Bereś' *Table II* (1968) (Figure 8.1) and *Table – I'm Sexy* (1969) could be compared to Alina Szapocznikow's *Desserts* (1970–71) (Figure 8.3). The first two works are wooden tables on which there are fragments of a female body, made of white-painted paper maché. In *Table II* there are a tablecloth and table utensils attached to the board, which turns the woman into a dish ready to be eaten. In *Table – I'm Sexy* we see the contour of a potential consumer's hands. In *Desserts* Szapocznikow used real platters and bowls on which she placed several female body parts cast in polyester. The whole composition resembles the way cakes or ice-creams are served.

A comparison of these pieces makes their differences evident. Although Pinińska-Bereś paid attention to her appearance and was considered to be fashionably dressed, and she used to read *Przekrój*—a popular weekly regarded as "a window into the West" (thanks to, among other things, its presentation of Western fashion), it is definitely not a world of glamour that was her point of reference. Unlike Szapocznikow she did not use

[16] "Podejmowanie wyznań – z Jerzym Beresiem (i Bettiną Bereś) rozmawia Natalia Kaliś," *Kultura i Historia*, No 18, 2010, www.kulturaihistoria.umcs.lublin.pl/archives/1885 (4 September 2015).

modern materials and techniques, but wood, papier maché, linen. Her works are not *étincelant* (Szapocznikow titled one of her lamps "Buste étincelant"—shining and sparkling) but rather poor in comparison. It refers both to earlier works by Pinińska-Bereś' that could be characterised as rough and to later ones that were much lighter. In that period, instead of rough unworked planks she started using pieces of painted plywood and papier maché. This can be perceived as signs that she distanced herself from the aesthetics of her everyday life, that is, from the Bereś' apartment, which was furnished with furniture made by her husband and resembling his works, which were also made of rough pieces of wood, and also from the gloomy cellars where the most interesting galleries in Cracow were found. At that time, the aesthetics of her work could be considered an expression of her aspirations towards a modern fashionable world, or at least a comment on it. Yet simultaneously they reveal the nature of what was available in communist Poland.

One of the interesting tropes for Pinińska-Bereś' version of pop can be found in the milieu of Piwnica pod Baranami, where—as has already been written—her first solo exhibition took place. It was an art club, but it was also a group of more or less professional artists who organised a cabaret. In 1965 they performed a programme titled "How we used to live, how we live, what we will bring to our apartments." Its poster, whose designer is unknown, was an obvious reference to Richard Hamilton's work from 1956, *Just What Is It that Makes Today's Homes So Different, So Appealing?* A difference in aesthetics between them—for example the lack of colour in the former and its handicraft quality—can serve as support for the comparison made in the previous paragraph between Szapocznikow and Pinińska-Bereś, stressing the significance of the conditions in which they worked. It is also a good illustration of the technical arguments, discussed earlier in this text, raised by Szapocznikow and Cieślewicz, when they explained their reasons to leave Poland. Here, yet, I want to stress a different aspect of the poster. Its title—*How we used to live, how we live and what we brought to our apartments*—was, according to Olczak-Ronikier, related to a discussion among members of Piwnica pod Baranami that dealt with a family life and its influence on functioning of the cabaret group.[17] For a long time, a philosophy of focusing on the present moment dominated what made the group's members

> ashamed of earning money, achieving professional success, spending money on a washing machine instead on a banquet [...] and above all of "family life" and attempts put into its sustaining.[18]

This explanation clearly indicates that at that time in Poland, for many artists, also for Pinińska-Bereś and her husband, the way of life that is ruled by consumption was also a subject of critique. Even if that consumption was on a poor level, often hardly extending basic life standard. A washing machine that one could spent money on, after many necessary efforts because of shortage of consumer goods, was the only one he/she had, not a new and better one.

The same could be said of the apartments and their furnishings, which is important here since by the beginning of the 1970s Pinińska-Bereś concentrated on this subject, creating a series called *Psycho-small-furniture*. The communist government significantly limited the possibilities of private investors to build houses and offered instead a large (but not sufficient) number of small apartments in blocks of flats. Also, appropriate furnishing was offered. In the beginning of the 1960s, a massive production of a newly designed style of a set of furniture began. The set consisted of multiple modules, among which a pulled in desk and a bed were very characteristic and useful because of the small living space. It was called "the Kowalski Furniture," which has a double meaning—referring to their designers, Bogusława and Czesław Kowalski, but also to an everyman, since "Kowalski" is used in Polish in that sense.[19] This project was a good example of modern design, yet with time it became the symbol of the unification of the living conditions caused by the communist government policy.

The Bereś obtained such a small apartment from the government in 1960 and they moved there with their two-year old daughter. It was a studio/apartment, consisting of the studio where he worked, and one

[17] Joanna Olczak-Ronikier, *Piwnica pod Baranami, czyli koncert ambitnych samouków*, Warsaw: Pruszyński i S-ka, 1997, p. 195.
[18] Olczak-Ronikier, 1997, p. 198.
[19] Jacek Kowalski, *Meble Kowalskich. Ludzie i rzeczy*, Poznań: Wydawnictwo Dębogóra, 2014.

room where they all lived, where many people used to spend a lot of time (as hippies mentioned in one of Bereś' recollections quoted above) and where Pinińska-Bereś worked. When the first pieces of furniture appeared in Pinińska-Bereś' art (*Table* pieces) they did not refer to her current situation but they were metaphors of her family history and referred to her recollections of having grown up in a milieu that was dominated by an "ultra-Catholic mentality with the chief sin of a body and the vision of damnation," as has already been said.[20] Later, the issue of eroticism was still crucial, yet a problem of space, especially of a lack of intimate space, became central. Such works as *Cupboard I* (1970) or *Screen* (1973) are important in this context. The latter is a somewhat miniaturised version of a real screen and has a handwritten slogan on it: "A screen is good for everything." However, apparently it cannot hide everything since viewers can spot a pink, soft, sensual form placed behind it. *Cupboard I*, which offers an uncanny experience as a seemingly ordinary cupboard with a clean plate remaining, turns out to be as if taken up by a woman or rather by a woman's breasts. This piece encourages one to think of possible relations to Richard Hamilton's works that deal with domesticity.

Most critics writing on Hamilton stress his interest in new forms of consumer culture. Yet, according to Ben Highmore, what played a more significant role in his art were "the social and sensorial perceptions through which such life was experienced."[21] Writing about such works as *$he* (1958–61), Highmore concentrated on the depiction of a relationship between female body parts and machine tools and he claimed that we actually deal with an uncanny space.[22] The phrase "the social and sensorial perceptions through which such life was experienced" could be used in reference to Pinińska-Bereś' works from this period as well. Yet, with the reservation that by "such life" we do not mean an apartment filled with modern electronic appliances, but simply the apartment she lived in.

[20] Maria Pinińska-Bereś, "ak to jest z tym feminizmem?," in J. Ciesielskiej and A. Smalcerz (eds.), *Sztuka kobiet*, Bielsko-Biała: Bielska Gallery, 2001, pp. 194–195.

[21] Ben Highmore, "Home Furnishings: Richard Hamilton, Domesticity and the Post-avant-garde," in (ed.), David Hopkins, *Neo-avant garde*, Amsterdam: Editions Rodopi, 1997, p. 252.

[22] Highmore, 1997, p. 256.

The reference to Hamilton's work might be surprising in a country that is always considered to have been isolated from the Western art world. Especially if we deal with artists such as Pinińska-Bereś, who did not travel abroad and who lived in Cracow, which is known for its inclinations towards the Paris art scene, not to British contemporary art. Yet, there existed different channels for the transfer of ideas, such as people travelling and publications being sent. For example, we know that in the 1960s the Bereś received *Art in America* (the sender has not yet been identified).[23] Obviously, Alina Szapocznikow had much better access to the international art world because she spent most of her time in Paris, not in Warsaw. It was also easier for her to get life style magazines, especially since her husband cooperated with *Elle*. Pinińska-Bereś, who read *Przekrój*, was also in touch with popular culture and the beauty industry, although with a poorer communist version. Yet she reacted to it in a work from 1972—*Is a woman a human being?* Once again she undertook the theme of the corset but this time formulating a statement that referred to contemporaneity. She made a form that oscillated between a fashionable swimsuit and a fragment of the female torso and attached a note to it with a date of production and an expiry date, thus making a reference to contemporary culture's expectations towards women.[24] The same year Pinińska-Bereś made one more piece with a similar massage—a bitter-sweet house appliance titled *Keep Smiling*. It is an ordinary trashcan with a female face in it. Made of papier maché painted white, it has one colour element—red lips.

In 1972 when Pinińska-Bereś created *Keep Smiling*, Alina Szapocznikow did *Ashtrays for the Grass Widower*. They belong to her design pieces, in which casts of female body parts were used, this time for example two breasts form an utensil into which ash can be flicked. Although in both cases we deal with a combination of trash and fragments of a female figure, they refer to different aspects of the feminine experience. This time it is Pinińska-Bereś, who concentrated more on commenting on the way women are treated in the consumer culture. Alina Szapocznikow's pieces

[23] In formation from the artist's family.

[24] For more on this piece see Maria Hussakowska-Szyszko, *Inny nieco aspekt lat siedemdziesiątych*, in Tomasz Gryglewicz and Andrzej Szczerski (ed.), *Sztuka w okresie PRL-u: Metody i przedmiot badań*, Cracow: Jagiellonian University Press, 1999, pp. 135-146.

have a much more personal nature. They can be considered a dying woman's farewell gifts to her husband. She was diagnosed with breast cancer in 1969, underwent surgery treatment, and after a short period of remission she had her second operation in July 1972. Several months later the artist died.

During her illness, Szapocznikow worked intensively, and in some pieces from that period references to death is clear (for example, *Great Tumour* 1969). Yet, the works in which she used female body casts had changed character earlier. Already in 1968 she exhibited pieces from the *Expansion* series, consisting of casts of female body parts immersed in black polyurethane. Trying to describe what had happened in Szapocznikow's art, Restany claimed (in the 1968 solo exhibition catalogue) that "the vision of Alina Szapocznikow has elevated to higher dimension, allowing the decorative aspects give way to the cosmic breath of energy."[25] My argument is that these were the political events of 1968—that is, what is referred to as the incidents of March '68 in Poland, and the Warsaw Pact forces invading Czechoslovakia—which had a strong impact on Szapocznikow. At the beginning of 1968, social disturbances arose among students and the intelligentia caused by the censorship of the performance of Adam Mickiewicz's *Forefathers' Eve*. In March, the students' protests against censorship started to be represented by the government-controlled media as having been triggered by Jewish intellectuals. The government unleashed a campaign of anti-Semitism; citizens were controlled (for the purpose of determining who was Jewish) and general repression and persecutions against them arose (losing one's job or prohibition of publication, etc.) with the aim of forcing them to leave Poland. When leaving, they received a document stating that they were no longer Polish citizens. In March 1968, Alina Szapocznikow—of Jewish origin, a former prisoner of the ghettos and concentration camps, who after the war very strongly believed in the possibility of building a new communist society—was in Poland and, as her friend recalled, was terrified by seeing a repetition of what she knew from the past.[26] Luckily, she was not in Prague during the

[25] Pierre Restany, "La nature moderne est amour," in *Alina Szapocznikow*, ex. cat., Galerie Cogeime, Brussels, 1968, n.p.
[26] Tadeusz Łodziana in a documentary on Alina Szapocznikow: *Każdy dotyk zostawia ślad*, director Joanna Turowicz and Anna Zakrzewska, 2009.

forced entrance of the Warsaw Pact army (that is the Soviet Union and its main allies, also Poland) into Czechoslovakia in August 1968, with the aim of stopping reforms being introduced by Alexander Dubček in order to improve the communist system, which in their opinion could have weakened the Communist Bloc. However, we know from archival documents that she followed these tragic events with concern taking place in a country that was much more than just one of the brotherly countries for her (as the Eastern Bloc countries used to be called.)[27]

Rather one would expect Pinińska-Bereś, spending time in Cracow, to be under the influence of the political events taking place in the Eastern Europe. Yet it seems that for her, living in a prudish Poland, not for Szapocznikow living in Paris, these elements of 1968, which dealt with the sexual revolution, were of greater importance. Szapocznikow's art seems not to have been influenced by it.

The juxtaposition of two sculptors that function as Polish artists—Alina Szapocznikow and Maria Pinińska-Bereś—does not offer a clear picture of the Polish take on pop art. The case of Szapocznikow, who lived, worked, and exhibited across the Iron Curtain, both in the West and in the East, shows how problematic it is even to let our thinking about pop art (and more generally about art, obviously) be dominated by political and economic regions. She was immersed in the Western popular culture, yet at certain points there were events from the East that influenced her reactions to it. When we put her art into a dialogue with the art of Pinińska-Bereś it becomes even more clear to what a large extent their relationship to popular culture was conditioned by numerous aspects of private life, sometimes related to more general financial or political factors (as in case of living conditions), sometimes independent from them (as in case of illness). Globalising art tendencies, for example pop art, often seems to mean going beyond its narrowly defined borders. In some exhibitions—for example, those mentioned at the beginning of this text—we find an attempt to look simultaneously from a far distance to catch a general view of "international Pop" and from close-up to see details of particular parts of "the world that goes pop." This text advocates taking an even closer look, from the perspective of the personal, as this reveals that political and

[27] Postcards to Wojciech Fangor, the artist's archive.

financial factors, so crucial in the case of the art that refers to popular culture, whose development and reception is conditioned by them, do not explain all.

References

Primary sources

"Podejmowanie wyznań – z Jerzym Beresiem (i Bettiną Bereś) rozmawia Natalia Kaliś," *Kultura i Historia*, No. 18, 2010, www.kulturaihistoria.umcs.lublin.pl/archives/1885, 4 September 2015.

"Roman Cieślewicz. Na maksimum wyobraźni. Rozmowa," in *Autoportrety: O sztuce i swojej twórczości rozmawiają z Wiesławą Wierzchowską*, Warsaw: Agencja Wydawnicza Interster, 1991, p. 75.

Andrzej Osęka, "Alina Szapocznikow," *Kultura*, No 12, 1973, p.12.

Maria Pinińska-Bereś, Piwnica pod Baranami, Cracow 1970, a leaflet accompanying the exhibition.

Maria Pinińska-Bereś, "Gorsety i wieże," 1994, MS, the artist's archive.

—. "Jak to jest z tym feminizmem?," in J. Ciesielskiej and A. Smalcerz (eds.), *Sztuka kobiet*, Bielsko-Biała, 2001, pp. 194–195.

Pierre Restany, "Alina Szapocznikow par Pierre Restany", in *Alina Szapocznikow*, ex. cat., Galerie Flocence Houston-Brown, Paris, 1967.

—. "La nature moderne est amour," in *Alina Szapocznikow*, exh. cat., Galerie Cogeime, Bruxelles, 1968.

"Z Paryża pisze Alina Szapocznikow," *Współczesność*, No. 5, 1966, p. 8, trans. Anna Szyjkowska-Piotrowska.

Secondary sources

Marek Beylin, *Ferwor: Życie Aliny Szapocznikow*, Warsaw-Cracow: Museum of Modern Art, Karakter, 2015.

Ben Highmore, *Home Furnishings: Richard Hamilton, Domesticity and the "Post-avant-garde,"* in David Hopkins (ed.), *Neo-avant garde*, Editions Rodopi, Amsterdam, 1997, pp. 243–262.

Maria Hussakowska-Szyszko, "Inny nieco aspekt lat siedemdziesiątych," in Tomasz Gryglewicz and Andrzej Szczerski (ed.), *Sztuka w okresie PRL-u. Metody i przedmiot badań*, Kraków: Jagiellonian University Press, 1999, pp. 135–146.

Agata Jakubowska, "Ambiguous liberation: The Early Works of Maria Pinińska-Bereś," *Konsthistorisk Tidskrift/Journal of Art History*, Vol. 83, No. 2, 2014, p. 168–182.

Anke Kempkes, "Black Drips and Dark Matter - The Luxury Cap - Concept Individuel - Quarry Desert," in Agata Jakubowski (ed.), *Alina Szapocznikow: Awkward Objects*, Warsaw: Museum of Modern Art., 2011, pp. 161–186.

Alicja Kępińska, *Nowa sztuka: Sztuka polska w latach 1945–1978*, Warsaw, 1981

Kalliopi Minioudaki, "Feminist Eruptions in Pop: Beyond Borders," in: Jessica Morgan and Flavia Frigeri (eds.), *The World Goes Pop*, exh. cat., Yale University Press, 2015, pp. 73–92.

Joanna Olczak-Ronikier, *Piwnica pod Baranami, czyli koncert ambitnych samouków*, Warsaw: Pruszyński i S-ka, 1997.

Piotr Piotrowski, "The Global NETwork: An Approach to Comparative Art History," in Thomas DaCosta Kaufmann, Catherine Dossin, and Béatrice Joyeux-Prunel (eds.), *Circulations in the Global History of Art*, Ashgate, 2015, pp. 149–165.

Sid Sachs, "Beyond the Surface: Women and Pop Art 1958-1968", in Sid Sachs and Kalliopi Minioudaki (ed.), *Seductive Subversion: Women and Pop Art 1958–1968*, Abbeville Press, 2010, pp. 18–87.

Kamil Sipowicz, *Hipisi w PRL-u*, Warsaw: Baobab, 2008.

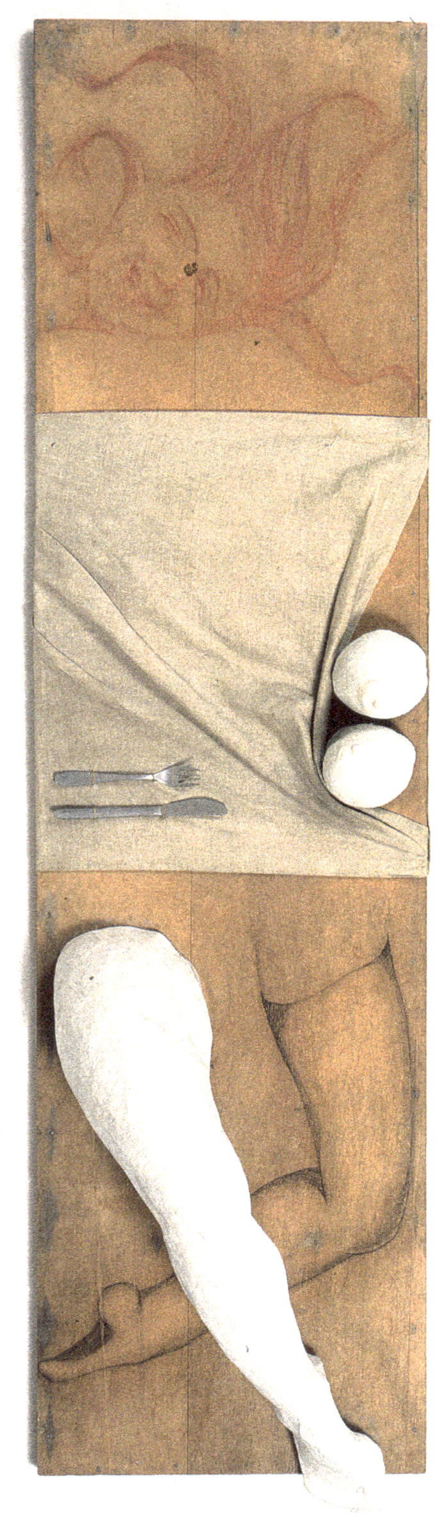

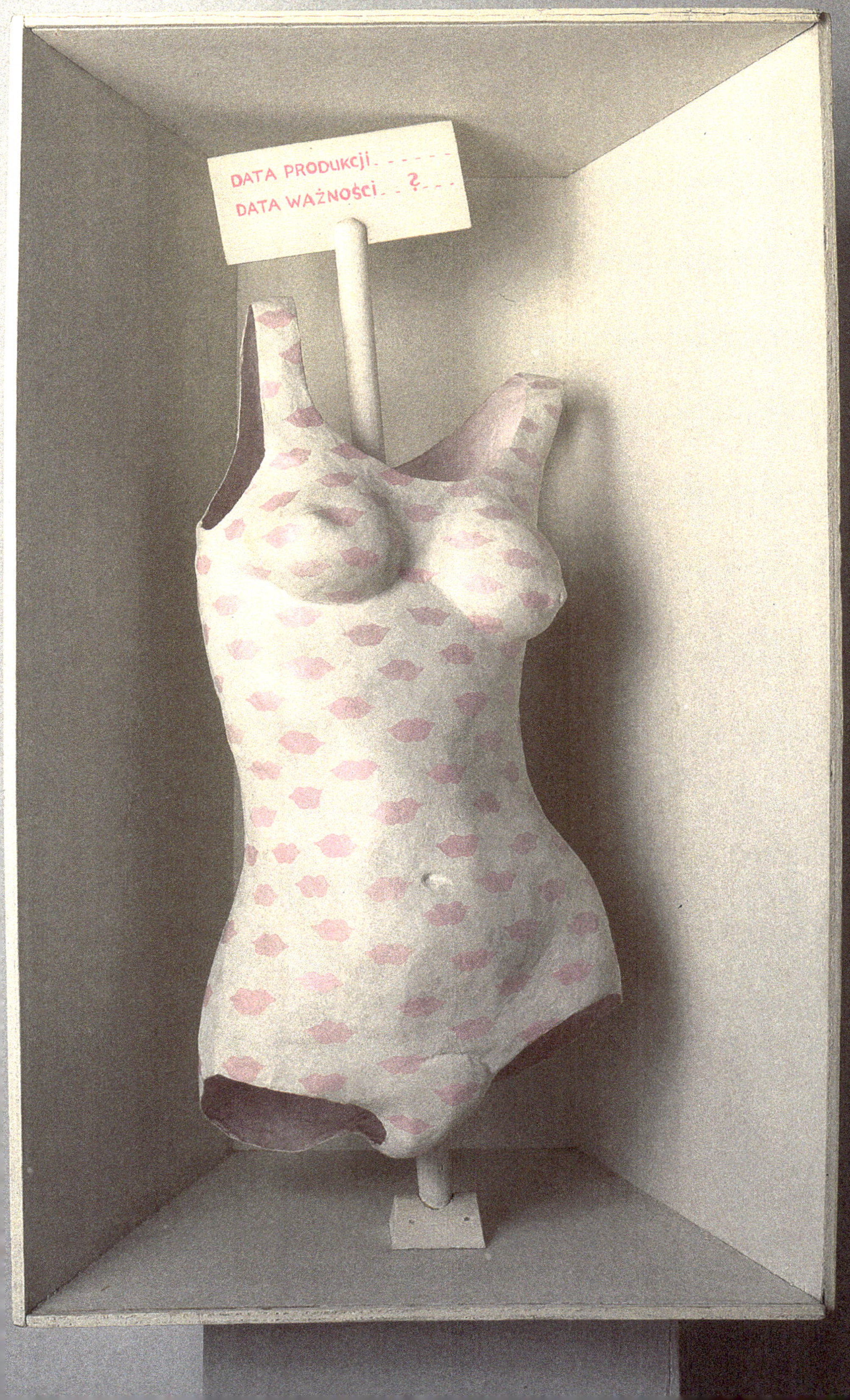

DATA PRODUKCJI
DATA WAŻNOŚCI ?

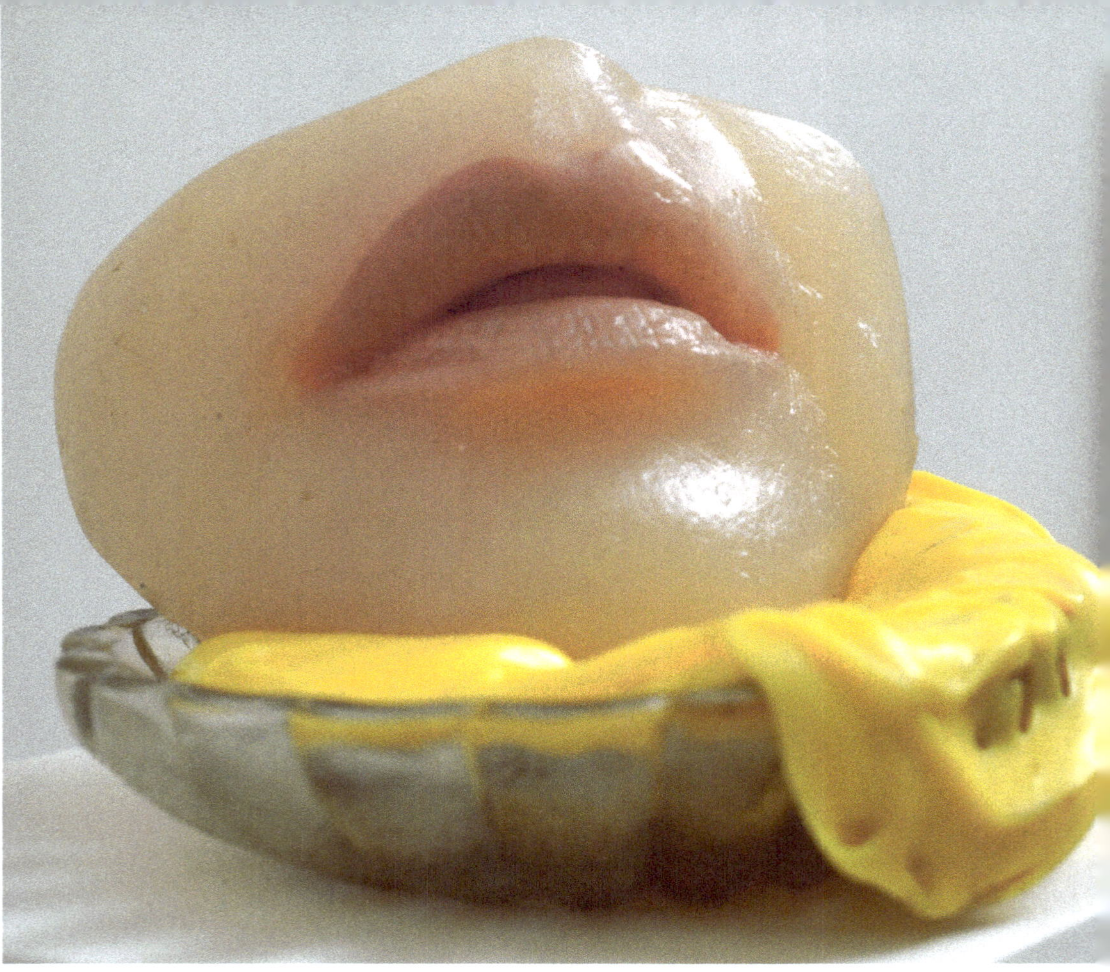

Figure 8.1 (previous spread, left): Maria Pinińska-Bereś, *Table II – The Feast,* 1968. Wood, papier maché, linen, drawing, Museum of Contemporary Art in Radom. Photo: Marek Gardulski. © Jerzy Bereś and Maria Pinińska-Bereś Foundation.

Figure 8.2 (previous spread, right): Maria Pinińska-Bereś, *Is a Woman a Human Being?*, 1972. 102,5 x 58,5 x 38 cm: plywood, glass, papier maché, acryl, Museum of Contemporary Art in Radom. Photo: Marek Gardulski. © Jerzy Bereś and Maria Pinińska-Bereś Foundation.

Figure 8.3: Alina Szapocznikow, *Dessert I*, 1970–1971. 8 x 11 x 13 cm: polyester, glass plate. Photo: Broadway1602 Gallery. © Piotr Stanisławski and ADAGP Paris.

Figure 8.4: Alina Szapocznikow, *Gold inger*, 1965, 183 x 76x 57 mm, Gold-patinated cement and car part. Photo: Muzeum Sztuki, Łódź, © Piotr Stanisławski and ADAGP Paris.

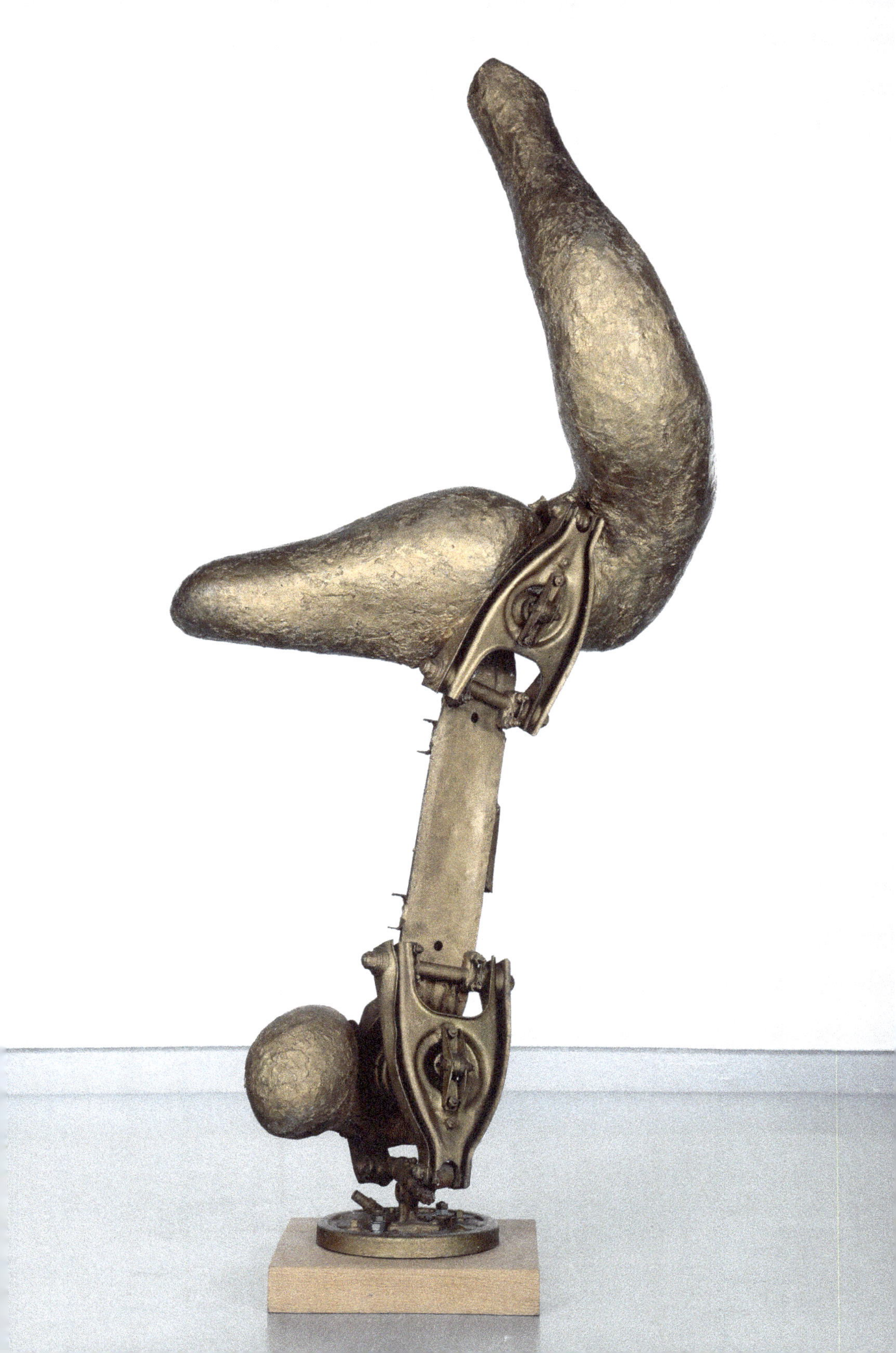

9
The Domestic Paradox[1]

Katarina Wadstein MacLeod

[1] This article reflects the research project The Domestic Paradox and relates to the following previously published articles: "Den obäddade sängen: Anna Sjödahl och sjuttiotalet," in Anders Burman and Lena Lennerhed (eds.), *Möjligheternas tid: Politik, filosofi och estetik på 1960- och 1970-talen,* Atlas förlag, 2014, pp. 389–416; "Body, Home, Object: The Living Room in Marie Louise Ekman's work," in Tone Hansen and Maria Lind (eds.), *No Is Not an Answer: A Reader on Marie-Louise Ekman, Berlin:* Sternberg Press, pp. 96–119.

1.

The paradox in the title of this chapter refers to the complexity of representations and receptions of domesticity in art. As several thinkers have explored, to have a home, or to be at home, or the longing for home, is a shared human experience across cultures and generations. Or is it? When Walter Benjamin pondered over capitalist society, the domestic environment was a key point and individual space was pronounced in the masculine.

Through the July Revolution, Benjamin states, bourgeois society established the private individual. "The private individual, who in the office has to deal with reality, needs the domestic interior to sustain him in his illusions. From this arises the phantasmagorias of the interior—which, for the private man, represents the universe. In the interior, he brings together the far away and the long ago. His living room is a box in the theatre of the world."[2] In his private universe, the individual can retreat from the realities of the world, a necessary retreat to keep functioning in an official capacity. The private realm is also where he expresses his personality;

[2] Walter Benjamin, "Paris, Capital of the Nineteenth Century" (1935), in *The Arcades Projects*, translated by Howard Eiland and Kevin Mclaughlin, Cambridge, Massachusetts, and London, England: The Belknap Press of Harvard University Press 1999, pp. 8–9.

through the things he collected and his everyday utilities we can follow the specificities of the middle-class man.

Historically, the theme of home and domestic scenes relates to such different representations as interior decoration and life style; backdrops for social scenes; or the formation of modernity and identity in art and design.[3] To represent the home during the turn of the century was à la mode and domestic interiors became metaphors for bourgeois identity. The division between private life and official affairs organised society, according to the school of thought by Jürgen Habermas. Bourgeois domesticity, albeit with regional differences, was a transnational phenomenon across the North American and European continents.[4] In Sweden, the importance of the domestic interior and home environment at the turn of the nineteenth century was pervasive and reached a nationwide audience through artists such as Carl Larsson and thinkers such as Ellen Key.[5]

When Gaston Bachelard, half a century later, tried to understand the deeper echelons of the human psyche, he did so through revisiting his childhood home. Bachelard's domestic space is enveloped in the feminine—it is a maternal space. It is a place the individual has once left and tries to retrieve and is therefore, in tandem with Bachelard's contemporary world, a subject equal to masculinity. Bachelard's critics have pointed out that for a woman during the mid-20th century, who never really left the

[3] K. H. Adler and Carrie Hamilton, *Homes and Homecomings: Gendered Histories of Domesticity and Return*, Chichester: Wiley-Blackwell, 2010; Akiko Busch, *Geography of Home: Writings of Where We Live*, Princeton: Princeton Architectural Press, 1999; Sherrie A. Inness (ed.), *Kitchen Culture in America: Popular Representations of Food, Gender, and Race*, Philadelphia: University of Pennsylvania Press, 2000; Janet Carsten and Stephen Hugh-Jones, *About the House, Lévi-Strauss and Beyond*, Cambridge: the Cambridge University Press, 1995; Griselda Pollock, "Modernity and the spaces of femininity," in *Vision and Difference: Feminism, Femininity and the Histories of Art* (1988), London and New York: Routledge Classics, 2003; Kirstein Ringelberg, *Redefining Gender in American Impressionist Studio Paintings*, Farnham: Ashgate, 2010.

[4] Susan Sidlauskas, "Psyche and Sympathy: Staging Interiority in the Early Modern Home," in Christopher Reed (ed.), *Not at Home: Resisting Domesticity in Early Modernism*, London: Thames and Hudson, 1996, pp. 65–80.

[5] See e.g. Michelle Facos, "The Ideal Swedish Home: Carl Larsson's Lilla Hyttnäs," in Christopher Reed (ed.), *Not at Home: Resisting Domesticity in Early Modernism*, London: Thames and Hudson, 1996; Ellen Key, *Beauty in the Home*, (1899), in Lucy Creagh, Helena Kåberg and Barbara Miller Lane (eds.), *Modern Swedish Design: Three Founding Texts*, The Museum of Modern Art, New York, 2008, transl. by Anne-Charlotte Harvey.

home, or for someone suffering domestic abuse, the psychological return to home may not really have been as rose-tinted.[6]

Poised between the idealised environments in Carl Larson's painting and the personal experiences in a globalised world in transition, characterised by migration such as in the work by the contemporary Iranian/Swedish artist Sirous Namazi's, we find the experimental, vibrating and local art scene of 1960s and 70s Stockholm. In countries in the West such as Sweden, where the women's movement changed society, domestic scenes set in the home where intertwined with issues of liberation, ideology, and aesthetics. Any myth about the home was deconstructed, any fallacy laid bare into cold light of day. Notably, the period from the mid-1960s to mid-1970s saw an intense resurgence of representations of home environments and domestic scenes within and beyond the women's liberation. In the hour of pop, the Stockholm art scene seems both to be on the global map *and* a peripheral place where a concern for the domestic is deeply grounded. The concern for this chapter is how art negotiates the domestic transfer across time and geography within the discipline of art history.

2.

The two Swedish artists in focus for this chapter, Marie-Louise Ekman (b. 1944) and Anna Sjödahl (1934–2001), illustrate the problems and traditions with the domestic during the era of Pop. Certainly, domestic objects are well integrated into a canon of pop art: toilets, TVs, bathroom cabinets. Or food: soup cans, spaghetti, hamburgers. But the domestic is a heterogeneous subject matter that seems dependent on context both in terms of time, place and art historical traditions. Of these two artists, Marie-Louise Ekman had a declared interest in pop art and pop culture. Her imagery is populated by cartoon figures such as Minnie Mouse, and in one of her most iconic pieces *Fishcakes in Lobster Sauce* (Figure 9.1) she has played with an Oldenburg vocabulary. In this piece, all food is made as textile objects in silk (fishcakes, prawns, lettuce, tomatoes), and attached onto a white plate against a pink background.

[6] Joshua M. Price, "The Apotheosis of Home and the Maintenance of Space of Violence," *Hypathia* 17, No. 4, 2002, 39–70.

Marie-Louise Ekman is well-known to the Scandinavian audience. Her body of work encompasses a variety of genres: film-making, art making, scenography, and between 1999 and 2015 she was Director of the Royal Institute of Art and the Royal Dramatic Theatre, Stockholm. The advance of an increasingly dispersed art history brings forth the relevance of making comparative analyses of Ekman's pop-aesthetics and her feminist work. Once the canon is dispersed to include women artists and artists from other geographies than the central hubs of the U.S. and Western Europe, an artist like Marie-Louise Ekman increasingly has a place in a more international canon. It is as if time caught up with Ekman's art. In other words, placed in a context of Pop Ekman's work translates comfortably into our own time.

Ekman's art from the 1960s and 1970s hinges on a narrative language that revolves around a number of characters: Disney figures, art history icons, and the so-called "lonely lady." The pastel colour scheme is bold and her art transgresses a sense of good taste or intellectual art.

In a series of paintings, the lonely lady is as often placed in her well tended home, with hair done, dress and heels the figure is respectable and neat. But the world around her, that is her flat, implodes and the narrative goes over the top. The lonely lady seems oblivious to dog shit shooting through the picture plane, being engrossed in a TV-programme. In one canvas, the TV-set takes on anamorphic shapes, with a fully erect penis, and ends up making love to the lonely lady (Figure 9.2).

Body parts, such as an ear, a nose, or a penis are just as likely to take a leading role as any man, woman, child, or cartoon figure. The stories told are often funny and at times play with toilet humour with excrements shooting through the image. In a small panting by Ekman titled *A Home* (1974) we enter an image that conflates two themes central to feminist art history: the body and the home (Figure 9.3). The scene set for the viewer is an ordinary environment with a standing lamp, an armchair and a dresser and its framing forces any viewer to peek. The typical scaffolding for the voyeur, a keyhole, curtain or window is in this image replaced with the female genitals. Ekman makes each viewer a Peeping Tom, but what is typically satisfying scoptophilic desire, the female body, becomes the structure for looking. The woman's womb is a well-known metaphor as a vessel for life, and female genitals on display meant to titillate the viewer's fantasy. In Ekman's version, life inside the uterus is neither a protected vessel for a foetus or the male organ, nor are the intimate parts particularly stimulating. Instead, the female inside is cosily furnished. In one gesture, this image collapses several tropes that have characterised art during the 20th century and which Ekman and her peers deconstructed during the 1970s. If the home had previously been structured by a patriarchal discourse, the home is in Ekman's hands a matter to be undone. Likewise, she takes apart the female body as an object of desire for the male gaze.

Ekman was formed as an artist at a moment in Sweden when the privacy of the home and representations of the body were being increasingly contested. She emerged with a debut at Galleri Karlsson (1967) in an art scene where her peers made art bold in expression and political in content. Kjartan Slettemark, one of her contemporaries, caused a series of media headlines with his happenings and interventions, for example performing naked in the street (in winter) or squatting Moderna Museet in 1970.[7] Carl Johan de Geer, at the time married to Ekman, ended up in court in 1967 and was sentenced with a heavy fine for exhibiting graphic prints with the Swedish flag matched with the word "cock." According to the gallerist Bo A. Karlsson, these were political times seeping into the everyday: not all exhibitions were outspokenly political, but many artists were.[8]

When Ekman made her art in the late 1960s and early 1970s, the feminist movement had begun to voice the importance of making the personal visible for public debate. Emancipation was to be addressed from within the home and from within family structures. When we are invited into the home in Ekman's art, it is through a language that is surrealist in tone and pop in style and it is through an artist described as at odds with contemporary political movements. In some of her work, Ekman undressed and posed naked, and poked fun at conservatism, political correctness, and not the least at a self-righteous and knowing art audience. Ekman was accused of being reactionary and bourgeois, not sufficiently feminist and not an artist enough—constantly transgressing genres. However, in hind-

[7] *KjARTan Slettermark: The Art of Being Art*, Nasjonalmuseet for kunst, arkitektur och design, Oslo 2013.

[8] Bo. A Karlsson, "Den svenska konsten 1964–1974," in Bo. A Karlsson, Ulf Kihlander and Ola Åstrand, *Hjärtat sitter till vänster*, exh. cat., Gothenburg Museum of Art, 7 March–1 June 1998.

sight it is precisely Ekman's pop aesthetics and feminist rhetoric that transfers into an international art history. Sylvia Eibelmayr illustrates in an article how similar impulses led to related work and she draws parallels between artist such as Ekman and Valie Export that had no relation during the 1960s and 70s. Yet, when looking back and mapping out a dispersed art scene there are clear affinities.[9]

3.

When we are at home with Ekman's contemporary Anna Sjödahl (1934–2001) it is equally in environments characterised by everyday life and everyday injustices, but rather than alter-egos and characters from popular culture, everyday reality and everyday people are in focus. In an exhibition catalogue from 1978, she published interviews with residents in one of Stockholm's new-built suburbs; high rise building holding a promise of a productive future for all its citizens. Sjödahl asked questions such as, "How much do you earn and what are your expenses?" "What does your day look like?"[10] The short interviews are illustrated with photographs from the newly built high-rise areas, domestic environments that are set against a radically different imagery, namely against a painting by Carl Larsson. Any Swedish resident would immediately understand the ideological pressure put on making everyday and family life the ideal in Larsson's imagery, and the interviews and related photographs show its impossibility.

Sjödahl's project had a resonance in the documentary film *Night-cleaners Part 1* (1972–75) by the British Berwick Street Film Collective, which also showed the impossible life-work equation of night shift work and full-time care for children. A tired woman, with tears in her eyes, answered the question, "Aren't you tired?" with a "yes, I am always tired." The inhabitants in Sjödahl's interviews are witnesses to similar struggles, and the daily routines are dire: difficult hard work, long days—or even worse, no work at all. Little money and lots of worries to deal with each

[9] Silvia Eibelmayr, "A Rebellious Uprising Against the Mythologies of Everyday Life," pp. 32–55, and Kalliopi Minoudaki, "Feminist 'Bad Girl' or Sweden's Bad Feminist?," pp. 56–95, in Tone Hansen and Maria Lind (eds.), *No Is Not an Answer: On the Work of Marie-Louise Ekman*, Berlin: Sternberg Press, 2013.

[10] *Vision och möda: Anna Sjödahl*, exh. cat., 1978.

day: cooking, cleaning, caring for kids, and agonising about the impact of their neighbourhood on their teenager children.

The domestic trap is a key theme in feminist critique. Simone de Beauvoir was explicitly negative towards "the home," which in the *Second Sex* is described as symbolic in culture for happiness and therefore in reality a prison, in particular for the married woman. "The ideal of happiness has always taken material form in the house, whether cottage or castle, it stands for permanence and separation from the world."[11] Others, like Iris Marion Young, pointed out the ambivalence for feminist philosophers in the idea of home and homemaking as precisely both repressive and liberating.[12] Bell Hooks showed how it is precisely the making of a home, or a home place, that is constructive for resistance in an oppressive structure, such as a racist organised U.S.A.[13]

When it comes to Anna Sjödahl's work, it is as if time and international comparisons help unpack her art, despite the artist herself predominantly acting in a national context. The paradoxical interpretations of Sjödahl's work, to be discussed below, are closely linked with the subject matters it deals with related to domesticity—and herein lies one of the problems of how Sjödahl's art has translated in an art historical narrative. If for Hooks, the domestic, or home place, can be constructive for liberation, for Sjödahl it is very clearly a site of oppression. If the individual pondering his home is synonymous to the masculine in both Benjamin and Bachelard's imagination, the radical aesthetics of Anna Sjödahl has become synonymous with the feminist movement, situated firmly in a specific period and possibly also bound to a certain geography—the Swedish art scene during the late 1960s and 1970s.

Sjödahl's exhibition *Var dags liv - mitt alternativ/EveryDay Life - My Alternative*, which in Swedish rhymes and reads as a slogan, was staged in different versions in the years 1973–75 (Figure 9.4). The installation

[11] Simone de Beauvoir, *The Second Sex* (1953), New York: Vintage Books, 1989, p. 501.

[12] Iris Marion Young, *Intersecting Voices: Dilemmas of Gender, Political Philosophy, and Policy*, Princeton: Princeton University Press, 1997. For a comment on this book, see for example Christine Di Stefano, "Intersecting Voices: Dilemmas of Gender, Political Philosophy, and Policy, by Iris Marion Young," *Political Theory*, 29, No. 3, 2001, pp. 469–478.

[13] Bell Hooks, "Homeplace: A Site of Resistance," in *Yearning: Race, Gender and Cultural Politics*, Boston: South End Press, 1990, pp. 41–49.

stretched from paintings on the walls to objects on the floor. Objects from the reality of the everyday were interlinked with paintings about power, violence and crushed expectations in a patriarchal society. On the floor and in-between paintings, Sjödahl had placed furniture such as a bureau overflowing with the things it meant to hide: socks, mittens, toys—an abundance of unsorted stuff that tends to multiply in a family household. Notes were pasted on the walls, between paintings, reminding of sports bags to pack and bills to be paid.

The scene staged in *Every-Day Life* was as if transposed from a home; as if a home environment had been dumped on the gallery floor. Next to the bureau was a single bed with the bedding all messed up, unsightly and intimate. With history in hindsight, another messed up bed is likely to be at the forefront; *My Bed*, the British artist Tracey Emin's contribution to the 1999 Turner Prize. As if transposed from a bedroom, it held evidence of personal debris: empty liquor bottles, dirty laundry, soiled sheets, used condoms. The British tabloids were outraged, protest groups gathered outside the museum stairs, and the installation was vandalised by a couple of art students. For some, this was a hoax. Others, such as the Turner Prize committee and several art critics, defended the piece.[14] Anna Sjödahl's installation has a similar history, albeit less violent; occasional visitors kicked the things on the floor according to the artist.[15] They were provoked, perhaps both by how the boundaries of "what is art" were pushed as well as the audacity of showing the dirty linen from private life.

For a few years, Anna Sjödahl was deeply embedded in the women's liberation movement and her art mirrors some of its key questions around patriarchal power structures and the distribution of labour in the domestic sphere. It was this close relationship that made her quit the movement; she felt that her art was interpreted as a vehicle for activism more than art.[16] A key piece for understanding the problems of translating the aesthetic achievements of Sjödahl's art beyond a political discourse is her bedroom

[14] Jennifer Doyle, *Sex Objects: Art and the Dialectics of Desire*, Minneapolis: University of Minnesota Press, 2006; John Kavanagh, "Love is what you want," http://artistsinsight.co.uk/archives/tracey-emin-love-is-what-you-want/, 19 September 2011; James Meek, "Art into Ashes," *The Guardian*, 23 September 2004.

[15] "Var dags liv: Ett samtal med Anna Sjödahl," (author unknown), *Synpunkt*, No. 4 1973, p. 9.

[16] Cecilia Gelin, "6 kvinnor blickar tillbaka," *Hjärtat sitter till vänster*, p. 113.

installation. The exhibition was received with mixed feelings amongst critics and visitors. Mostly, reports Sjödahl in an interview, it was those of the older generation who were upset: "The bureau aggravated some. I believe they perceived it as an insult towards their way of life. Maybe they spent a lot of time tidying up. Others may have been disturbed in their understanding of art."[17] The installation seems to suggest that a self-fulfilled life demands a messy home, and vice versa: that an ordered home is testament to an old-fashioned model where women's work is household work. The other section of the quote, on people being disturbed in their view on art, points to another complexity. Namely, how homes and domestic environments have been analysed across the 20th century.

Tracy Emin's *My Bed*, as well as Anna Sjödahl's installations, are preceded by an art historical discourse on beds—unmade and altered. The German realist Adolph Menzel made a small and intense drawing in 1845 of an unmade bed with pillows indented and sheets ruffled.[18] Menzel's recently inhabited bed comes across as a generic, single bed, without class, place or gender. Sjödahl too, created a generic, single bed in not having a personal imprint, as opposed to Emin who clearly manifested *her* bedchamber. The most important bed for art history and theory may be Robert Rauschenberg's assemblage *Bed* from 1955 which helped the critic and philosopher Arthur C. Danto to explain in 1964 the expanded notion of art in his article "The Art World."[19] Danto showed that if you analysed Rauschenberg's *Bed*, altered with paint and hung on the wall as a painting, we may also understand that a piece of art is far more than the sum of its materials. The bed as such has a theoretical trajectory, a staple in the art historical canon. Another fixture is the gesture of installation art that Anna Sjödahl experimented with, for example through the 1973–75 exhibitions. Some scholars have recognised the effect that Sjödahl herself opposed: that installations (or environments) in the 1970 tend to be interpreted too literally. An installation has at times tended to be taken for

[17] Cecilia Gelin, "6 kvinnor blickar tillbaka," *Hjärtat sitter till vänster*, p. 113.
[18] In Alte Nationagalerie, Berlin.
[19] Robert Raushenberg *Bed*, 1955, in MoMA, New York; Arthur C. Danto, "The Art World," *The Journal of Philosophy*, No. 19, 1964, pp. 571–584.

real, like the illusion of photography's inherent capacity to signify truth.[20] Sjödahl's installation has documentary qualities with socks, gloves, toys and reminders pasted on the wall. Yet it is also an aesthetic and experimental project in the tradition of Rauschenberg's Combines.

What is rarely mentioned in the articles at the time is the installation as such, and how it relates to a genre of making art through creating environments and installations. At the forefront is the woman's project. The domestic paradox is in this case how radical politics obscures the aesthetic gesture—both in contemporary critique and in art history. This stands in contrast to Anna Sjödahl's contemporary, Ola Billgren (1940–2001), and the reception of his many paintings of domestic scenes. His art belongs, in the words of one of his contemporary critics, to a tradition of realism. The domestic objects and environments in Billgren's paintings speak beyond the living room, the bedroom, the clothes piles, the flowerpot, and the dining table.[21] It is a reaction against bourgeois culture, but most of all it is *art*. There is a tendency in the writings of Sjödahl (and Ekman) to obscure the complexity of her (their) art with the feminist movement. Feminist issues, it seems, obliterate any other aesthetic importance. In fact, for Sjödahl it went so far that she left the women's liberation movement so as to be seen as artist, rather than a woman, or a feminist.

4.

It is tempting from a contemporary outlook to place Marie-Louise Ekman's and Anna Sjödahl's body of work in an international narrative, poised between the domestic as an entrapment to break free from and a culturally productive place. Examples of artists who address related themes in societies with similar problems are plentiful. For the exhibition *Doing What You Want*, 2012 at Tensta Konsthall in Stockholm, curated by Maria Lind, Marie-Louise Ekman's work was placed side by side with Sister Corita Kent (1918–1986), Mladen Stilinović (b. 1947), and Martha Wilson (b. 1947). The cross-over between artists from the U.S. and Serbia turned out fruitful and unexpected. The anarchism in Stilinović's pieces has a

[20] Briony Fer, "The Somnabulist's Story: The Installation and the Tableu," *Oxford Art Journal*, No. 2. 2001, pp. 77–92.
[21] See e.g. Douglas Feuk, "I vardagsrummet," *Konstrevy*, 1969, p. 236.

resonance in the non-abiding work by Ekman, the role-play by Martha Wilson has a counter-part in Ekman's paintings and films, and the pop-aesthetics in Ekman is echoed in the posters by Sister Corita Kent. The exhibition brought together artists largely unknown in each other's remits and the contemporary viewer could form an understanding of a dispersed art history formation through the wisdom of hindsight. One critic took the position that despite interesting artists, the exhibition was more a testament to time, however that Marie-Louise Ekman's work stood out in withstanding the test of time.[22] Regardless of point of view, the exhibition manifested the resilience of the local context. In one of Stilinović's exhibited pieces he states with letters embroidered on a pink banner: "An Artist who Cannot Speak English Is No Artist." Stilinović's metaphorical use of English points not only towards an access to language, but to the places where art happens. The margin is in itself a complexity, as the Stockholm critic, Stilinović's banner and the Tensta exhibition make visible. On the one hand, we understand art history through central locations and art hubs, yet each regional context is its own centre. It is its own measurement and at times therefore its own limitation, but there is also strength in the margins, as observed by Yuri Lotman.[23] This is where new intersections can take place, where new knowledge may form.

At the Marabou Konsthall in 2015, the synergetic effects were more overtly directed towards the theme of house-work and domestic labour. In the exhibition *From her House*, curated by Bettina Pehrsson, the German artist Margaret Raspé's (b. 1933) films and Anna Sjödahl's activist art and paintings on domesticity and emancipation were exhibited parallel to the North-American artist Mierle Laderman Ukeles (b. 1939) *Maintenance Art Works 1969–1980*. Ukeles brought house and family maintenance into city service sectors of cleaning thus relating labour economy to art making. Margaret Raspé's camera-helmet films explores aggressive aspects of making food, housework, and art by filming from her head what the hands whip, slash, gut, and paint. Ukeles recalls that as a young artist she had three great figures of inspiration: Jackson Pollock for how he used his body when painting, Mark Rothko for enabling another dimension

[22] Agneta Klingspor, "Göra som man vill: Tensta Konsthall," *Expressen*, 7 November 2012.
[23] Yuri Lotman, "On the semiosphere," *Sign Systems Studies*, No. 33, 2005 pp. 205–229.

through paint and canvas, and Marcel Duchamp for demonstrating the power of words.[24] Anna Sjödahl, too, was full of dreams and hopes when becoming an artist. In a pamphlet in 1978 written for the exhibition *Vision and möda* (Vision and Effort) at the age of 44, she wrote:

> About ten years ago I filled drawing pad after drawing pad with partly airy summer landscapes that I encountered, and partly romantic happy fantasies about Arcadia with sunshine, sea and greenery. [...] what became of the dream and what happens to our visions? I looked around, scrutinized my everyday and realised this is how it will continue for each and all of us: chores, illness, routines, disappointments, hard work.[25]

Similar to Laderman Ukeles, Sjödahl had a sharp awakening. With maternity dreams vanished, late night debates on the potential effects of materiality were replaced with around-the-clock responsibilities and chores. Nothing, Laderman Ukeles says, could have prepared her for the double role in the 1960s of being both a mother and artist; "Duchamp, Pollock and Rothko never changed nappies."[26]

Sjödahl, Raspé, and Laderman Ukeles all explore the symbolic value of domestic environments and labour in culture. As artists and feminists, they are in good company. The questions addressed in their art has prevalence in the different societies and art worlds their work inhabit; New York, Berlin, Stockholm, in the past and in the present. Their art shares similar societal concerns about division of labour and the potential to make art when there is little scope for art making. In hindsight, and when put side-by-side, their works are also a testament to how similar problems got different solutions in the different societies which they reflect: in Sweden, Germany and the U.S. The comparisons laid out in the exhibition show affiliations between artists and artworks, as well as the role of home and home-making in culture and society. It also shows the potential impact on art on society and the complex relationship between art and activism. Ukeles' impact on sanitation work is widely recognised, and Anna Sjödahl and her peers made several interactions that help form a

[24] Lecture by Marele Laderman Ukeles at Marabou Konsthall and Konsthall C, 23 March 2015.
[25] *Vision och möda: Anna Sjödahl,* 1978, cover (author's translation).
[26] Ukeles 2015

new and more equal society. It is also instructive in how what seems to look similar may be vastly different. It is a familiar narrative that the home in the 1960s and 1970s was a place to break free *from*: the mundane domestic life, chores, and problems to be brought out in public life. The home, as we've seen some few examples of, was a metaphor for portraying identity, class, political critique. But it is also clear that this narrative is firmly placed in a specific geography where the women's liberation emerged. The home as a place for family life, as Susan E. Reid has proposed, implies vastly different behavioural patterns depending upon where it takes place.[27] In the Khrushchev era behind the iron curtain, family life can be traced as deeply connected with specific and regulated behaviour. In art history in countries in Eastern Europe and the Soviet Union, the home is also a place to protect, where unofficial art can be made, seen, and discussed.

5.

The domestic in art has had a particular stronghold in Sweden and the impact of Carl Larsson's domestic scenes and Ellen Key's programme for creating a good home has marked the life lived in Swedish society. Perhaps it is not surprising that Anna Sjödahl was understood in her time through the lens of contemporary politics and activism, rather than through the aesthetic radicalism in her art. Yet, understanding the woman artist dealing with home environments has its own trajectory. When Carl Larsson's contemporary Fanny Brate painted home and family life at the turn of the nineteenth century, the home was a topic of its time. Politicians changed home environments and homestead politics enabled new ways of living. Ellen Key proposed new ideals for home decoration to replace the old, dark, and stuffy, with walls painted with light colours and with simple materials.[28] The suffragette movement developed, and women artists

[27] Lewis Siegelbaum (ed.), *Borders of Socialism: Private Spheres of Soviet Russia*, Palgrave, 2006; Claire E. McCallum, "The Return: Postwar Masculinity and the Domestic Space in Stalinist Visual Culture, 1945–53," *The Russian Review*, 74 (January 2015) pp. 117–43.

[28] Anonymous author(s), "Konsten att möblera ett hem 1," *Idun*, No. 16, 1897; "Konsten att möblera sitt hem II," *Idun*, No. 20, 1897, pp. 157–158, article continued in *Idun*, No. 21,

increased in the number. Like Larsson Brate painted ideal homes, both in terms of interior design and blissful family life. Brate can be described according to a typical narrative of the woman artist being stuck in the domestic trap; engaging with the less daring subjects of family life and interiors, or having to—once domestic responsibilities call.[29] Yet, Larsson's body of work confuse any such reading. It is unlikely that he was made to deal with domestic scenes and interiors. Larsson opted to paint what he did and he captured something in his time, and through his themes he explored new ways of making art. So too did Brate, Ekman, and Sjödahl—they captured their times and explored new ways of making art. As did the Swedish author Kristina Sandberg, in her trilogy on the housewife, Maj.[30] Sandberg captures the complexity of the domestic sphere from early twentieth century to the 1960s, and she does so in our present and in a world where once again the domestic sphere is increasingly becoming a politicised sphere.

The ideal domestic life represented by Larsson and Brate would later cause some shady corners for the people of Maj's generation, which in turn fostered Ekman and Sjödahl's generation. The character Maj belongs to the generation who may have been insulted by the bedroom mess in Sjödahl's work. The fictional character personifies the societal structures that the next generation had to break away from. When faced with artists' work relating to the domestic, it is important to keep the restraints of the actual domestic spheres, which artists such as Laderman Ukeles, Raspé, Sjödahl, and Ekman revolt against, in mind. But it is equally important to keep in mind how these artists furthered artistic expression, that content is never liberated from time, place, or form.

1897 p. 166–167; Isa, "Ett modernt hem," *Idun*, No. 45, 1897, pp. 359-360; Ellen Key, "Skönhet i hemmen," *Idun*, Christmas Special, 1987, p. 4.

[29] Beatrice Zade, "Fanny Brate - Familjelyckans konstnärinna," *Svenska Journalen*, No. 48, 1943.

[30] Kristina Sandberg, *Att föda ett barn*; *Sörja för de sina*; *Liv till varje pris*, Stockholm: Norstedts förlag 2010, 2012, and 2014.

Bibliography

K. H. Adler & Carrie Hamilton, *Homes and Homecomings: Gendered Histories of Domesticity and Return*, Chichester: Wiley-Blackwell, 2010.

Simone de Beauvoir, *The Second Sex*, (1953) New York: Vintage Books, 1989.

Walter Benjamin, *The Arcades Projects*, translated by Howard Eiland and Kevin Mclaughlin, Cambridge Massachusetts, and London: The Belknap Press of Harvard University Press, England 1999

Akiko Busch, *Geography of Home: Writings of Where We Live*, New York: Princeton Architectural Press, 1999.

Janet Carsten and Stephen Hugh-Jones, *About the House: Lévi-Strauss and Beyond*, Cambridge: Cambridge University Press, 1995.

Arthur C. Danto, "The Art World," *The Journal of Philosophy*, No. 19 1964, pp. 571–584.

Jennifer Doyle, *Sex Objects: Art and the Dialectics of Desire,* Minneapolis: University of Minnesota Press, 2006.

Michelle Facos, "The Ideal Swedish Home: Carl Larsson's Lilla Hyttnäs," in Christopher Reed (ed.) *Not at Home: Resisting Domesticity in Early Modernism,* London: Thames and Hudson, 1996.

Briony Fer, "The Somnabulist's Story: The Installation and the Tableu," *Oxford Art Journal*, No. 2. 2001, pp. 77–92.

Douglas Feuk, "I vardagsrummet," *Konstrevy,* 1969, p. 236.

Tone Hansen and Maria Lind (eds.), *No Is Not an Answer: On the Work of Marie-Louise Ekman*, Berlin: Sternberg Press, 2013.

Bell Hooks, "*Yearning: Race, Gender and Cultural Politics*," Boston: South End Press, 1990.

Cecilia Gelin, "6 kvinnor blickar tillbaka," in Bo. A Karlsson et al., *Hjärtat sitter till vänster*, p. 113.

Sherrie A. Inness (ed.), *Kitchen Culture in America: Popular Representations of Food, Gender, and Race*, Philadelphia: University of Pelsylvania Press, 2000.

Bo. A Karlsson, Ulf Kihlander, and Ola Åstrand, *Hjärtat sitter till vänster*, exh. cat., Gothenburg Museum of Art 7 March-1 June 1998.

John Kavanagh, "Love is what you want," http://artistsinsight.co.uk/archives/tracey-emin-love-is-what-you-want/ 19 September 2011.

KjARTan Slettermark: The Art of being Art, Nasjonalmuseet for kunst, arkitektur och design, Oslo, 2013, 2002, pp. 39–70.

Agneta Klingspor, "Göra som man vill: Tensta Konsthall," *Expressen,* 7 November 2012.

Ellen Key, *Beauty in the Home / Skönhet i hemmet*, Stockholm: Bonnier, 1989, also in Lucy Creagh, Helena Kåberg, and Barbara Miller Lane (eds.), *Modern Swedish Design: Three Founding Texts*, New York: The Museum of Modern Art, 2008, transl. Anne-Charlotte Harvey.

Ellen Key, "Skönhet i hemmen," *Idun*, Julnummer (Christmas special) 1987, p. 4.

Marele Laderman Ukeles, Lecture at Marabou Konsthall, Stockholm, 23 March 2015.

Yuri Lotman, "On the Semiosphere," *Sign Systems Studies*, 33, 2005, pp. 205–229.

Claire E. McCallum, "The Return: Postwar Masculinity and the Domestic Space in Stalinist Visual Culture, 1945–53," *The Russian Review*, 74 (January 2015), pp. 117–43.

James Meek, "Art into Ashes," *The Guardian*, 23 September 2004.

Griselda Pollock, *Vision and Difference: Feminism, Femininity and the Histories of Art* (1988), London and New York: Routledge Classics 2003.

Joshua M. Price, "The Apotheosis of Home and the Maintenance of Space of Violence," *Hypathia* 17, No 4.

Christopher Reed, (ed.), *Not at Home: Resisting Domesticity in Early Modernism*, London: Thames and Hudson, 1996.

Susan E. Reid, *Borders of Socialism: Private Spheres of Soviet Russia*, New York: Palgrave McMillan, 2006.

Kirstein Ringelberg, *Redefining Gender in American Impressionist Studio Paintings*, Farnham: Ashgate, 2010.

Kristina Sandberg, *Att föda ett barn*; *Sörja för de sina*; *Liv till varje pris*, Stockholm: Norstedts förlag, 2010, 2012, and 2014.

Lewis Siegelbaum, (ed.), *Borders of Socialism: Private Spheres of Soviet Russia*, New York: Palgrave McMillan, 2006.

Christine Di Stefano, "Intersecting Voices: Dilemmas of Gender, Political Philosophy, and Policy, by Iris Marion Young," *Political Theory*, 29, No. 3, 2001, pp. 469–478.

Vision och möda: Anna Sjödahl, exh. cat., Hellerup, 1978.

Iris Marion Young, *Intersecting Voices: Dilemmas of Gender, Political Philosophy, and Policy*, Princeton: Princeton University Press, 1997.

Isa, "Ett modernt hem," *Idun*, No. 45, 1897, p. 359–360.

Beatrice Zade, "Fanny Brate – Familjelyckans konstnärinna," *Svenska Journalen*, No. 48, 1943.

Anonymous author(s), "Konsten att möblera ett hem 1," *Idun*, No. 16, 1897; "Konsten att möblera sitt hem II," *Idun*, No. 20, 1897, pp. 157–158, article continued in *Idun*, No. 21, 1897 p. 166–167.

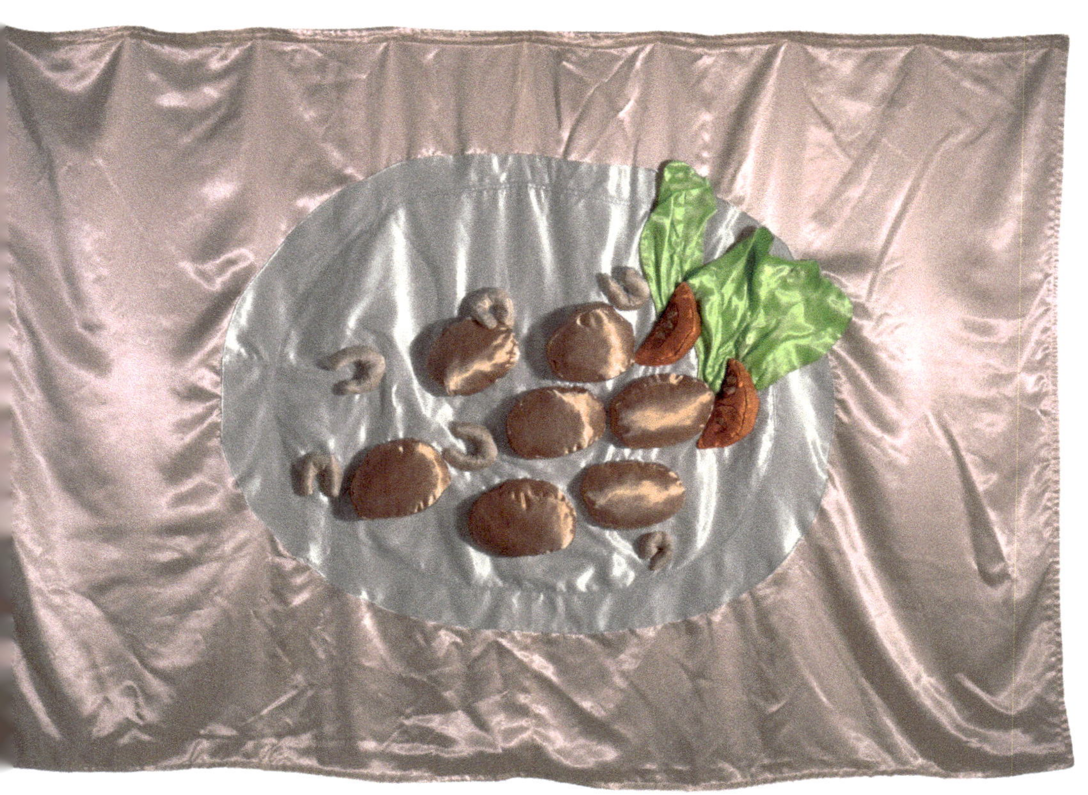

Figure 9.1: Marie-Louise Ekman, *Fiskbullar i hummersås* (Fishcakes in Lobster Sauce), 1968. 121 x 174 cm, Appliqué on satin. Purchased in 1968, Moderna museet. © Marie-Louise Ekman/Bildupphovsrätt 2016.

Figure 9.2 (next spread): Marie-Louise Ekman, *Hemma hos en dam (*At home at a Lady's), 1973. 50 x 62 cm, oil on canvas, mixed techniques, private collection. © Marie-Louise Ekman/Bildupphovsrätt 2016.

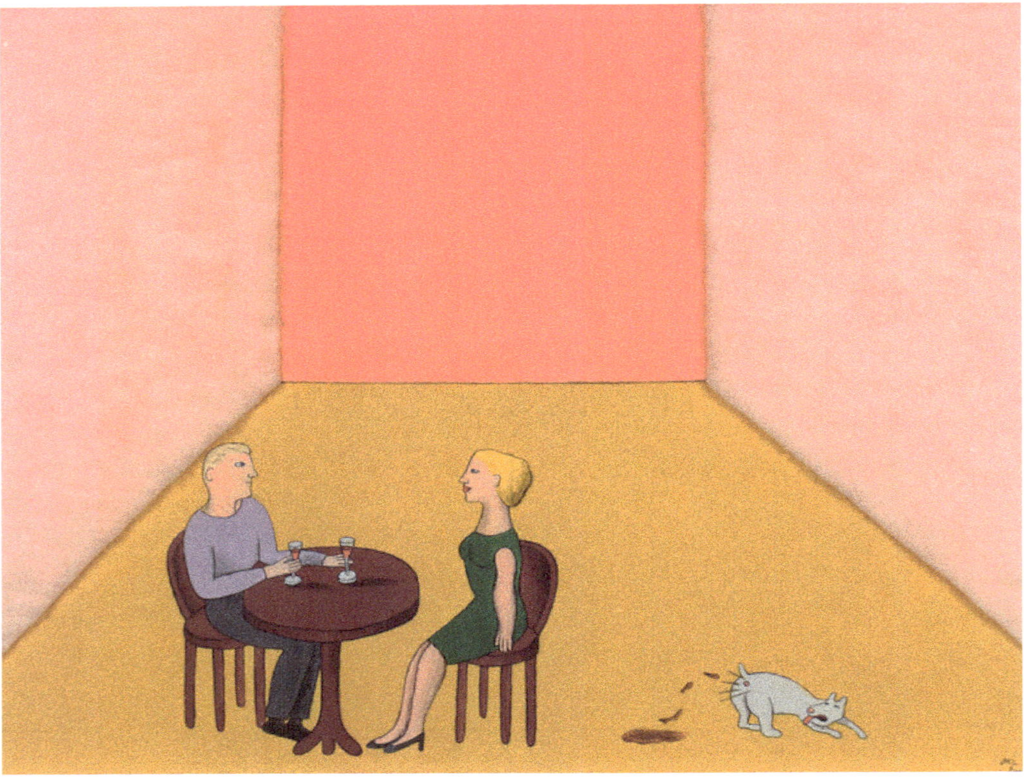

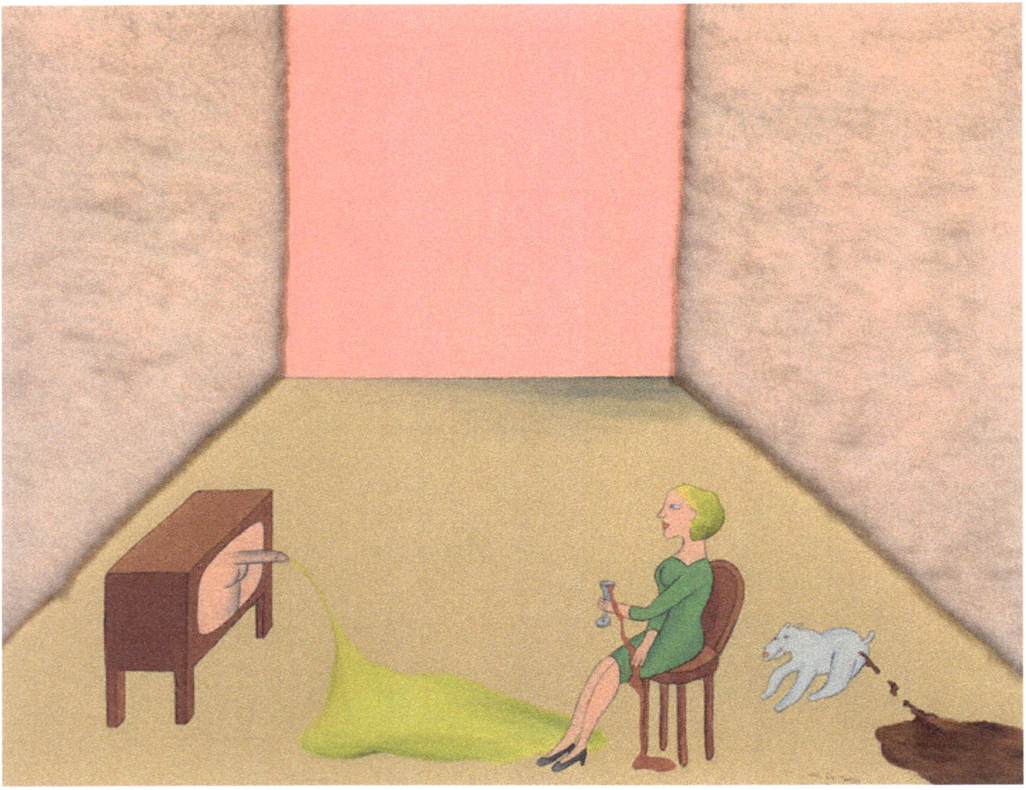

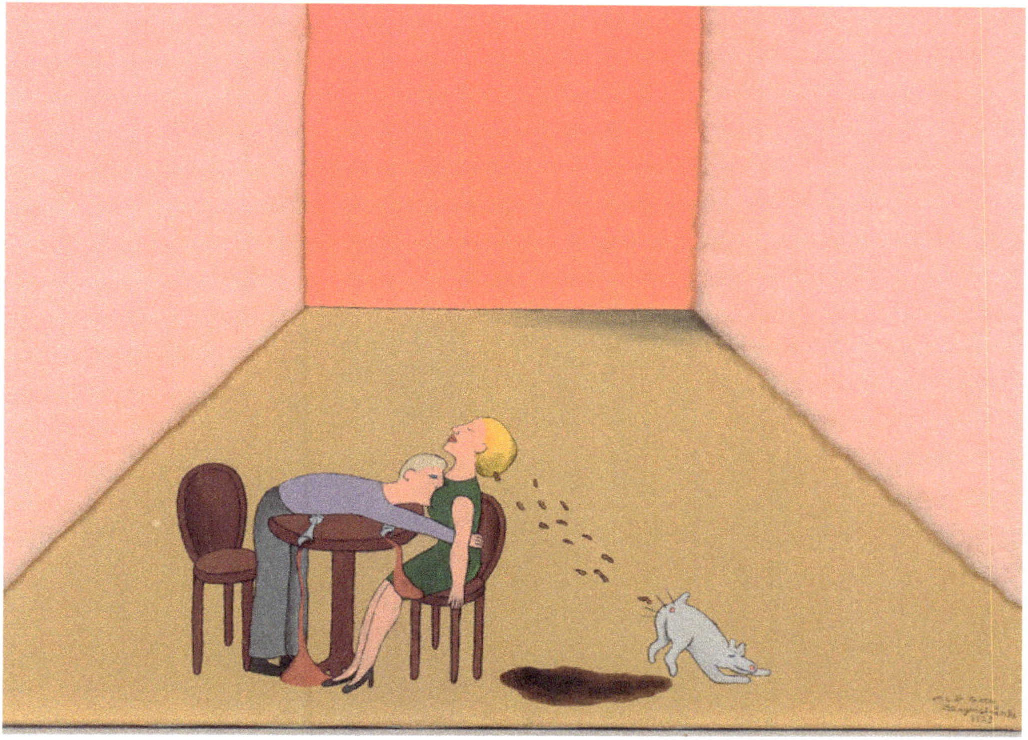

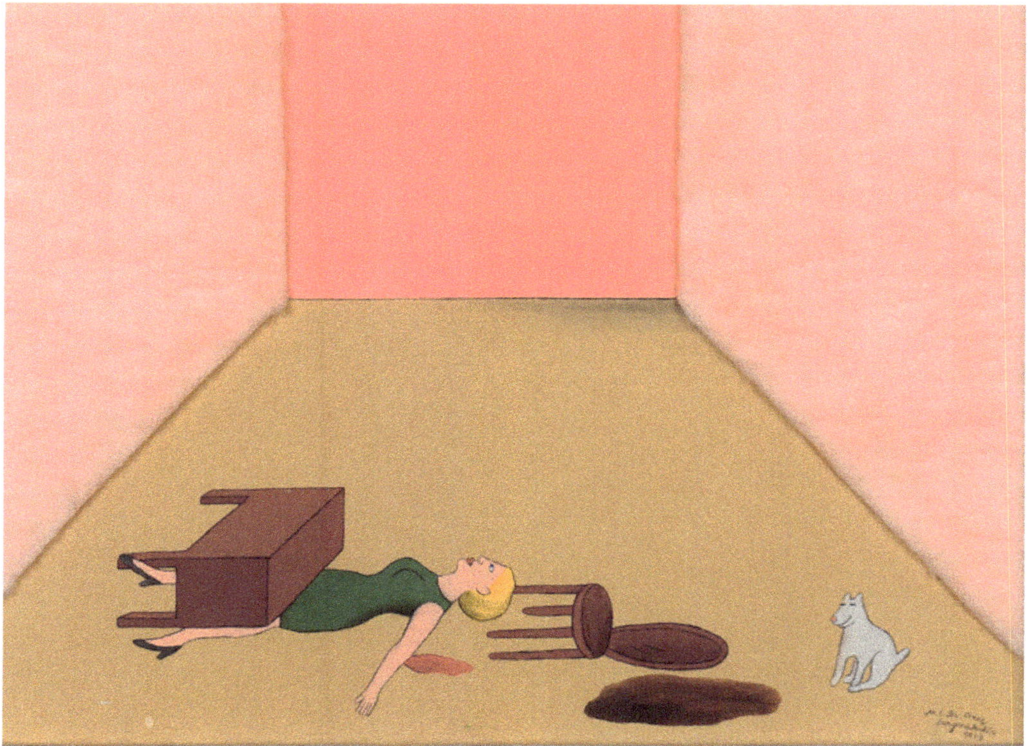

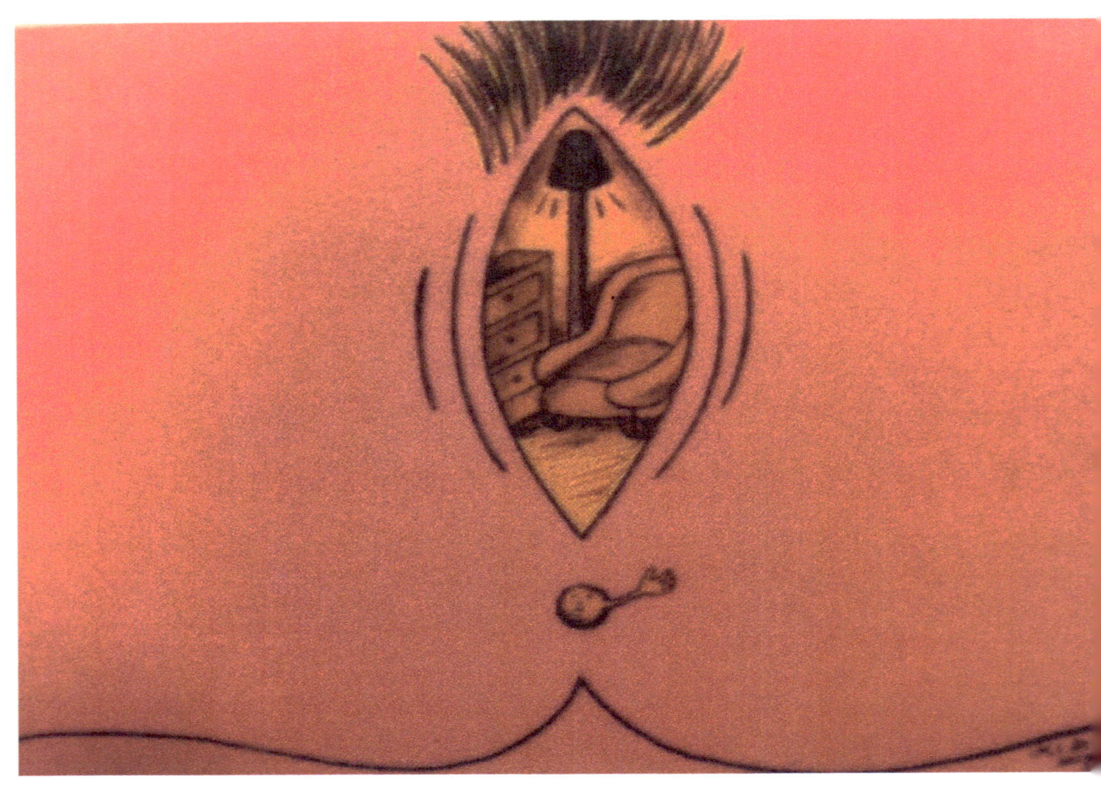

Figure 9.3: Marie-Louise Ekman, *A Home*, 1974. © Marie-Louise Ekman/Bildupphovsrätt 2016.

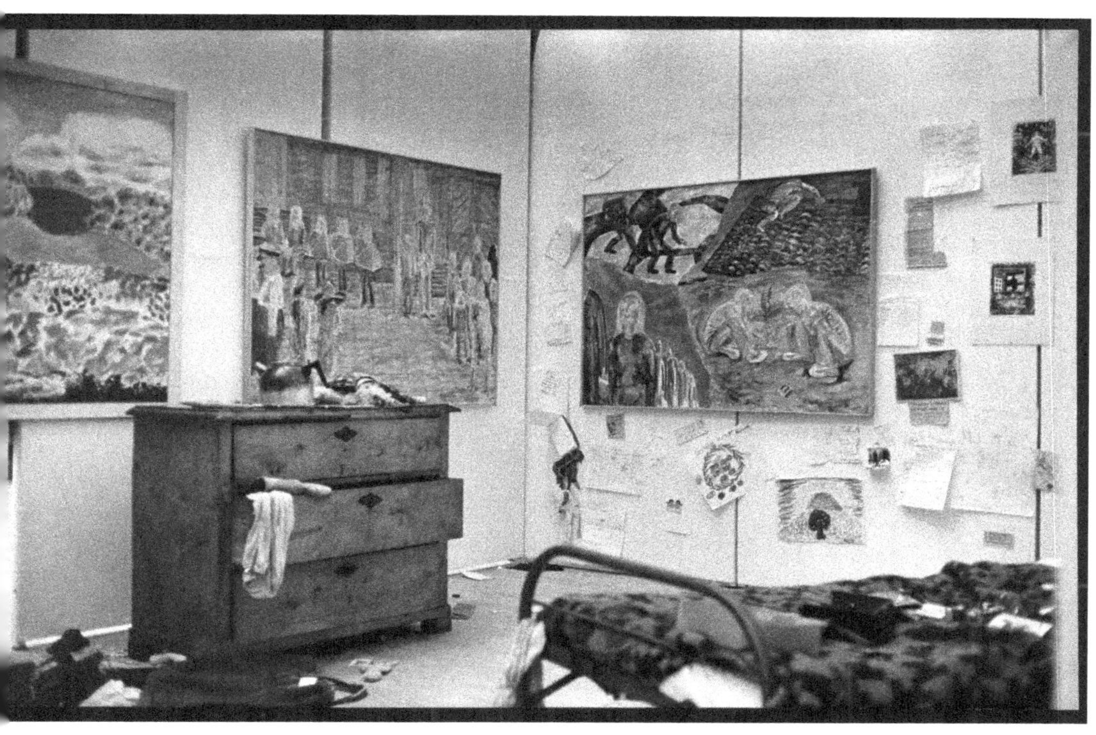

Figure 9.4: Anna Sjödahl, *Var dags liv – mitt alternativ/EveryDay Life – My Alternative*, 1973–75, installation shot *Kvinnoliv* at Malmö Konsthall, 1975. Photo: Anna Lena Lindberg.

10
Collective Modernism
Synthesising the Arts, Engaging in Society

Håkan Nilsson

After the artist/writer Gregory Sholette sent out an inquiry in 2008–9 to 211 art collectives world-wide, he concluded that the reason explaining why artists got involved working as a group rather than as individuals had to do with a change in how collective work is appreciated in the art world. "The two most salient results revolve around the changing nature of collectivism after modernism," writes Sholette, and he continues by stating that the "stigma against belonging to an artists' group or collective has decreased in recent years."[1]

As a professor teaching at an art academy, I do recognise the attitude described above. While individuality continues to play an important role, not the least for "branding" and maintaining an identity which the market can trust and predict, there is also a growing field of artists for whom this is increasingly uninteresting to them. These artists tend to find other ways and other forms of exhibitions, outside the established art scene. As a consequence, parts of the "Dark Matter" Sholette devotes his book to, i.e. the artist driven, alternative art scene, sometimes gets equally much attention as the established one. One could, for instance, point to the fact that the largest commercial art fair in Stockholm, called "Market", plain and

[1] Gregory Sholette, *Dark Matter: Art in the Age of Enterprise Culture*, New York: Pluto Press, 2010.

simple, both when it comes to attention from the press and from the crude numbers of visitors, is challenged from the alternative fair, tong-in-cheekily called "Supermarket", presenting mainly artist run initiatives.

However here I will look at Sholette's polarity between individualism and collectivism from another angle and ask what happened when the individualistic artists of post war modernism assembled in groups with collective ambitions, i.e. not preliminary uniting under some stylistic banner or movement, but gathering in order to achieve something together? Because, contrary what one would gather from Sholette's description above, this was a rather well-spread phenomenon in Europe (also, as Piotr Piotrowski has shown, in some countries in the eastern bloc)[2] during the first decades after the War. In short, their ambitions were to "synthesise" the art forms, but this should be understood as more than a mere merging of different art forms in a mutual expression; it was also an attempt to form a new artistic language for a new and democratic world. But if this was well spread, why do we so seldom read about it? Perhaps the geographical position can hint at some explanation to this; art history surveys of recent decades have had us looking at the U.S., rather than to Europe for the development of late modernism. By this change of focus, many things that happened in the "old world" got lost. Indeed, if one follows this trail of thought for a while, one can follow how already back then, American artists thought of their art as something different, and perhaps also more in tune with time, than what was left of not only European modernism but of Europe at large, which lay in ruins after the devastating war. Barnett Newman simply said good riddance to the European quest for "beauty" and instead pointed towards another drive, that he felt had hitherto been pushed aside; the "sublime" which Newman described to be at the core of contemporary American art.[3] In Europe, however, the non-figurative modernist art from the period between the wars would after the war play the role of a vessel for democracy, having been banned by the fascist. It therefor seemed to hold the future in its hands. In fact, many saw the new times as a revenge for abstraction, not only after the ban from

[2] Piotr Piotrowski, *In the Shadow of Yalta: Art and the Avant-garde in Eastern Europe, 1945–1989*, London: Reaktion Books, 2009.

[3] Barnett Newman, "The Sublime Is Now" (1948), in John P. O'Neill (ed.), *Barnett Newman: Selected Writings and Interviews*, Berkeley and Los Angeles: University of California Press, 1990.

fascism, but also after a long neglect from the official art scene: The first manifesto for *du Salon des Realites Nouvelles* from 1948 (thus the same year as Newman's essay) understands this scene for abstract art as a response to the "systematic exclusion of abstract art" that had been going on for thirty years, with the Venice biennale of 1948 as the most recent example.[4]

Of course, every kind of distinction based on geographical sites must be results of crude simplifications, and so is, no doubt, the one I am suggesting here between the modernisms labeled "European" and "American." I will, however, stick to this distinction for what one could call "operative" reasons. Firstly, it can be helpful for discussing differences between that what might be described in terms of "collective" and "individualistic" modernism, where the latter would be more privileged in the United States. Not only because the U.S. is the centre for the cult of the self-made man. The individuality of American modernism was also emphasised in the cold war politics, where it would be used in the propaganda as an antidote to communistic "collectivism."[5] Secondly, the difference between "collectivistic" and "individualistic" challenges another, more established idea about the differences between European and American modernism: namely the one between "idealism" and "pragmatism." European art is often labeled "idealistic" and thus clinging to an obsolete idea that has its roots in romanticism (not unlike the ideas promoted by Barnett Newman in 1948). This very duality has also often been used to measure how relevant and/or radical occasional European modernist artists have been. If they can be said to pass as "pragmatic," they are understood as more important and more contemporary than their "idealistic" colleagues.[6]

[4] *Premier Manifeste du Salon des Réalités Nouvelles* (1948) p. 2, "Depuis trente ans les œuvres abstraites sont éliminées systématiquement de toutes les manifestations officielles, en France et á l'étranger, la Biennale de Venise de 1948 est le dernier en date de cet escamotage."

[5] See for example Frances Stonor Saunders, *Who Paid the piper?: The CIA and the Cultural Cold War*, London: Granta, 1999, or Christopher Lasch, *The Agony of the American Left*, London: Lowe and Brydone Ltd., 1966.

[6] The non-idealism of post-war American art has of course been questioned, not least through the exhibition *Trace du Sacre* at Centre Pompidou in Paris 2005, where the spiritual/religious sides of artists such as in Pollock and Barnett Newman were put into focus. However, this discussions lays outside the scope of this paper.

I concur with Gregory Sholette on that focus from the art field and from art history has for a long time been solely on the individual artists. However, as Michel Foucault's genealogy reminds us, we always look after that in history, which confirms what we know about the present.[7] Maybe the history writing of authors such as Sholette allows us also to re-think the importance of the art groups during modernity.

Belonging

If history was a landscape in ruins for Barnett Newman, returning to the ideals of pre-war era served as a way of looking to the future for many European artists and architects. Here, they were striving to find a language that would work for all kinds of artistic expressions. Not simply to find the lowest common denominator which would mean that differences in style would only be variants of an underlying theme of "art." At least during the first decade after the war, the ambition seems to have been to find a mutual "theme" also in style, a visual Esperanto, a grammar that would suit painting, sculpture and architecture equally well. But the groups were not limited to these art forms, they also tended to embrace everything from dance to music and handicraft; a plurality that in itself seem to have carried another kind of idea of what the idea of a mutual artistic platform could mean, suggesting a quite open atmosphere. An important question is how "pluralistic" this all-embracing was: the "synthesis of the arts" seems to advocate a totality that would limit the possibility of variety of expressions. One can sense a dispositive of "discipline" here which opted both for an inclusion of any kind of art form and a narrow scope of visual (and audial) expression at the same time. One of my hypothesis is that this slightly paradoxical situation is closely connected to the political ambitions of the groups; creating a modern world, freed from traditional values and built on mutual understandings of rationality and democracy would do away with the very grounds of fascism itself.

Nevertheless, both Dutch architect and situationist Constant and Swedish artist Carl-Fredric Reutersvärd, who one would find difficult to

[7] Michel Foucault, "Nietzsche, Genealogy, History," in *Language, Counter-Memory, Practice*, Oxford: Blackwell, 1987.

label even slightly "modernist," joined the French *Groupe Espace* and the Swedish aspect, respectively, for short while; I will look more closely here at these two groups. This raises questions about belonging and why artists (or indeed anyone) joins a group at all. Without being able to develop the topic, one could perhaps discern between four different reasons. The first reason follows what Gregory Sholette described above; that the artists in question do not wish to partake in the commercialism following that the focus on individual artists and fix stars. We could call this the collective reason. The second reason would be that the individual artist in question approves the ideals behind the group; we could call this the ideological reason. Yet another, and perhaps as common reason, could be that the artist feels that s/he can benefit from joining or forming the group, be it financial support or a possibility to exhibit; we could call this the strategic reason. The fourth and possibly the most difficult one to pinpoint would be when the artist feels attracted to the momentum of the group to a greater extent than the ideology behind it. The group might appear as a place where things happen, that it carries a promise of any outcome imaginable. Following Gilles Deleuze, we could call this the virtual reason. Deleuze understood the virtual not as a possibility, but rather more as a situation, a part of the same real as the actual. In fact, they are interdependent of each other as a "circuit," writes Deleuze, who also states that a purely actual object does not exist.[8] One could perhaps describe the virtual as all those possibilities that are given in a certain situation. Which in this case, would mean that someone might join a particular group because it seems to offer a potentiality beyond their own understanding. This energetic, virtual field is probably the reason for why the above-mentioned artists joined modernist movements, and one should perhaps always be open to the situation that any member may be attracted by any of and/or all these reasons (and perhaps even others that I have not considered here).[9] Regardless of why anyone joins a group, it also asks what kind of impact this has on the development of the individual artist. Of course, every artist always belongs to a context that influences him or

[8] Gilles Deleuze, "The Actual and the Virtual," *Dialogues II*, London & New York: Continuum, 2002.

[9] I am here indebted to my colleagues at Konstfack for important input, most notably Katja Aglert and Thomas Elovsson.

her in one way or another, but one could assume that the effects are more readily visible upon actually joining a group. It would indeed be interesting to scrutinise more thoroughly the relationship between, for instance. Swedish artist Olle Bærtling's (to whom I will return later on) notion of "open form" and the discussions of spatiality in associations such as *Groupe Espace* and *aspect*, both to which he belonged.

Collective modernism

I will now turn to the formation and faiths the two different artist groups, already mentioned above: *Groupe Espace* and *aspect*. I will do so partly from the perspective of Swedish artist Olle Bærtling (Figure 10.5–10.6), who today is probably the most prominent Swedish modernist artist. Bærtling is well-known for the abstract, geometrical paintings and sculptures he developed during the years around 1950 when he turned away from figurative. Initially he would give his paintings titles like "Creation d'espace" and "Force Noir," but slowly he would also use abstract titles, where the names only intended to hint kinship within a series of paintings (like "Neli," "Nelamk," "Nero," etc). Bærtling opted for an art where nothing; not the colours, not the forms, not even the titles would resemble anything in "nature."

Bærtling was an autodidact artist who provided for himself as a banker, an occupation he would leave in the mid-1950s. He had troubles with becoming accepted among other Swedish abstract artists, but quite early in his career did exhibit extensively abroad. His production from when he started to explore the non-figurative world in the 1950s until his demise in 1981 is best understood as whole. As he wrote in his "Prologue to a manifesto of open form" he insisted that his paintings and sculptures belonged to the same world, being "of kindred spirits."[10] "Open form" was a concept Bærtling would develop during his entire career, which apart from painting and sculpture also included some architectural projects.

[10] "[D]e är båda samma andas barn." Olle Bærtling, "Prolog ur ett manifest till öppen form," *Bærtling, den öppna formens skapare*, Malmö, 1981, p. 40 and p. 49.

Groupe Espace

Groupe Espace was formed by artists who already regularly participated in *Salon des Réalités Nouvelles*, founded in 1946. The salon was a yearly exhibition[11] which during its first decade took place at the Musée d'art Modern Ville Paris.[12] It was constituted by members of the pre-war organisation *Abstraction-Création* (formed in 1931) such as Auguste Herbin, Félix del Marle and Albert Gleizes and was conceived of as a continuation of it. The Salon became successful rather quickly. From 1946 to 1948 the numbers of exhibitors had gone from 89 to 366, and it thus became an important context for showing and arguing for abstract art (hence the manifesto of 1948).[13] Bærtling exhibited there already in 1950, only a year after his first solo exhibition at Galleri Samlaren in Stockholm.

Groupe Espace was formed because the initiators didn't feel that the Salon did provide enough space or possibilities for an abstract art that concerned itself with spatiality. Félix del Marle (secretary of the Salon and unsigned author (with Auguste Herbin) of Salon's Manifesto mentioned above) had at this late stage of his career taken interest in the synthesis between art and architecture, and started a section for architecture at the Salon in 1950.[14] At this time, paintings hanging on the wall no longer interested Del Marle. In 1957 Art historian Marcel Brion would describe how del Marle fled the "imprisonment" of two dimensionality,[15] and Daniel Schidlower writes that del Marle left the flatness the painting to grasp what he called "the space."[16] (Same flatness that during the same period was seen as one of the "limiting condition"; the threshold, challenge and demarcation line for the painting of American modernism, promoted

[11] Already in 1939, Sonia and Robert Delaunay and some other artists did a show under this name at the Charpentier gallery in Paris. Sonia Delaunay was also involved in starting the post-war exhibition, which show took place at Palais des Beaux-Arts de la Ville de Paris 1946.

[12] It has since then changed location a few times, but is still running.

[13] See Domitille d'Orgeval, "L'histoire du Salon des réalités nouvelles de 1946 à 1956," p. 2.

[14] Felix del Marle past away in 1952, at the age of 63.

[15] Marcel Brion, La peinture moderne: De l'impressionnisme à l'art abstrait, Stuttgart: Editions d'Art Somogy, 1957, p. 83.

[16] "Del Marle va progressivement quitter le plan du tableaux pour ce qu'il appelle 'l'espace'..." Daniel Schidlower, *F. del Marle: la polychromie dans l'espace 1945–1952* (1986) p. 5.

by Clement Greenberg.)[17] As several artists felt inclined to go beyond the scope of the easel painting, del Marle joined André Bloc, founding editor of *L'Architecture d'aujourd'hui* and *Art d'aujourd'hui* (Figure 10.2), to form *Groupe Espace* in 1951. The manifesto would be published in Art d'aujourd'hui #3 1951 (Figure 10.1). André Bloc had since long been interested in the synthesis between art and architecture. Before starting Art d'aujourd'hui he had a long-time co-operation with le Corbusier (through L'Architecture d'aujourd'hui) and they both also attended the VIe Congrès International d'Architecture Moderne (CIAM) in 1947 and 1951, events which both took upon this theme.[18] And in 1949 they formed l'Association pour une synthèse des arts plastiques with Henri Matisse as chair. However, a disagreement between Bloc and le Corbusier in 1950, where Bloc opted for more collective works and solutions, led to that Bloc instead sought out other partners and thus came to form *Groupe Espace* with del Marle.[19] There might also have been other reasons for the fall-out: in a letter from André Bloc to Olle Bærtling, the French artist writes that *Groupe Espace* never consults le Corbusier since the Swiss architect was "anti-abstract."[20]

It was thus various ideas of spatiality that formed the collective interest for the members of *Groupe Espace*; how this is expressed in various art forms and how these can work together to reach new heights, aesthetic but also social. The idea of a synthesis of the arts, preliminary a sort of joint venture between art, architecture and sculpture, is of course not entirely new. We find it at the advent of modernism, in Weiner Werkstädte, in neo-plasticism and in Bauhaus. *Groupe Espace* must of course be understood in this context and their members were aware of its history. Indeed,

[17] In the essay "After Abstract Expressionism" (1962), Greenberg wrote: "the irreducible essence of pictorial art consists in but two constitutive conventions or norms: flatness and the delimitation of flatness…", in *Collected Essays and Criticism IV*, p. 131.

[18] See Domitille d'Orgeval, "Groupe Espace - Groupe Mesure: Une histoire de la synthèse des artsdans la France des années 1950 et 1960," *Groupe Espace - Groupe Mesure: L'esthétique constructiviste de 1951 à 1970, une aventure du XXème siècle*, Paris: Galeri Drouart (2010), pp. 12–45.

[19] Véroinique Wiesinger, "La Synthèse des arts et le Groupe Espace," *Abstractions en France et en Italie*, pp. 119–121.

[20] "[L]e Corbusier n'ayant jamais été consulté pour le Groupe Espace, en raison de sa position anti-abstraite." Letter of 31 January 1955.

at the very basis of *Groupe Espace* lay the ideas that Mondrian promoted in his "Plastic Art and Pure Plastic Art" namely that Constructivist art should unite with architecture, in order to create a new environment in tune the new society that was to emerge in the modern age.[21] Yet, it seems like the challenge that came with a Europe in ruins, made the ambition of spatial manifestations not only feasible (compare with the spatial ambitions neo-plasticism, which is executed in a few buildings only, where Rietvelds *Schröder Haus* from 1924 stands out) but a reality. The artists, architects and others who belonged to the group also felt it necessary, not to say morally compelled, to engage in the spatiality of the built environment.

Thus, moving towards a synthesis of the arts, gave the artists of *Groupe Espace* a feeling of being more in tune with the times (not to say the future) than their peers, stuck,, as they were, by their easels. In contrast to *Salon des Réalités Nouvelles*, *Groupe Espace*, rather than mere organising exhibitions, seems to have moved on to a more theoretical level. This might have come naturally since they already had a journal which gave them visibility: *Art d'aujourd'hui* (and which continued to be published until 1954), the first periodical to be devoted solely to abstract art.

One can only imagine the excitement Bærtling must have felt. In 1950 he had exhibited at the Salon three times, and it was turning out to be a hub of rapid changes and intense discussion about the very *raison d'être* of abstract art. And with the forming of *Groupe Espace,* the arguments extended beyond the scope of aesthetics: In fact, abstraction was understood to be essential for the new world and the artists were encouraged to participate "directly with the human community," as it is stated in the manifesto.[22] That the move from two to three dimensions also was a move from aesthetics to politics, seems to have been generally agreed. Art being obliged to partake in the reconstruction of Europe, and space as a vehicle to "discipline" a new, democratic, anti-fascist man seem to have been two reasons for this. But one can sense a more phenomenological understanding of the move to three-dimensional space by necessity included the beholder in a kind of social bond. Not unlike the way American artist

[21] Piet Mondrian, "Plastic Art and Pure Plastic Art" (1937), in *Art in Theory: 1900–1990*, Oxford: Blackwell, 1992.

[22] "[P]ar d'effectives réalisations (participer) à une action directe avec la communauté humaine."

Robert Morris would explain how his sculptures functioned, in his seminal essays "notes on sculpture" I–II.[23] Further down in the passage about Fèlix del Marle quoted above, Daniel Schidlower describes how creating *Groupe Espace* was to promote "an art in life, an art for mankind" that opted for a reunion of all the arts, and that was meant for everyone, not just an elite.[24] Gallerist Daniel Cordier reasons in a similar vein when he describes (in a catalogue) the art of Jean Dewasne: by moving towards objects, rather than paintings, Dewasne was understood to experiment with presence and "the forces of modern life."[25] Marc Ducourant writes apropos of *Groupe Espace* that they made a "radical move" when they tried to "reintroduce art into every-day life."[26]

The concept of *Groupe Espace* engaged many artists, both of those who had been known before the war (for instance, Fernand Léger and Sonja Delauney) and younger artists such as Jean Dewasne, as well as numerous of foreign artists, such as Olle Bærtling. Marc Ducourant states that by 1954 *Groupe Espace* had over 150 members, from 16 different countries.[27] The concept was also repeated in many other countries. Art historian Domitille d'Orgeval mentions branches in Italy, Belgium, Finland, Switzerland, Great Britain, Tunisia and Germany.[28] Sweden is not mentioned, but an exchange of letters from late 1954 until early 1955 between André Bloc and Olle Bærtling indicates that such a branch did exist. This was however organised without Bærtling's knowledge, which made him furious and only strengthened him in his belief that the Swedish artists were doing whatever they could to fight him. In one letter, Bærtling explains that he and some colleagues have been preparing a "radical art group" for a long time, whereupon he concludes that the initiators behind the Swedish *Groupe Espace* have declared "a war" against him. But it was a

[23] Robert Morris, "Notes on Sculpture," in Gregory Battcock, *Minimal Art: A Critical Anthology*, Los Angeles and London: University of California Press, 1995.

[24] "[…] creé le Groupe Espace pour promouvoir l'art dans la vie, l'art pour homme […]," "[…] non d'une élit, mais de l'homme, de tous les hommes […]," Schidlower, pp. 6–7.

[25] "Dewasne exprime le sensibilité de la présence de l'object et des forces de la vie moderne", Daniel Cordier *Jean Dewasne* (cat) 1963.

[26] "Sa stratégie consiste réintroduire l'art dans la vie quotidienne…," Marc Ducourante, *L'art d'Edgard Pillet*, Musée de Grenoble, 2001, p. 14.

[27] Ducourante, p. 36.

[28] "L'histoire du Salon des réalités nouvelles de 1946 à 1956," p. 9.

war waged by only "second rate artists and architects" with whom Bloc should be careful to engage with.[29] Bloc replied that although *Groupe Espace* never interferes in the internal business of branches, they were of course interested in working only with artists who were at the frontline. He encourages Bærtling to remain in the French *Groupe Esapce*, but that he also sees the importance of starting a branch in Sweden with the best artists and architects.[30]

There is much research remaining to be done about *Groupe Espace*, about their branches, and what goals they managed to achieve. Some essays do exist. One also finds more or less elaborated passages in monographies, and then there is of course a rich material in the house organ *Art d'aujourd'hui*. As for built environments, it is difficult to discern projects that included various members and projects initiated as a consequence of *Groupe Espace*. One example is André Bloc's villa/studio in Meudon (1952), where not only art, sculpture and architecture collaborate, but so do interior, furniture, the garden, et cetera, to form a totality that Véronique Wiesinger has called the "[Bloc's] substitute for the laboratory of synthesising the arts that never came about together with le Corbusier."[31] Another quite well-known project is the Renault factory in Flins, close to Paris, which was inaugurated in 1952. It was the work of architect Bernard Zehrfuss who was appointed vice-president in *Groupe Espace* in 1951 (together with Fernand Léger) in collaboration with Félix del Marle. However, as it was completed in 1952, it could not be the result from a collaboration within *Groupe Espace*. But perhaps such a distinction is unnecessary. The group was formed to provide a forum for ideas that of course already existed, i.e. the *Groupe Espace* is better understood as a *result* of certain ideas about art, society and collaboration than the other way around.

[29] "Après un interview de moi dans un journal ici le Groupe Espace Suédoise [...] a visiblement déclaré la guèrre [*sic*] contre moi et comme en contre mes amis dans le groupe radical. [...] Le Groupe Espace Suédoise est constitué [...] par artistes et architectes de deuxième ordre." Letter of 22 November 1954.

[30] "[J]e pense qu'il faudrait arriver à créer en Suède un Groupe Espace comprenant les meilleurs artistes et les meilleurs architectes," Letter of 25 November 1954.

[31] "[L]e substitut du laboratoire de synthèse des arts qu'il n'avait pu réaliser avec le Corbusier," Wiesinger, pp. 54–55.

For the same reasons it is also difficult to say for how long *Groupe Espace* exists, at least in terms of influence. When André Bloc stop publishing *Art d'aujourd'hui* there seems to have been a drop of interest. Not least from Bloc himself, who seem to be more devoted to his own art (mainly sculpture) than to group activities. In 1956 he also left the chair of *Groupe Espace* to Georges Breuil.[32] In the correspondence with Bærtling, which lasted until at least 1961, he is also mostly concerned with exhibitions.

Not only did Bloc de-associate himself with *Groupe Espace;* many of the early members seem to have left the cooperation in the years following the mid-1950s. Many seem to have started to doubt the possibility of a synthesis of the arts. Already in 1954, artist/theorist Michel Seuphor posed the question in an essay called "Le Synthèse des Arts est elle possible?" in *Art d'aujourd'hui,* and two years later an essay with the same name appeared in *Prisme des Arts,* signed by the artist Jean Gorin.[33] Due to some disagreements between painters and architects, the latter left *Groupe Espace* in 1957.[34] It also seems that Gorin thought that the group had abandoned its ideals; that it thus did not exist in spirit anymore.[35] Other artists left for other reasons. Edgart Pillet, for instance, moved to the United States, where he became a professor—first to Louisville, then to Chicago.

aspect

As *Groupe Espace* was dissolving in Paris, a sibling to it was beginning to be formed in Sweden: *aspect: föreningen för konstarternas samverkan* (*aspect*: The association for collaborations between the arts). According to their first annual report, *aspect* was founded on the 11 May 1959 during a public meeting at Moderna Museet, attended by some 100 persons.[36] The formation had a background history from a few years prior when a group consisting primarily of artists and architects had been gathering in meetings in Helsingborg in order to create a manifestation for the progres-

[32] Wiesinger, p. 129.
[33] Michel Seuphor, "Le Synthèse des Arts est-elle possible?," *Art d'aujourd'hui,* Vol 5, No. 4–5, (1954) pp. 9–11 Jean Gorin, "Le Synthèse des Arts est-elle possible? La Polychromique architectural et le groupe 'Espace,'" *Prisme des arts,* No. 5 (1956).
[34] *Jean Gorin,* Stedelijk Museum Amsterdam (1967).
[35] Brion p. 116.
[36] "Verksamhetsberättelse för arbetsåret maj 1959 – maj 1960."

sive arts, something they felt hadn't been done since the Stockholm Exhibition in 1930.[37] The group consisted of Editor Gunnar Hellman, artist Eric H. Olson,[38] artist Nils Nixon, artist Bengt Orup, architect Olaaf Liisberg, architect Hans Matell and later on, also editor Åke Danielsson. They had approached the people in charge of the exhibition area at H55,[39] but the financial situation was still difficult, as it lacked funding. The group the contacted art patron Theodor Ahrenberg, who turned out being less keen on financing the project than taking it to a more national level, forming a group called "Radical Forum for Culture," a name that was never meant to be anything else than a working title, according to the minutes from the first meeting on 18 March 1959, which consequently was changed to "*aspect*" at the constitutional meeting of the 11 of May, suggested by Åke Danielsson.

Thus, this interim society was in existence only for two months, it set the agenda for the larger meeting at the Moderna Museet in May. The minutes from the March meeting reveal some more details about the background story. It seems that editor Gunnar Hellman had been the driving force behind the efforts in Helsingborg, where he was seeking for some kind of manifestation/exhibition of "experimental and radical forms" for every form of art. It also seems like Hellman was the driving force behind this first gathering in March, consisting of 19 persons, mostly artists and architects but one also finds director Per Edström, composer Ingvar Liedholm, curator K.G. Hultén, editor Åke Danielsson, Miss Ingrid Cornéer and Laborator (!) Tryggve Johansson among the participants. Olle Bærtling is among the artists present, and he would later also become member of the Board of *aspect*.

In the debate that followed the opening of the March meeting, two opinions are made clear: the arts would benefit from a mutual exchange

[37] Where the International Style was presented in full scale, something that had immense impact not least on the development of architecture in Sweden; over night, it seems, many of the most influential architects in the country left the neoclassicist ideals behind and became "modern."

[38] According to the letter correspondence referred to above, Eric H Olson seems to have been one of the founders of the Swedish Groupe Espace, which made Bærtling so furious. Olson was also a member of French Groupe Espace.

[39] An architecture and housing exhibition that took place in Helsingborg in 1955, consisting also in some permanent dwelling areas.

not having to live in splendid isolation, as many voices were seen as being the case presently; this was only made possible by forming an association, which also was the result of the meeting. Artist/professor Eric Grate was asked to be the chairman.

The appointment of Grate as chairman is interesting. From one perspective, the choice was logical: Grate was among the older in the group and he held a position as a professor at the Royal Academy of the Arts in Stockholm, both dignifying him with some authority. The connection to younger artists through his position at the academy could be said to place him in the "future" of the arts. But as an artist, Grate is not the obvious choice as someone "experimental and radical" in the year of 1959. Looking at the other artists, one gets an idea of what was meant by this description. Most of them stand in a modernist tradition; only artist Per-Olof Ultved diverts from this, as he already then moved towards a kinetic art. Grate acted chairman only during the interim period, and became vice chairman on the new Board where architect Viking Göransson was elected chairman.

One can draw some conclusions from the first year of forming *aspect*. Many of the claims and actions of *aspect* reveal how small and neglected the cultural sector was in Sweden back then. It also shows how small the country was. When the Swedish government didn't find the means to send composer Karl-Birger Blomberg (who was a member of *aspect*) to participate personally in the opera festival in Edinburgh, where his master piece "Aniara" was set up, *aspect* reacted and collected the money to cover cost of the airplane ticket. The situation became a bit of a newspaper story, where finally Tage Erlander, the prime minister, declared that he found it essential that Blomdahl should go to Edinburgh and that he had been in contact with the Minister of Trade to sort out the matter.[40]

In the light of such stories, one gets the feeling that *aspect* was formed out of a desperate need just to do *something*, in an area neglected by the public authorities. It also reveals a discrepancy between the artistic development and the institutional support. *Aspect* organised a public meeting at Konstakademin on 3 September 1959, where Theodor Ahrenberg held a talk on "The Poverty in Art in the Welfare State" (which would be a theme at several of *aspect*'s public gatherings), where he commented

[40] "Verksamhetsberättelse för arbetsåret maj 1959–maj 1960," p. 3.

not only about the step-motherly treatment of the arts from the public authorities, but also about the slumber in which many arts associations were in at the time. Ahrenberg also suggested that investing in art should be tax deductible, in a manner similar to the way things work in the United States, and he also advocated a new public lottery which would contribute to funding for the arts.[41] The Minister of Ecclesiastical Affairs Per Edman attended the meeting and suggested that *aspect* should continue to point out a failed appreciation of the situation, and that they should do so in written a presentation. *Aspect* took the suggestion ad nutum, and on 22 October they presented a letter from *aspect* to the King of Sweden, signed by the chairman Viking Göransson and secretary, Åke Danielsson.

The resolution points to many interesting things. The *aspect* association wanted to make the King aware of that, while there had been enormous development in Sweden concerning the social welfare in general, the situation for the artists and sculptors rather has deteriorated during the same years. As a consequence, the letter states, they cannot be expected to contribute to society's development at the same level as other professions: "It [the occupational group] can thus not be expected contribute to the progressive construction and development of contemporary society at full of power."[42] *Aspect* also reacts to the fact that studies in art do not find the same kind of public funding in form of student study loans and student housing, for instance.

In the formation years, *aspect* seem to have been involved in most fields of the arts, ranging from engagement in the Swedish dance scene to various different appeals, not only to the King, but also to the Ecclesiastical Minister Per Edman concerning the situation for students of the fine and performing arts. Their gatherings were set at various locations, including poetry reading and other performing art events such as Carl Fredrik Reutersvärd's "Bankrån i Dublin" (Bank Robbery in Dublin). During the

[41] Konstens armod i Välfärden.

[42] "En från föreningen aspect ställd skrivelse till KONUNGEN 22 oktober 1959," resolution delivered to the King by a committee consisting of Åke Danielsson, Viking Göranson, Gunnar Hellman, and Hans Matell. Quote from the third paragraph, first page. ("Den kan därmed inte förväntas medverka i det samhälleliga uppbyggnads- och utvecklingsarbetet till sin fula kraft.")

first year, several debates concerning the situation for the arts in the country, the status of our museums (Are they archives? Or, Are they living institutions?), and on the co-operation between art and architecture at the Moderna Museet (12 April 1960), with a focus on education on the one hand and commissions on the other.

At this later occasion, Gunnar Hellman, the moderator, seems to have been rather critical about the status of exiting collaborations, where he criticised the artists for being too egotistic. He also questioned the ways The National Public Art Council Sweden (presently, the Public Art Agency) worked. Hellman stressed the need to think about where these projects were going, where the aim must be a totality, a comprehensive environment (*helhetsmiljö*) following "strict artistic principles."[43]

The "cooperation" between the different art forms (which seems to have excluded craft) that is stated in all the material sent out saying "The Association Aspect for the Collaboration of the Arts" (Föreningen Aspect för Konstarternas Samverkan) seem to have two different meanings. On the one hand, there is this multitude of expressions and the mutual will to meet and form some platform for any kind of experimental art. On the other, the collaboration is often thought of in terms (not unlike the ones we can find in *Groupe Espace*) where the working together is understood as a synthesis of different art forms, usually manifested in architecture.

The question about art and architecture was also addressed in the letter to the King, mentioned above. In the letter, *aspect* comments upon the fact that the "Engbergsk 1 percent rule" that was decided upon in the Riksdag (parliament) before the War (a rule that said that 1 percent of all public building costs should be invested in art) was abandoned due to the extreme circumstances during War, but was at the time not yet reinstalled. And, the authors write "Since private housing construction either has decreased considerably or has been transformed into municipal housing companies," funded with governmental loans, pressing costs, and other cut-backs has rendered "artistic contributions in societal environments superfluous or something that can be postponed."[44]

[43] "Verksamhetsberättelse för arbetsåret maj 1959–maj 1960," p. 6

[44] "[...] konstnärlig medverkan vid samhällsmiljöns utformning är något överflödigt eller något som kan anstå." From the perspective of 2015, it is interesting to see how *aspect* points to the decrease in private funded buildings as a source for the diminishing presence of arts

The organisation also points to how democratic decision-making can be the source of these problems: As the majority of the people in such assembly have no artistic education, they will often support a conservative line, leaving that some of "our most talented and progressive artists only occasionally under their lifetime are offered official assignments [...]"[45] Instead, *aspect* proposes that special art and cultural boards are created, where knowledge in the field will be essential for all members.

Again, we find that the demarcation line goes between the artists and the others, not between the different art forms. Although many ideas behind the association and the projects clearly belong to modernism, there seems to be no will to promote one art form over the other, or to say that some artists wouldn't have felt included. Perhaps this is due to the situation for the arts at the time; internal gabble had to stand aside in order to organise against other threats. This would mean that the gathering in *aspect* was not preliminary based on a desire for a mutual program, but on a shared need to put the art agenda on the table. Thus, it followed a strategic, as much as an ideological agenda. Still, at the time, in *aspect* there seems to have been little or no need to make a difference between the upcoming "open" art scene of the coming 1960s and the dying, depleting aesthetics and ideals of modernism. This is probably due to the fact that modernism then still was a radical movement in many ways.

Looking at the housing situation in Stockholm in 1959 also helps to explain why modernism was seen as radical. The reconstruction of the city centre was just finishing, in which *aspect* member David Helldén had been the guiding force behind the five high rises and the shaping of the *Sergels Torg* square at the very core of Stockholm. Helldén was the architect behind the first high rise, where the entrance was designed by him and Olle Bærtling jointly; indeed it was a co-operation between the arts, as promoted by *aspect*—although initiated before. In his article "Estetiskt rum—Immateriell rymd" Bærtling describes the jointly achieved project, where they strived not only for an aesthetic expression, but also tried to

in newly built architecture. Today, as the municipal had been selling out its rental apartments to private households and letting private interests be responsible for the major bulk of new buildings, the complaints goes the other way around.

[45] "Våra mest begåvade och progressiva konstnärer endast undantagsvis under sin livstid erhålla officiella uppdrag [...]"

arrive at a spatiality that could "contribute to a more constructive and progressive way of thinking."[46] Still, this was to become the only fully realised joint-venture project Bærtling took part in, although there are other suggestions signed by both Bærtling and Helldén and later on by Bærtling and the German architect Gerd Fesel. Other co-operations consisted of Bærtling providing for paintings and sculptures for buildings and/or public spaces (Figure 10.7).

One reoccurring theme in the discussions held by the association was the need to make *aspect* and its members more visible. They reach an agreement on starting a magazine (again close to the workings of *Groupe Espace*), but never find the means to actually do so. Another way of visualisation is of course to make an exhibition and a committee has been working on finding a suitable spot. They negotiated with Liljevalchs konsthall, the kunsthalle of the City of Stockholm, and then agreed on making a "jury free" exhibition for all the arts in 1961(Figure 10.3–10.4).

This exhibition was to be become the most important task *aspect* managed to accomplish. It is also interesting in that it points to a rupture between two different meanings of cooperation, the totality of "artistic principles" and the infinity of many different projects. The exhibition seems to have balanced in-between the two. The catalogue contains a homage to Otto G. Carlsund, the Swedish artist who belonged to *Art Concret*, and who saw to it that there was a selection of abstract art presented at the Stockholm Exhibition (1930); the exhibition that had been so important for the artists when they were striving to create an association for the radical arts in the years that predated the advent of *aspect*. The exhibition contained a separate part, celebrating the newly constructed Brazilia in Brazil, and there is also an essay in the catalogue by Olle Bærtling called "Rymdålderns konst" (The art of the space age), where the artist in a futuristic vein claims that the modernist aesthetic belongs to a new, even coming age.[47] These entries are arguments for the same kind of modernist synthesis of the arts we found in *Groupe Espace*. But then the exhibition at Liljevalchs spoke another language altogether. *Aspect -61*

[46] Olle Bærtling, "Estetiskt rum – Immateriell rymd," *Konstperspektiv*, No. 2, 1960, pp. 11–14; "[...] positivt medverka till ett mera konstruktivt, mera framåtskridande tänkande," p. 14.

[47] Olle Bærtling, "Rymdålderns konst," *Document aspect 61*, Stockholm: Lilljevalchs konsthall, 1961, n.p.

counted no less than 202 exhibitors, presenting a multitude of art expression. Judging from this variety, it almost seems like just anything could fit the profile for what *aspect* stood for. Maybe this also explains why Bærtling later on left the association. He felt it was not developing in the right direction, as he states in an unsigned letter, hereby following the reasons Jean Gorin gave for leaving *Groupe Espace* half a decade earlier.[48]

Conclusions

As the influence of modernist aesthetics and ideology began to diminish in the beginning of the 1960s, the art scene shifted, to borrow the concepts from Emmanuel Lévinas, from a "totality" of some visual Esperanto towards an "infinity" of many styles.[49] By then, most of the groups opting for a "synthesis of the arts" had been dissolved. However, the Swedish group *aspect* evolved with the changing art scene and for a short while became a platform for any artistic expression, most notably in the jury-free exhibition *aspect -61*. This transformation of *aspect* is interesting when it comes to the question of what happened to late modernist collectivism. One answer is of course that it became obsolete and disappeared. Another answer would be that the democratic ideals survived, but in a visual multitude. The transformation of *aspect* seems to suggest this; the group could be faithful to the ideals and yet changing expression. A third answer is that it actually survived, where it had its foremost expression in the construction of many suburbs constructed in the 1960s and 1970s. The cooperation in the residential area of Flemingsberg between artist Gert Marcus and architect Hans Matell, both members of *aspect*, is such an example. The fact that the municipality of Huddinge (where Flemingsberg is located) invested money in such high-brow co-operation was widely understood as an effort to make a difference. But when it was completed in 1974, already at its inauguration it was being criticised as being inhuman, as was indeed most suburbs after 1968, the year when journalists and the cultural elite in Sweden started to criticise what it until then had embraced as a quest for democracy. The author Per Wirtén, who grew up in the neighbourhood,

[48] Olle Bærtling, Letter to *aspect*, 1962.
[49] Emmanuel Lévinas, *Totality and Infinity: An Essay on Exteriority*, Pittsburgh: Duquesne University Press, 1969.

recounts the shift from curious praise to bashing, something he also connects to the fact that when Flemingsberg was completed, the housing shortage that it was meant to solve no longer existed, and it thus it became very difficult to find tenants to occupy the new apartments. In the media, Flemingsberg was described as a "fiasco," where nobody moved, an area that was plagued with rampant crime, et cetera.[50] Interestingly, in 1982 Gert Marcus was allowed four pages to describe the housing project in Flemingsberg in an article in the East German magazine *Farbe und Raum*.[51] The totality of "the syntheses of the arts" had gained the attention of totalitarianism (although the editor wrote that it was questionable if architecture was a suitable carrier of one person's individualistic artistic expression).

From the perspective of the suburbs of the 1970s, it is easy to think about the endeavours of the artist groups from the 1950s as think tanks for what Michel Foucault called "the society of discipline." The society of discipline did perhaps get its most well-known description in *Discipline and Punish*, where Foucault developed his thoughts on the panopticon, where we all would monitor ourselves, in fear of some kind of big brother.[52] In *The Production of Space* Henri Lefebvre reasons in similar veins when he describes architecture as something that produces an ideological space, often used as a means of monitoring and controlling the citizens. Foucault also seem to have thought along those lines when he argued that "architecture belongs to discipline" in the lecture series at Collège de France in the end of the seventies, posthumously published.[53]

One can argue that artist groups such as *Groupe Espace* or *aspect* (at last initially) moved on the level that Lefebvre called "conceived space," i.e. more on a level of abstract planning. One can also argue that this is connected to the dispositive "discipline." Both of these would feel very alien to contemporary art groups who instead operate on small scale in

[50] Per Wirtén, *Där jag kommer ifrån – kriget mot förorten*, Stockholm: Albert Bonniers förlag, 2010.
[51] Gert Marcus, "Farbe in Västra Flemingsberg," *FARBE und RAUM*, No 9, September 1982, VEB Verlag für Bauwesen, Berlin, DDR, pp. 10-14.
[52] Michel Foucault, *Discipline and punish: The Birth of the Prison*, New York: Vintage Books, 1995.
[53] Michel Foucault, *Security, Territory, Population: Lectures at the Collège de France, 1977–1978*, Houndmills, Basingstoke, Hampshire: Palgrave Macmillan, 2007.

reaction to the "lived space" of the inhabitants. Still, the "discipline" in the art groups cannot be easily translated to the "discipline" of society. It might be that they are connected in many ways, but this does not mean that they operate with the same goals and/or agendas. The discipline of a (totalitarian) society and the discipline opted for by an art group, striving for a totality of arts, is no more connected than is, the neo-liberal society of "control," as Foucault called the other dispositive, with the rhizomaticly connected alternative art groups of today. The likeness is a likeness of means, which doubtlessly can turn into a problem when the radical alternative finds how easily it can be adopted by the very powers it understands as its enemy.

The discussion of "conceived space" and "society of discipline" must be balanced with questions about what kind of *force* the groups represented. The members of *Groupe Espace* did obviously want to take a step further from easel painting and they did see art as a tool that could and should have social and political implications. Perhaps there are reasons to discuss to what extent the aesthetics of these groups also reflects their possibilities, their virtuality, for returning to Gilles Deleuze. Here it also becomes relevant to look into the downfall of the associations, which begs the more complicated questions: when is it no longer productive to remain in a certain context? Did Bærtling leave *aspect* because he didn't feel related to the other artistic expressions that in the end were allowed, or did he leave because the association no longer provided the same potentiality in a more profound way?

Works cited

Olle Bærtling, "Estetiskt rum – Immateriell rymd," *Konstperspektiv*, No. 2, 1960, pp. 11–14.

—. "Rymdålderns konst," *Document aspect 61*, Stockholm; Lilljevalchs konsthall, 1961, n.p.

—. "Prolog ur ett manifest till öppen form," *Bærtling: Den öppna formens skapare,* Malmö, 1981.

Marcel Brion, *La peinture moderne: De l'impressionnisme à l'art abstrait,* Stuttgart: Editions d'Art Somogy, 1957.

Daniel Cordier, *Jean Dewasne,* exh. cat., Paris: Galerie Daniel Cordier, 1963.

Marc Ducourante, *L'art d'Edgard Pillet,* Grenoble: Musée de Grenoble, 2001, p. 14.

Gilles Deleuze, "The Actual and the Virtual," *Dialogues II*, London and New York: Continuum, 2002.

Michel Foucault, *Discipline and Punish: The Birth of the Prison*, New York: Vintage Books, 1995.

—. *Security, Territory, Population: Lectures at the Collège de France, 1977–1978*, Houndmills, Basingstoke, Hampshire: Palgrave: Macmillan, 2007.

—. "Nietzsche, Genealogy, History," in *Language, Counter-Memory, Practice*, Oxford: Blackwell, 1987.

Jean Gorin, "Le Synthèse des Arts est-elle possible? La Polychromique architectural et le groupe 'Espace'," *Prisme des arts*, No. 5, 1956.

Jean Gorin, Amsterdam: Stedelijk Museum, 1967.

Clement Greenberg, "After Abstract Expressionism," in John O'Brian (ed.), *Collective Essays and Criticism IV*.

Christopher Lasch, *The Agony of the American Left*, London: Lowe and Brydone, (1966).

Emmanuel Lévinas, *Totality and Infinity: An Essay on Exteriority*, Pittsburgh: Duquesne University Press, 1969.

Gert Marcus, "Farbe in Västra Flemingsberg," *FARBE und RAUM*, No. 9, September 1982, Berlin, DDR: VEB Verlag für Bauwesen, pp. 10–14.

Piet Mondrian, "Plastic Art and Pure Plastic Art" (1937), in *Art in Theory 1900-1990*, Oxford: Blackwell, 1992.

Robert Morris, "Notes on Sculpture," in Gregory Battcock, *Minimal Art: A Critical Anthology*, Los Angeles & London: University of California Press, 1995.

Barnett Newman, "The Sublime Is Now" (1948), in John P. O'Neill (ed.), *Barnett Newman: Selected Writings and Interviews*, Berkeley and Los Angeles: University of California Press, 1990.

Domitille d'Orgeval, "Groupe Espace - Groupe Mesure: Une histoire de la synthèse des artsdans la France des années 1950 et 1960," *Groupe Espace - Groupe Mesure: L'esthétique constructiviste de 1951 à 1970, une aventure du XXème siècle*, Paris: Galeri Drouart, 2010?.

Piotr Piotrowski, *In the Shadow of Yalta: Art and the Avant-garde in Eastern Europe, 1945–1989*, London: Reaktion Books, 2009.

Frances Stonor Saunders, *Who Paid the Piper? The CIA and the Cultural Cold War*, London: Granta, 1999.

Daniel Schidlower, *F. del Marle: la polychromie dans l'espace 1945–1952*, 1986.

Michel Seuphor, "Le Synthèse des Arts est-elle possible?," *Art d'aujourd'hui*, Vol 5, No. 4–5, 1954.

Gregory Sholette, *Dark Matter: Art in the Age of Enterprise Culture,* New York: Pluto Press, 2010.

Véroinique Wiesinger, “La Synthése des arts et le Groupe Espace,” in *Abstractions en France et en Italie.*

Per Wirtén, *Där jag kommer ifrån - kriget mot förorten,* Stockholm: Albert Bonniers förlag, 2010.

Manuscripts

Lund: Landsakivet. Olle Bærtling-arkivet

Stockholm: Private collection: *aspect* Verksamhetsberättelse, *aspect* stadgar, *aspect* exhibition catalogue

Web sources

Domitille d’Orgeval, “L’histoire du Salon des réalités nouvelles de 1946 à 1956,” www.realitesnouvelles.org/pdf/dorgeval-fullenght.pdf

Premier Manifeste du Salon des Réalités Nouvelles (1948), www.realites nouvelles.org/pdf/manifest48.pdf

Le Groupe Espace

La dissociation des arts plastiques : peinture, sculpture, architecture, est un fait déplorable, mais tellement admis par les artistes, les critiques et le public, que les essais les plus timides pour replacer les arts dans la vie courante apparaissent, à beaucoup, comme des audaces inutiles.

Cependant, un groupe s'est formé en France pour aborder cette tâche difficile de synthèse, sans laquelle aucune civilisation ne peut affirmer sa présence.

Des conditions favorables vont permettre les premières expériences. Les grandes réalisations de la reconstruction entrent dans une phase décisive. Les architectes, qui ont été chargés des travaux essentiels, ont compris qu'ils pouvaient utilement associer, à leurs études, d'autres plasticiens.

Ensemble, ils viennent de signer un manifeste où ils exposent leur programme. Les artistes, qui ont semblé s'intéresser spécialement aux nouveaux problèmes, ont été invités à se réunir. Les premières signatures, groupées sur le manifeste, ne constituent que le début d'un ralliement.

L'idée est lancée et elle fait son chemin. En France, au Brésil, au Danemark et en Italie, on note les premières réalisations. La Triennale de Milan montre de quelle façon intelligente peuvent collaborer les architectes et les plasticiens.

Le groupe « Espace », désormais constitué en Association, ne sera pas une chapelle. Ses membres ne rechercheront pas une publicité personnelle, mais aborderont, avec l'humilité qui convient aux véritables artistes, les risques qui s'attachent à des expériences fondamentales.

Manifeste

Pour se dégager définitivement de certaines survivances néfastes qui imprègnent autant la masse du public qu'un grand nombre d'artistes, les Architectes, les Constructeurs et les Plasticiens soussignés créent

LE GROUPE ESPACE

ils préconisent

un Art non-figuratif procédant des Techniques et Méthodes actuelles pour des Buts rénovés

un Art qui s'inscrive dans l'Espace réel, réponde aux nécessités fonctionnelles et à tous les besoins de l'homme, des plus simples aux plus élevés

un Art soucieux des conditions de vie, privée et collective, un Art essentiel même à l'homme le moins attiré par les valeurs esthétiques

un Art constructif qui, par d'effectives réalisations, participe à une action directe avec la communauté humaine

un Art devenu spatial par la pénétration sensible et modulée de la Lumière dans l'œuvre, un Art dont la conception et l'exécution s'appuient sur la simultanéité des aspects dans les trois dimensions non suggérées, mais tangibles

un Art où la Couleur et la forme soient enfin indissolublement liées par leurs qualités intrinsèques et architecturales dans une expression idéale de rapports et de proportions.

ils constatent

que d'immenses tâches de construction sont trop souvent confiées à des personnes que rien ne qualifie pour engager l'avenir d'un groupe d'habitations, d'une ville, voire même d'un pays

que l'Urbanisme et la Construction des Cités exigent de ceux qui en sont responsables, non seulement des qualités techniques, mais aussi des connaissances sociales, psychologiques et une certaine culture artistique

que ces connaissances et cette culture sont généralement insuffisantes, qu'on assiste trop souvent à la Reconstruction de nos Cités sur des plans imparfaits et avec une plastique contestable

que la plupart des Architectes n'ont pas été préparés aux tâches nouvelles

que ceux qui ont la responsabilité de créer le milieu dans lequel vivront les générations futures doivent pouvoir s'entourer de Techniciens et d'Artistes plasticiens familiarisés avec les problèmes spatiaux et, de plus, soutenus et aidés par les lois et règlements.

ils proposent

la création de liens étroits entre tous ceux qui peuvent être appelés à concourir aux grandes tâches contemporaines et en particulier, aux :

Études d'Urbanisme, Études de Plans-Masses, Études de la Plastique architecturale y compris tous les prolongements dans la vie courante, Incidences de la couleur dans l'Architecture.

Ainsi, pour familiariser le public avec les nécessaires innovations plastiques, il est souhaitable que les Artistes du Groupe Espace soient appelés à prêter leur concours, notamment lors des Festivals, Expositions et lors des grandes Fêtes publiques. Des démonstrations plastiques, d'envergure, seront admises plus facilement à l'occasion de ces Manifestations et ouvriront ainsi la voie aux réalisations permanentes.

Les Commissions suivantes seront créées immédiatement pour l'étude des problèmes particuliers et devront comprendre chacune des Architectes, Peintres, Sculpteurs et Plasticiens :

URBANISME, PLANS-MASSES, COULEUR, EXPOSITIONS, FÊTES, PLASTIQUE APPLIQUÉE AUX OBJETS

ils réclament

POUR L'HARMONIEUX DÉVELOPPEMENT DE TOUTES LES ACTIVITÉS HUMAINES LA PRÉSENCE FONDAMENTALE DE LA PLASTIQUE

L'Assemblée générale constitutive de cette Association a eu lieu, le 17 octobre 1951, au Grand Palais, sous la présidence d'honneur de M. Eugène Claudius-Petit, Ministre de la Reconstruction et de l'Urbanisme, et la présidence effective de M. André Bloc, Directeur des revues « L'Architecture d'Aujourd'hui » et « Art d'Aujourd'hui ».

Etaient présents à cette Assemblée :

Mmes Sonia DELAUNAY, FAHR-EL-NISSA-ZEID, Jeanne COPPEL, Simone SERVANES, Nicolaas WARB-HELD.

MM. Luc ARSENE-HENRY Paul AYNES, André BRUYERE, Jean GEORGE, Paul HERBE, Lionel MIRABAUD, Walter MUNZ, Marcel ROUX, Jean SEBAO, Bernard-Henri ZEHRFUSS, Architectes.

MM. Aagard ANDERSEN, Etienne BEOTHY, André BLOC, Félix DEL MARLE, Roger DESSERPRIT, Cicero DIAZ, A. R. FLEISCHMAN, Georges FOLMER, Emile GILIOLI, Bernard LAFFAILLE, Pierre LACOMBE, Berto LARDERA, LE CHEVALIER, Fernand LEGER, Claude PARENT, Edgard PILLET, P. E. SARISSON, Ionel SCHEIN, Nicolas SCHOFFER, Plasticiens.

S'étaient excusés :

Madame KANDINSKY

MM. Xavier ARSENE-HENRY, Wladimir BODIANSKY, Silvano BOZZOLINI, Henri CALSAT, G. DEDOYARD, Piero DORAZIO, Pierre FAUCHEUX, Jean FAYETON, G. LAGNEAU, Jean GINSBERG, Jean GORIN, Robert LE RICOLAIS, Marcel LODS, Alberto MAGNELLI, MONNET, NATIVI, Richard NEUTRA, Micaël PATOUT, Serge POLIAKOFF, Jean PROUVE, Alfred ROTH, André SIVE, YONGERMANN.

Au cours de cette réunion, lecture a été donnée des statuts de l'Association et, notamment de l'article premier qui définit les buts : ceux-ci ont été énoncés par M. André Bloc qui a ouvert la séance et rappelé les diverses tentatives modernes, heureuses ou malheureuses, de synthèse des arts.

Article premier. — L'Association dite « Groupe Espace », fondée au cours de l'Assemblée générale du 17 octobre 1951, a pour but de préparer les conditions d'une collaboration effective des architectes, peintres, sculpteurs, plasticiens et d'organiser, par la plastique, l'harmonieux développement des activités humaines.

Sa durée est fixée à 99 ans.

Elle a son siège à Boulogne-sur-Seine, 5, rue Bartholdi.

L'Assemblée a, en outre, procédé à l'élection des membres du Bureau et des membres du Comité, qui se trouvent ainsi constitués :

BUREAU :

Président d'Honneur : M. Eugène CLAUDIUS-PETIT, Ministre de la Reconstruction et de l'Urbanisme.

Président actif : André BLOC.

Vice-Présidents : Paul HERBE, Fernand LEGER, Bernard ZEHRFUSS.

Secrétaire général : Félix DEL MARLE.

Trésorier : Bernard LAFFAILLE.

Délégués à la propagande : Luc ARSENE-HENRY, Edgard PILLET.

COMITE :

MM. Sonia DELAUNAY, Etienne BEOTHY, Silvano BOZZOLINI, Cicéro DIAS, Jean FAYETON, Pierre FAUCHEUX, Jean GORIN, Berto LARDERA, Robert LE RICOLAIS, Paul NELSON, Marcel ROUX.

Enfin, elle aborda la mise au point des méthodes de travail : création des diverses Commissions constituées par des Groupes chargés d'études précises, qui s'étendront aux problèmes les plus divers, allant des plans d'urbanisme aux recherches plastiques, dans le domaine des objets les plus usuels.

COMMISSIONS :

— *Urbanisme et Plans Masse.*

— *Expositions et Fêtes.*

— *Plastique appliquée aux objets (les industriels seront invités à cette Commission).*

En outre, sera constituée une Commission « de la Dimension » chargée d'un des problèmes essentiels pour lequel la collaboration des ingénieurs est très importante.

Dès sa constitution, l'Association est saisie de plusieurs demandes de collaboration, notamment pour la mise en couleur de diverses constructions (extérieur et intérieur), pour les études de volumes, pour des concours de peintures murales et de sculpture en accord avec l'architecture.

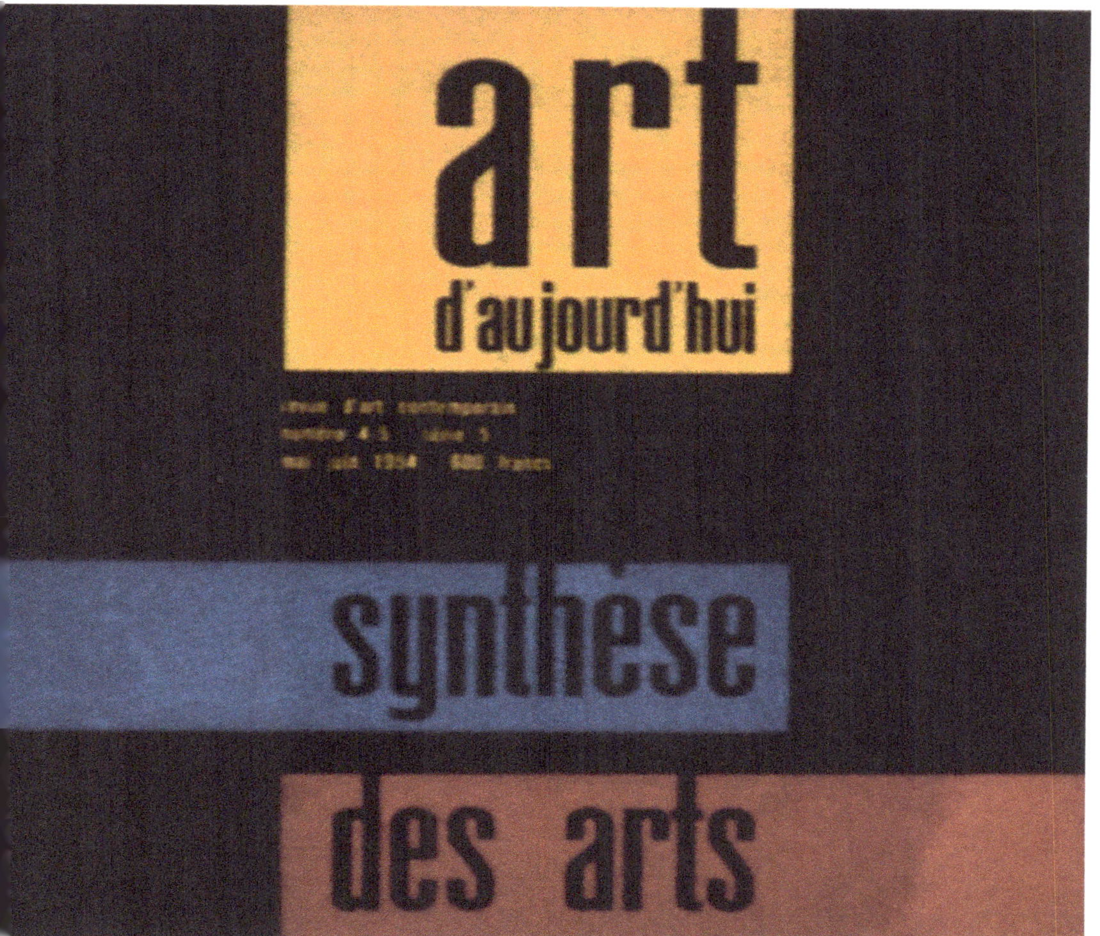

Figure 10.1 (previous page): Manifeste Groupe Espace in *Art d' aujourd'hui*, October 1951, page V.

Figure 10.2: Cover of the journal, *Art d'aujourd'hui, revue d'art contemporain*, No. 45 June 1954.

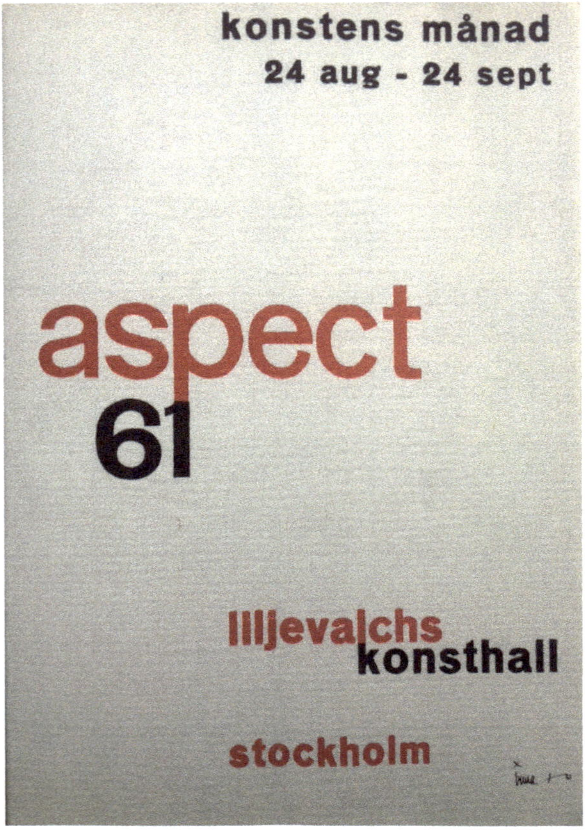

konstens månad
24 aug - 24 sept

aspect
61

liljevalchs
konsthall

stockholm

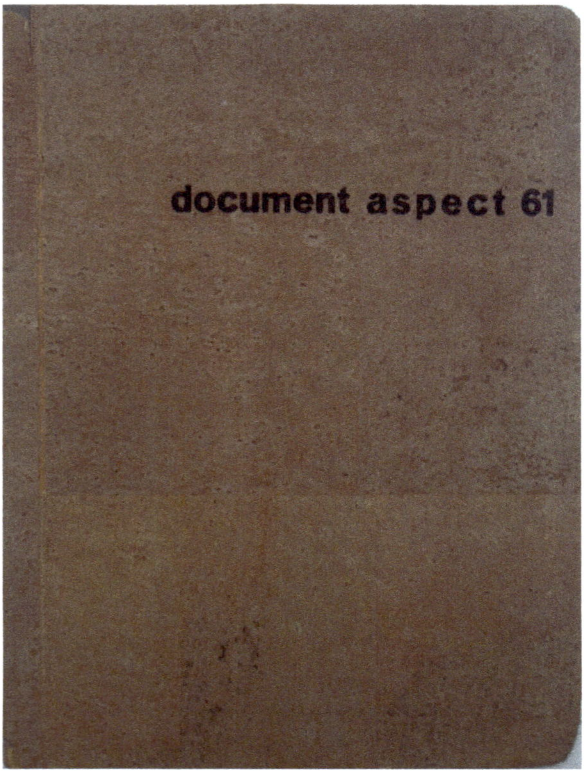

document aspect 61

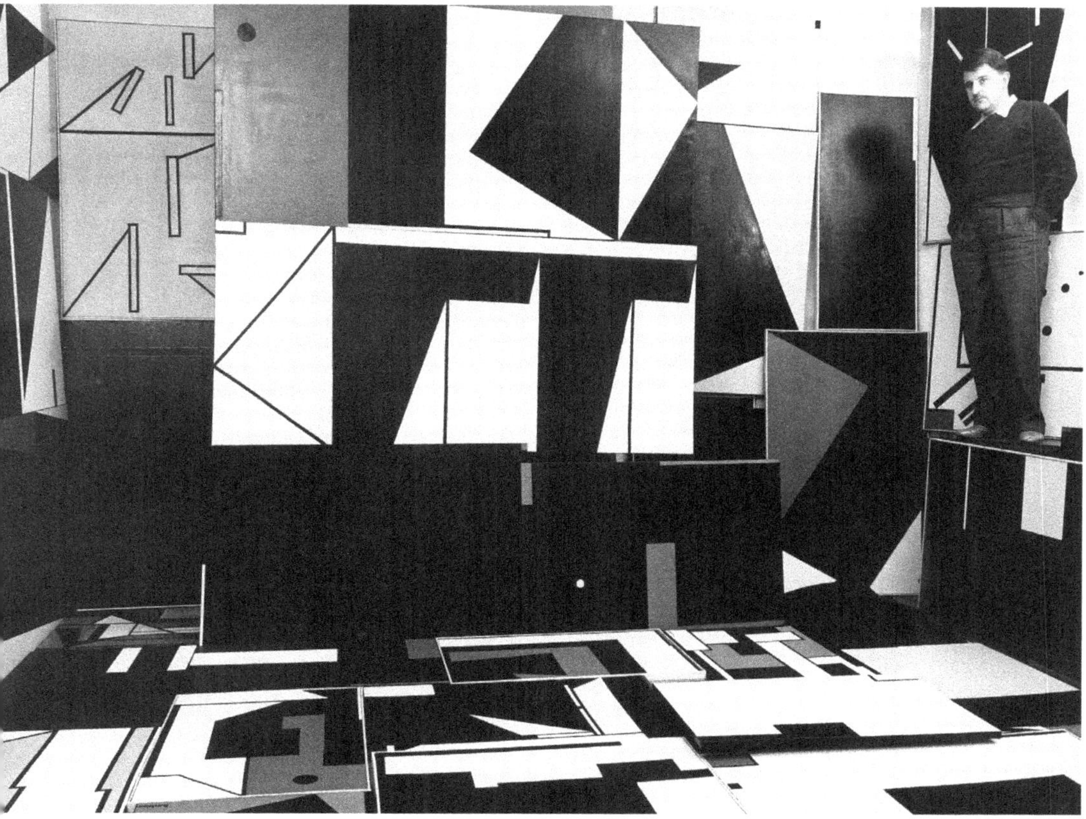

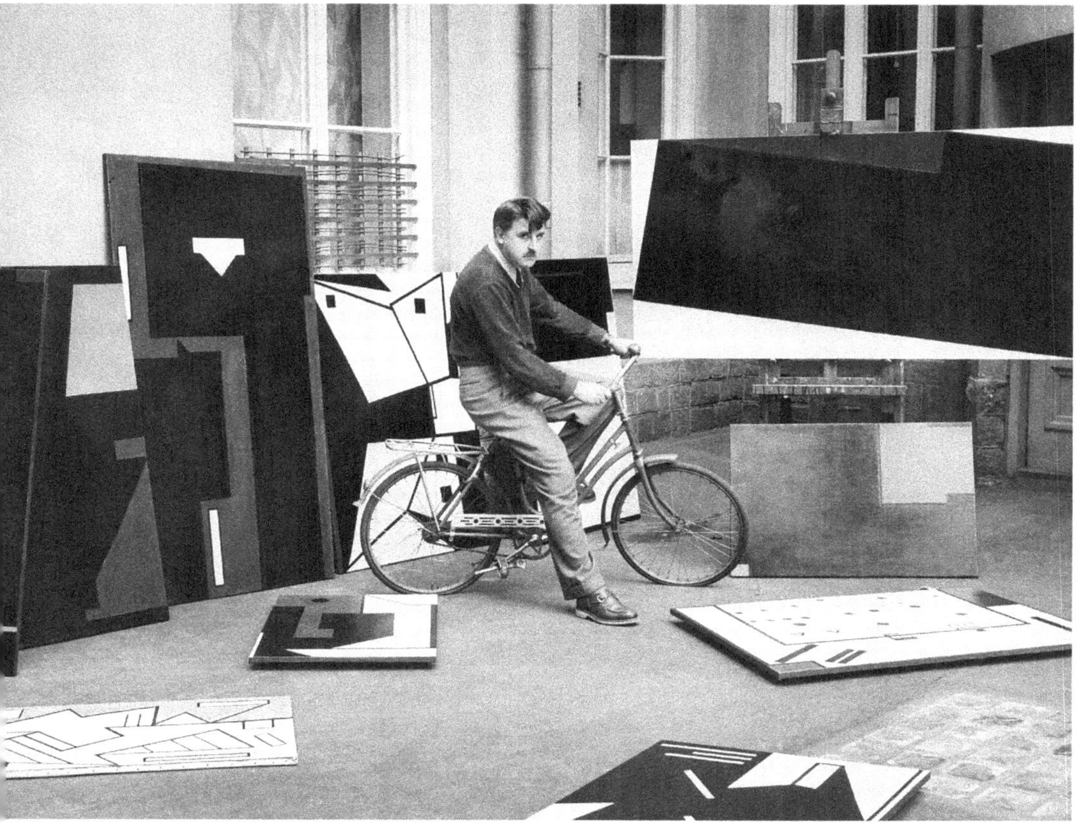

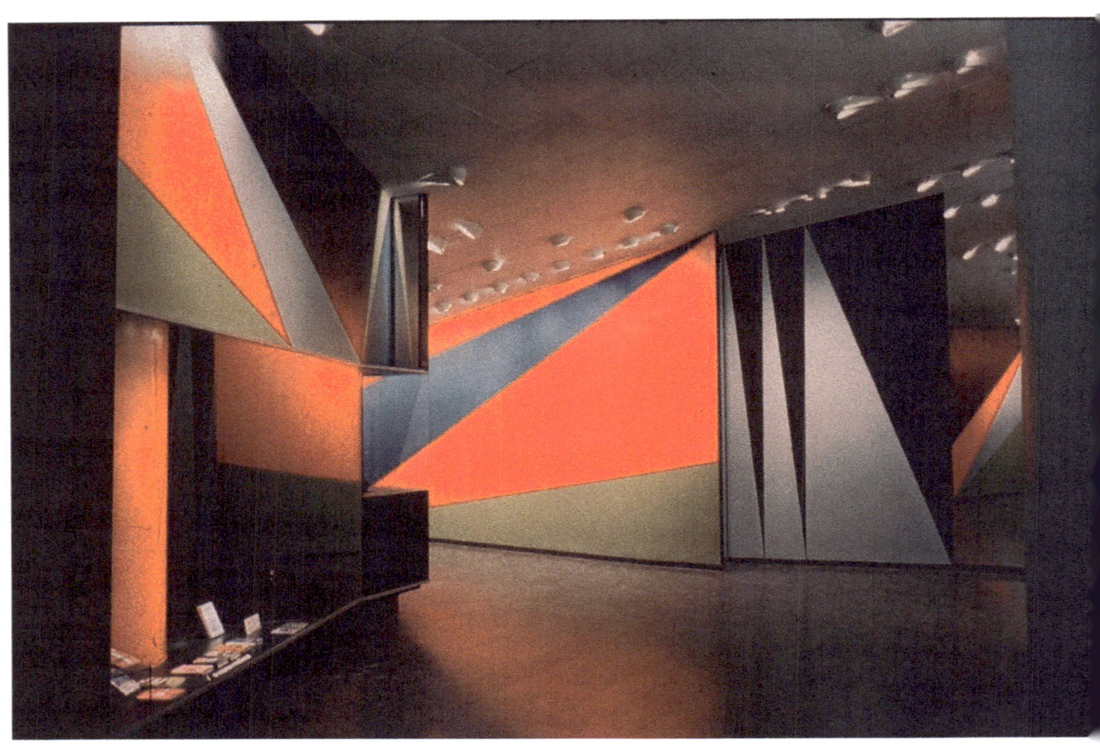

Figure 10.3 (previous spread, top left): Exhibition catalogue, *aspect 61 med brasilia*, kat 254, Liljevalchs konsthall, Stockholm, 1961.

Figure 10.4 (previous spread, bottom left): Åke Danielsson (ed.) *document aspect 61*, Stockholm: Liljevalchs konsthall, 1961.

Figure 10.5 (previous spread, top right): Olle Bærtling in his studio, undated (probably 1955). Photo: Lennart Olson. © Hallands konstmuseum.

Figure 10.6 (previous spread, bottom right): Olle Bærtling in his studio, 1951. Photo: Lennart Olson. © Hallands konstmuseum.

Figure 10.7: *The Aesthetic Rom*, entrance to the first high-rise at Hötorget, Stockholm, by Olle Bærtling and David Helldén, 1959. Photo Lennart Olson. By kind courtesy of the Bærtling foundation. © Hallands konstmuseum.

Manifeste

Pour se dégager définitivement de certaines survivances néfastes qui imprègnent autant la masse du public qu'un grand nombre d'artistes, les Architectes, les Constructeurs et les Plasticiens soussignés créent

LE GROUPE ESPACE

Ils préconisent

Ils constatent

Ils proposent

URBANISME, PLANS-MASSES, COULEUR, EXPOSITIONS, FÊTES, PLASTIQUE APPLIQUÉE AUX OBJETS

Ils réclament

POUR L'HARMONIEUX DEVELOPPEMENT DE TOUTES LES ACTIVITÉS HUMAINES
LA PRESENCE FONDAMENTALE DE LA PLASTIQUE

Architectes

Constructeurs

Plasticiens

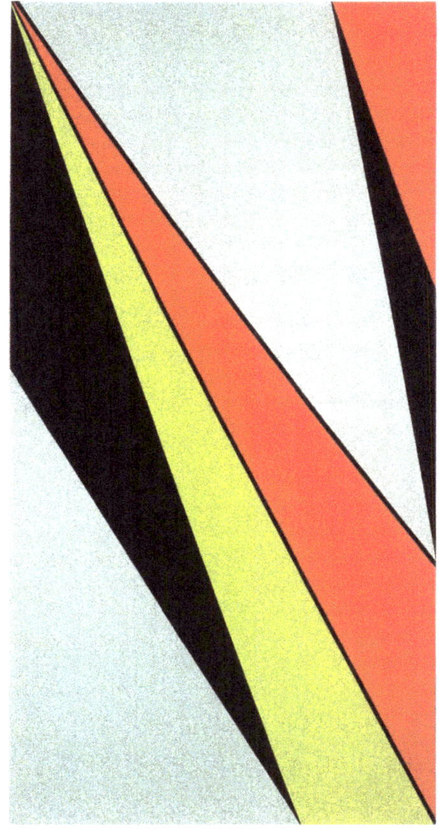

Figure 10.8: Poster of the Groupe Espace Manifest, 1951.

Figure 10.9: Olle Bærtling, *Irgy*, 1958, Oil on canvas. By kind courtesy of the Bærtling foundation. © Olle Bærtling/Bildupphovsrätt 2016.

11
Terminology in the Making
Pop and Minimalism in the 1960s

Tania Ørum

During the 1960s there was a lot of contact and collaboration between the Nordic countries, both at an institutional level as well as through informal self-organised networks formed by groups of artists from all the arts. The Moderna Museet in Stockholm was a beacon for all of the Nordic countries in this period: American artists invited to Stockholm went on to visit Denmark, Norway, and Finland as well, and there was an established collaboration between the Moderna Museet in Sweden, the Louisiana Museum of Modern Art in Denmark and the Stedelijk Museum Amsterdam in the Netherlands, allowing exhibitions to travel from one country to another. Introductions to new American art as well as other recent movements in the Danish museum journal *Louisiana Revy* were very often written by people from the Moderna Museet. Indeed, most pop art came to Denmark via Sweden.

For instance, the 1964 exhibition *Amerikansk pop-konst: 106 former av kärlek och förtvivlan* (American Pop Art: 106 Forms of Love and Despair) at the Moderna Museet continued on to Louisiana, where it was presented with some trepidation—after the roar of public protest created by a previous exhibition imported to Louisiana from the Stedelijk and the Moderna Museet, *Rörelse i Konsten* (Movement in Art) in the summer of 1961. The initial cause of this outrage was the accidental killing of a pigeon in Jean Tinguely's self-destructing sculpture "Study for the End of the World," but it grew into a display of public hostility against modernist art in general and the Louisiana Museum in particular. [1]

Pop art was first introduced in the *Louisiana Revy* in 1963 by the director of the Moderna Museet, Pontus Hultén. His lead article "On Painting in New York after Pollock, i.e. On Pop Art"[2] presented pop art as the dominant new American art movement after abstract expressionism, "America's most remarkable contribution to world art after Pollock." Hultén's introduction was accompanied by a very skeptical editorial note cautioning readers about "the new art movement in the United States known as pop art. Although hardly viable as painting, it is an interesting sign of the times" that artists should use the language of comics, advertising or recreate trivial objects of everyday life, so the note said.[3] And when the Moderna Museet's pop art exhibition opened in Denmark in April 1964, it was introduced very defensively and apologetically in the *Louisiana Revy* by the owner and director Knud W. Jensen who evidently anticipated renewed protests: The older generation of artists and art lovers were sure to accuse Louisiana of betraying the quality of art and pandering to vulgar tastes, Jensen wrote, while the general public would surely ask whether this was supposed to be art. And he did not venture an opinion of his own:

> What we at the museum feel about this exhibition we have no idea, as I write these lines. Only a few examples have yet come into view, and they seemed annoying, ugly, idiotic, beautiful, inciting and convincingly right in some way—all at the same time, so there must be *something* in this particular kind of pop or art…[4]

[1] See for example Uffe Harder's editorial comment in the art and literature magazine *Hvedekorn*, No. 5, 1961, also quoted in Tania Ørum, *De eksperimenterende tressere: Kunst i en opbrudstid*, Copenhagen: Gyldendal, 2009, pp. 28–29.

[2] K.G. Hultén, "Om maleriet i New York efter Pollock dvs. OM POP-KUNSTEN" (On Painting in New York after Pollock, i.e. ON POP ART), in *Louisiana Revy*, No. 1, September 1963, pp. 10–15.

[3] *Louisiana Revy*, No. 1, September 1963, pp. 10. The note was probably written by Knud W. Jensen.

[4] Knud W. Jensen, "Pop-kunst på Louisiana" *Louisiana Revy*, No. 4, April 1964, p. 3, (my translation).

The opening towards mass culture—including the comics, advertising and trivial objects of everyday life mentioned in the Louisiana note—was part of the attempt to bridge the contemporary chasm between high and low culture that was a hallmark of pop art and other new art movements in the 1960s, such as for example French nouveau réalisme. This opening met with considerable resistance and skepticism from dominant modernist artists, critics and students of culture in Denmark, while discussions of cultural democracy in the early 1960s perhaps paved the way for a more open attitude in Sweden.[5] Knud W. Jensen clearly found pop art's inclusion of themes, techniques and figures from popular culture and everyday life difficult to handle.

The Warhol exhibition held at the Moderna Museet in 1968 did not continue to Denmark, therefore many Danish artists travelled to Stockholm to see both the exhibition and especially the films that had a huge impact on the Danish art and film scene.[6]

The institutional contacts between museums also fed into the artist-run networks. For instance, the French nouveau réalistes travelling to Stockholm for the exhibition *Rörelse i konsten* (Movement in Art, 1961) stopped over in Copenhagen where Niki de St. Phalle mounted an exhibition in the small gallery run by the Copenhagen based German artist Arthur Köpcke, who had an extensive European network.[7] Other members of the nouveau réalisme group, especially Daniel Spoerri and Robert Filliou, were in Copenhagen now and again and kept up correspondence and collaboration with Köpcke, as did Dieter Roth, who mostly lived in Iceland in the 1960s.[8] Köpcke was in touch not only with the nouveau réalisme group, who might be seen as the more messy French equivalent of Anglo-Saxon pop art, but also with the beginnings of the transcontinental Fluxus movement, which included several people from the

[5] See Christer Ekholm, "The Social Avant-Garde: The 'Democratisation' of Literature in the Early 1960s in Sweden," and Tania Ørum, "Culture Wars in Denmark," in Tania Ørum and Jesper Olsson (eds.), *A Cultural History of the Avant-Garde in the Nordic Countries 1950–1975*, Amsterdam and New York: Brill, 2016, pp. 101–105 and 106–111 .

[6] See Ørum, 2009, pp. 503–505.

[7] See Ørum, 2009, pp. 83–88.

[8] See Anna Jóhannsdóttir, "Exile, Correspondence, Rebellion," in Ørum and Olsson (eds.), 2016, pp. 239-250.

nouveau réalisme group. It was due to Köpcke's network that the second Fluxus concert took place in Copenhagen in 1962. This event recruited a number of Danish participants, so there were several Fluxus members in Denmark,[9] but only one Fluxus member from Sweden, Bengt af Klintberg, who got in touch with Fluxus during a research stay in Copenhagen in 1962 that happened to coincide with the Fluxus festival.[10]

These are just a few examples of the many networks connecting Denmark and Sweden to each other and to the rest of the world. But although there was a significant amount of contact and collaboration among the Nordic countries, interesting differences can also be observed. One of these is the different conception of pop art and minimalism in Sweden and Denmark in the 1960s, which will be the main focus of this essay.

Swedish Pop

On the back cover of the 1966 Swedish edition of texts by the American composer John Cage—selected and translated by two influential figures in the Swedish art world of the 1960s, the writers and critics Torsten Ekbom and Leif Nylén—the two editors introduce Cage as "an important inspiration for the entire modern current of American art normally called pop art."[11] The two editors go on to explain that what they term pop art includes "open art," art that leaves the recipient to form his own opinions, but makes him aware of the reality surrounding him.[12]

This goes to show the very wide sweep of what was referred to as pop art in Sweden in the 1960s. The subjects covered in the Cage volume include

[9] Initial members were Arthur Köpcke and the two composers Henning Christiansen and Eric Andersen. The first Fluxus concerts in Copenhagen were organised by Arthur Köpcke and the Association of Young Composers (DUT). Some early Fluxus practitioners left the movement around 1964 for various reasons. In Denmark the Fluxus label was appropriated by Eric Andersen who quarrelled with everyone else. See Ørum, 2009, pp. 64–88.

[10] Bengt af Klintberg, *Svensk Fluxus/Swedish Fluxus*, Stockholm: Rönnels Antikvariat, 2006., p. 12.

[11] John Cage: *Om ingenting*, Stockholm: Bonniers, 1966. "John Cage är en viktig inspiratör för hela den moderna amerikanska konstriktning som brukar sammanfattas under namnet popkonst."

[12] *Open Art* (1994) is also the title of Leif Nylén's memoirs from this period. Here the term pop art is no longer used.

sound art, cross-aesthetic art, chance composition and the open work. It is certainly true that the composer John Cage was behind much of what happened in all the arts in the U.S. from the early 1950s onwards. But today it hardly seems self-evident to describe Cage or the diversity of new experimental strategies in the arts that he helped introduce—from happenings to chance music and Fluxus—under the general heading of pop art.

In his introduction to pop art in the *Louisiana Revy*, Pontus Hultén made a similar reference to Cage as the central influence on pop art: "A careful reading of Cage's book *Silence* would probably lead to the conclusion," he wrote, "that some of the basic ideas of Johns, Rauschenberg, and the pop artists" had already been published in the postwar years and the 1950s. Hultén describes the New York art scene in the early 1960s as made up of three or four parallel groups: Abstract expressionism (de Kooning, Motherwell, Frankenthaler, Rothko), a "cooler abstract art verging on the geometrical" (Noland, Barnett Newman, Morris Louis, Stella), "pre-pop art" (Jasper Johns and Robert Rauschenberg), and the pop artists proper who are the same age as Johns and Rauschenberg but have appeared later. Hultén evidently prefers the "pre-pop" of Johns and Rauschenberg, whom he compares to Picasso and Braque, to the pop artists, who are assigned the secondary place of the later and minor cubists (such as Gleizes, et al.). The paintings by Johns and Rauschenberg have "almost all the elements of pop art, but their paintings are more versatile and multifaceted." And while Hultén sees Rauchenberg and Johns as critical, controversial and interested in the formal aspects of painting, the pop artists are described as lacking any political consciousness, wholly emotional in their approach, without programme and "neither critical nor revolutionary." So although one may "glimpse Marcel Duchamp behind many of the early paintings by Rauschenberg and Johns, it makes no sense to describe pop art as "Neo-Dada."[13]

Hultén's introductory essay in the *Louisiana Revy* seems to indicate that Ekbom and Nylén's broad definition of pop art as comprising the new tendencies in the 1960s originating in Cage was a shared perception in the Swedish art world.

[13] K. G. Hultén, 1963, pp. 10–15. The quotations are from pp. 14, 10 and 11, and have been translated by me.

By 1968 Leif Nylén had become the editor of the leading Swedish art journal *Paletten* (The Palette), and in this capacity he visited Lund's Konsthall to review an exhibition of minimal art called "Anonymiteter" (Anonymities) by members of The Experimental Art School and other Danish minimalists.[14] In a later article Nylén remembers finding it hard to see what the exhibition was about:

> [I]t looked like old-fashioned non-figurative art. But Hans-Jørgen [Nielsen] talked about "primary structures," as what was later labelled minimalism was called at the time, he referred to articles by Robert Smithson, to work by Don Judd, Sol LeWitt, Robert Morris and many others. And soon I had grasped that this was not about old looks but about new models, based on repetition rather than variation, entropy rather than harmony.[15]

Apparently minimalism, and its contemporary synonyms, were not strong concepts in Nylén's Swedish environment. The American artists whose names Nylén got from his Danish friend, the writer and critic Hans-Jørgen Nielsen, were not those exhibited at the Moderna Museet nor transmitted to Denmark by Swedish art historians or artists, but especially Smithson, Judd, and Morris were much discussed in the less institutionalised Danish context—for instance in the journal *Billedkunst* (Visual Art, 1966–1969) as well as in the little magazine *ta'* (take, 1967–1968), both dominated by members of the Experimental Art School.

And while there was a turn towards minimal and conceptual art in Denmark in the late 1960s, Swedish experimental artists such as Leif Nylén and others in the *Svisch* group turned to political pop music, and the group around the magazine *Puss* (Kiss, 1968–1974) took the figural style of pop in a more explicitly political direction aimed at a broader public. This turn to political agitation was as incomprehensible to the Danish critic Hans-Jørgen Nielsen as Danish minimalism was to Nylén. Nielsen clearly saw both the

[14] The participants were: Hein Heinsen, Kasper Heiberg, Steen Høyer, Mogens Møller, Niels Guttormsen, Steffen Jørgensen, Egon Fischer, Peter Bonnén. The Ex-school artists were: Stig Brøgger, Hans-Jørgen Nielsen, Paul Gernes, Peter Louis-Jensen, Per Kirkeby, Bjørn Nørgaard. See Ørum, 2009, pp. 374–379.
[15] Nylén, "Alt var ligesom i bevægelse," in Ørum (ed.), 2001, p. 210, (my translation).

figural style and the direct political messages as a re-traditionalisation, and hence just as old-fashioned as Nylén found minimal art.[16]

These examples seem to indicate that in Sweden the new art of the 1960s was generally seen as pop art, whereas in Denmark minimalism would seem to be the general term for what went on in the 1960s, linking up to other American artists than the Swedish connections that often came via the Moderna Museet. While Danish avant-garde artists were as keen as their Swedish colleagues to break down the barrier between "high art" and "low" mass culture, the avenues they chose were different.

Danish Minimalism

Per Kirkeby has later described his encounter with the Experimental Art School (1961–1974, often just called the Ex-School, since it stopped being a proper school after a few years) as an encounter with the "iconoclasm of the sixties" and with minimalism. Kirkeby talks about minimalism as a train departure. At certain times in art history, he says, it is important to get on the train in time, or you will be left behind:

> Minimalism is one such train departure. Minimalism in the sense of a very broad basis of shared attitudes. A very large train that departed at the start of the sixties. It had a fluxus-carriage, a box carriage, a pop carriage, a party carriage with music and dancing. There was even a whole carriage of those of us from remote areas.[17]

Kirkeby's idea of minimalism is as broadly defined as Nylén's idea of pop art. They are both generalising about the new tendencies of the 1960s, but significantly use different terms. Kirkeby's term seems to represent the whole process of reduction that took place in the arts during the 1960s. He sees minimalism as characterised by "a very broad basis of shared attitudes"—so broad that his train metaphor can include a wide spectrum of "carriages" or trends, ranging from pop to Fluxus and "box" (i.e. the sculptural tradition of LeWitt or Judd), and even including popular

[16] See H.-J. Nielsen, "Kritik af den svenske intelligens" (Critique of the Swedish Intelligentsia), *Paletten,* No. 4, 1968, p. 50, and Ørum, 2009, pp. 380–382.
[17] Kirkeby, *Håndbog* (Handbook), Copenhagen: Borgen, 1991, pp. 84–85, (my translation).

culture such as rock music and youth culture ("music and dancing"). According to Kirkeby, these tendencies, including the varieties produced by artists in peripheral areas, all belonged to the same general art historical "train" or line of development that he calls minimalism. Such a definition of minimalism makes sense in relation to the development that took place among the tightly knit group of individual artists in the Danish Ex-School who made different choices within this spectrum of "carriages," and also chose to go their separate ways later on.

The Experimental Art School started out in 1961 from the strong tradition of "concrete art"—carried into the postwar era by the artist group *Linien II* (Line No. 2) and especially Albert Mertz, Poul Gadegaard and Gunnar Aagaard Andersen. This tradition was continued by one of the founders of the school, the painter Poul Gernes. Another founder, the art historian Troels Andersen, brought along his personal knowledge of Russian constructivism, at the time hidden away in the USSR and largely forgotten in the West. And because of Andersen's teaching, Ex-School artists tended to view the work of their American contemporaries in the light of Russian artworks and aesthetic/political discussions of the 1910s.[18] To this legacy of concrete art and constructivism, impulses from French nouveau réalisme and the Fluxus movement, as well as American influences, were added. The minimalism that emerged from this background easily led into conceptual art in the second half of the 1960s.

One of the first students at the Ex-School, Peter Louis-Jensen, had already painted a series of op art paintings in early 1961 before entering the self-organised school, and he and Poul Gernes continued from grid painting, collage and assemblage into minimalist painting from 1962. But although Peter Louis-Jensen and Poul Gernes represented the most minimalist wing in the school, their work does show occasional elements of what could be called Pop.

Especially in connection with his performative practice, Louis-Jensen talked about the necessity for the contemporary artist of engaging with figures of popular mythology in order to approach a wider public while still

[18] See Troels Andersen, *Moderne russisk kunst 1910–1925* (Modern Russian Art 1910–1925), Copenhagen: Borgen, 1967, and his memoirs: *Ude af øje* (Out of Sight), Copenhagen: Forlaget Vandkunsten, 2014

keeping up an experimental line of work.[19] His happening, "Stars and Stripes for Ever" (1965), thus centred on a mannequin representing Jacqueline Kennedy; the striped room where the performance took place was turned into an American flag when a section of stars were lowered on to the striped wall during the performance, and the audience was offered Coca Cola, while "cowboy" music was played and "cowboy" films were shown. The striped room itself was Louis-Jensen's contribution to a largely minimalist exhibition in which Poul Gernes exhibited, for example, his series of striped portraits of all the letters in the alphabet. On its own, the room was a minimal environmental work, but the iconic American features of the performance were closer to the figurative and cultural meanings of pop art, thus indicating the links between pop and minimalism.

Poul Gernes' early work also has pop (or *nouveau réalisme*) elements, for instance in his giant collages commenting on current affairs that included clippings from magazines, everyday objects and life-size figures wearing contemporary clothes. His large plaster sculptures of cakes have an unmistakable pop quality to them. And his serial paintings of numbers and of the letters of the alphabet hover between minimalism and a touch of pop, not least in the bold pop colours of the stripes.

Three other members of the Ex-School, John Davidsen, Per Kirkeby, and Stig Brøgger, have obvious pop art characteristics. John Davidsen started using cut-out elements from popular and commercial culture, mostly images of women, in his paintings from 1962, but these elements are mostly overlaid by geometrical shapes and structures in a combination of pop and minimalism. His naked self-portrait in the pose of a Playboy centre-fold girl (1966) is pop art, while his later use of his own body and clothes and his series of works involving roses hover between pop and conceptual art. Stig Brøgger used pop elements in his sculptures and painting from 1965 and soon turned them into material of his conceptual strategies.

Per Kirkeby developed his version of the cut-out elements from 1963 to 1968, mixing pop, minimalist grid structure and painterly gestures. In his artistic practice and reflections Kirkeby was constantly struggling to find

[19] Louis-Jensen, Radio interview, DR, July 1965. Quoted in Christine Buhl Andersen (ed.), *Peter Louis-Jensen Retrospektiv*, Sorø: Vestsjællands Kunstmuseum 2003, p. 67.

his balance in the eternal conflict of the "pure" versus the "impure" that was a recurring theme at the Ex-School, and which was also a tension between the minimalist and collective standards of the Ex-School (represented by Poul Gernes and Peter Louis-Jensen especially) on the one hand, and Kirkeby's own romantic inclinations and love of both classical painting and the opulence of kitsch culture on the other hand. One solution that Kirkeby found to this conflict was the use of cut-out templates, another was the serial concept—both represent cool, impersonal, formal principles that keep the romantic and pop impulses under control.

Kirkeby has described how this minimalist approach helped him tone down personal ambitions as an artist in favour of collective work and more impersonal conceptual strategies. The cut-out templates helped minimise the hand-made, painterly quality of his drawings and paintings. And by arranging his work in series, he could reduce the pretensions of a closed self-contained work of art, and thus conceive of the individual drawings, paintings or sculptures as "points in a constant flow" or parts of a larger conceptual whole, with no separate, absolute value of their own.[20]

One can see in Kirkeby's work of the 1960s and 1970s the tension between minimalism and pop as a successful balance. The romantic icons (Brigitte Bardot and other celebrities) and the motifs from popular culture (cars, the wild west, sunset) are there, floating in rich fields of colour, but they are kept in place by a minimalist structure, whereas from the later 1980s gestural painting takes over, largely obliterating both the pop figures and the minimalist structures.

Mixing styles, moving on

Such broad definitions of pop and minimalism as voiced by Nylén and Kirkeby may seem like the well-known lack of strict adherence to the artistic styles and schools of the centres that is often noticeable in peripheral areas before World War II, and which allows provincial artists to freely or eclectically mix styles that are kept separate in the centres.[21] Another reason

[20] Kirkeby, "Collioure-serien," in *Naturens blyant* (Nature's crayon), Copenhagen: Borgen, 1978, pp.115–117, (my translation).

[21] For the case of the Nordic artists in the period 1900–1925, see van den Berg, et al. (eds.), *A Cultural History of the Avant-Garde in the Nordic Countries 1900–1925,* Amsterdam and

for artists to move from one trend to another is, of course, that the Nordic artists rarely got canonised as for example minimalists or pop artists or conceptual artists in the way artists from the centres did. So while Oldenberg remained a pop artist, Judd a minimalist, and Kosuth a conceptual artist, the more unrecognised Danish or Swedish artists moved on with the times and were free to explore new strategies: In both Denmark and Sweden and the other Nordic countries there was a general move from the aesthetic experiments of the early 1960s to the social/environmental projects of the mid-1960s to the political projects of the late 1960s and early 1970s. And during these transitions Nordic artists also moved from one medium to another.[22] However, in the case of pop and minimalism, it may be more complicated than peripheral artists mixing styles: According to the American art historian Rosalind Krauss, minimal art and pop art share a common source in the rediscovery of the Duchampian readymade.[23] Both exploit cultural "readymades," but whereas pop art uses pictorial elements that are already heavily culturally marked, minimalists use elements with a less specific content, functioning as abstract components. Minimalists make use of the readymade concept in a less "anecdotal" way, you might say, than do pop artists and relate to its structural rather than its thematic implications.

Because of this common source and strategy, pop art and minimal art can coexist, and in fact have many overlapping elements. Within for example the Danish Experimental Art School pop and minimal art existed alongside each other—some artists worked predominantly with pop elements, while others mainly used anonymous industrial components, but there were also many instances of crossover between the two tendencies.

The overlap between pop and minimalism is, however, not just a peripheral, Nordic phenomenon. When you look at the early American efforts to define pop art and minimalism as distinctive movements in art, their outlines do not seem quite as clear as we often tend to assume today.

New York: Rodopi, 2012. See also Piotr Piotrowsky, "Toward a Horizontal History of the European Avant-Garde," in Sascha Bru, et al. (eds.) *Europa! Europa? The Avant-Garde, Modernism, and the Fate of a Continent.* New York: De Gruyter 2009, pp. 49–58. Per Bäckström and Benedikt Hjartarson, (eds.), *Decentring the Avant-Garde* (Avant-Garde, Critical Studies, 30), Amsterdam and New York: Rodopi, 2014.

[22] See Ørum, 2009, Ørum and Olson (eds.), 2016.

[23] Krauss, "The Double Negative: A New Syntax for Sculpture," *Passages in Modern Sculpture,* Cambridge Mass. and London: The MIT Press, 1993, p. 243.

The Scope of Minimalism

Kirkeby's very broad and comprehensive definition of minimalism is actually quite close to that of the art historian James Meyer, who, from his retrospective American perspective, notes that minimalism is not a proper movement with a common programme, not one minimalism, but a number of partly overlapping minimalisms.[24]

As the American critic Anne M. Wagner points out in her introduction to the 1995 reprint of the seminal anthology *Minimal Art* edited by Gregory Battcock (1968), the original essays collected here "reveal the haphazardness and breadth, uncertainties and unfinish of the critical language of the day."[25] Not only do the critics use different terms, ranging from "systemic painting" (Alloway), to "serial art" (Bochner), "minimal art" (Leepa, Wollheim) or "minimal abstracts" (Perreault), to "ABC art" (Rose) and "literalist art" (Fried, Mussman)—not to mention "Primary Structures," the title of the noted exhibition curated by Kynaston McShine at the Jewish Museum in New York in 1966. Several of the artists and works included under these terms would hardly be called minimalist today. Anne M. Wagner takes the example of Lucy Lippard: Among "the artists she names, nowadays only Eva Hesse would be said to have much to do with minimalism; the others—Claes Oldenburg, Yayoi Kusama, Lucas Samaras, Lindsey Ecker—hardly fill the bill."[26] Indeed, I would say that several of these artists seem rather to belong under the heading of pop art. The critics of the time, Wagner notes, were clearly "convinced that sensibilities had shifted and certain that the changes must be accounted for, but they were equally aware of the problems involved in explaining them"[27] and took widely divergent views of whether minimalist works of art were erotic, involved bodily responses or relentless reflexivity, whether they were concerned with ideation or mere objecthood. As Wagner comments,

> minimal art was evidently, in 1968, a loose and capacious enough term to allow both stuffed vinyl appliances and sprayed acrylic surfaces to be included within

[24] Meyer, *Minimalism*, London: Phaidon Press, 2000, p. 18.
[25] Anne M. Wagner, "Reading Minimal Art," in Gregory Battcock (ed.), *Minimal Art*, Berkeley, Los Angeles, and London: University of California Press, 1995, p. 5.
[26] Anne M. Wagner, 1995, p. 13.
[27] Anne M. Wagner, 1995, p. 9.

> it. It could also be used to name what had already become a kind of artistic koine: the shaped canvas, its angled edges extended or abruptly curtailed; the wedge of plywood, performing a connection between wall and floor, or floor and ceiling; the rod of steel or acrylic or aluminium, enacting a shape it certainly had no business assuming.[28]

Anne M. Wagner and the critics included in Battcock's anthology speak only about American art. In a global perspective, things of course look different, and even the blurred, contradictory and uncertain perspectives drawn up by the critics in the anthology have to be supplemented. From a Danish perspective, I would suggest that minimalism is less a "new style" or a self-contained -ism than a general impulse to strip away what was seen as superfluous institutional characteristics and metaphysical assumptions about art, the artist and the creative act, in order to arrive at a more impersonal kind of art, open to interaction with the audience and in step with contemporary cultural reality. And as a general impulse, it could include figurative pop elements as well as nonfigurative minimalist features.

In the Danish context, minimalism in the arts (especially in the visual arts and in music) was the result of a constructive move following the (self-declared) "destructive" phases of neo-realist and Fluxus experiments in the early 1960s.[29]

The Danish composer Henning Christiansen (known internationally for his close collaboration with another ex-Fluxus artist, Joseph Beuys) thus left Fluxus in 1964 to engage in more "constructive" collaboration with the poet Hans-Jørgen Nielsen and the visual artists from the Experimental Art School—simultaneously crossing into other art forms such as visual poetry, performance, installation art and film. And for some of the visual artists in the Ex-School, minimal art, or "literalist art," was an attempt to create new kinds of art "after zero," i.e. after stripping away the

[28] Anne M. Wagner, 1995, pp. 8–9.

[29] Fluxus cannot be defined as a destructive movement. But some of the Danish artists who left Fluxus around 1964 declared that they wanted to turn to more constructive activities, trying to build new kinds of art rather than questioning the concept of art. The Experimental Art School defined their early experimental work in 1961 and 1962 as "destructive," i.e. as an attack on standard conceptions of the artwork, the creative process and the art institution.

metaphysical assumptions about art.[30] The ambition was to produce open works that would have a more democratic role to play in society.

The American critic Barbara Rose has suggested that what kept the overlapping minimalist currents together was a common sensibility that was not just a continuation of what the influential American art critic Clement Greenberg had defined as the "modernist reduction" with its constant formal self-reflection.[31] The artists of the 1960s that Rose considers were, she says, "more related in terms of a common sensibility than in terms of a common style."[32] This collective new sensibility, belonging, Rose suggests,[33] to a particular *Zeitgeist*, tended to prefer the factual to the symbolic, and ordinary objects to art objects, and to value "non-expressive," "neutral," "anonymous" and "impersonal" forms which must hence, she thinks, be read as statements of a philosophical, existential, social—or even mystical content.[34]

As a "common sensibility" of the kind that Rose suggests, Danish minimalism could accommodate both constructivist and pop art elements, as long as they were kept within the range of "non-expressive," "neutral," "anonymous" and "impersonal" forms indicated by Rose. This interpretation is borne out by the writings of Hans-Jørgen Nielsen. In one of his essays he adopts Judd's minimalist wall sculpture as a key to interpreting minimalist texts,[35] and his reading is very similar to that of Barbara Rose: When looking at something as spare, reduced, anonymous and empty as Judd's boxes, he says, you must ask: What does it imply to prefer the empty and the indifferent? Even to find it attractive or beautiful?—or, in Rose's terms, how can you read them as statements of a philosophical or existential content.

[30] See for instance the programmatic statement by Peter Louis-Jensen "Omkring Zero" (Around Zero) in the first number of the little magazine *ta'*, 1967.

[31] Rose, 1965, in Battcock (ed.), 1995, pp. 278–281.

[32] Rose, 1965, pp. 280–281.

[33] Rose, 1965, p. 282.

[34] I would want to add that the "mystical" content of the 1960s tends to be not the anthroposophical current of the prewar period, but rather the Zen Buddhist or Wittgensteinian cult of emptiness and language games leaving the metaphysical questions unspoken.

[35] Hans-Jørgen Nielsen, "Fortolkning i entropiens tidsalder" (Interpretation in the age of entropy), in *Selvsyn,* 1969, (my translation). Nielsen speaks of Judd's work as a sculpture, whereas Judd himself only refers to his works as "untitled" and generally tends to avoid the term sculpture, which is freely used by the Danish minimalists.

The reading strategy Nielsen proposes is to first look at the surfaces of such artworks or texts and see how they have been made to be as lacklustre as they are, and next to perceive these lacklustre qualities as a positive statement. This is a reading strategy in the spirit of McLuhan, reading the medium as the message.[36] Nielsen sees this minimalist aesthetics as signifying a certain "sense of life" or sensibility, as Rose calls it, resulting in art that is neither "pure formalism" ("the wrong kind of emptiness and anonymity"), nor "literary," i.e. without formal relevance— thus keeping up the desired balance between the "pure" and the "impure." According to Nielsen this art is "both formal and existential" and signals a sense of "the break-down of the old human order," i.e. it responds to the great technological, economic and cultural changes in the Western societies in the 1960s and tries to revise traditional modes of perception and interpretation.

Viewed from Rose's and Nielsen's contemporary perspective, the minimalist currents—which in retrospect are often seen as purely formalist experiments within the white cube of the art institution—are quite compatible with Peter Bürger's notion of the avant-garde as non-formalist movements intent on changing the world (or at least the conceptions of art, communication and artistic creation) rather than on developing a new style. This "common sensibility" is also one of the reasons why minimalism tended to encourage cross-aesthetic experimentation. From this broad definition of minimalism, it was easy to move on to both conceptual art and political activism—two things that were not necessarily very far apart at the time.

Definitions of Pop

In the first sentence of her anthology on *Pop Art* (1966) Lucy Lippard claims it as "an American phenomenon," although she does acknowledge that "It was born twice: first in England and then again, independently, in New York."[37] And in her final chapter on pop art in Europe and Canada,

[36] "The medium is the message" was one of the slogans of the influential media theorist Marshall McLuhan and the title of the first chapter in his bestselling book *Understanding Media* (1964). McLuhan was widely read in both Sweden and Denmark.

[37] Lucy Lippard, "Introduction," in Lippard (ed.), *Pop* Art (1966), London: Thames and Hudson, 1994, p. 9.

she says: "There is no hard-core Pop Art in Europe, although there are a few artists in Germany, Italy, and France who approach either its subject matter or its techniques." This is due to the fact "that a different tradition and living conditions produce different art," and "a healthy diversity of attitude."[38] Lippard consequently sees nouveau réalisme and pop art as "two totally separate visual impetus behind" the European and the American trends.[39]

Pop subject matter has a long list of precedents, she notes, from folk art to cubist collage, to the still lifes and found objects of Picasso and surrealism, but Lippard sees all of this European tradition as more "introverted" and philosophical than the American pop art that is "based on a tough, no-nonsense, no-preciosity, no-refinement standard appropriate to the 1960s"[40] and motivated by the "decision to approach the contemporary world with a positive rather than a negative attitude."[41] Pop "chose to depict everything previously considered unworthy of notice, let alone of art" and it did not respect "the time-honoured methods of creating art": often artists "did not even 'invent' their images" and "did nothing about them once they had selected them."[42] These are the features that the director of the Danish Louisiana Museum of Modern Art objected to. They are also features that connect easily to the "shared sensibility" behind minimalism pointed out by Rose and Nielsen and to the shared roots of minimalism and pop in the Duchampian readymade, as mentioned by Rosalind Krauss.

In this broad sense of pop as an opening towards themes and figures from popular culture, pop was present in most new 1960s art, signaling the end of the high/low divide in the new art and culture of this period and the wish to create a more "democratic" and accessible art incorporating contemporary cultural material. Such aims were part of the "significant similarities in the impetus behind" the European and the American trends that Lucy Lippard points out.

[38] Lippard, "Europe and Canada," in Lippard (ed.), 1994 p. 173.
[39] Lippard, 1994, p. 174.
[40] Lippard, 1994, p. 11 and 10.
[41] Lippard, 1994, p. 9.
[42] Lippard, 1994, p. 82.

As for the stylistic characteristics of pop art, Lippard argues that the five artist in New York that she admits as "hard-core Pop artists," "all employ more or less hard-edge, commercial techniques and colours to convey their unmistakably popular, representational images,"[43] and are committed to de-personalisation, detachment and recognition of "common clichés" and "common stock responses" as a valuable part of both public and personal life.[44] Again, except for the representational images, these are characteristics that are quite close to minimalism, and might be seen as further examples of the shared sources of pop and minimalism in the Duchampian readymade and the "similarities in impetus" behind the American and the European artists.

Apart from the few "hard-core Pop artists," who each had a fairly individual style, Lippard points out second and third wave pop artists as well as several artists who straddle "the gap between Pop iconography and abstraction" (such as Robert Indiana[45]), and she also notes a trend towards abstraction that has merged with "the anti-sculptural structures of Donald Judd and Robert Morris" and spawned a "dissimulated Pop" including use of industrial materials as "an abstract sculptural medium, fusing aspects of Pop, Surrealism, and non-objective art." She predicts that in the near future (i.e. in the late 1960s) such "cross-fertilisation with non-objective art will have multiplied."[46] According to Lippard the clear-cut distinctions between pop art and minimalism thus seem to become progressively less clear in the American context. So the mixing of critical terms and artistic styles in the Nordic countries does not seem more pronounced than in the U.S. in this period.

In today's global context, the pop history centring on New York is perceived to have edited out "alternative pops—and pop in other places—before they were even understood to exist." A global perspective thus opens the door to further broadening and diversifying of the definition of

[43] Lippard, 1994, p. 69. The five artists are: Warhol, Lichtenstein, Wesselmann, Rosenquist, and Oldenburg.

[44] Lippard, 1994, p. 10. The clichés and stock responses are Lippard's quotations from G.R. Swenson.

[45] Lippard, 1994, p. 122.

[46] Lippard, 1994, p. 126, 136–138

pop art. In the words of Jessica Morgan for the introduction to the 2015 exhibition catalogue *The World Goes Pop*,

> this process of exclusion can be read as a direct or deliberate echo of the convergence of critics, market and exhibitions that established abstract expressionism as the dominant art movement in the postwar United States.
>
> Yet around the world, "pop" did not just signify North American popular culture. Pop arose in singular forms and designations, but in no singular lineage. Many pops emerged simultaneously [...] This was global yet specific pop. [...]
>
> Just as "pop style" encompasses various strategies of composition and process, so there is no one universal pop art but rather hundreds of iterations around the globe that share a populist concern.[47]

If we accept Morgan's definition of global pop art as "largely a response to diverse strains of local and international commercial media" reflecting "a desire to create a truly populist art form,"[48] we are not far from the broad definitions of pop art and minimalism current in Denmark and Sweden in the 1960s. Nor from Barbara Rose's notion of the art of the 1960s as "more related in terms of a common sensibility than in terms of a common style." Not only were Hans-Jørgen Nielsen and Leif Nylén close friends and allies during the early and mid-sixties, both were championing concrete poetry, McLuhan's media theory and a materialist aesthetics. They belonged to artistic groups that shared fundamental new orientations and "sensibilities." The Swedish Svisch group and the Danish Ex-School group both engaged in cross-aesthetic experimentation, they shared an interest in new technologies and sought to create open works in literature, art and music that were in touch with contemporary reality. They also shared what Rose calls a "collective new sensibility" that tended to prefer the factual to the symbolic, ordinary objects to art objects, and to value "non-expressive," "neutral," "anonymous," and "impersonal" forms. After all, the "ordinary

[47] Jessica Morgan, "Political Pop: An Introduction," in Morgan and Frigeri (eds.), *The World Goes Pop*, London: Tate Publishing 2015, pp. 15–27. The quotations are from pp. 15 and 16. Among "artists and movements with a pop strategy" Morgan includes "nouveau réalisme, neo-dada, Otra and Nueva Figuración, Saqqakhaneh or Spiritual Pop, and Equipa Crónica, as well as such singular figures as Öyvind Fahlström, Keiichi Tanaami, and Erró" (p. 16).
[48] Morgan, 2015, p. 17.

objects" of minimalism that Rose mentions are not far from the everyday objects of pop art. And since what could be seen as more "expressive" and "personal" elements of pop art are borrowed from commercial media, they are not very personal at all, but cultural clichés quoted with some degree of irony or affection.

The best-known Swedish pop artist, Öyvind Fahlström, started out as a poet and wrote his famous 1953 manifesto of concrete poetry that became an inspiration for Leif Nylén and the 1960s generation of Swedish concrete poets. He also designed the cover for the little magazine *Rondo* (1961–1964), edited by the writers Torsten Ekbom, Björn Håkanson, Leif Nylén, and Torkel Rasmusson, that launched "open art" (as it was called) as a recurring theme. *Rondo*'s concept of "open art," highlighted in the two editors' introduction to the Swedish selection of Cage's texts, included new media, mixed media, and intermedia as well as open forms and the relationship between everyday language and poetic language. And this theme was continued into the subsequent magazine *Gorilla: Konst: Media* (Gorilla: Art: Media, 1966–1967) that expanded into the visual arts and mixed media.[49] Together a number of artists from these circles formed the performative group *Svisch*.[50] And although Öyvind Fahlström has been classified as a pop artist in art history, his various and multiform work in several media tends to elude easy classification, combining different modes, genres and media and straddling a set of contested binaries: art and life, aesthetics and politics, form and ideology, high and low, national and international. His visual artwork that moved from semi-abstract sign painting to figural elements in collages, games, maps, puzzles, and installations can only be characterised as impure.[51]

So perhaps the term pop art in Sweden and the term minimalism in Denmark are less indications of a specific style, than makeshift markers of far more heterogeneous art practices in both Sweden and Denmark. Even

[49] For a more detailed analysis of Fahlström's manifesto and the little magazines *Rondo* and *Gorilla* se Jesper Olsson's essays in Ørum and Olsson (eds.), 2016.

[50] The members of the *Svisch* group were: Öyvind Fahlström, Carl Fredrik Reuterswärd, Elis Eriksson, Torsten Ekbom, Åke Hodell, Leif Nylén, Mats G. Bengtsson, and Bengt Emil Johnson.

[51] I quote Jesper Olsson's description of Fahlström's art in "Politics and Art: The Impure Arts of Öyvind Fahlström," in Ørum and Olsson (eds.), 2016, pp. 53–63.

though the critical discourses were not the same in the two countries, these moveable, multiform and impure art practices seem to be a shared characteristic of Danish and Swedish art in the 1960s. And as briefly indicated above, somewhat similar problems of developing a terminology and agreeing on a description of the new art movements in the 1960s seems to be carried over from the U.S.

Bibliography

Christine Buhl Andersen (ed.), *Peter Louis-Jensen Retrospektiv*, Sorø: Vestsjællands Kunstmuseum, 2003.

Troels Andersen, *Moderne russisk kunst 1910–1925*, Copenhagen: Borgen, 1967.

—. *Ude af øje*, Copenhagen: Forlaget Vandkunsten, 2014.

Per Bäckström and Benedikt Hjartarson (eds.), *Decentring the Avant-Garde*, Avant Garde Critical Studies 30, Amsterdam and New York: Rodopi, 2014.

Gregory Battcock (ed.), *Minimal Art: A Critical Anthology*, Berkeley, Los Angeles, London: University of California Press, 1995.

Hubert van den Berg, et al. (eds.), *A Cultural History of the Avant-Garde in the Nordic Countries 1900–1925*, Amsterdam and New York: Rodopi, 2012.

Sascha Bru, et al. (eds.), *Europa! Europa? The Avant-Garde, Modernism, and the Fate of a Continent*, New York: De Gruyter, 2009.

John Cage, *Om ingenting*, Stockholm: Bonniers, 1966.

Hultén, K. G., "Om maleriet i New York efter Pollock dvs. OM POP-KUNSTEN," *Louisiana Revy*, No. 1, September 1963, pp. 10–15.

Knud W. Jensen, "Pop-kunst på Louisiana," in *Louisiana Revy* no. 4, April 1964, p. 3.

Per Kirkeby, "Collioure-serien," in *Naturens blyant*, Copenhagen: Borgen, 1978.

—. *Håndbog*, Copenhagen: Borgen, 1991.

Bengt af Klintberg, *Svensk Fluxus/Swedish Fluxus*, Stockholm: Rönnells Antikvariat, 2006.

Rosalind Krauss, "The Double Negative: A New Syntax for Sculpture," in *Passages in Modern Sculpture*, Cambridge, Mass., and London: The MIT Press, 1993, pp. 243–288.

Lucy Lippard (ed.), *Pop Art*, London: Thames and Hudson, 1994.

Peter Louis-Jensen, Radio interview, DR July 1965. Quoted in Christine Buhl Andersen (ed.), 2003, p. 67.

Marshall McLuhan, *Understanding Media* (1964), London & New York: Routledge, 2001.

James Meyer, *Minimalism*, London: Phaidon Press, 2000.

Jessica Morgan and Flavia Frigeri (eds.), *The World Goes Pop*, London: Tate Publishing, 2015.

Hans-Jørgen Nielsen, "Fortolkning i entropiens tidsalder" (Interpretation in the age of entropy), in *Selvsyn,* 1969.

Leif Nylén, "Alt var ligesom i bevægelse" in Ørum (ed.), *Portræt af et forfatterskab: Hans-Jørgen Nielsen,* 2001.

—. *Den öppna konsten*, Stockholm: Sveriges Allmäna Konstföreningen, 1998.

Jesper Olsson, "Politics and Art: The Impure Arts of Öyvind Fahlström," "Rondo and Gorilla: Magazine and Calendar," and "Hätila ragulpr på fåtskliaben: Conceiving of Concrete Poetry," in Tania Ørum and Jesper Olsson (eds.), Leiden: Brill Academic Publishers, 2016, pp. 53–63, pp. 195–201, pp. 477–485.

Piotr Piotrowski, "Toward a Horizontal History of the European Avant-Garde," in Sascha Bru, et al. (eds.), 2009, pp. 49–58.

Barbara Rose, "ABC Art" originally printed in *Art in America*, October-November 1965. Reprinted in Battcock (ed.) 1995, pp. 274–297.

ta', Copenhagen: Borgen, 1967–1968.

Anne M. Wagner, "Reading Minimal Art," in Gregory Battcock (ed.), 1995, pp. 3–18.

Tania Ørum (ed.), *Portræt af et forfatterskab: Hans-Jørgen Nielsen,* Copenhagen: Forlaget Spring, 2001.

Tania Ørum, *De eksperimenterende tressere,* Copenhagen: Gyldendal, 2009

Tania Ørum and Jesper Olsson (eds.), *A Cultural History of the Avant-Garde in the Nordic Countries 1950–1975,* Amsterdam and New York: Brill, 2016.

12
Pop Beyond Pop
Some Exhibitions of the Hungarian "Iparterv-Circle"

Dávid Fehér

"No isms in Hungary." This was the title of an essay by art historian Éva Körner, published in the magazine *Studio International* in 1974 under a pseudonym.[1] The brief statement reflects the difficulties of using the terminology of a West-centred art history for describing local artistic production of art scenes that are treated as marginal. The title refers to a conceptual work of Hungarian artist, János Major entitled *Cubist Concept* (1971).[2] The work consists of a photograph of the tombstone of an unknown person called Lajos Kubista (Louis Cubist) accompanied by the artist's satirical comments in 17 points. Major describes his homeland as a "necropolis of ideas."[3] He points out that "No 'ism' has yet been born in Hungary," but several trends "came to Budapest to die." In the first draft of the concept written in German the artist states that "Pop art was born in the USA, and it died in Hungary." Later, in the English version of the text the artist softened this statement by claiming "Pop art was born in the

[1] Anik Cs. Asztalos (Éva Körner), "No isms in Hungary," *Studio International*, No. 964, 1974, pp. 105–111.

[2] See Dániel Véri, *"Leading the Dead": The World of János Major*, exh. cat., Budapest: Hungarian University of Fine Arts, 2013, pp. 51–53.

[3] See the German translation of the text made by the artist: "Budapest ist ein Ideen-Nekropolis."

USA, its influence irradiated also to Hungary." The ironic artwork can be interpreted as a symptomatic reflection to the essential differences between notions of "Western" history of art, and their reception in East Central Europe.[4]

Major's statement on the "irradiating influence" of pop art refers to important trends in Hungarian art that bear (formal) affinities with British and American instances of pop art. It was already a crucial question of Hungarian art critique in the 1960s whether we could speak of Hungarian pop art per se concerning these tendencies. Hungarian artworks that are related to pop art did not reflect the spectacle of consumer culture, which did not exist in the local scene. Rather, they were instances of a unique form of figuration that resonated international trends of art, but also inseparable from the local discourses on realism. This essay investigates some art events that can be interpreted as paradigmatic cases of pop art's local reception, and peculiar instances of *cultural transfer*. I explore phenomena that can be described as "pop beyond pop" through presenting artworks that bear formal affinities with pop art, but their local context is essentially different. I aim to explore these differences, and to create a framework in which this superficial formal similarities and essential differences can be described. I will touch on some dilemmas that have already occurred in Hungarian and international scholarship and in curatorial projects concerning the extension and re-thinking of pop art's (local and/or international) notion, and after that I will present some major exhibitions and artworks from the 1960s that reflect a peculiar understating of pop art.

The most important contribution to this question is Katalin Keserü's exhibition and book *Variations on Pop Art* organised and published in 1993,[5] in which she used a radically expanded notion of pop art to describe the artistic production of the Hungarian art scene. Keserü's book was harshly criticised in Hungary because of the contradictory usage of terminology that eliminates the essential differences between the local

[4] See in this context: David Crowley, "Pop Effects in Eastern Europe under Communist Rule," in Jessica Morgan and Flavia Frigeri (eds.), *The World Goes Pop*, exh. cat., London: Tate Modern, 2015, p. 33.
[5] Katalin Keserü, *Variations on Pop Art: Chapters in the History of Hungarian Art Between 1950 and 1990*, Budapest: Ernst Museum, 1993

contexts in Hungary and in the United States. In a groundbreaking essay, art historian Katalin Timár claimed that such unreflective usage of Western terms for the local production can make art history a "self-colonizing" tool.[6] Nevertheless, the situation seems to be even more complicated, as the "Western" term of pop art was already used by the artists themselves, and—as Piotr Piotrowski suggested—the wish for such "colonisation" was not far from their own intentions.[7]

However, the problem of "self-colonisation" might be eliminated, if we interpret Hungarian artworks that bear affinities with pop art not only as instances of "artistic import," but rather as a peculiar case of *cultural transfer*, a unique way of *translation*, as I proposed in my recent essay on Hungarian transformations of pop art.[8] The already existing *local* narratives of pop art, like the Hungarian and the Estonian[9] one, should be situated in the *global* history of internationalisation of pop art, mainly in the trends of what is referred to as the "*Europop*" of the 1960s Europe, that include such figurative—sometimes also politically engaged -movements such as German *Capitalistic Realism*, French *Figuration Narrative*, and Belgian-Dutch *Nieuwe Figuratie*. Several comparative exhibitions, mostly the one in Zürich in 2008 and the one in Nijmegen in 2012[10] investigated the question of pop art's internationalisation in the European context, albeit relevant examples of the "Eastern bloc" were missing from these surveys. Such phenomena as "*Europop*" have little in common with what art critic Lucy Lippard called "hard core" pop art in America.[11] The above-

[6] Katalin Timár, "Is Your Pop Our Pop? The History of Art As a Self-Colonizing Tool," *Artmargins online*, 15 March 2002, www.artmargins.com/index.php/archive/323-is-your-pop-our-pop-the-history-of-art-as-a-self-colonizing-tool (most recently accessed: 20 August 2015).

[7] Piotr Piotrowski, *In the Shadow of Yalta: Art and the Avant-garde in Eastern Europe, 1945–1989*, London: Reaktion Books, 2009, p. 166.

[8] Dávid Fehér, "'Where is the Light?': Transformations of Pop Art in Hungary," in Darsie Alexander and Bartholomew Ryan, *International Pop*, exh. cat., Minneapolis: Walker Art Center, 2015, pp. 135–152.

[9] For Estonian examples see Sirje Helme, *Popkunst Forever: Estonian Pop Art at the Turn of the 1960s and 1970s*, Tallinn: Eesti Kunstimuseum, KUMU, 2010.

[10] Tobia Bezzola and Franziska Lentsch (eds.), *Europop*, exh. cat., Kunsthaus Zürich, Cologne: DuMont, 2008; Frank van de Schoor (ed.), *Pop Art in Europe*, exh. cat., Nijmegen: Museum het Valkhof, 2012.

[11] According to Lucy Lippard, only five New York artists can be treated as a real "hard core" pop artist; these are Andy Warhol, Roy Lichtenstein, Tom Wesselmann, James Rosenquist and Claes Oldenburg. Lucy R. Lippard, *Pop Art*, London: Thames and Hudson, 2001 (1966), p. 69.

mentioned European trends can be seen as local responses to hegemonic trends of American art. The precondition of presenting the diverse trends of "*global pop*" or "*international pop*" is to characterise the various forms and histories of "*local pop*": the different cases of transfer and the diverse forms of understanding and re-interpreting the notions that are related to pop. In order to describe the correlation between "local pop" and "global pop," it seems to be necessary to investigate the various channels of information flow, the *global circulation* of magazines, images and notions in the international pop era. If the hegemonic term of (British and American) pop art is substituted by such umbrella terms as "*global pop*" or "*international pop*," as it is proposed by two major exhibition projects of the Walker Art Center in Minneapolis and Tate Modern in London, the parallel narratives of local "*popisms*" will be seen in the context of a "horizontal" and "polyphonic" art history that deconstructs the hierarchy between centres and peripheries.[12]

Although it is hardly possible to find artworks from East Central Europe that thematise the problems of a (non-existent) consumer culture, there are several works of art that can be seen as reflections to international phenomena of pop (for instance the works of East-German Willy Wolff, Polish Jerzy Ryszard "Jurry" Zieliński, Slovakian Jana Želibská, Stano Filko, Július Koller and Alex Mlynárčik, Czech Jiři Kolář, Estonian Leonhard Lapin and others). The peculiar examples of local "*popisms*" are substantially *different* from American pop art. They can rather be seen as cases of "international pop" with specific local attributes. To characterise these local attributes, it seems essential to reconstruct the original context in which these artworks were created and presented, and also to investigate the dynamics of the processes of *cultural transfer* and *translation*, or even *hybridisation*.

Countries of East Central Europe can be described as "close Others"[13] of the two superpowers of the Cold War era. Although there are essential differences between the particular art scenes of the region, and it would be dangerous to homogenise this heterogonous group of countries, the

[12] For "horizontal art history," see Piotr Piotrowski, "Toward a Horizontal History of the European Avant-Garde," in Sascha Bru (ed.), *Europa! Europa? The Avant-Garde, Modernism and the Fate of a Continent*, Vol. 1. (2), Berlin: De Gruyter, 2009, pp. 49–58.
[13] See Piotrowski, 2009, p. 52.

analysis of the nature of their "close Otherness" seems to be a productive point of departure, as the activity of progressive artists was both defined by a "Western orientation" and the local discourses on realism.

For a reconstruction of the original context of East Central European "popisms," it seems unavoidable to explore how they were presented and received in their own time. There are several exhibition projects in the region that could be investigated as instances of local "popisms," like the *Danuvius '68* (1968) festival in Bratislava, Jana Želibská's solo shows in Bratislava (1967) and Prague (1969),[14] or the *Soup '69* group exhibition in Café Pegasus in Tallinn that was the founding event of the phenomenon that was called by its initiator Leonhard Lapin "*Union pop*."[15] A complex analysis should also investigate such exhibition projects and events that presented "Western" trends in the "Eastern bloc," like the big exhibition of American art in Bucharest and Cluj in 1969,[16] the year when Richard Nixon visited Romania. Such events as the performances of the Merce Cunningham Dance Company in Prague, Ostrava, Warsaw and Poznań, organised within the framework of their "world tour," are also of major importance,[17] just like the visit of Derek Boshier and Joe Tilson, two major figures of British pop art, to Prague, Bratislava, and Budapest in 1968.[18] In Prague, they initiated the *Smith/Novak event*, an emblematic action of the Cold War period; in Budapest, they gave a public lecture on the trends of British pop art.

Nevertheless, an analysis of "cultural exchanges" should also characterise the role of contemporary "Western" curators and art critics who contributed to the international reception of East Central European trends that are related to pop art. German art historian Dieter Honisch dis-

[14] For details on Jana Želibská's exhibitions see Lucia Gregorová, "Her View of Him and Her," in Vladimíra Büngerová and Lucia Gregorová (eds.), *Jana Želibská: No Touching*, Bratislava: Slovak National Gallery, 2012, pp. 42–59.

[15] Helme, 2010, pp. 41–44.

[16] The exhibition project was initiated by the Smithsonian Institute, see its catalogue: *Dispariția și reapariția imaginii: pictura americană de după 1945* (The Disappearance and Recurrence of the Image: American Painting after 1945), Washington, D.C.: Smithsonian Institute, 1969.

[17] On the world tour of the Merce Cunningham Dance Company and Robert Rauschenberg's role, see Hiroko Ikegami, *The Great Migrator: Robert Rauschenberg and the Global Rise of American Art*, Cambridge, Mass.: The MIT Press, 2010 (for their visit to Eastern Europe, see in particular p. 6).

[18] Fehér, 2015, p. 136.

covered progressive Hungarian art when he visited the first and the second Iparterv exhibitions in Budapest in 1968 and 1969. Evelyn Weiss (one of the advisors and close associates of art collector Peter Ludwig) discovered László Lakner's art by visiting his first solo show during her visit to Budapest in 1969. French art critic Pierre Restany played an important role in the international presentation of such artists as Alex Mlynárčik and Jana Želibská. In addition, in the period of the Moderna Museet's legendary director, Pontus Hultén, alongside major exhibitions of American pop artists, a one-man show of Polish artist Władysław Hasior had been shown in Stockholm.[19]

Although the complex history of East Central European "popisms" and their international relations could be investigated through analysing such art exhibitions and other events that are mentioned above, this chapter will examine only the Hungarian scene that was one of the liveliest ones with respect to the reception of pop art. In the late 1960s several exhibitions opened in Hungary that reflected local discourses on recent questions of pop art. These art events can be seen as paradigmatic cases of *local* reactions to *international* art phenomena. The focus of this study will be the "Iparterv circle," named after two legendary semi-official group exhibitions held in Budapest. In what follows, I will investigate how pop art in the two exhibitions appeared and was received, and to what extent the exhibitions can be interpreted as peculiar local responses to international phenomena, and as instances of *cultural transfer*. After describing the two "Iparterv exhibitions," I will also present three solo shows of "Iparterv-artists" (György Kemény, Endre Tót, and László Lakner), which were directly related to the contemporary questions of pop art and how such relations were also addressed in the contemporary art critique. I will go on to analyse how these artists transformed the "Western" notion of pop art in a specific way and how they related to the local artistic traditions.

The Iparterv Exhibitions (1968, 1969)

The two Iparterv exhibitions are key events of Hungarian art history of the 1960s, and the most often referred exhibitions of Hungarian art of the

[19] Wladislaw Hasior, Moderna Museet, Stockholm, 9 November–15 December 1968.

Cold War, because the exhibitions were the first common appearance of a new generation of artists who reflected on recent trends of international art and local traditions of classical modernism as well.[20] The shows summarised several trends that had already begun in the first years of the decade. Both exhibitions were held at the main hall of an architectural firm called "Iparterv" in the downtown of Budapest. Later, not only the exhibitions, but the whole generation of artists was named "Iparterv." The exhibitors of Iparterv were young artists (born in the 1930s) who were interested in the most recent trends of the international art scene (the exhibitors of the first Iparterv exhibition are: Imre Bak, Krisztián Frey, Tamás Hencze, György Jovánovics, Ilona Keserü, Gyula Konkoly, László Lakner, Sándor Molnár, István Nádler, Ludmil Siskov, and Endre Tót, on the second Iparterv show also appeared: András Baranyay, János Major, László Méhes, and Tamás Szentjóby). Although they had only restricted access to images of "Western" art, they started to collect information about the recent developments of international art in the beginning of the 1960s. Besides the few opportunities of travelling abroad, the main sources of information were Western art magazines in local libraries, mainly the library of the Fészek Art Club. Its director, Éva Molnár, consulted with several Iparterv artists (mainly with László Lakner) concerning the list of the ordered international magazines. The attitude of the young Iparterv artists, and their ways of acquiring information and reactions to it were aptly described by contemporary art critic Géza Perneczky in a retrospective essay written in the 1990s:

> I don't think I would be off track if I said that the artists of the Iparterv in effect completed their master classes at the foreign language bookstore in Váci Street, as this was the only place where the books and catalogues so vital for them could be found. [László] Lakner was in the vanguard in this respect, and he was almost provocative in pushing a competition as to who would be the first to learn about something important and decisive from the Western »scene« and who would make use of it in his studio, whether it be a technical innovation or something concerning the approach to art. But even so, sometimes [Gyula]

[20] See the most recent publication on the Iparterv exhibitions: Csaba Varga (ed.), *Groupe Iparterv – Le Progrès de l'Illusion: La troisième génération de l'avant-garde hongroise*, Paris: Institut Hongroise de Paris, 2010; see also my previous summary on the first Iparterv exhibition: Fehér, 2015, pp. 138–140.

> Konkoly or [György] Jovánovics would paint or sculpt, or rather "arte poverize" something fresher. It sounds harsh when put this way, but behind this attitude lay the fact that in the sixties New York took the baton from Paris with such force that if one was even mildly interested in what was happening in the world, he or she was truly compelled to update his or her knowledge on a daily basis. It was like a teeming market. It is thus understandable that in any region of Europe, artists who wanted to be taken seriously could not afford to disregard catalogues from New York.[21]

As Perneczky explains, the instant reaction and the challenge of interiorisation of the most recent international trends was of key importance for the artists of Iparterv. Their major goal was to relate to the international discourses of contemporary art, and to create works of art that could be "understood" from the perspective of such international discourses without losing its local specificity.

This attempt of "timeliness" could be the common denominator of the very heterogeneous group of artists that was shown at the Iparterv exhibitions. Although such exhibitions as the 1964 Venice Biennale and the *Pop, etc.* exhibition in Vienna in 1964 proved to be formative experiences for several Iparterv artists whose work can be related to pop art, the point of departure for a common exhibition project was the *4. documenta* in 1968. Imre Bak and István Nádler, who had a common exhibition in the well-known Müller Gallery in Stuttgart in the same period, and László Lakner, who spent a short-term residency in Museum Folkwang in Essen, had the chance to visit the *documenta* in Kassel. The show was dominated by trends of *pop art*, *post-painterly abstraction* and artworks that are related to *op art* and *kinetic art*. The Hungarian artists realised that such a co-existence of contemporary (post-painterly) abstraction and figuration can also be detected in the Hungarian art scene. The first Iparterv exhibition was an attempt to present the parallel trends of figuration and abstraction in the same physical and discursive space, as a local response to the recent *documenta*. The relationship between the first Iparterv exhibition and the *documenta* was manifested by the title of an unofficially published cata-

[21] Géza Perneczky, "Produktivitásra ítélve? Az Iparterv-csoport és ami utána következett Magyarországon" (Sentenced to Productivity? The Iparterv-Group and what followed it in Hungary), *Balkon*, 1996/1 and 1996/2., www.c3.hu/~perneczky/articles/IPARTRV (most recently accessed: 20 August 2015).

logue that followed both Iparterv exhibitions in 1970. The booklet was entitled *Dokumentum* meaning "evidence" in Hungarian, and expresses a claim to document the current trends of young Hungarian art that are nearly invisible for a broader audience, since they are barely tolerated by the official cultural politics, and have little space in the centralised (and state-controlled) institutional system.

In the preface to the catalogue of the first Iparterv exhibition that was opened on 12 December 1968, art historian Péter Sinkovits, who organised the exhibition, briefly described the programme of the show:

> The exhibition of these eleven artists documents the strivings that are tied to the world's best avant-garde tendencies. They attempt to shoulder the painfully difficult but always fruitful task of keeping pace. They tie themselves to tendencies labelled Pop Art, Art Informel, New Abstraction, Abstract Illusionism, and Abstract Impressionism [sic!]. Their task is not simply to adopt the recognised accomplishments, it is not slavish copying, but rather a personal, emotionally charged individual adaptation. A homogenous approach is only beginning to take shape. This exhibition is an experiment in providing a possibility to clarify the most recent tendencies.[22]

The phrase of "keeping pace" paired with the term "individual adaptation" in the statement of Sinkovits seems to be a symptomatic approach towards the work of the exhibited artists. The claim of "keeping pace" was later mentioned by art historian László Beke as "possibly a quite inadequate formulation from a tactical point of view,"[23] because it strengthened such critical voices that described most works of the exhibition as not more, than "a copy of fashionable, international trends," which is "incapable of finding its own voice and create its own style and form," as influential art historian Lajos Németh wrote in his review on the exhibition.[24] This dilemma leads us back to the matter of self-colonisation through art his-

[22] Péter Sinkovits, "Bevezető" (Introduction), in *Kiállítás az Iparterv dísztermében (*Exhibition in the Iparterv Hall), exh. cat., Budapest, 1968, n.p.
[23] László Beke, "12 Years of Iparterv," in László Beke, Péter Sinkovits, and Lóránd Hegyi, *Iparterv 68–80*, exh. cat., Budapest: "Iparterv Home Printing House," 1980, VIII.
[24] Lajos Németh, "Új törekvések a magyar képzőművészetben: A 68-as őszi évad tárlatairól" (New Tendencies in Hungarian Art. On the Exhibitions of the Fall Season in 1968), *Kritika*, No. 4, 1969, repr. in Beke, Sinkovits, and Hegyi, 1980, p. 47.

torical terminology that was not far from the intentions of the initiators of the show.

Although the first "Iparterv exhibition" presented a wide array of artistic trends, it was mostly dominated by "pop-effects"[25] to the extent that several art critiques simply called it as a "pop-show." Imre Bak's and István Nádler's post-painterly abstraction was dominated by strident colours resembling the aesthetics of an industrial landscape, but also evoking some motifs of local *folk art* and *vernacular culture*. Their Hard-edge paintings can be seen as attempts to create works of art that have both local attributes and global relevance. Their attitude can be compared to that of Ilona Keserü, whose sewed motifs and vibrant forms are in some cases direct quotes of folk art objects. The abstraction of Bak, Nádler and Keserü is not only a local reflection on Hard-edge painting and other new forms of geometric abstraction, but also a successor of the local "post-surrealist" art of the so-called "European School" (mostly the painter Dezső Korniss). Members of the Hungarian artists' group "European School" often evoked motifs of local folk art to create a specific form of modernism in the late 1940s. One of the key point of reference for them was the composer Béla Bartók, who also often appropriated folk music in his practice. Although artists of the "European School" were silenced in the repressive period of the 1950s, they became unofficial masters, and major reference points for several members of the Iparterv-circle.

The link between geometric trends in the Iparterv-circle and "international pop art" was more than the association of the contemporary critique. Most of the above-mentioned artists had experimented with combining abstraction with figurative motifs that evoke typical works of pop art. Imre Bak's painting *Marika* (1967) paired an abstract composition of diagonal lines with repeated silkscreen motifs of a young girl in the spirit of Peter Blake and Andy Warhol. Ilona Keserü's painting *Couple* (1967) is one of the major examples of international trends of *female pop*: she situated a naked couple paired with plastic roses in the middle of an ornamental composition derived from folk art. The artist depicts the two figures as "New Adam" and "New Eve" of the beat culture and hippie

[25] What I mean by "pop-effects" is stylistic elements that evoke "Western" pop art and pop culture. For the term, see Crowley, 2015, pp. 29–37.

culture, presented in the spirit of the aesthetics of "*flower power*." The faces of the figures were formed of newspaper-clippings that depict Ringo Starr and Julie Christie. The juxtaposition of Hungarian folk art and celebrity culture of "swinging London" describes well the dual—both local and Western—orientation of the Iparterv-artists. Although *Marika* and *Couple* were not shown in the Iparterv exhibitions, they underline the fact that even the abstract exhibitors had strong links to international trends of pop art, and this relation is not exceptional, if we have in mind the statement of Lucy Lippard: "Pop Art has more in common with the American 'post-painterly-abstraction' of Ellsworth Kelly and Kenneth Noland, than with contemporary realism."[26]

Most of the artworks shown at the two Iparterv exhibitions combined several forms of expression that are typical for "Western" trends, which the artists saw in foreign art exhibitions and periodicals. Although Krisztián Frey's—and also Endre Tót's—art was mostly linked to *informel* painting and a peculiar form of post-abstract-expressionism, Frey often applied everyday objects on his pictorial surfaces. His work *In memorian Francesca Belloni* (1968)—shown at the first Iparterv exhibition—is an overpainted mannequin that can be compared to works of French "new realism" and trends of neo-dadaism. The usage of letters and numbers, and the modes of appropriating everyday imagery is strongly linked to contemporary trends of pop art. György Jovánovics exhibited plaster casts on both Iparterv exhibitions. Although his works can be compared with plaster works of George Segal, his attitude is closer to such artists as the Slovenian Marko Pogačnik, who created similar plaster casts (entitled *Pop objects*) in the same years. The sculptures of Jovánovics evoke art historical tradition, and re-think dilemmas of realistic and illusionistic artistic depiction. Although Jovánovics' illusionism is generally different from the realistic attitude of pop art, the usage of "Western" media images played an important role in his practice, creating a link between his activity and contemporaneous trends of pop art.[27]

[26] Lucy R. Lippard, *Pop Art* (1966), London: Thames and Hudson, 2001, p. 9.
[27] Regarding on Jovánovics' relationship to George Segal, see Márta Kovalovszky, "György Jovánovics," in Hafner Zoltan (ed.), *Jovánovics*, Budapest: Corvina Kiadó, 2004, p. 26.

There were only a few artists on the two Iparterv exhibitions who consistently applied "pop-effects." One of them was Ludmil Siskov, a painter of Bulgarian origin but living in Hungary at the time. Siskov depicts typical "Western" motifs of 1960s: rugby players (*Rugby*, 1968) and astronauts (*Astronauts*, 1968). The figures are often painted with air-brush technique, his harsh colours, stylised backgrounds and imitated raster points form a peculiar version of "hand-painted pop"[28] that bear affinities with such artists as Peter Saul.

The "hand-made" character is also dominant in the case of László Lakner and Gyula Konkoly, the two foremost figures of Hungarian quasi-pop painting. The point of departure for both of them was a peculiar form of "magical realism" that appeared in Hungary in the late 1950s as a peculiar reaction to the art of socialist realism. The early work of Lakner (the first Hungarian artist who experimented with a figuration that resembles pop art) was inspired by both Max Ernst and Ben Shahn in the 1950s. His surrealistic paintings are characterised by both a French and an American orientation, as Lakner himself stated in an interview conducted in 1988:

> around this time [the late fifties] I began to perceive a parallel between American and Hungarian art! [...] *They too have no traditions* in art in the sense that the French, the Italians, the Germans have. [...] Our beginning is a tabula rasa, much as it is for the Americans. There are, there can be advantages to a *lack of tradition*.[29]

The interest in American pop art was a self-evident consequence of Lakner's American orientation (which was manifested in paintings that were based on American magazine clippings and paid tribute to such American artists as Ivan Albright, Ben Shahn, and Louise Nevelson). Lakner's works painted around 1963–64 that resemble pop art (for instance, *News*, 1964, Figure 12.1) are continuations of his earlier surrealistic painting that thematised

[28] Russell Ferguson (ed.), *Hand-painted Pop: American Art in Transition 1955–62*, exh. cat., The Museum of Contemporary Art, Los Angeles, New York: Rizzoli, 1992.
[29] Edit Szentesi, "Beszélgetés Lakner Lászlóval" (A conversation with László Lakner), in Ildikó Nagy (ed.), *Hatvanas évek: Új törekvések a magyar képzőművészetben* (The Sixties: New Approaches in Hungarian Visual Arts). exh. cat., Hungarian National Gallery, Budapest: Képzőművészeti Kiadó, Magyar Nemzeti Galéria, and Ludwig Múzeum, 1991, p. 128.

everyday imagery and historical traumas, and was often based on photographic prototypes. His painting *Bones* (1968) shown at the first Iparterv exhibition is based on the varied repetition of an enlarged photograph of a bone, evoking compositions of Andy Warhol. However, Lakner paints the duplicated bone that resembles an x-ray photograph free-hand. Lakner's art is rooted in realistic traditions of painting: the sensual painterly surfaces are generally different from that of Andy Warhol.

In the late 1960s, Gyula Konkoly—who started his career as a figurative painter—created large "soft-sculptures" in the spirit of Claes Oldenburg. His *Academic Study* (1968) depicts a distorted hand paired with a cage: the work often interpreted as an ironic inversion of the socialist topos of the clenched fist,[30] in which case the title can be seen as a critique of the ideological character of the official academic instruction in Hungary. The "softness" of Konkoly's works shown at the first Iparterv show (*Softened Egg*, 1968) differs from that of Oldenburg. It might recall the process of "softening" of socialist dictatorship in the late 1960s. In some cases, Konkoly cites local references. His work *Rose* (1968) depicts a "softened" or withered flower. Konkoly's sculpture can be compared to László Lakner's brownish *Rose*-paintings and monumental *Rose*-sculpture from the same year that turn a vivid pop-motif into a colourless and decayed entity. Konkoly's work refers to the lines of a kitschy song of a well-known Hungarian operetta: "a rose speaks more beautifully than any love letters…."[31] In this sense, Konkoly's rose evokes Hungarian "low art" and everyday culture, and on the other hand makes an ironic comment on the conservatism of Hungarian society.

The contribution of the Iparterv-circle can only be understood, if we investigate such artistic production in its local context. The young artists used the visual language of pop art and new figuration to relate themselves to international discourses on art, but their activity was rooted in local traditions of realism and abstraction. In the system of what is referred to as the "three Ts" (támogatott, tűrt, tiltott—meaning: supported, tolerated, and banned), which defined cultural politics of Hungary at the time, most

[30] Emese Révész, "Figura, história, táj: Figurativitás Konkoly Gyula festészetében" (Figure, History, Landscape: Figurativity in Gyula Konkoly's Art), in *Konkoly: Figuratív képek* (Konkoly: Figurative Paintings), exh. cat., Budapest: Ernst Museum, 2003, n.p.
[31] Keserü, 1993, cff. 21.

of the artists were in the category of "tolerated": they had sporadic chances to present their works in (semi-)official exhibitions, but remained underrepresented in the art scene. The situation of such artists as Lakner was a peculiar one: his realistic paintings implied a leftist critique of the Vietnam War (*The Protest of Buddhist Monks of Saigon,* 1965, Figure 12.2), and represented a peculiar form of realism, but still remained ideologically problematic because of their "Western" orientation.

The second Iparterv exhibition in 1969 signalled a major shift in the progressive art scene. If the main source of influence of the first show was the *4. documenta*, then the second exhibition can be interpreted as an immediate reaction to the influential exhibition *When Attitudes Become Form* (curated by Harald Szeemann), and signalled the end of the period of "international pop." In the second Iparterv show Gyula Konkoly exhibited an environment called *Monument* (1969) formed of ice, potassium permanganate, cotton-wool and gauze.[32] As soon as the ice started to melt, red spots appeared on the gauze's white surface. Through imitating a bleeding body, the work evoked the traumatic defeat of the Hungarian Uprising of 1956 (the second Iparterv show opened on 24 October, one day after the twelfth anniversary of the uprising, which fact self-evidently referred to the uprising). The 1956 uprising was a taboo in János Kádár's society; the *Monument,* which broke this taboo and provoked the authorities, who were able to read between the lines. Although the work of Konkoly continues the artist's former series of "soft" sculptures, it signals a shift to a political form of conceptual art. Lakner's exhibited work the *Rope* (1969) juxtaposes a real rope with its painterly depiction: it is a composition of two symmetric parts (just like *Bones* one year before) but also shows a stronger conceptual interest, and a move toward photorealism.[33]

In 1969, the list of exhibitors was expanded with artists such as Tamás Szentjóby, who had initiated the first Hungarian happening (*The Lunch. In*

[32] This work is well-known as an early Eastern European instance of conceptual art: Tony Godfrey, *Conceptual Art* (1998). London: Phaidon, 2006, p. 267.

[33] Regarding Rope's many contexts, see Dávid Fehér, "Kötél és identitás: Megjegyzések Lakner László Identitás (Kötél) című alkotásához" (Rope and Identity: Remarks upon László Lakner's Work Identity (Rope), in Annamária Szőke and Tamás Ullmann eds., *Tanulmányok. Filozófiatudományi Doktori Iskola.: Művészettörténet-tudományi Doktori Iskola (Asteriskos 4.)* (Studies of Doctoral Schools of Philosophical Studies and Art History: Asteriskos 4], Budapest: Eötvös Loránd University, 2013, pp. 311–327.

Memoriam Batu Khan, 1966) with Gábor Altorjay. Szentjóby's exhibited objects (*New Unit of Measurement*, 1965; *Cooling Water*, 1965) are emblematic instances of an artistic production that can be related to the Fluxus movement, although their original idea is related to a planned (but never realised) 1965 exhibition, where Szentjóby and Altorjay would have presented "pop-objects" that imply ironic critique of pop art. The trends of happening, fluxus and pop art were (worldwide) strongly related to each other, and the second Iparterv show underlined such connections in the Hungarian scene, and also signalled the beginning of a new artistic attitude that followed the "Golden Age" of pop art.

Although the two Iparterv exhibitions had hardly any coherent curatorial concept, and the process of their organisation was also determined by mere coincidences, their significance lies not only in the exhibited artworks themselves, but also in their manifestations as ground-breaking exhibition projects. Both shows can be interpreted as local adaptations of important international exhibitions (*documenta 4*, *When Attitudes Become Form*), and in that sense they can be seen as attempts to transfer phenomena of the international art world to the local scene. To this extent not only the exhibited artworks, but also the exhibitions per se are instances of a complex process of *cultural transfer* and *translation*—a process in which the understanding of pop art played a major role. The act of *translation* in the context of the Ipaterv shows didn't mean mere imitation of already existing trends, but rather the gesture of combining local traditions with stylistic elements that are typical for recent art movements of "Western" art scenes. In what follows, I will briefly present three solo exhibitions of three Iparterv artists from the same years that thematised the questions of pop art in a more direct way, than the Iparterv exhibitions did.

Appropriating Pop Art
(György Kemény's solo show, Fészek Art Club, Budapest, 1968)

György Kemény's solo show at the Fészek Art Club was one of the most pop art-like exhibitions of 1960s Hungary, therefore it is one of the key examples of a peculiar understanding and translating trends of international pop in the context of a local scene. Although György Kemény was not an exhibitor at the two Iparterv exhibitions, he is the person of this circle whose activity was the closest to American pop art, with which he became acquainted during his trip to Paris in 1963, when Kemény had the chance to visit several exhibitions of the Sonnabend Gallery among other venues. He was one of the leading graphic designers of Hungary in the 1960s. Among numerous important posters and books, he designed also the catalogue of the first Iparterv exhibition and the poster of the second. The frivolous female nude on the poster evokes the aesthetics of pop art, and could be compared with Tom Wesselmann or works by German graphic designer Heinz Edelmann. The late 1960s was one of the golden ages of Hungarian graphic design, with such remarkable figures as György Kemény and Árpád Darvas, who consequently appropriated visual effects of pop art, just like their Polish colleagues (Jan Lenica, Henryk Tomaszewski, Roman Cieślewicz, Waldemar Świerzy). Although it was barely possible to present artworks related to pop art in official art exhibitions, the products of graphic design were treated in a different way. Making posters, illustrations and other forms of decoration became a source of income for several leading figures of the progressive art scene: László Lakner, Gyula Konkoly designed several important "pop-posters," and the conceptual artist Miklós Erdély executed lots of "photo-mosaics" in public spaces that echoed trends of pop art.

Although György Kemény is mostly known as an emblematic figure of Hungarian graphic design, he also created works of "high art." His solo exhibition opened on 15 October 1968 in the Fészek Art Club (Figure 12.3), a well-known locale of progressive Hungarian artists, which in the 1960s wasn't a venue for art exhibitions, rather a club and a library for artists, therefore its exhibition programme wasn't under a strict control. Kemény's exhibition showcased different types of artworks: sculptures made of cans overpainted with bright colours that formed a *Laocoon Group*, a collage that multiplied the figure of Twiggy (*Twiggy As Jeanne d'Arc*, 1967, Figure 12.4), an assemblage that depicts the *Assassination of Kennedy,* several paintings that evoke the visual effects of comics (*Car Crash*, 1968) and installations formed of vividly coloured plastic fruits and animal toys. Some works evoked "Western" *consumer culture* (like an assemblage that consists of packets of Philip Morris cigarettes, or another one that includes applied utensils on its surface in the spirit of Daniel Spoerri), and some other works thematised political issues of the Cold War (*Hommage à Oppenheimer*, 1968).

During the exhibition, art historian László Beke conducted a long interview with the artist, in which he touched on several major questions concerning the reception of pop art in East Central Europe.[34] Beke asked Kemény whether he thought of making an exhibition that presents motifs of Hungarian daily life instead of thematising the visual world of "supermarkets" and the figure of Twiggy. The answer reflects well Kemény's relation to Western consumer culture:

> Twiggy is looked at by Hungarian girls with the same fascination [as she is looked at by girls in the "West"] [...] they are looking at her haircut, her clothes [...] and the whole atmosphere that she brought as a novelty into the world's fashion. Why cannot we treat Twiggy as a Hungarian problem [...].[35]

Kemény's answer seems to confute the commonplace that the emblematic motifs of "Western-type" consumer culture cannot be subjects of artworks in the Eastern bloc. Nevertheless, Kemény depicts Twiggy from a different perspective, as a fetishised subject of desire that represents "Western" culture.

In his answer, Kemény also refers to the major piece of his exhibition, *Childhood Self-Portrait* (1968) that presents a specific "Hungarian problem." The painting evokes personal traumas by using stylistic elements of pop art: it depicts the artist as a child painted in the style of comics. The painting's harsh, frivolous Pop elements allude perplexingly to the absurd situations of the traumatic past: Kemény experienced World War II as a Jewish child—on his montage-like composition, he coordinates memory-fragments. The waterfront refers to childhood vacations as well as the place where Jews who were shot then fell into the Danube. As a nine-year old child, the artist miraculously survived such an event. The tense figres in the background, painted on the basis of documentary photographs of the ghetto in Warsaw, are referring to this situation. Paradoxically, the absolute commonplace of "Pop," known from its occurrence in works by Roy Lichtenstein, the burning Mickey Mouse, is placed in this context—recalling a loved storybook from the artist's childhood, from which the adult guardian of the persecuted children read in the evenings. In this case

[34] László Beke, Interview with György Kemény, Budapest, 24 October 1968, manuscript (a transcript of the recording is in the archive of György Kemény).
[35] Beke, 1968, manuscript, p. 6.

Kemény radically reinterprets the tools of Pop art, which became the subject of a peculiar *memory-work*, completely distinct from its American counterparts. Kemény's attitude might be compared with some works of the Polish artist Alina Szapocznikow, who also thematised traumatic experiences of the Holocaust by using the "visual language" of *Nouveau Réalisme* (*Souvenir I*, 1971; *Grande Tumeur I*, 1969).[36]

Childhood Self-Portrait is not the only work of Kemény that radically reinterprets elements and motifs of pop art. His sculpture *Conservative Chair* (1969) was made for a subsequent exhibition at Fészek Art Club that had been never realised. Kemény's chair is formed of empty cans recalling an emblematic motif of Andy Warhol. The cans are deprived of their brand-logos, just like on Leonhard Lapin's soup-can poster made for the *Soup '69* exhibition in Tallinn. In both cases, the cans devoid of brand marks become emblems of a non-existent consumer culture. Kemény's work is not lacking humour and irony: the sculpture's title is pun on the word *konzerv*, which in Hungarian means "can," while *konzervatív* means "conservative." The play on words evokes the distance between the Warholian cans and the conservatbism of Hungarian society.

One year later, Kemény painted a grand secco in a tiny room in an apartment in the downtown of Budapest. On the walls of the room, which used to serve as a meeting point for the democratic opposition of late socialism, one finds a unique leftist iconography: the portrait of Marxist philosopher György Lukács next to the head of Leon Trotsky, on the neighboring wall the Chocolate grinder of Marcel Duchamp's *Large Glass* is floating beside a female nude, who stands in a psychedelic landscape. In the visionary composition one finds iconic figures of leftist ideology, like Angela Davis and Karl Marx, and emblematic motifs of the Cold War era, such as peace and yin-yang symbols. The iconographical programme was created by a closed circle of dissident leftist intellectuals. The style of the wall-painting recalls the visual culture of comics and even Western Pop art, not only American examples, but also paintings of French "Figuration narrative" (for instance the works of Erró), the Latin-American or Spanish

[36] See Griselda Pollock, "Too Early and Too Late: Melting Soldis and Traumatic Encryption in the Sculptural Dissolutions of Alina Szapocznikow," in Agata Jakubowska (ed.), *Alina Szapocznikow: Awkward Objects*, Warsaw: Museum of Modern Art, 2011, p. 85.

transformations of Pop art (such as the group El Equipo Crónica), or even critical pop-artists from Asia, like the Japanese Keichii Tanaami. The "poppy" political secco of György Kemény, which was painted in 1970–71, can be seen not only as a summary of the ideology of a dissident intellectual group, but also as a conclusion of the local trends related to Pop art, which had blossomed some years before, not only in Hungary, but also in several other parts of Central Eastern Europe. The work is a peculiar *transformation* of "Western" pop art that revisits the questions posed in Kemény's solo-show in Fészek Art Club concerning the relation between the local and the international, and should be interpreted as a major instance of a politically engaged pop.

Emptying Pop Art
Endre Tót's solo show, Mednyánszky Hall, Budapest, 1969

Endre Tót is one of the central figures of the Iparterv circle, whose works were shown on both Iparterv exhibitions. In the early phase of his career he was—alongside Tamás Hencze—the most important artist of Informel painting in Hungary. In the middle of the 1960s he started to combine abstract expressionism with letters and American newspaper clippings that recalled the work of such Neo-Dadaist artists as Jasper Johns and Robert Rauschenberg. In 1968 on his solo-show in Ferenczy Museum in Szentendre (a small town neighbouring Budapest) he presented a new series of graphic works that focused on everyday motifs (mostly running athletes and football-players). The figures were marked with silhouettes and were combined with numbers and letters. The repetition of the figures on the drawings recalls the visual effects of pop art. "Directness is a decisive experience for me. I am interested in the most trivial reality,"[37]—states the artist in the catalogue of the exhibition; and this statement might be a point of departure of his next series he showed in his subsequent solo exhibition in 1969.

The circumstances of the 1969 presentation reflect well the differences between "Western" forms of "popisms" and their "Eastern" transformations. The Mednyánszky Hall was a gallery of the so-called Képcsarnok

[37] János Frank, *Endre Tót*, exh. cat., Szentendre: Ferenczy Museum, 1968.

Vállalat (Picture Hall Company) that ran a network of for-profit galleries owned by the state. Képcsarnok was in a monopolised position in Hungary's centralised art market. Although the galleries of Képcsarnok mostly showed "state supported artists," in some cases they also organised exhibitions of tolerated figures of the progressive art scene. Endre Tót also reflected, in his exhibition, the ambivalence of Hungary's non-existing art market. In the storefront of the gallery he showed his work "*Four times four hats are sixteen heads*" (Figure 12.8) that depicted sixteen hand-painted silhouettes of stylised hats in the spirit of Warholian pop art, yet in a small scale and made with ink on paper. According to urban legend, the leader of the Mednyánszky Hall was mocked by his colleagues for opening a hat shop. With his ironic gesture of putting his painting in the shopwindow, Endre Tót poses questions on the complex relation between commodities, artworks and the market in the context of a dysfunctional and state-controlled quasi-market.[38] He creates an ironic inversion of pop art by quoting its visual elements.

Such questions had been clearly reflected in the review written by Géza Perneczky, the leading art critic of the period:

> The structure of Endre Tót's pictures, and the material of their motifs is inspired by visual reminiscences of advertisements, poster-design, and shop window decorating. [...] Indeed, Tót has recently returned from London, where he might had been inspired by the beauty of modern technique and the work of pop artists. While Antonioni's *Blow-Up* mapped the irrational way of living in a consumer society in London, and the works of pop artists express a protest of a human who is fed up with the exaggerated forms of consumption, for Endre Tót the cityscape has remained not more than a visual impulse: a harmonic form of joy, movement, and alteration.[39]

[38] Tót's humorous gesture might be compared with the concept of Claes Oldenburg's *Store* (1961), in which art-objects were shown in a store-like environment. In the "Eastern Bloc," Slovakian artists Július Koller and Peter Bartoš organised a "series of exhibitions" in front of a shop-window of a communal tights repair company in 1968–69, which can be also compared to Tót's artistic "shop-window."

[39] Géza Perneczky, "Fiatalok gondjai" (Problems of Young People), *Élet és Irodalom*, No. 23, 1969, p. 8.

Perneczky's review reflects well how pop art was perceived in Hungary by art historians, and how consciously were the general differences thematised in the contemporaneous press. He emphasises that for Tót "the technique is not a threatening power, but a promise of a freer and joyous feeling." Tót doesn't criticise consumer culture, rather creates an imagery that represents "western" design as an object of desire. In this sense, as Perneczky points out, Tót's series "is more related to Op Art, than to Pop."

The works shown at Endre Tót's exhibition in the Mednyánszky Hall Budapest (Figure 12.7) show the impact of the artist's 1968 travel to London, as the artist recalls:

> In the sixties, every Hungarian artist went to Paris, but I went around Paris, and travelled to London because of pop art (it wasn't easy to organise such a trip at the time). I was attracted by the world of hippies, I spent fantastic nights under the famous statue of Piccadilly Circus. The square was full of hippies until the rise of day.[40]

Although Endre Tót saw only a few instances of British pop art, his new exhibition was dominated by harsh colours, geometric forms and figures that are derived from everyday imagery, as art historian Péter Sinkovits points out in his introductory text published on the flyer that accompanied the exhibition:

> These paintings are crystallized forms of pop art that are results of a consequent artistic progress. Besides the inner motivations, the artist's travel in the summer of 1968 to London might have played an important role in their creation. He might have gotten major impulses from the strongest personalities of the third generation of pop: among whom Kitaj, Peter Phillips, David Hockney are the most important artists.[41]

The paintings shown at the Mednyánszky Hall (usually painted with water colour or acrylic paint) were reduced variants of the artist's earlier ink drawings that focus on one single motif: a seemingly abstract circle that refers to the emblem of London's subway, an empty form of a running

[40] Endre Tót's e-mail to Dávid Fehér, dated 27 August 2015

[41] Péter Sinkovits, *Endre Tót*, Budapest: Mednányszky Terem, 1969, n.p.

athlete that appear twice on a diptych, stylised contours of multiplied hats and empty silhouette-portraits of attractive women (Figure 12.5). Tót combined the emptied figurative forms with geometric compositions formed of horizontal or diagonal parallel lines that recall Hard-edge painting—mostly the works of Kenneth Noland.

Although the works shown in the Mednyánszky Hall represent a very short period of transition in the work of Endre Tót, they signal a major turn in his activity that proved to be a decisive one. Tót started to empty his painting, until he arrived at the conceptual representation of nothingness that is still today a major motif of his art. The representation of "invisibility," "emptiness," "loss" or "nothingness" has in the work of Endre Tót both an ontological and a political aspect. It signals both the conceptual null-point of painting, and the ambivalent joys of a society that is determined by the economy of shortage. The emptied forms of Endre Tót's "emptied pop art" are ambivalent emblems of shortage. This shortage was manifested more explicitly in Tót's painting "*What is inside?*" (1969), painted soon after the exhibition in the Mednyánszky Hall. The painting depicts an empty (even invisible) money bag accompanied by a short question stencilled onto the pictorial surface: "what is inside?" The painting is dominated by a geometric composition of lines and squares. Three horizontal lines in the geometric centre are painted with red, white and green, evoking the Hungarian national flag, a recurring motif in Tót's art. The central, yet hidden, motif of the Hungarian flag alludes to complex questions of the "local" and the "international." The occurrence of the tricolour underlines that the stylised forms and signals still refer to a specific Hungarian situation.

Hand-Painted Pop Art
László Lakner's solo show, Institute for Cultural Relations, Budapest, 1969

László Lakner's solo show at Budapest's Institute for Cultural Relations (Figure 12.9) is a legendary event of the late 1960s that became formative experience of several young artists that emerged in the 1970s. The exhibition summarised and simultaneously concluded the artist's pop-period. It was opened one month before the second Iparterv exhibition, where Lakner exhibited a work in which he already moved away from the "pop-approach" that characterised his earlier works. The catalogue and the poster of Lakner's exhibition were both designed by György Kemény, just like in the case of the Iparterv exhibitions.

In the Institute for Cultural Relations, Lakner exhibited paintings that depict two single motifs, which are typical for pop art: roses and mouths magnified to monumental scales. On the opening ceremony of the exhibition, instead of a usual opening speech, Lakner projected one of his experimental films. The film entitled *Toy* (1969) showed a Soviet plastic children's toy that models a spaceship. The unpredictable movements of the wobbling toy models Cold-War relations in the period of the Moon landing, meanwhile it also thematises question of daily life and popular culture in the spirit of pop art. Lakner's experimental film also touched upon questions concerning the fate of classical easel painting, as the boundaries of the area in which the plastic spaceship could move was marked by wood stretchers.

Indeed, the works shown on Lakner's exhibition were thematising the fate of classical painting. One of the central pieces of Lakner's exhibition presents a single rose multiplied, like Andy Warhol's famed flowers, but nevertheless painted by hand in deep brown and olive green Rembrandtian hues, as if providing examples of "hand-painted Pop art." The question of Lakner's relation to American pop art was addressed in the contemporaneous press. In his important review entitled "Hungarian Pop Art?," Géza Perneczky wrote the following on Lakner's roses:

> Lakner's treatment is the closest to the methods of American artists, his Hungarian identity is shown by certain technical questions. Namely, Andy Warhol repeats his cans (flowers and lynching scenes) by using reproductive methods, and thus underlines that the presented issues are strongly linked to mechanisms of consumer culture's mass production. Lakner paints even the second and third copies free-hand, and uses a kind of "handicraft" method.[42]

By painting every single rose by hand, Lakner transfers Warholian pop art to the terrain of classical painting. The brownish tones of Lakner's flowers

[42] Géza Perneczky, "Hungarian Pop Art?" *Élet és Irodalom*, No. 40, 1969, p. 9.

evoke the artist's Rembrandt series, in which the deep tones of Rembrandtian painting appeared as a metaphor of a peculiar human condition. On an ironic etching, Lakner wrote under a rose motif: "instead of a real rose please accept this grey one," which statement reflects well the general differences between "Western" pop art and its counterparts in the Eastern bloc.

However, Lakner's Rembrandtian brownish paintings and environments (for example the shaped canvas: *Zig-zag Rose* (Figure 12.8), and a rose-environment made of felt) were compensated by several paintings at the exhibition dominated by the vivid colours of pop art. One of the central pieces of the exhibition was *Mouth with Stairs* (1969, Figure 12.7). On the top of the painting, a monochrome blue mouth appears, meanwhile the lower part is filled with a horizontal stripe sequence painted with intense colours. The painted stripes are extended with similarly coloured real steps, and above the blue mouth a smaller tableau hung, one that depicts a stylised sky painted with paint roller. Although the combination of geometric stripe sequences with naturalistic details recalls several works of Peter Blake, and the usage of the stair motif can be compared with works of Allen Jones, Lakner's work is essentially different from its counterparts. *Mouth with Stairs* appeared in Lakner's exhibition as an erotic altar with sacral connotation, meanwhile it combined several trends of painting: it evoked naturalistic imagery (the mouth motif), elements of post painterly abstracttion (geometric stripe sequences), trends of environmental art (the stair), and also trends of op art (stylised sky-motif).

In *Tondo Mouth* (1969), Lakner situates a realistic male mouth in the centre of a target-like concentric stripe sequence, and confronts the brownish tones of the mouth with the intense colours of the geometric structure. On this painting, the silence of the closed mouth alludes simultaneously to the spirituality of Zen and the compulsion to remain silent. "Whereof one cannot speak, thereof one must be silent." Lakner cites Wittgenstein's adage in one of his later conceptual work (*Wittgenstein Citation*, 1971), which is permeated beyond the analytical content with political implications. Lakner's deep brown male mouth, enlarged to a landscape size and recalling the female genitalia (as well as summoning the mouth motif popular among surrealist artists, like Man Ray), is not lacking in political connotations, as the mouth is that of the German revolutionary, Fritz Teufel, which the artist had enlarged from a documentary photograph he came across in the German leftist magazine *Stern*.

From this point of view, the work can be seen as an expression of a new-leftist political stance, and is radically different from the mouth pictures of Andy Warhol or Tom Wesselmann. Its approach is much more akin to the peculiar European derivations of Pop art, especially to the representatives of the Capitalist Realism movement who had "Eastern" roots, such as Konrad Lueg, Sigmar Polke and most of all, Gerhard Richter. Lakner's mouth pictures can be interpreted alongside other Eastern European works, such as Jerzy "Jurry" Zieliński's stylised mouth depictions or the Norwegian-Swedish painter Kjartan Slettemark, an artist who was also working in a region that can be regarded as peripheral, if perhaps for different reasons. Kjartan Slettemark likewise represented the stance of the new left, protesting the Vietnam War with his famous mouth picture (*From a report from Vietnam: Children are splashed with napalm. Their skin is burnt into black wounds and they die*, 1965).

Lakner's *Mouth* series presented in the Institute for Cultural Relations is one of the most important instances of a peculiar form of "popism" that can be compared with British and American pop art, however it is mostly based on traditions of realistic painting. The *Mouth* paintings represent a transition between Lakner's pop-related period and his photorealistic series that can be interpreted as peculiar form of "post-pop."

"Pop Art and Non-Pop Art" (Instead of a Conclusion)

In his essay *Pop art and Non-Pop Art* first published in 1964,[43] Robert Rosenblum posed several questions about the problems of pop art's terminology. After the global extension of art historical geography, such questions of terminology appear more often than ever.

In this essay, I did not aim to prove that pop art existed in Hungary. My goal was rather to present some trends that can be interpreted as local reactions to pop art. The exhibitions I presented were dominated by artworks that used stylistic elements of "international pop," but transformed them in a specific way through evoking several elements of a local

[43] Robert Rosenblum, "Pop Art and Non-Pop Art," in John Russell and Suzi Gablik (eds.), *Pop Art Redefined*, London: Thames and Hudson, 1969, pp. 53–56.

imagery. Exhibitions of György Kemény, Endre Tót and László Lakner were perceived as "pop-exhibitions" in their own time, but their relationship to pop art had already been subject to debates in the local art critique of the 1960s.

It is the task of further research to investigate the particular contexts and attributes of local popisms, and characterise their discrete otherness. I am convinced that modern art history can be written as a history of exhibitions. In this essay, I presented some exhibitions that are essential for understanding pop art's reception in Hungary. Hopefully exhibitions of the Iparterv-circle will be situated in the global history of exhibitions, and will be the subject of further comparative studies that investigate "pop beyond pop."

References

Anik Cs. Asztalos (Éva Körner), "No isms in Hungary," *Studio International*, No 964, 1974, pp. 105–111.

László Beke, Interview with György Kemény, Budapest, 24 October 1968, manuscript (transcript of the recording in the archive of György Kemény).

László Beke, Péter Sinkovits, and Lóránd Hegyi, *Iparterv 68–80*, exh. cat., Budapest: "Iparterv Home Printing House," 1980.

Tobia Bezzola and Franziska Lentsch (eds.), *Europop*, exh. cat., Kunsthaus Zürich, Cologne: DuMont, 2008.

Vladimíra Büngerová and Lucia Gregorová (eds.), *Jana Želibská: No Touching*, Bratislava: Slovak National Gallery, 2012.

David Crowley, "Pop Effects in Eastern Europe under Communist Rule," in Jessica Morgan and Flavia Frigeri (eds.), *The World Goes Pop*, exh. cat., London: Tate Modern, 2015, pp. 29–37.

Dávid Fehér, "Kötél és identitás: Megjegyzések Lakner László Identitás (Kötél) című alkotásához" (Rope and Identity. Remarks upon László Lakner's Work Identity (Rope)), in Annamária Szőke and Tamás Ullmann (eds.), *Tanulmányok: Filozófiatudományi Doktori Iskola. Művészettörténet-tudományi Doktori Iskola (Asteriskos 4.)* (Studies of Doctoral Schools of Philosophical Studies and Art History: Asteriskos 4), Budapest: Eötvös Loránd University, 2013, pp. 311–327.

—. "'Where is the Light?': Transformations of Pop Art in Hungary," in Darsie Alexander and Bartholomew Ryan, *International Pop*, exh. cat., Walker Art Center, Minneapolis, 2015, pp. 135–152.

Russell Ferguson (ed.), *Hand-painted Pop: American Art in Transition 1955–62*, exh. cat., The Museum of Contemporary Art, Los Angeles, New York: Rizzoli, 1992

János Frank, *Endre Tót*, exh. cat., Szentendre: Ferenczy Museum, 1968.

Tony Godfrey, *Conceptual Art* (1998), London: Phaidon, 2006.

Sirje Helme, *Popkunst Forever: Estionian Pop Art at the Turn of the 1960s and 1970s*, Tallinn: Eesti Kunstimuseum, KUMU, 2010.

Hiroko Ikegami, *The Great Migrator: Robert Rauschenberg and the Global Rise of American Art*, Cambridge, Mass.: The MIT Press, 2010.

Katalin Keserü, *Variations on Pop Art: Chapters in the History of Hungarian Art Between 1950 and 1990*, Budapest: Ernst Museum, 1993.

Márta Kovalovszky, "György Jovánovics," in Hafner Zoltan, ed., *Jovánovics*, Budapest: Corvina Kiadó, 2004, pp. 26–41.

Lucy R. Lippard, *Pop Art*, London: Thames and Hudson, 2001 (1966).

Géza Perneczky, "Fiatalok gondjai" [Problems of Young People], *Élet és Irodalom*, No. 23, 1969, p. 8.

—. "Hungarian Pop Art?" *Élet és Irodalom*, No. 40, 1969, p. 9.

—. "Produktivitásra ítélve? Az Iparterv-csoport és ami utána következett Magyarországon" (Sentenced to Productivity? The Iparterv-Group and what followed it in Hungary), *Balkon*, 1996/1 and 1996/2, URL: www.c3.hu/~perneczky/articles/-IPARTRV.html (date most recently accessed: 20 August 2015).

Piotr Piotrowski, *In the Shadow of Yalta: Art and the Avant-garde in Eastern Europe, 1945–1989*, London: Reaktion Books, 2009.

—. "Toward a Horizontal History of the European Avant-Garde," in: Sascha Bru, (ed.), *Europa! Europa? The Avant-Garde, Modernism and the Fate of a Continent*, Vol. 1. (2), Berlin: De Gruyter, 2009, pp. 49–58.

Emese Révész, "Figura, história, táj: Figurativitás Konkoly Gyula festészetében" (Figure, History, Landscape: Figurativity in Gyula Konkoly's Art), in *Konkoly: Figuratív képek* (Konkoly: Figurative Paintings), exh. cat., Budapest: Ernst Museum, 2003, n.p.

Robert Rosenblum, "Pop Art and Non-Pop Art," in John Russell and Suzi Gablik (eds.), *Pop art redefined*, London: Thames and Hudson, 1969, pp. 53–56.

Frank van de Schoor (ed.), *Pop Art in Europe*, exh. cat., Nijmegen: Museum het Valkhof, 2012.

Péter Sinkovits, "Bevezető" (Introduction), in *Kiállítás az Iparterv dísztermében* (Exhibition in the Iparterv Hall), exh. cat., Budapest, 1968, n.p.

—. *Endre Tót*, Budapest: Mednányszky Terem, 1969, n.p.

Edit Szentesi, "Beszélgetés Lakner Lászlóval" (A conversation with László Lakner), in Ildikó Nagy (ed.), *Hatvanas évek: Új törekvések a magyar képzőművészetben* (The Sixties: New Approaches in Hungarian Visual Arts), exh. cat., Hungarian National Gallery, Budapest: Képzőművészeti Kiadó, Magyar Nemzeti Galéria, and Ludwig Múzeum, 1991, pp. 125–137.

Katalin Timár, "Is Your Pop Our Pop? The History of Art as a Self-Colonizing Tool," *Artmargins online,* 15 March 2002, www.artmargins.com/index.php/archive/323-is-your-pop-our-pop-the-history-of-art-as-a-self-colonizing-tool (date most recently accessed: 20 August, 2015).

Csaba Varga (ed.), *Groupe Iparterv - Le Progrès de l'Illusion: La troisième génération de l'avant-garde hongroise*, exh. cat., Paris: Institut Hongroise de Paris, 2010.

Dániel Véri, *"Leading the Dead" - The World of János Major*, exh. cat., Budapest: Hungarian University of Fine Arts, 2013.

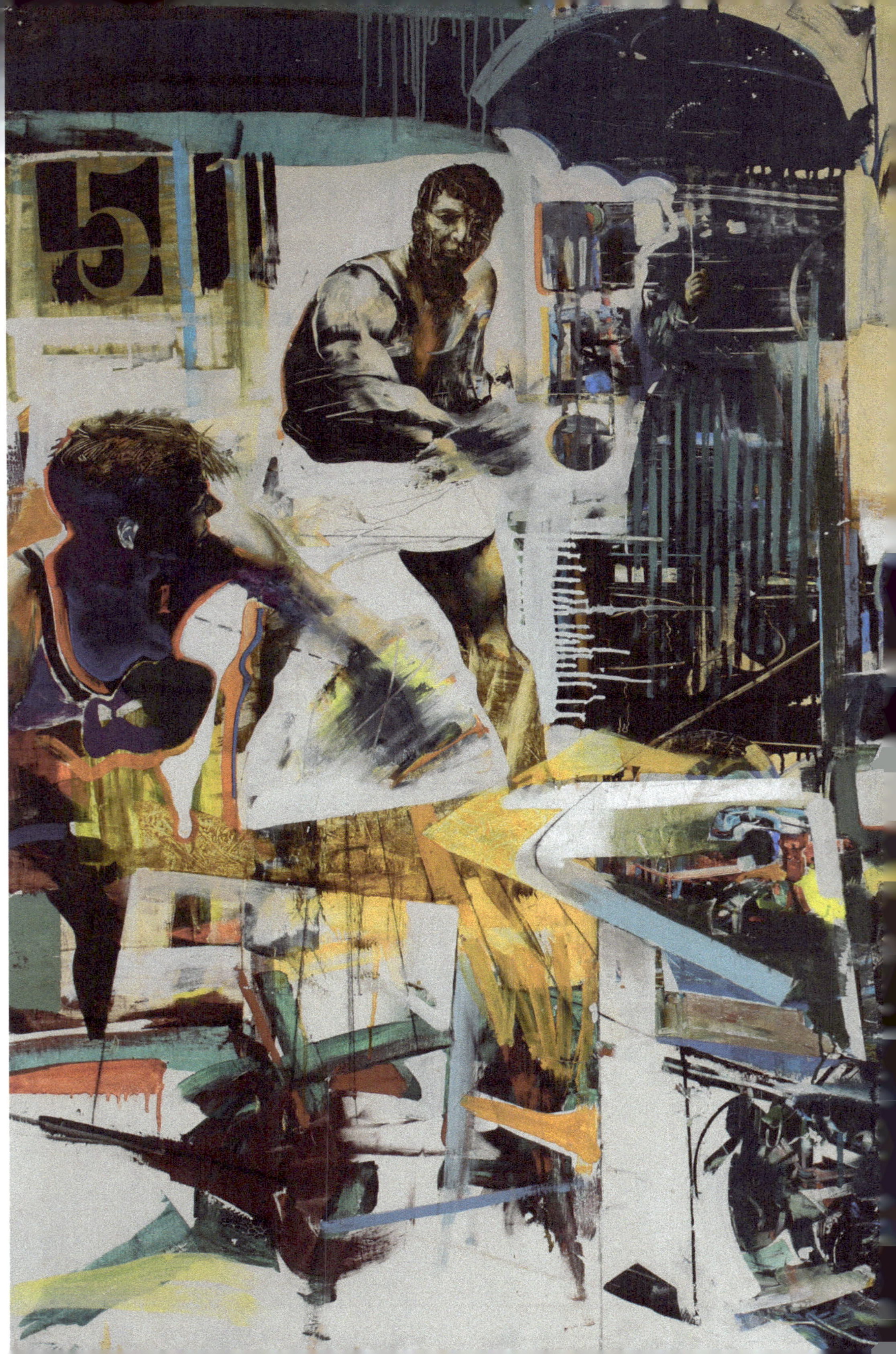
5

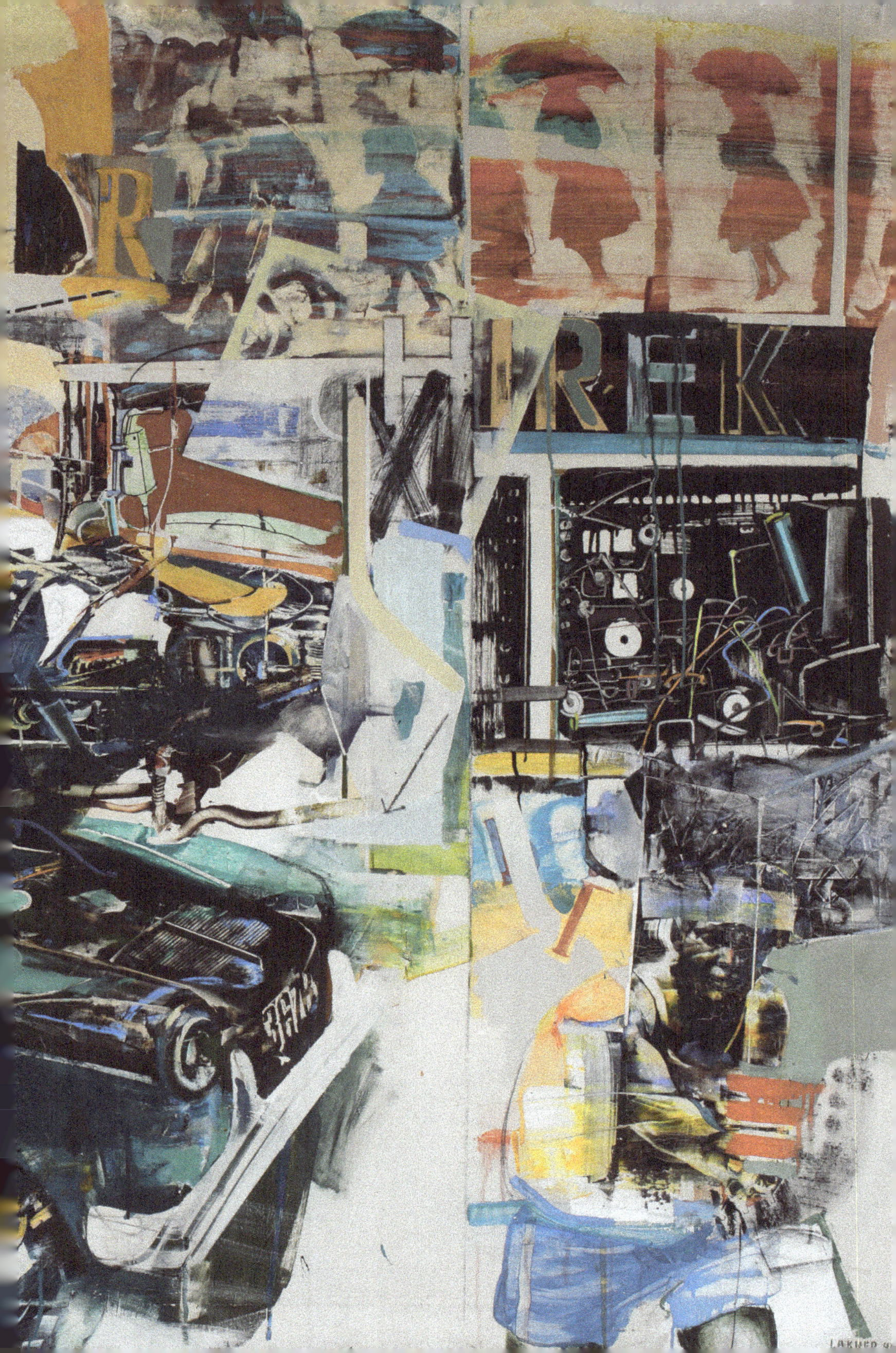

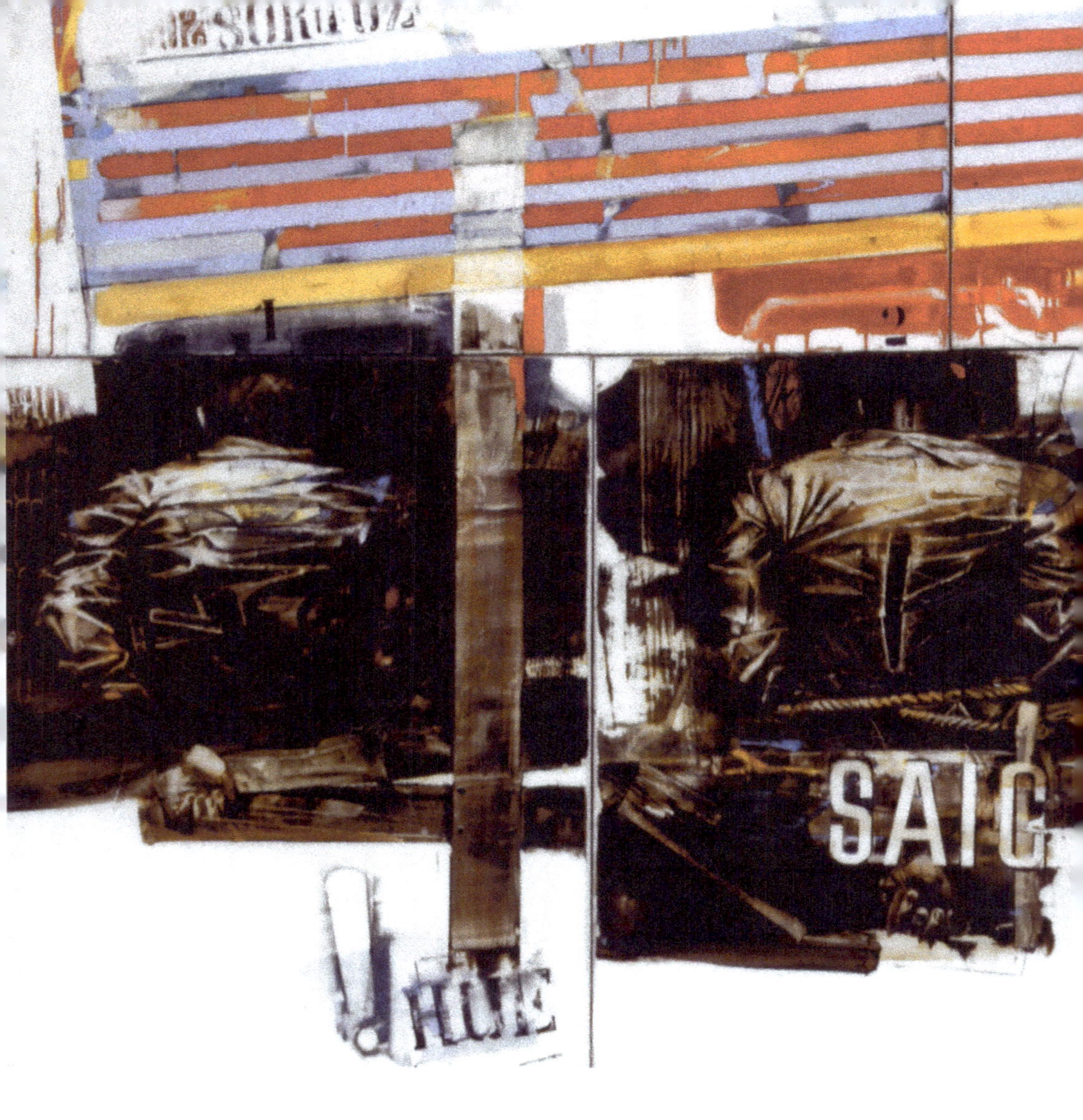
SAIC

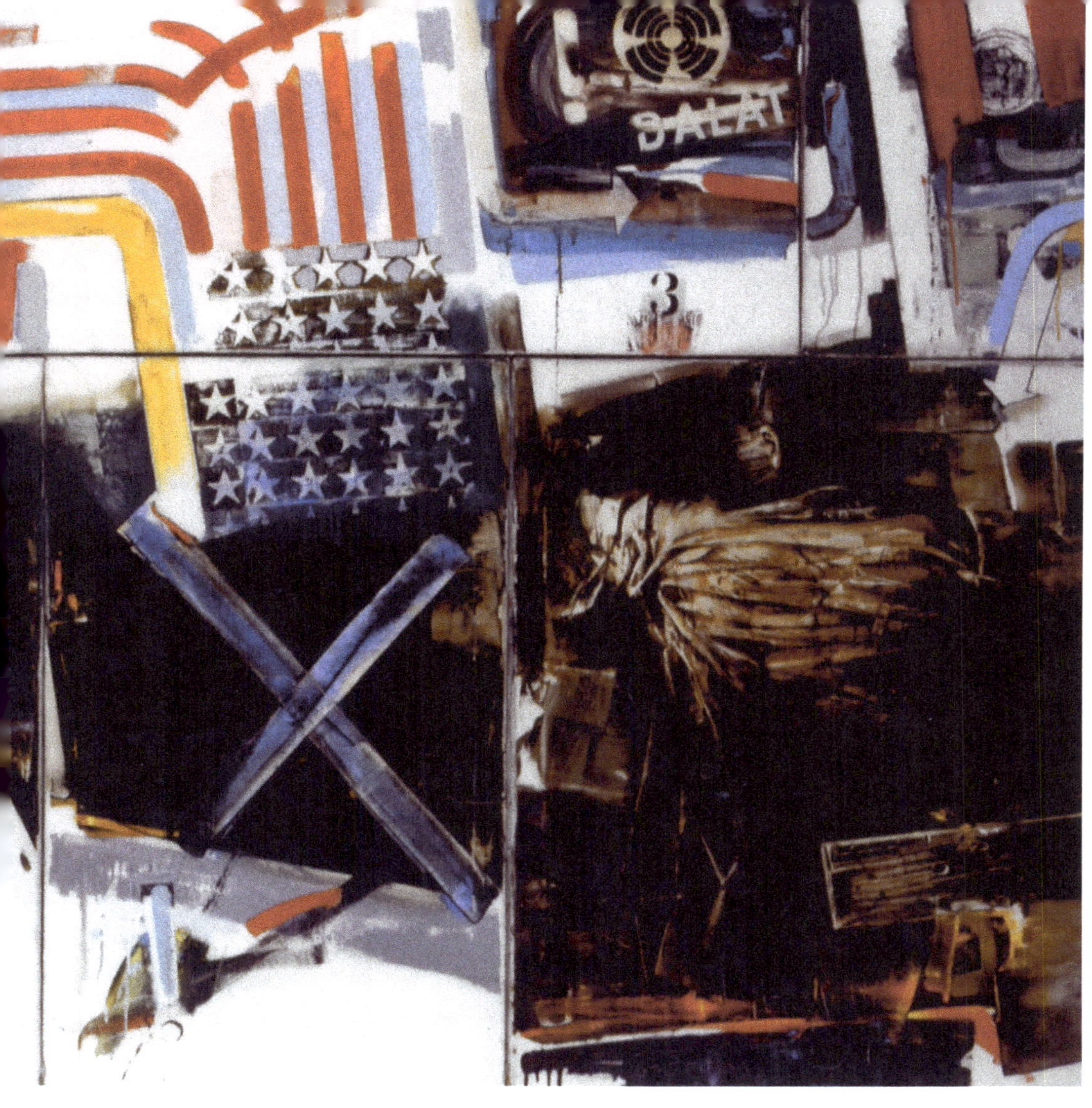

Figure 12.1 (previous spread): László Lakner, *Hírek* [*News*], 1964 oil on canvas, 130 × 150 cm private collection, Budapest. Photo: Miklós Sulyok. © László Lakner.

Figure 12.2: László Lakner, *Saigon (Saigoni buddhista szerzetesek tiltakozása)* [*Saigon (The Protest of Buddhist Monks of Saigon)*], 1965 oil on canvas, 100 × 240 cm Thury György Museum, Nagykanizsa (on loan from JPM – Modern Hungarian Gallery, Pécs). Photo: István Füzi. © László Lakner.

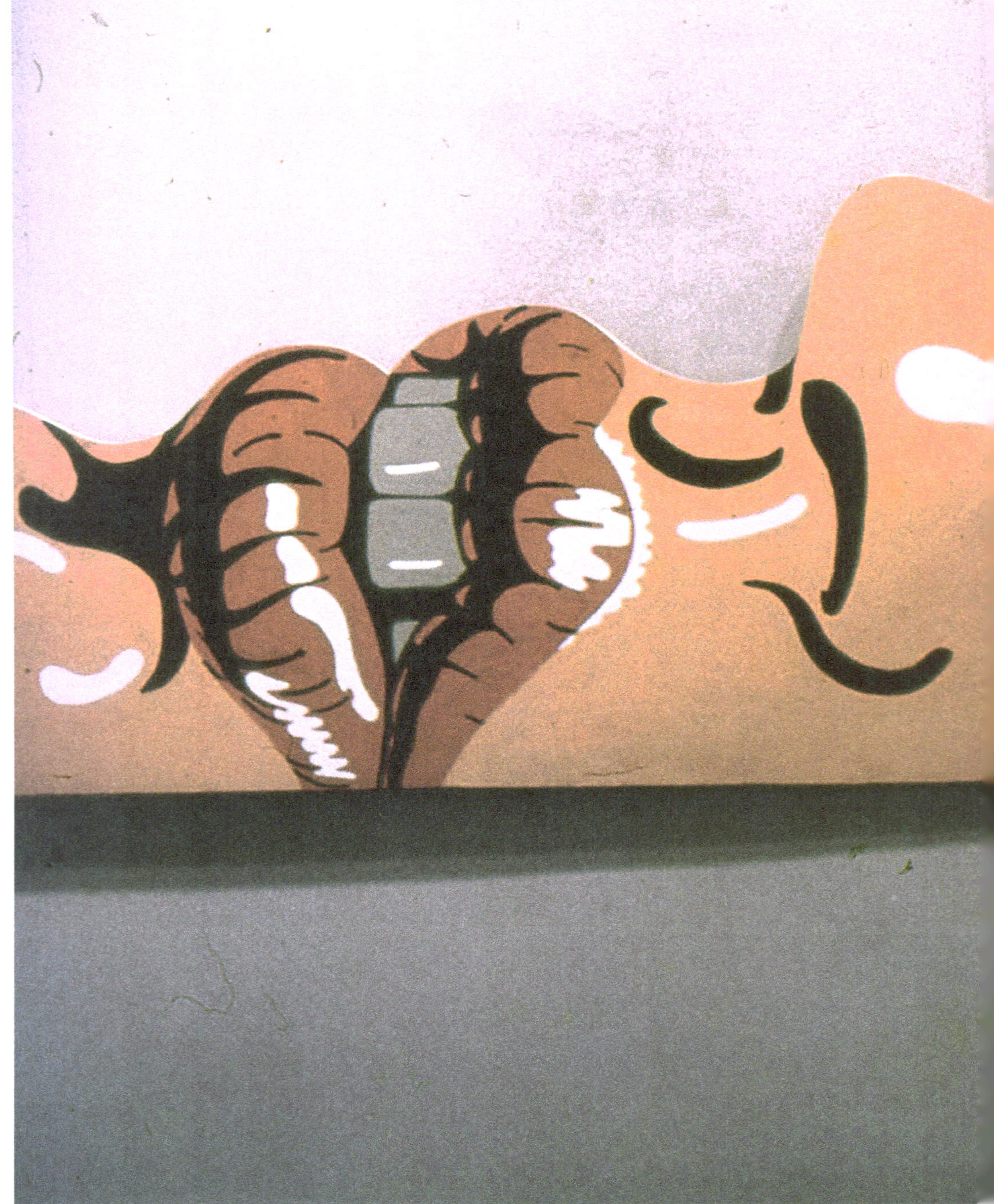

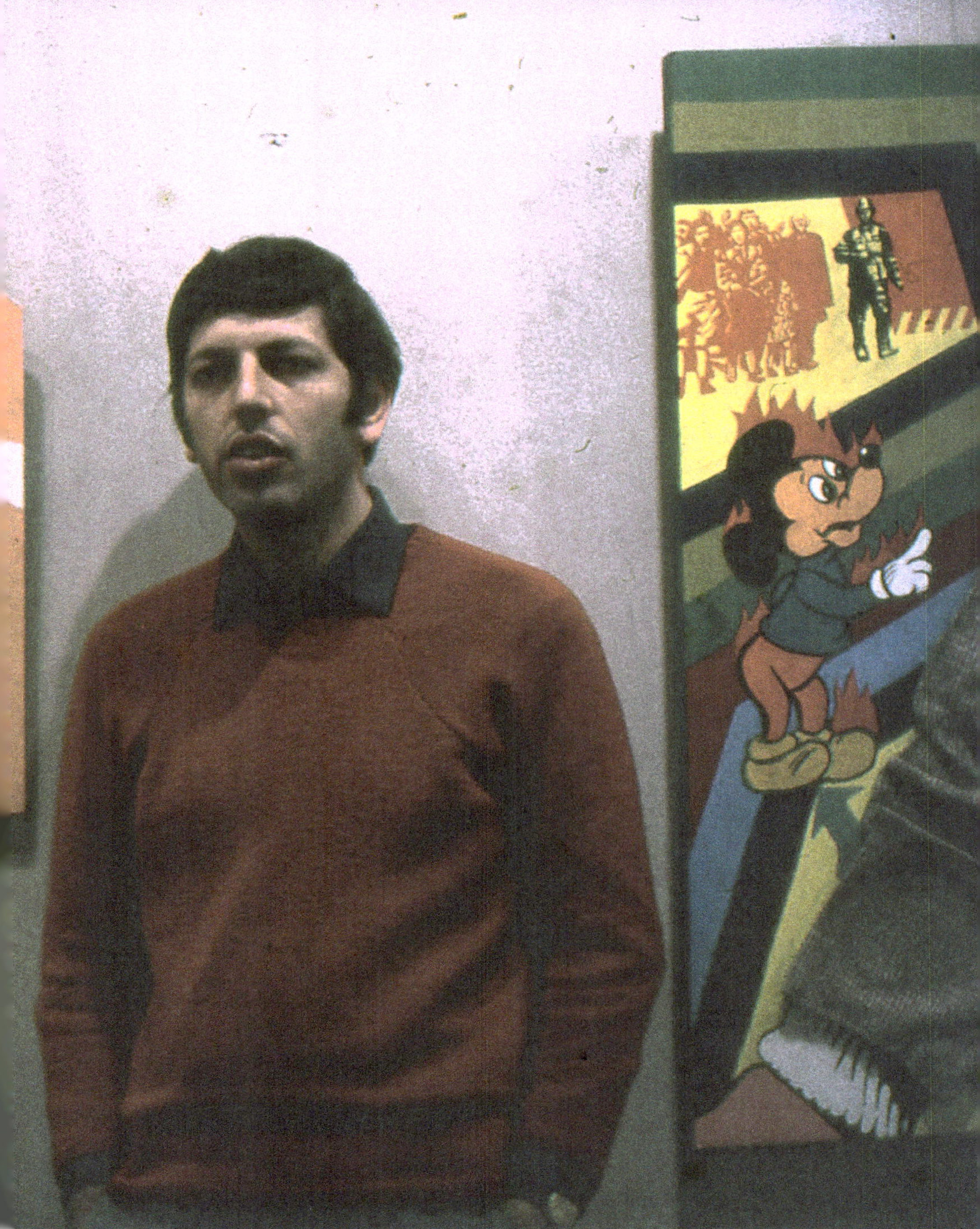

Figure 12.3: György Kemény in front of his "Selfportrait" (1968) and "Childhood Self-portrait" (1968) at his solo show in Fészek Art Club, Budapest, 1968, photo: archive of György Kemény. © György Kemény.

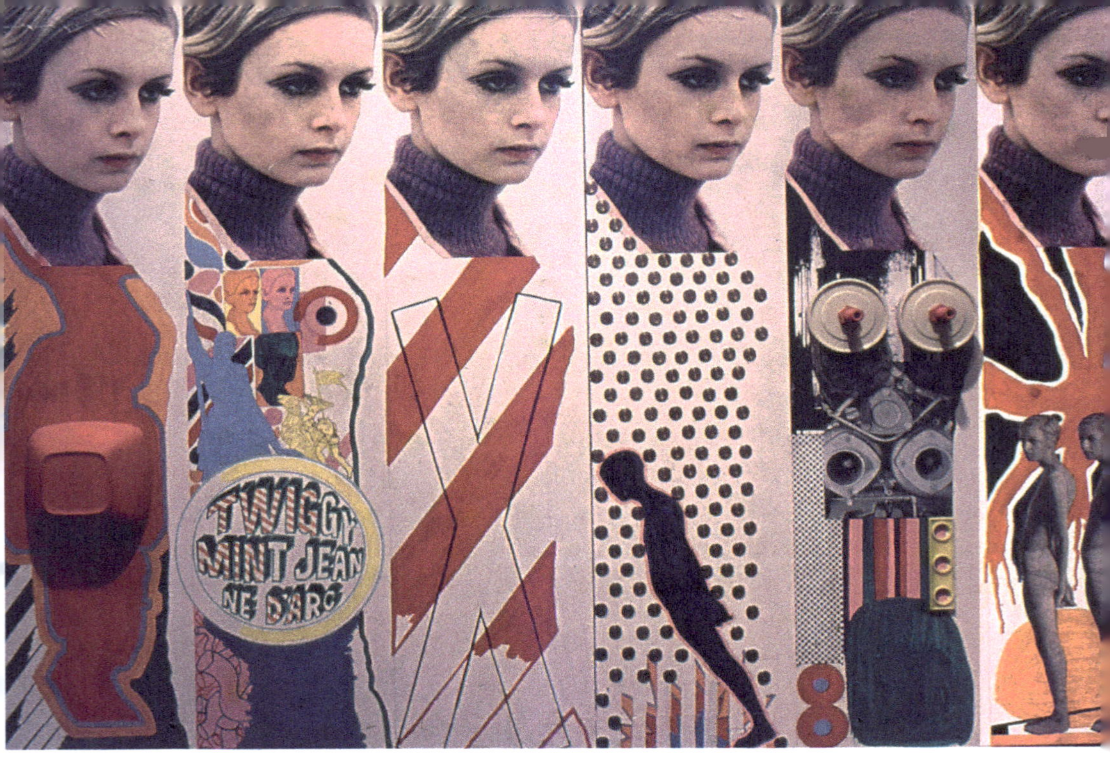

Figure 12.4: György Kemény, *Twiggy mint Jeanne d'Arc* [*Twiggy as Jeanne d'Arc*], 1967 wallkyd, plastic, application on wood, 100 × 72 cmcourtesy of the artist. Photo: archive of the artist. © György Kemény.

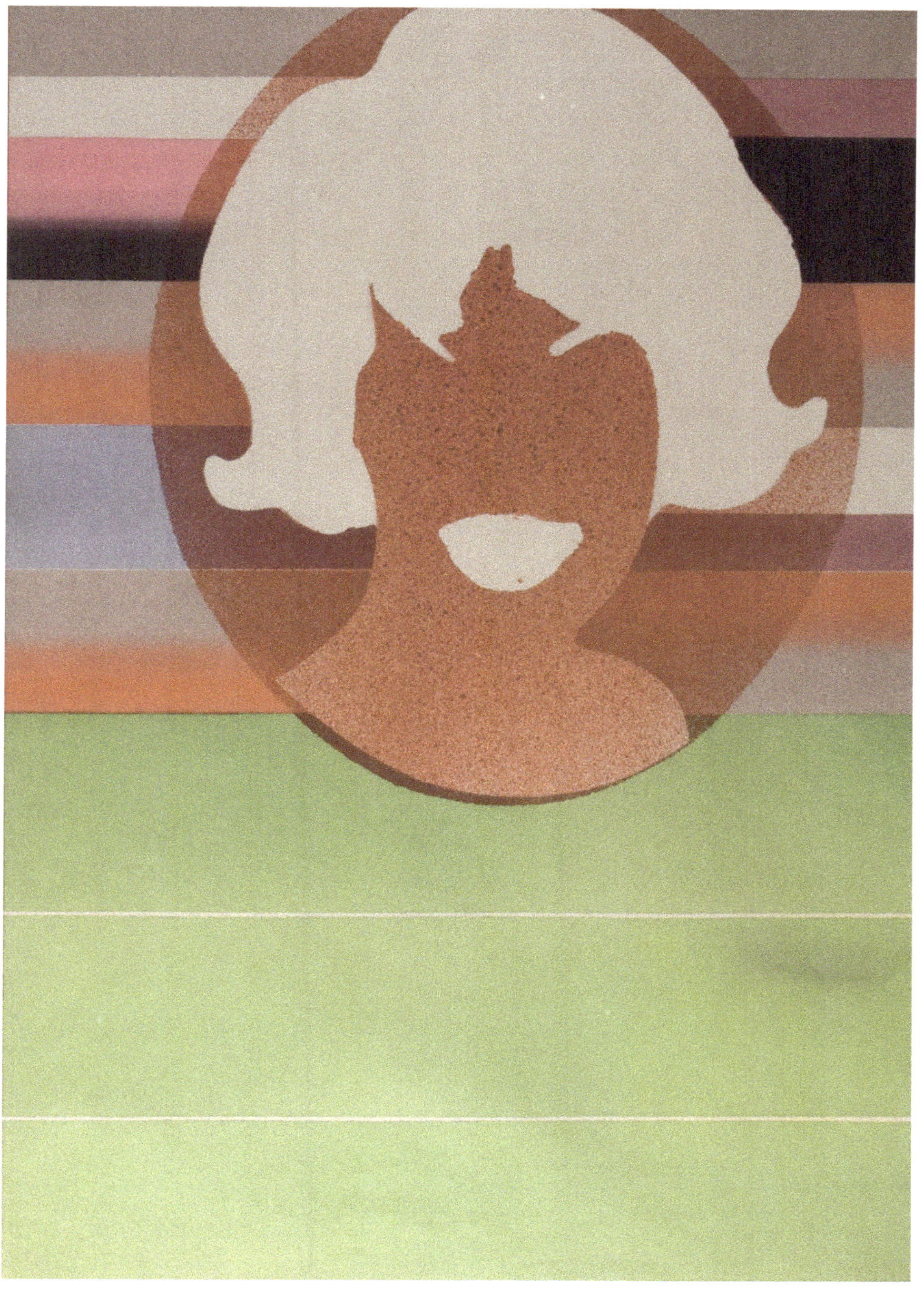

Figure 12.5: Endre Tót, Régi szép idők [Good Old Times], 1968 watercolour on paper, 980 × 690 mm. Collection of László Zimányi. Photo: György Zima. © Endre Tót.

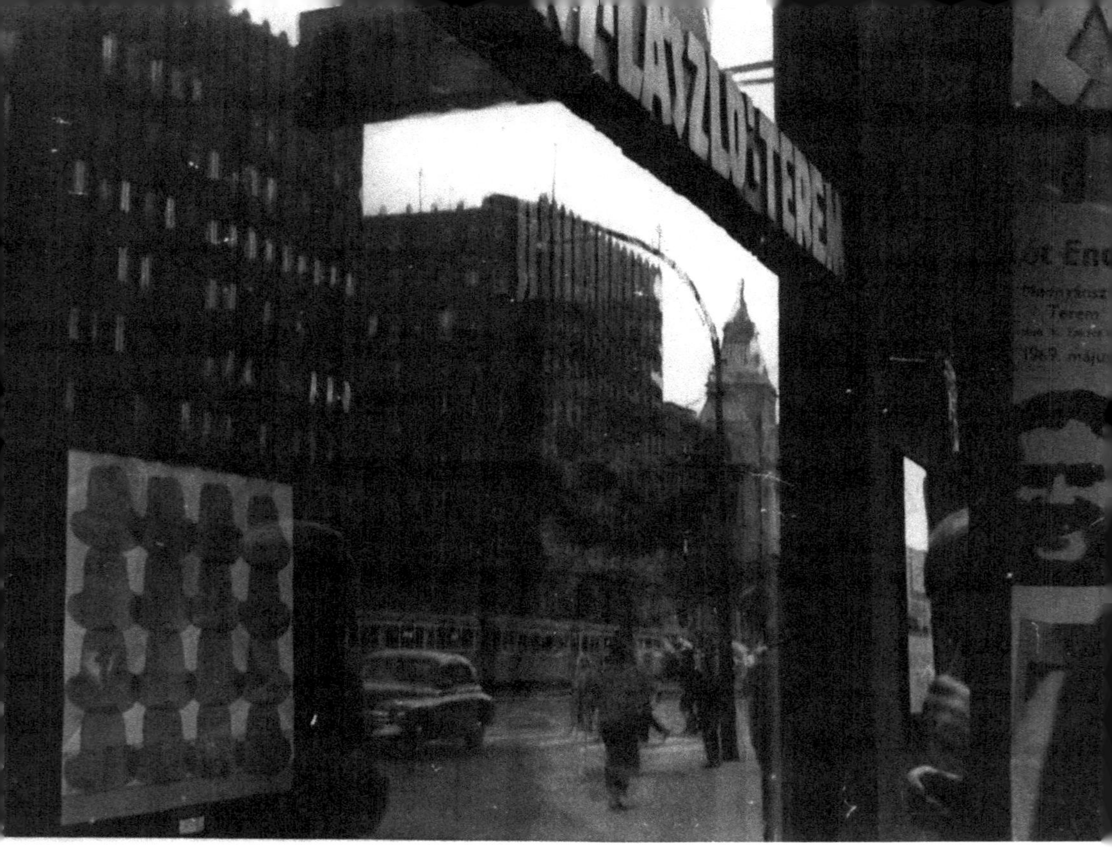

Figure 12.6: The storefront of Mednyánszky Hall with Endre Tót's "Four Times Four Hats are Sixteen Heads", Budapest, 1969. Photo: archive of the artist. © Endre Tót.

Figure 12.7 (following page): László Lakner, Lépcsős száj [Mouth with Stairs], 1968/2015 oil on canvas, painted wood, 133 × 140 × 34 cm, 167 × 140 cm, 75 × 175 cm. Private Collection, Budapest. Photo: Miklós Sulyok. © László Lakner.

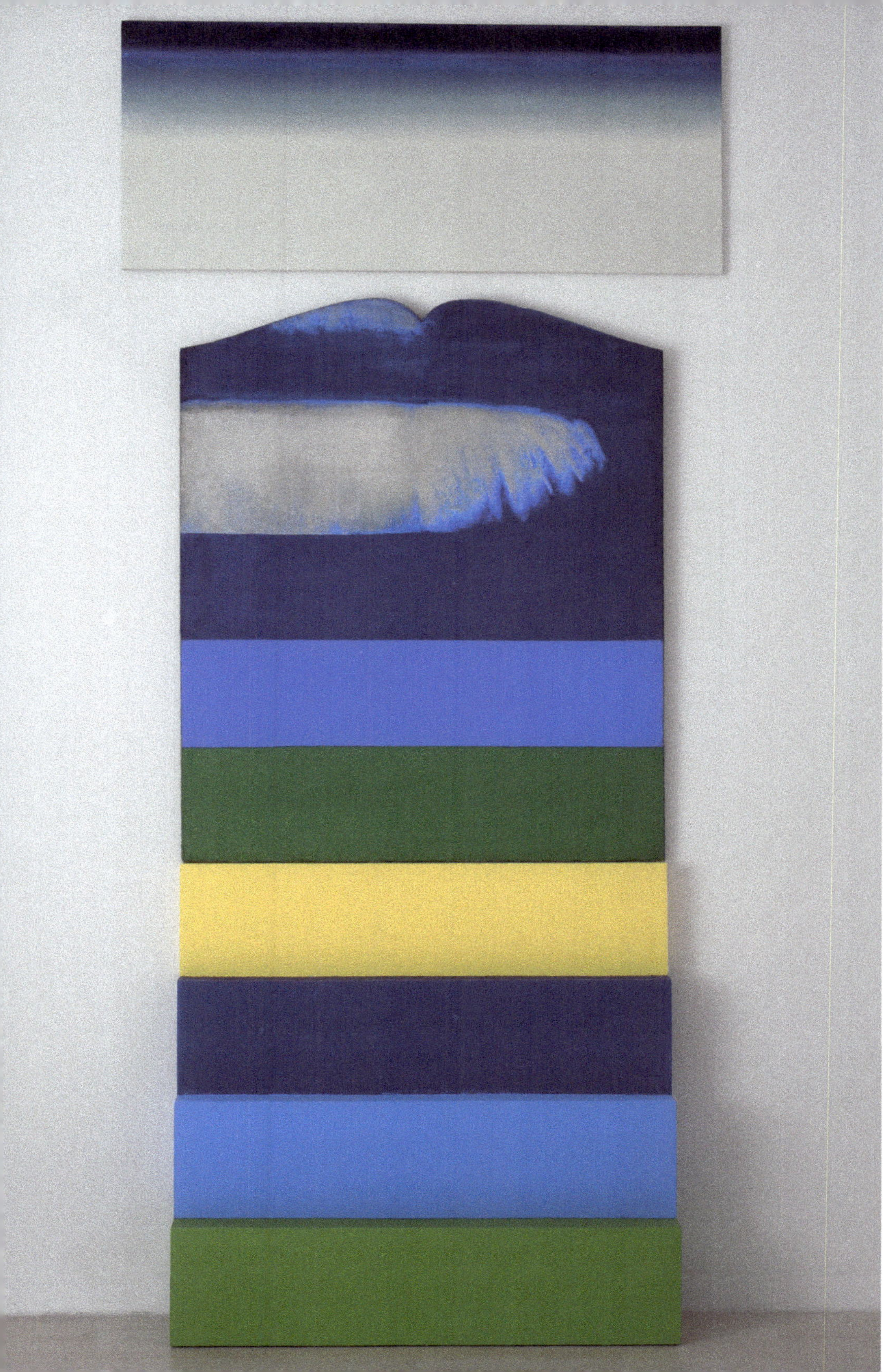

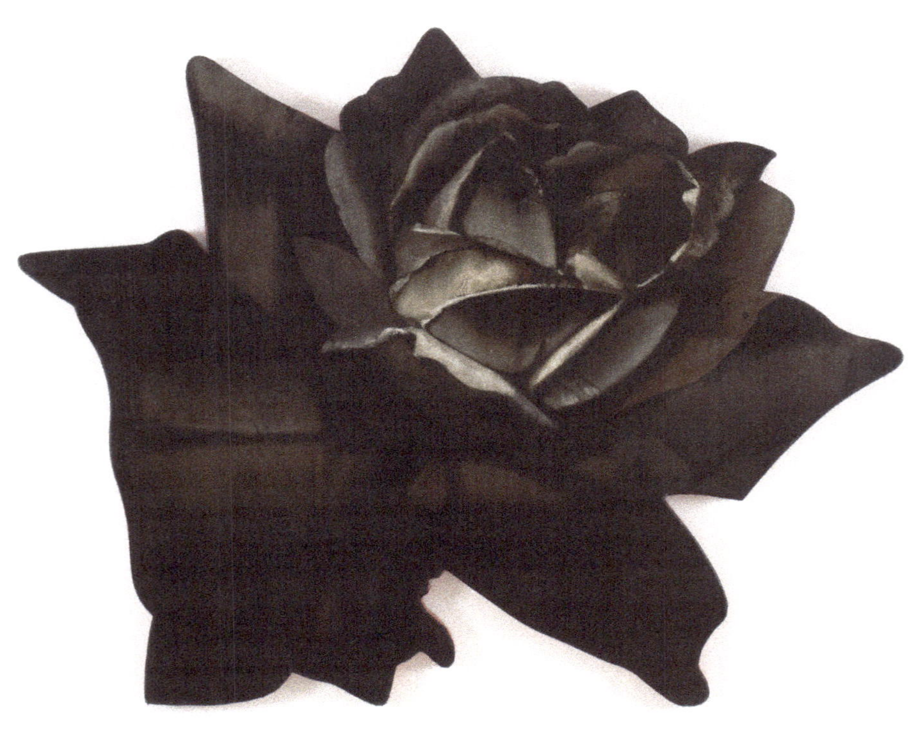

Figure 12.8: László Lakner, *Cikk-cakk rózsa* [*Zig-zag Rose*], 1969 oil on canvas, 100 × 126 cm Szombathely Gallery, Szombathely. Photo: Miklós Sulyok. © László Lakner.

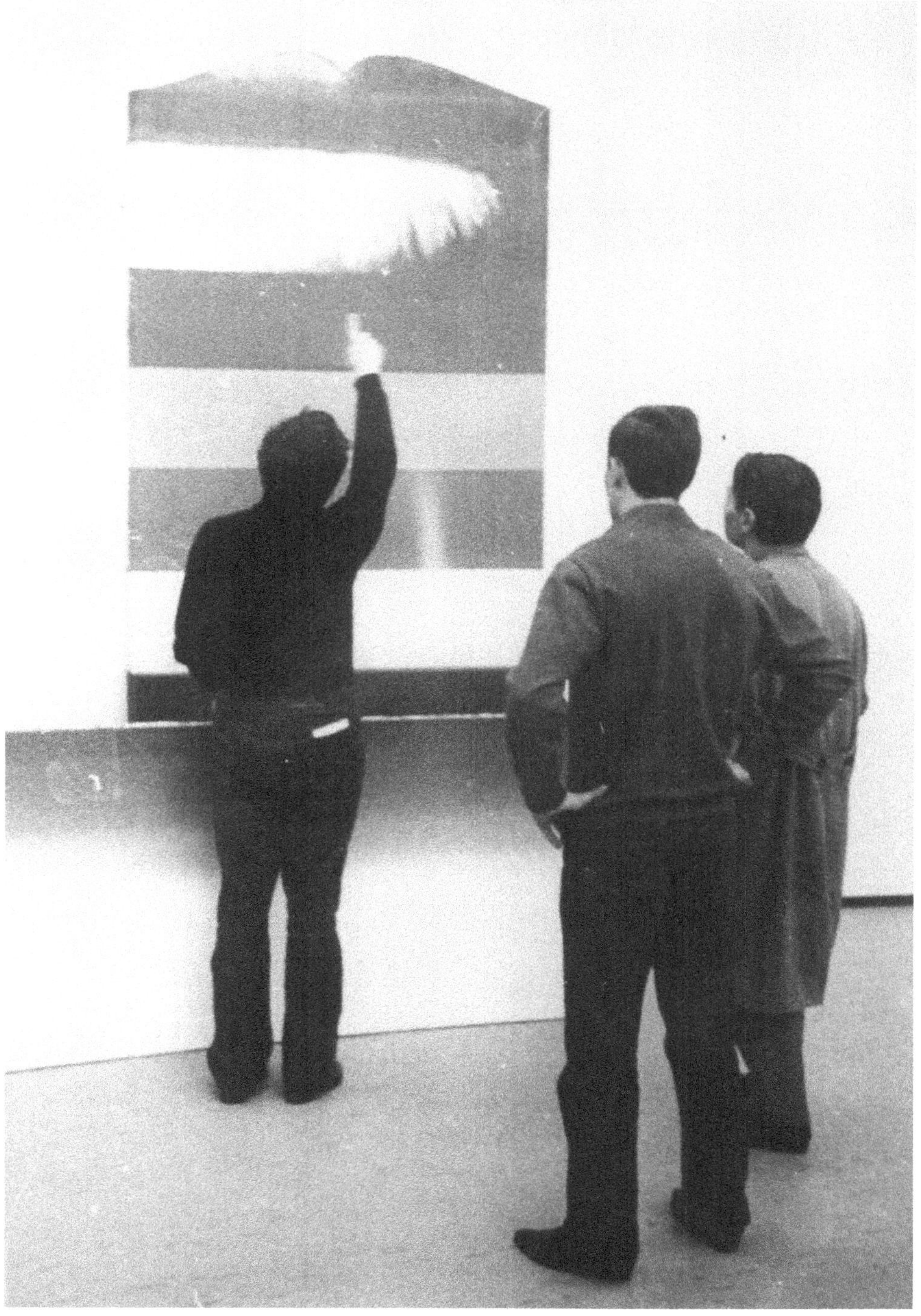

Figure 12.9: László Lakner (left) is installing his work "Mouth with Stairs" (1968) during the preparations of his solo show at the Institute for Cultural Relations, Budapest, 1969. Photo: archive of Kunsthalle Budapest. © László Lakner.

Contributors

Hannah Abdullah holds a PhD and an MSc in the Sociology of Art and Culture from the London School of Economics (LSE) and a BA in Art History and Spanish from University College London. Her research focuses on artistic developments in East and West Germany before and after the fall of the Berlin Wall, on art and the post-socialist condition, as well as methodological debates in the Sociology of Art. She has taught at the Department of Sociology at the LSE and lectured at the Institute of Art History at the University of Leipzig. Her writings have appeared in *Theory, Culture & Society*, *The British Journal of Sociology* and *Sociologie de l'Art - OPuS*. Since 2015 she is Cultural Program Curator at the Goethe-Institut New York.

Mathilde Arnoux is a Research Director at the Centre allemand d'histoire de l'art in Paris, and PI of the project *To Each His Own Reality: The Notion of the Real in the Art of France, West Germany, East Germany and Poland Between 1960 and 1989* (funded by the ERC Starting Grant Program). Focusing on the artistic exchanges in Europe in the XIXth–XXth century Arnoux has published *La peinture allemande dans les musées français 1871–1981*, Paris, 2007 and, with Anne Panzani and Thomas W. Gaehtgens, *Correspondance entre Henri Fantin-Latour Otto Scholderer*, Paris,

2011. Arnoux's research currently deals with cross-cultural analyses of Cold War Europe. On this subject, she has published various articles in *Etudes Germaniques, Perspectives, Revue de l'art, Art beyond borders in communist Europe (1945–1989)*, ed. by J. Bazin, P. Dubourg-Glatigny and P. Piotrowski, and online Lettres du Séminaire Arts & Sociétés de Laurence Bertrand-Dorléac, Sciences Po, www.artsetsocietes.org/f/farnout.html, in M. Gispert, M. Murphy (ed.), *Voir, ne pas voir. Les expositions en question*, actes de journées d'étude Université Paris 1 – Panthéon Sorbonne – HiCSA et INHA, 2014, http://hicsa.univ-paris1.fr/documents/file/Arnoux.pdf

Sophie Cras is an Assistant Professor at Université Paris 1 Panthéon-Sorbonne. Her research considers how money, finance, and economics in general became a focus for artistic experimentation in the 1960s to 1980s. Her writings have appeared in *American Art, Texte zur Kunst, Histoire de l'art* and *Les Cahiers du Musée National d'Art Moderne.* Cras is currently preparing a book entitled *The Artist as Economist: Art and Capitalism in the 1960s.*

Catherine Dossin is an Associate Professor of Art History at Purdue University, Vice-Director of ARTL@S, and Chief Editor of the *ARTL@S Bulletin.* Dossin is the author of *The Rise and Fall of American Art, 1940s–1980s: A Geopolitics of Western Art Worlds* (Ashgate 2015) and the co-editor with Thomas DaCosta Kaufmann and Béatrice Joyeux-Prunel of *Circulations in the Global History of Art* (forthcoming), and serves as President of the European Post-War and Contemporary Art Forum (Epcaf).

Dávid Fehér is Associate Curator at the Museum of Fine Arts, Budapest, in the Department of Art after 1800, a lecturer at the University of Arts Budapest, and a PhD candidate in the Department of Art History at ELTE University, Budapest. His research focuses on the art history of Hungary and Eastern Europe 1960–1980, mainly the reception of photorealism, pop art and conceptual art. His work on photorealism and his survey of the transformations of Pop Art in Hungary and Eastern Europe has been published respectively in the exhibition catalogs *East of Eden: Versions of Reality* (Ludwig Museum, Budapest) and *International Pop* (Walker Art Center, Minneapolis) as well as in major Hungarian journals. He also publishes regularly in the art press. In 2013 he held a lecture at Tate Modern's *Global Pop-symposium.* Fehér curated the exhibittion *László Lakner: Seamstresses Listen to Hitler's Speech* at the Museum of Fine Arts, Budapest, and Imre Bak's recent retrospective show at Art Gallery of Paks (*Imre Bak: Timely Timelessness. The Layers of an Oeuvre / 1967-2015*). He was the co-curator of the Museum of Fine Art's most recent permanent exhibition of 20th Century and Contemporary art. In 2011-2012, he received the Ernő Kállai Scholarship for art historians and art critics; in 2014, the Eötvös State Scholarship for young scholars, and was a DAAD-fellow at the Freie Universität Berlin for the academic year 2013-2014. He is the board member of the Hungarian section of AICA.

Hiroko Ikegami is an Associate Professor at the Graduate School of Intercultural Studies of Kobe University, specialises in post-1945 American art and global modernisms. Her main publications include *The Great Migrator: Robert Rauschenberg and the Global Rise of American Art* (The MIT Press, 2010) and *Shinohara Pops! The Avant-Garde Road, Tokyo/New York* (New Paltz: Samuel Dorsky Museum of Art, 2012). In 2015, she served as a consulting curator for the Japanese section of "International Pop" exhibition at Walker Art Center.

Agata Jakubowska is an Associated Professor at the Department of Art History at Adam Mickiewicz University in Poznań. Jakubowska is the author of, among others, *On the Margins of the Mirror: Female Body in the Art of Polish Women Artists* (in Polish, 2004), *Multiple Portrait of the Work of Alina Szapocznikow* (in Polish, 2008), *Awkward Objects: Alina Szapocznikow* (editor, Museum of Modern Art, Warsaw, 2011). Currently she is working on a project devoted to a history of "women-only exhibittions" and on a book on the Polish sculptor Maria Pinińska-Bereś (1931–1999). Since 2009 she has been the vice-president of the Polish Section of AICA.

Katarina Wadstein MacLeod is Associate Professor and a lecturer in Art History at Södertörn University, Stockholm. She graduated in 1999 with an MA in Politics of Representation, Art History, UCL, London and 2006 with a PhD *Lena Cronqvist: Reflections of Girls Girls* (Sekel förlag, 2006) in Art History, University of Lund, Sweden. In her research she has published on topics such as representations of bodies, femininity and girls in art; the domestic impulse in Nordic art at the turn of the 19th century, 1960s and 1970s and contemporary art; narratives of Easter Europe as peripheral after 1989, and the production of cultural heritage value.

Håkan Nilsson divides his time between being a Senior Lecturer at the Department of Art History at Södertörn University and a Professor of Art History and Theory at the Fine Arts Department at Konstfack, University College of Arts, Crafts and Design, Stockholm. He is also a regular art critic in the Swedish newspaper Svenska Dagbladet and is the author of many essays, catalogue texts, and books such as *Clement Greenberg och hans kritiker* (dis) (2000) and *Måleriets Rum* (2009

Annika Öhrner is a Senior Lecturer at the Department of Art History, School of Culture and Education, Södertörn University. In 2010, she defended her dissertation *Barbro Östlihn & New York*, at Uppsala University, published by Makadam. It deals with a painter who worked in New York in a neo-avantgarde context, as well as with issues of transfer of American pop art to Sweden. Her research scope also includes the classical avant-garde. Öhrner was Dean of the Valand Academy, Faculty of Fine, Applied and Performing Arts, Gothenburg University, 1996–2001. She has curated numerous exhibitions, for example retrospectives of Meret Oppenheim (2004) and Siri Derkert (2011) at the Moderna Museet, Stockholm. Öhrner is working presently within the research project *Art, culture, conflict: transformations of museums and memory culture in the Baltic Sea region after 1989*, funded by *The Foundation for Baltic and East European Studies.*

Tania Ørum is an Associate Professor emerita from the Department of Cultural Studies and the Arts, University of Copenhagen. Director of the Nordic Network of Avant-Garde Studies (www.avantgardenet.eu) supported by the Nordic Research Council Nordforsk 2005–2009. Chairman of the European Network for Avant-Garde and Modernism Studies (www.eam-europe.ugent.be) 2007–2008. Ørum has been a member of the Steering Committee of EAM from 2007, and is the primary editor of the four volumes of *Cultural History of the Avant-Garde in the Nordic Countries* published by Rodopi/Brill, Amsterdam & New York 2012–2018.

Piotr Piotrowski (June 1952–May 2015) was a long-time Professor *Ordinarius* at the Art History Department, Adam Mickiewicz University, in Poznan, Poland, which he had been chairing between 1999 and 2008. He was Research Fellow of the Graduate School for East and South-East European Studies, Ludwig-Maximillians-Universität, München/Regensburg Universität. Piotrowski was also the co-editor of the annual journal *Artium Quaestiones* (1994–2009), Director of the National Museum in Warsaw, 2009–2010, and Senior Curator of Contemporary Art at the National Museum in Poznan, 1992–1997. His visiting professorships include Humboldt University (2011–2012), Warsaw University (2011, 2012–2013), the Center for Curatorial Studies, Bard College USA (2001), and the Hebrew University of Jerusalem (2003). He was a fellow of the Center for Advanced Studies in the Visual Arts, Washington D.C. (1989–1990), Columbia University, NYC (1994), the Institute for Advanced Study, Princeton NJ (2000), Collegium Budapest (2005–2006), and the Clark Art Institute, Williamstown, MA (2009) among other institutions. He is the author of over a dozen books including: *Meanings of Modernism* (Polish 1999, 2011), *In the Shadow of Yalta. Art and the Avant-garde in Eastern Europe*, (Polish 2005, English 2009, Croatian 2011), *Art after Politics* (Polish 2007), *Art and Democracy in Post-Communist Europe* (Polish 2010, English 2012), and *Critical Museum* (Polish 2011, Serbian 2013), as well as editor, co-editor or co-author of many others. For his scholarly achievements, Professor Piotrowski received among others the Jan Dlugosz Award (Krakow 2006), and the Igor Zabel Award for Culture and Theory (Barcelona 2010), among others.

Oscar Svanelid is a PhD Student in Art History at Södertörn University. His research project studies the Brazilian post-history of Russian constructivism in the post-World War II period. Previously he worked at the Department of Art History at Södertörn as a lecturer on undergraduate courses. Svanelid was also the organiser of the Art in Transfer conference held in November 2014.

Södertörn Studies in Art History and Aesthetics

With an introductory essay by Professor Piotr Piotrowski and contributions from twelve international scholars and experts in the field, Annika Öhrner, Senior Lecturer, Södertörn University, Stockholm, edited this volume for the series Södertörn Studies in Art History and Aesthetics.

1. Håkan Nilsson (ed.), *Placing Art in the Public realm*, 2012.

2. Charlotte Bydler & Cecilia Sjöholm (eds.), *Regionality/Mondiality: Perspectives on Art, Aesthetics and* Globalization, 2014.

3. Annika Öhrner (ed.), *Art in Transfer in the Era of* Pop, 2017.

Södertörn Academic Studies

1. Helmut Müssener & Frank-Michael Kirsch (eds.), *Nachbarn im Ostseeraum unter sich. Vorurteile, Klischees und Stereotypen in Texten*, 2000.
2. Jan Ekecrantz & Kerstin Olofsson (eds.), *Russian Reports: Studies in Post-Communist Transformation of Media and Journalism*, 2000.
3. Kekke Stadin (ed.), *Society, Towns and Masculinity: Aspects on Early Modern Society in the Baltic Area*, 2000.
4. Bernd Henningsen et al. (eds.), *Die Inszenierte Stadt. Zur Praxis und Theorie kultureller Konstruktionen*, 2001.
5. Michal Bron (ed.), *Jews and Christians in Dialogue*, ii: *Identity, Tolerance, Understanding*, 2001
6. Frank-Michael Kirsch et al. (eds.), *Nachbarn im Ostseeraum übwer einander. Wandel der Bilder, Vorurteile und Stereotypen?*, 2001.
7. Birgitta Almgren, *Illusion und Wirklichkeit. Individuelle und kollektive Denkmusterin nationalsozialistischer Kulturpolitik und Germanistik in Schweden 1928–1945*, 2001.
8. Denny Vågerö (ed.), *The Unknown Sorokin: His Life in Russia and the Essay on Suicide*, 2002.
9. Kerstin W. Shands (ed.), *Collusion and Resistance: Women Writing in English*, 2002.
10. Elfar Loftsson & Yonhyok Choe (eds.), *Political Representation and Participation in Transitional Democracies: Estonia, Latvia and Lithuania*, 2003.
11. Birgitta Almgren (eds.), *Bilder des Nordens in der Germanistik 1929–1945: Wissenschaftliche Integrität oder politische Anpassung?*, 2002.
12. Christine Frisch, *Von Powerfrauen und Superweibern: Frauenpopulär-literatur der 90er Jahre in Deutschland und Schweden*, 2003.
13. Hans Ruin & Nicholas Smith (eds.), *Hermeneutik och tradition. Gadamer och den grekiska filosofin*, 2003.
14. Mikael Lönnborg et al. (eds.), *Money and Finance in Transition: Research in Contemporary and Historical Finance*, 2003.
15. Kerstin Shands et al. (eds.), *Notions of America: Swedish Perspectives*, 2004.
16. Karl-Olov Arnstberg & Thomas Borén (eds.), *Everyday Economy in Russia, Poland and Latvia*, 2003.

17. Johan Rönnby (ed.), *By the Water. Archeological Perspectives on Human Strategies around the Baltic Sea*, 2003.

18. Baiba Metuzale-Kangere (ed.), *The Ethnic Dimension in Politics and Culture in the Baltic Countries 1920–1945*, 2004.

19. Ulla Birgegård & Irina Sandomirskaja (eds.), *In Search of an Order: Mutual Representations in Sweden and Russia during the Early Age of Reason*, 2004.

20. Ebba Witt-Brattström (ed.), *The New Woman and the Aesthetic Opening:Unlocking Gender in Twentieth-Century Texts*, 2004.

21. Michael Karlsson, *Transnational Relations in the Baltic Sea Region*, 2004.

22. Ali Hajighasemi, *The Transformation of the Swedish Welfare System: Fact or Fiction? Globalisation, Institutions and Welfare State Change in a Social Democratic Regime*, 2004.

23. Erik A. Borg (ed.), *Globalization, Nations and Markets: Challenging Issues in Current Research on Globalization*, 2005.

24. Stina Bengtsson & Lars Lundgren, *The Don Quixote of Youth Culture: Media Use and Cultural Preferences Among Students in Estonia and Sweden*, 2005.

25. Hans Ruin, *Kommentar till Heideggers Varat och tiden*, 2005.

26. Ludmila Ferm, *Variativnoe bespredložnoe glagol'noe upravlenie v russkom jazyke XVIII veka* [Variation in non-prepositional verbal government in eighteenth-century Russian], 2005.

27. Christine Frisch, *Modernes Aschenputtel und Anti-James-Bond: Gender-Konzepte in deutschsprachigen Rezeptionstexten zu Liza Marklund und Henning Mankell*, 2005.

28. Ursula Naeve-Bucher, *Die Neue Frau tanzt: Die Rolle der tanzenden Frau in deutschen und schwedischen literarischen Texten aus der ersten Hälfte des 20. Jahrhunderts*, 2005.

29. Göran Bolin et al. (eds.), *The Challenge of the Baltic Sea Region: Culture, Ecosystems, Democracy*, 2005.

30. Marcia Sá Cavalcante Schuback & Hans Ruin (eds.), *The Past's Presence: Essays on the Historicity of Philosophical Thought*, 2006.

31. María Borgström & Katrin Goldstein-Kyaga (ed.), *Gränsöverskridande identiteter i globaliseringens tid: Ungdomar, migration och kampen för fred*, 2006.

32. Janusz Korek (ed.), *From Sovietology to Postcoloniality: Poland and Ukraine from a Postcolonial Perspective*, 2007.

33. Jonna Bornemark (ed.), *Det främmande i det egna: filosofiska essäer om bildning och person*, 2007.
34. Sofia Johansson, *Reading Tabloids: Tabloid Newspapers and Their Readers*, 2007.
35. Patrik Åker, *Symboliska platser i kunskapssamhället: Internet, högre lärosäten och den gynnade geografin*, 2008.
36. Kerstin W. Shands (ed.), *Neither East Nor West: Postcolonial Essays on Literature, Culture and Religion*, 2008.
37. Rebecka Lettevall & My Klockar Linder (eds.), *The Idea of Kosmopolis: History, philosophy and politics of world citizenship*, 2008.
38. Karl Gratzer & Dieter Stiefel (eds.), *History of Insolvency and Bankruptcy from an International Perspective*, 2008.
39. Katrin Goldstein-Kyaga & María Borgström, *Den tredje identiteten: Ungdomar och deras familjer i det mångkulturella, globala rummet*, 2009.
40. Christine Farhan, *Frühling für Mütter in der Literatur?: Mutterschaftskonzepte in deutschsprachiger und schwedischer Gegenwartsliteratur*, 2009.
41. Marcia Sá Cavalcante Schuback (ed.), *Att tänka smärtan*, 2009.
42. Heiko Droste (ed.), *Connecting the Baltic Area: The Swedish Postal System in the Seventeenth Century*, 2011.
43. Aleksandr Nemtsov, *A Contemporary History of Alcohol in Russia*, 2011.
44. Cecilia von Feilitzen & Peter Petrov (eds.), *Use and Views of Media in Russia and Sweden: A Comparative Study of Media in St. Petersburg and Stockholm*, 2011.
45. Sven Lilja (ed.), *Fiske, jordbruk och klimat i Östersjöregionen under förmodern tid*, 2012.
46. Leif Dahlberg & Hans Ruin (eds.), *Fenomenologi, teknik och medialitet*, 2012.
47. Samuel Edquist, *I Ruriks fotspår: Om forntida svenska österledsfärder i modern historieskrivning*, 2012.
48. Jonna Bornemark (ed.), *Phenomenology of Eros*, 2012.
49. Jonna Bornemark & Hans Ruin (eds.), *Ambiguity of the Sacred: Phenomenology, Politics, Aesthetics*, 2012.
50. Håkan Nilsson, *Placing Art in the Public Realm*, 2012.
51. Per Bolin, *Between National and Academic Agendas: Ethnic Policies and 'National Disciplines' at Latvia's University, 1919–1940*, 2012.

52. Lars Kleberg & Aleksei Semenenko (eds.), *Aksenov and the Environs/Aksenov iokrestnosti*, 2012.
53. Sven-Olov Wallenstein & Brian Manning Delaney (eds.), *Translating Hegel: The Phenomenology of Spirit and Modern Philosophy*, 2012.
54. Sven-Olov Wallenstein and Jakob Nilsson (eds.), *Foucault, Biopolitics, and Governmentality*, 2013.
55. Jan Patočka, *Inledning till fenomenologisk filosofi*, 2013.
56. Jonathan Adams & Johan Rönnby (eds.), *Interpreting Shipwrecks: Maritime Archaeological Approaches*, 2013.
57. Charlotte Bydler, *Mondiality/Regionality: Perspectives on Art, Aesthetics and Globalization*, 2014.
58. Andrej Kotljarchuk, *In the Forge of Stalin: Swedish Colonists of Ukraine in Totalitarian Experiments of the Twentieth Century*, 2014.
59. Samuel Edquist & Janne Holmén, *Islands of Identity: History-writing and identity formation in five island regions in the Baltic Sea*, 2014.
60. Norbert Götz (ed.), *The Sea of Identities: A Century of Baltic and East European Experiences with Nationality, Class, and Gender*, 2015.
61. Klaus Misgeld, Karl Molin & Jaworski *Solidaritet och diplomati: Svenskt fackligt och diplomatiskt stöd till Polens demokratisering under 1980-talet*, 2015.
62. Jonna Bornemark & Sven-Olov Wallenstein (eds.), *Madness, Religion, and the Limits of Reason*, 2015.
63. Mirja Arnshav & Anna McWilliams, *Stalins ubåtar: en arkeologisk undersökning av vraken efter S7 och SC-305*, 2015.
64. Carl-Gustaf Scott, *Swedish Social Democracy and the Vietnam War* (forthcoming).
65. Jonna Bornemark & Nicolas Smith (eds.), *Phenomenology of Pregnancy*, 2016.
66. Ulrika Dahl, Marianne Liljeström & Ulla Manns, *The Geopolitics of Nordic and Russian Gender Research 1975–2005*, 2016.
67. Annika Öhrner (ed.), *Art in Transfer in the Era of Pop*, 2016.

www.ingramcontent.com/pod-product-compliance
Lightning Source LLC
LaVergne TN
LVHW052349100826
845147LV00013B/797

* 9 7 8 9 1 8 7 8 4 3 6 4 8 *